Women in Retrospect

By the Same Author

Blitzkrieg and Books: British and European Libraries As Casualties of World War II

The Magic Glass: The Individual and Society As Seen in the Gams of Herman Melville's **Moby-Dick**

Renaissance Spain in its Literary Relations with England and France: A Critical Bibliography

Women in Retrospect

A Research Guide
to Studies

in English and Romance
Languages

Hilda Urén Stubbings

Rubena Press
Bloomington, Indiana

Copyright ©1994 by Hilda Urén Stubbings. *All rights reserved, including rights of translation*. No part of this publication may be reproduced or transmitted in any form or by any means, electronic or mechanical, without permission in writing from the author except for brief portions used for purposes of review or research.

First published 1994. Printed in the United States of America at the Book-Mart Press, North Bergen, New Jersey.

Cataloging-in-Publication Data
    Stubbings, Hilda Urén
        Women in retrospect
        Includes index, p. 345-
            1. Women's studies—Bibliography. 2. Women—History—Bibliography.—3. Women and literature—Bibliography. I. Title.
        Z7963 S78   301.41
        ISBN 1-880622-04-1 (alk. pa.)
        Library of Congress Card Number 93-85424

Rubena Press, 2500 East Eighth Street, Bloomington IN 47408-4215

To my daughters
Katharine and Suzanne
and to
Dr. Robert S. Chauvin

Who can find a virtuous woman? For her price is far above rubies.

The heart of her husband doth safely trust in her, so that he shall have no need of spoil

She will do him good and not evil all the days of her life.

She seeketh wool, and flax, and worketh willingly with her hands.

She is like the merchants' ships; she bringeth her food from afar.

She riseth also while it is yet night, and giveth meat to her household, and a portion to her maidens.

She considereth a field, and buyeth it; with the fruit of her hands she planteth a vineyard.

She girdeth her loins with strength, and strengtheneth her arms.

She perceiveth that her merchandise is good; her candle goeth not out by night.

She layeth her hands to the spindle, and her hands hold the distraff.

She stretcheth out her hand to the poor; yea, she reacheth forth her hands to the needy.

She is not afraid of the snow for her household; for all her household are clothed with scarlet.

She maketh herself coverings of tapestry; her clothing is silk and purple.

Her husband is known in the gates, when he sitteth among the elders of the land.

She maketh fine linen, and selleth it; and delivereth girdles until the merchant.

Strength and honour are her clothing; and she shall rejoice in time to come.

Proverbs xxxi, 10-25

Table of Contents

Preface	*xi*
Women in Society	*3*
Women in Literature and the Arts	*207*
Index	*345*

Preface

It is hoped that this book will serve as a doorway to wider vistas for the serious researchers in women's studies who have already found that much work waits to be done. They have undoubtedly found that an international approach is germane to women's situation, for women's experiences differ markedly from men's, about whom the traditional history books have been written. It has been taken for granted that there are events and currents of thought that have affected all inhabitants of the earth throughout this history. It is also generally taken for granted, as when we talk of what has happened to "man" and "mankind," that these events and currents of thought have affected everyone in a general sense in the same way.

But there are some people—and they are increasingly numerous—who have come to realize that history has not been the same for women as it has for men. Much of the literature bringing out that fact had for a long time been largely ignored or consigned to oblivion. Therefore our research into what women throughout the ages have said about their actions, their conditions of life, their feelings, and their hopes has a ring of modernity. We ponder their writings and can only imagine what has been left out. Since the entirety of women's history is impossible to know, the logic of the situation leads us to the conclusion that our knowledge of history will always be less complete than even traditional historians have been willing to admit. To cite only one example, Roman women left us no record of their lives. Or if they did, nothing is left of the records, for, as Germaine Brée points out, collectors of records have historically been male.

Yet we have a wealth of retrospective materials at hand, with more to be discovered, giving almost boundless information and interpretation to make us more fully aware that women have had a kind of history which has been both derivative of men's and yet independent, especially in its psychological aspects. We realize now that to understand only what has happened to one-half of humanity is not to understand history at all.

As the twentieth century comes to a close enlightened people are aware that the "woman question" exists in a very vital way. But among them many still believe that it is a relatively new question, brought into focus by the contemporary emphasis on civil and human rights. There are others who believe that the centrality of the woman issue was spotlighted by Mary Wollstonecraft as she declared openly for the rights of women in England with her 1790 manifesto.[1] Lately a smaller number have come to realize that even earlier such American women as Abigail Adams, the wife of John Adams, were exercised about not officially sharing in the "inalienable rights" accorded to "all men" by the Declaration of Independence. However, to launch an organized protest would have been absurd, burdened as they were with a multiplicity of responsibilities. How could they have predicted the consequences, when political freedom at that time

---

[1] In her *Vindication of the Rights of Women.*

meant freedom from the one who personified a desperate struggle, King George III?[2]

Students of literature may have seen that as far back as the era of ancient Athens women rebelled against their subservient place in the scheme of things, as in Aristophanes' *Lysistrata* (where women are ridiculed, of course). Or perhaps some have reflected upon Euripides' realistic Medea who, enraged at her philandering husband, rebelled against her situation, not silently but with shocking aggression. Male novelists find fascination in delineating women characters, but so often they are stereotyped as good or bad—witness the unfeeling daughters in Balzac's *Le Père Goriot*, and their opposite, the noble self-sacrificing Agnes in Dickens' *David Copperfield* (or the sweetly pathetic Dora).

As people have become more aware of women's unique but heretofore forgotten history, much has been made of their protests and lamentations. It is important now that their achievements be signalled even more, however. It is not always easy to discover them, for as Joan Morris says in *Against Nature and God*, "History may be hidden in many ways." She rescues from comparative neglect the role of abbesses like Brigid of Kildare and Hilda of Whitby in the establishment of the Christian Church in Britain. Other writers of women's history point out that nuns as well as monks, especially in Ireland, shared the great civilizing work of

---

[2] We may note William L. O'Neill's naïve question in *Everyone Was Brave: A History of Feminism in America* as to why American women did not ask to be included in the Declaration of Independence, where "all men" were created equal. He sees the more recent change in family structure to that of the "nuclear" family as the precipitating factor in women's "rebellion."

copying and embellishing the manuscripts that carried classical and biblical learning forward during the so-called Dark Ages. Recent revivals are the writings of Hroswitha of Gandersheim and Hildegard of Bingen, two nuns whose works lay forgotten. It was a man who found Hroswitha's dramatic works. It is a man who writes of Hildegard. [3]

Medieval women, too, are being given well-deserved attention. In France, for example, Christine de Pisan, sometimes known as "France's first feminist," has awakened keen interest for the modernity of her ideas. Widowed at an early age, Christine took to writing and consequently became the first Frenchwoman to earn money by her pen, as many Englishwomen did in their turn. Christine's ideas were not what today we would deem "feminist," for part of her philosophy counseled resignation in the face of society's imponderable forces ranged against women of her time. She urged women to respect their special gifts within their own circle, however.

The Renaissance period has attracted such a multiplicity of scholars that much more is known of the women who made their mark on contemporary life in several countries—in Italy, for example, Isabella d'Este, in Spain Queen Isabella of Castile, and in England the redoubtable Queen Elizabeth I. Women of this era and succeeding centuries in France are well-known to scholars, even if their fame has not spread noticeably world-wide. As leaders of the *salons* over the years they became undeniably

---

[3] The index to this Guide has a reference, "women, forgotten," which might be of interest.

influential in literature and social accomplishments. Some of the most important cultural improvements (even the idea for the *Académie Française*) were brought about by French women, notably the *salonières,* but their reputation was diminished by the ridicule of Molière in such plays as *Les Femmes savantes.* He still, however, is more celebrated in French studies than they. Yet no critics will deny the importance of Mme de LaFayette's *La Princesse de Clèves* to the development of the psychological novel: some say that it is the first one.

For research in all fields where concentration is upon their concerns, women owe a debt of gratitude to champions of their cause in times past, and many of these have been male, men who have considered it very much worth their while to write books about women. The analysis of the nature of women has intrigued many and frustrated some. Scholars like Robert Briffault spent years researching into the origins of society and came to the conclusion that women's inherent nature and the basic values they developed have proved to be the determining factors in the development of social life.[4] While he was conducting his researches, as he commented in his preface, his colleagues scorned his theses and he had to work alone. [5]

Many prominent Frenchmen have been encouraging of women's education and enhanced status. It would be gratifying to report that for this reason women in France have as a matter of

---

[4] See *The Mothers: A Study of the Origins of Sentiments and Institutions* (1927)
[5] See for example *Unsung Champions of Women* by Mary Cohart and many references in the index under "feminists, male."

course enjoyed a greater degree of freedom from the usual constraints, especially legal. But their complaints, even today, indicate otherwise. In the nineteenth century we notice the arrogant diatribes of P.-J. Proudhon against feminists Jenny d'Héricourt and Juliette Lambert, and even in the twentieth century Simone de Beauvoir and Germaine Brée, productive scholars, find the prejudices in *academia* burdensome.

When we speak of the "Renaissance woman" we cannot apply the concepts implicit in the expression, the "Renaissance man." Although many women were exposed to the expansive ideas of the times, they often lamented that restraints were put upon their intellectual growth.[6] Thus we can note Marie de Gournay's essay, *L'Égalité des hommes et des femmes*, written in 1622, in which Marie insists upon the natural equality of men and women and regrets bitterly that society would not acknowledge women's right to be treated as equals.[7]

As for Spanish women, even though many of them were learned and as *sabias* enjoyed the respect of male contemporaries for their gifts, very little of their intellectual record remains. Spanish literary men have not generally earned commendation for their championing of women, probably because Moorish ideas in regard to women lingered long after the Moors were chased from the peninsula. Yet a brilliant exception was Juan Luis Vives,

---

[6] R. Maulde la Clavière shows is very clearly in *The Women of the Renaissance: A Study of Feminism*, which documents the obstacles put in the way of women who tried to augment their chances of becoming full participants in social life.

[7] Marie was the adoptive daughter of Montaigne, whose *Essais* are widely read and studied internationally.

the Spanish humanist who, while living in England as tutor to Queen Catherine of Aragon, wrote influential books advocating the classical education of women (then, of course, of the upper classes only), adding his voice to those of Erasmus and Sir Thomas More, Margaret Roper's father. True, "piety" was always an integral part of the educational essentials for women, considering that in all times, it appears, "chastity" was a *sine qua non* for women in the minds of men.

Margarita Nelken reminds us that as a rule little attention has been paid to women writers in Hispanic cultures. In the twentieth century Hispanist Barbara Matulka analyzed the delineation of women in the literature of the Golden Age, the time when the greatest writers, such as Miguel Cervantes and Tirso de Molina made their appearance. For those whose interests lie in researching drama, these female characters offer a challenge. Spanish studies call out for researchers like Matulka (whose life was cut all too short) to interpret the women who are, regrettably, only reflected in pages written by men, as P. W. Bomli points out in *La Femme dans l'Espagne du siècle d'or.* Yet we must not overlook the writings of Gregorio Martínez Sierra, who encouraged nineteenth-century Spanish women in their struggle for equality.

Portugal suffered from the same myopia in regard to women, as witnessed by Maria Barreno in *The Three Marias.* Unfortunately, the Hispanic legacy was transported to the New World, where the ideas of *honra* and *machismo* confronted literary women with almost insurmountable problems, cutting off any number of talented women from fulfilling their promise and making the cause of feminism a disheartening one. As for Italy, we see appearing in the Renaissance some women of great brilliance who were universally admired. Usually they were women of high station; they feature in the works of Boccaccio, Dante, and Castiglione. Regarding the general ambience in which Italian women have lived historically, however, Gina Lombroso-Ferrer comes to discouraging conclusions in *The Soul of Woman: Reflections on Life*.

In England, whose surface culture was more liberal, in the sixteenth century Mary Astell had articulated her frustrations and at the same time put forth constructive ideas for the future of more liberated women: she felt that their hope lay in the path of advanced education and in their determination not to remain chattels in marriage. Yet four centuries later, Virginia Woolf was echoing the same concerns in *A Room of One's Own*. In the United States, Margaret Fuller (Ossoli) wrestled with the problem of being an intellectual woman in the nineteenth century—problems which she never succeeded in resolving. Realizing that things had to change for the better, Fuller joined the utopian community Brook Farm, where gathered some of the now-greats of American intellectual life. But evidently her presence was found to be disruptive.

Studies coming from the British and American heritage reflect a more realistic attitude as the growing effects of the Industrial Revolution became subjects for literature. Its effects upon working class women are documented by Mrs. Gaskell's novels, while such writers as Jane Austen, George Meredith, and, in the United States, Edith Wharton, tried to portray how women's lives had been affected—sometimes for the better, sometimes for the worse. Herman Melville, cognizant of the difference between women's and men's inherent values, regretted the tearing of the fabric of traditional American society—his short story describing women at work in a textile factory, "The Tartarus of Maids," was symbolic of his fears.

Social critics such as Mary Wollstonecraft and John Stuart Mill analyzed the injustices inherent in society in relation to women. Social change accelerated with the advent of capitalism and the machine, along with the compassionless rationalizations for the sake of efficiency. The requirements of the marketplace began to take over all aspects of society.

For women a serious problem appeared in this technological age: the worth of woman's work and the primacy of her values were diminished in the rising commercialization of life's activities. Rewarding work that had once been indispensable was taken from women, work which had been accomplished in the home. Certain "cottage industries" which had been shared by both partners in a marriage lost ground. In the years up to 1800 middle class women had often found greater prestige in work, as Alice Clark shows in her *Working Life of Women in the Seventeenth Century.* Her study deals with Englishwomen, but on the American scene we find this even truer, for everyone's effort was needed on the successive frontiers.

With the advent of the factory system, men (and in cases of the poor, women also) were forced to find a way to make a living outside the home. Moreover, universal education took children out of the home at any early age. Often they were exposed to values not countenanced in the home. This development, too, made the mother's role in education of less importance. Eventually many sociologists came to realize that alienation and isolation were growing problems among women. When this was added to the traditional reluctance of men in authority to offer women the same opportunities for education and career challenges then reserved for males only, the problems were compounded. That these problems were not addressed or could not be under the circumstances was attested to as late as the 1960's, when in the United States Betty Friedan's *The Feminine Mystique* became overwhelming popular among women, if not men.

Clark shows that the zenith of women's usefulness in economics was reached before the advent of the Industrial Revolution. This fact points up a broader issue: the fact that women, in spite of the advances which humanity has achieved, had not succeeded greatly in their efforts to be considered much higher than second class citizens without full legal status with men. That could be seen as the key factor around which all other considerations revolved. Even under early twentieth century Communism in Russia, where the new system of government seemed to promise women a better life, hard work in factory or mine became the lot of thousands. Harsh reality, in the form of the dearth of men caused by war and the need of their country to industrialize made "freedom" for them an empty word.

Legal equality became a goal for which nineteenth century women in the United States and Britain worked. To trace the laws which have impinged mercilessly upon women's lives one may take as examples the epics and sacred writings of India, tribal Teutonic (Anglo-Saxon and German) laws, Napoleon's *Code Civile,* and the Anglo-American laws based upon the interpretations of Edward Coke and William Blackstone. In the United States, dedicated to political freedom, it was illegal for women to vote. In 1872 feminist Susan B. Anthony defied the law by

Preface

voting—her purpose was to turn a spotlight upon the injustices perpetrated in the United States. After being reprimanded, however, she was denied the punishment she sought.[8]

As women in Western countries have made enviable advances in their situation, women on other continents have looked to the West for encouragement with their struggles for a modicum of freedom. India and Africa are two examples. Indian women had occasion to be familiar with the West when it was part of the British Empire and there was mutual exchange for education. It was not until 1895 that Pundita Ramabai Sarasvati broke the "silence of a thousand years" to reveal, in a book published in Germany, the sufferings of even high-caste Hindu women, let alone the ordeals of the women from the "untouchables." Other women have been bound by the Koran and in some cases where some freedom was achieved, the return of a theocratic government, such as that in Iran, took away even those vestiges of liberation.

When we turn to Africa, also familiar with the West because of colonization, we see the work of women anthropologists documented by Denise Paulme and the Talbot sisters. The Talbots were encouraged in their work with women of the Ibibios in Southern Nigeria by British male anthropologists, who were astute enough to realize that what they knew of African women had always been filtered through conversations with men. African women, too, looked to the West for knowledge and hope. As for

---

[8] See Anthony, *An Account of the Proceedings on the Trial of Susan B. Anthony on the Charge of Illegal Voting at the Presidential Election in Nov., 1872.*

Australia and New Zealand, they shared the basic culture of the West, for weal or woe. A definite pattern runs through the studies found here: in all ages, in all countries, women share the history of men, but they also share an "existential situation" which men can hardly understand. Perhaps it is a situation which women themselves do not always understand clearly. This is one of the purposes of women's studies—to make clear that which heretofore has been an area of darkness.

For those who are curious about epigraphs, the one I have chosen, consisting of some verses from the Hebrew Old Testament's *Book of Proverbs,* bids fair to be unique in the annals of ancient writings. Since those verses come at the very end of *Proverbs* and are in marked contrast to much of what goes before, one is inclined to believe that these verses in the epigraph were added by a woman—or at least by a man of unusual understanding.

Although throughout the centuries many virtues were ascribed to a pious woman, including meekness and passivity, in this passage we find praise not only for piety but for her administrative ability as an equal in marriage, her imaginative and practical talents, and for a vision which extends beyond the narrow confines of a household. In the ambience of freedom in which she evidently lived (and which seemed to be ignored by later biblical interpreters who preferred to emphasize the wickedness of the "scarlet woman"), she had no reason to be in competition or subservient to men: the idea of "liberation" is extraneous. This ancient paragon of feminine virtue is truly a *woman* who can live in the past, present, and future.

Preface

This guide, while being far from exhaustive, has been designed to be inspiring as well as useful—and objective as far as objectivity is important. I have examined all the books and articles referenced here, with one or two exceptions. Each item is included because after review I decided that it had special qualities of interest or original thought.

The entries are not limited to certain geographical areas, for as is noted above, the situations of women have more similarities than differences, and the influence of the West is global. The only requirement is that each entry must appear in English, French, Spanish, Portuguese or Italian. The work is divided into three parts: (1) *Women in Society,* which consists of studies dealing with the relations of women and their place in society in different cultures, whether these be written by women or men; (2) *Women in Literature and the Arts,* preponderantly about women who create literature or those who are reflected in literature, with some studies concerning women in music and art; (3) the index, which is very detailed because it is the key to the entries in which titles, persons, places, and subjects are mentioned. Too, in the index are noted certain books whose translations may be of interest to comparatists especially. Purists may complain that authors' names are duplicated in this work—that there are no dashes to indicate several works by the same person. For my part, I dislike dashes in place of personal names. Every author, I think, deserves to have his or her full name written out as many times as necessary.

The researcher might be helped by noticing copyright dates, original and of later vintage (including reprints), for each entry that seems to be relevant to the projected use. This is important in order to place the word "contemporary" in its proper context, for one thing. For another, it makes it easier to appreciate the uniqueness and originality of the writer's contribution. Because so many of the works referenced here hark back for centuries, noting the sometimes surprising dates of their first publication can enhance our respect for these women and men of the past.

As this work nears its publication, I think gratefully of the many friends who have been part of it, either because of their moral support or because of actually sharing in its development. Therefore, thanks to the noted Hispanist, the late Dr. Gerald E. Wade, who gladly welcomed women into the fold of scholarship; to Barbara Anderson, *la asistante importante,* for good times at libraries and bookshops; to Wilma and Bill Colbert for help with research at UCLA and the University of Southern California; to Kathy Abramson for her unflagging enthusiasm; to Dr. Jean Katz Cawardine of St. Thomas University for good talk on literature and life; to Dr. Albert Stone of the University of Iowa for his encouragement; to Jean Hartman for finding tantalizing titles; to librarian Betty Terry for sharing trips to old bookshops; to librarian Anne Hurst for appreciating bibliography; to Dr. Ruth Grace Zibart of Vanderbilt University for being an admirable example; to Dr. Frances Hardie of Vanderbilt University for a share in her convivial luncheons; to my cousins Ellaleen and Geoffrey Procter for their warm understanding; to the women honors students at Stetson University who shared their thoughts on the subject; to George who helped keep the wheels of industry turning, and finally to Robert, Carl, Douglas, and Seth for paying attention.

H. U. S.

Women in Society

Women in Society

Abbott, Edith. *Women in Industry: A Study in American Economic History.* New York: Source Books Press, 1970. (Originally published in 1909.) 409 p.

Drawing conclusions from her minute studies of working women in in the United States in the early years of the twentieth century, Abbott remarks that the advances of the women's rights movement had accrued mainly to professional women. Working class women, she declares, still experienced a world "very much as her great-grandmother left it." The basic assumptions underlying her analysis are that the rebellion begun by such women as Susan B. Anthony should by the twentieth century have borne more fruit for the women who carried on the struggle, although perhaps these pioneers, too optimistic, were unaware of how much yet remained to be done. In 1909 when Abbott published her study women had not even been granted the vote, and this became a *sine qua non* of the political power which was necessary to achieve many real economic advances for women.

Abbott includes bibliographical notes, a good bibliography (pages 392-399), and a list of occupations in which women were gainfully employed in 1900.

Adams, Henry. *Mont-Saint-Michel and Chartres.* Atlanta, Georgia: Cherokee, 1990. (Reprint of Houghton Mifflin's 1935 edition.) 377 p. (Originally published in 1905.)

An extended interpretation of the architecture of the cathedrals of Mont-Saint-Michel and Chartres forms the idealistic framework around which Adams builds his thesis of the power of woman. He juxtaposes the heavenly powers, represented by the Virgin Mary and symbolized by the cathedral of Chartres, with the earthly powers displayed in the lives of three French queens, Eleanor de Guienne (1122-1204), Marie de Champagne, her daughter (1145-1198), and Blanche de Castile, Eleanor's granddaughter (1187-1252).

Adams sees the basic reason for the "courts of love" developed by these women originating in the feminine desire to soften the barbaric manners of their men by setting forth a code of manners. He shows not only woman's aptness for refinement, however; he also points out her potential in the use of power and concludes that "the proper study of mankind is woman." (See Mary Beard, *Woman as Force in History* [below] for a careful critique of *Mont-Saint-Michel and Chartres.*) A French translation was published in 1955 by R. Laffont, Paris, with George Fradier and Jacques Brosse as translators.

Addams, Jane. **Democracy and Social Ethics.** Edited by Anne Firor Scott. (The John Harvard Library.) Cambridge: Harvard University Press, 1964 [1902]. 281 p.

Addams' seminal work was first published in 1902 to explicate the ideas central to her thought as she pioneered in social work in Chicago's Hull House. In the rapidly industrializing nineteenth century many socially sensitive people throughout the world saw the need for reform in the situation of women, most of whom had little economic and political power and few opportunities for education. Tending toward social Darwinism in thought, Addams sympathized as well with the young middle-class woman's need to grow away from the protection of her parents to find maturity in a "moral enterprise" of her own.

Scott provides a good biographical and critical introduction to this work.

Addams, Jane. ***The Long Road of Woman's Memory***. New York: Macmillan Company, 1917 [1916]. 168 p.

Chapter V, "Challenging War" grew out of Addams' conversations in France with women in moral revolt against their bereavements during World War I. Many were convinced that a commitment to feminism could discourage the destructive militarism which resulted in massive slaughter of men on the battlefields in Europe..

Throughout the book Addams is groping for a new interpretation of woman's place in civilization, hoping that the budding Woman's Movement (and its counterpart in Germany) might find a way to mitigate the violence and injustices which were especially brutalizing to women and children.

Afetinan, A. ***The Emancipation of the Turkish Woman***. Amsterdam: Drukkerij, 1962. 63 p.

This UNESCO study surveys the social revolution which had been brought about since 1925 by the emancipation of women in Turkey. Afetinan played a leading role in this movement in Anatolia, and here she presents not only first-hand accounts of those times but also an overview of the past, dating from the pre-Islamic era. Thus it is of interest for women everywhere, for it sheds light on the struggles undertaken by Turkish women in their hope to attain some of the freedoms enjoyed by most women in advanced countries. Afetinan highlights the contrast between the Turkish *mores* of yesterday and those of her own time as to their effects upon women's personal and social situations.

Alliluyeva, Svetlana. *Twenty Letters to a Friend.* Translated by Priscilla Johnson McMillan. New York: Harper & Row, 1967. 246 p.

These letters form an unprecedented and unique account of a woman's life in the former USSR, an account which can never be replicated. Svetlana Alliluyeva's letters are to an anonymous friend—perhaps they were merely a vehicle through which she, as Stalin's daughter, could relax enough to express her ambivalent feelings about the world around her as it looked from the Kremlin, which she called "home." To her these memories became "an intolerable burden."

The controlling image for Alliluyeva was her father, and the event around which her thoughts turn here are his death. To millions he was the cruel despot, for all around her people were being repressed, sent into exile or executed. But until she was sixteen he was kindly, and she felt that he loved her (two affectionate letters from him are printed on page 97). When the Nazi armies invaded, he became a different man—a tyrant with no time for family life, a paranoid man who trusted no one.

The most important influences in her affective life, however, were women: her gifted and misunderstood mother—a "perfect wife" who committed suicide at the age of thirty-one when Svetlana was six; her wise and loving nurse, Alexandra Andreevna, who was with her for thirty years; and, when the "evil days" came, a peasant girl assigned to be her housekeeper (and a spy, yet who was also a "helpless pawn") by Beria ("a terrifying evil genius"), Stalin-appointed head of Internal Affairs. Svetlana Alliluyeva's freedom disappeared.

No one interested in the history of twentieth century Russia—and in women's lives there—should overlook this amazing little book.

Alvarez Quintero, S. y J. ***La Mujer española: una conferencia y dos cartas***. Madrid: Biblioteca Hispania, 1918 (?). 89 p.

Although the purpose of this book is to present the text of a lecture on the subject of women by Alvarez, the kernel of interest is in the two letters written by him in reply to the protest against his ideas by the famous woman author, Emilia Pardo Bazán.

In Alvarez's text one recognizes the traditional Spanish *ethos* in regard to women: they should be the inspirers of men, beautiful and protected at home, following the examples of Queen Isabella and Santa Teresa (who was, however, a very strong woman, hardly "protected at home"). If this beatific state of affairs is disturbed, he warns," we [men] shall emigrate to another planet"—Venus or Mars. But when he comes to the letters he has written to Señora Pardo Bazán, we see less bombast, out of respect for her prestige. Here in delicate wording he shows that he realizes the necessity for staying on earth to justify his position! Unfortunately, the text of Bazán's letter which prompted Alvarez's veiled apology is not included in this slim volume.

Alvarez Vignoli de Demicheli, Sophie, ed. ***Derechos civiles de la mujer; antecedentes parlamentarios***. Tome I. (Série "Juridicas y sociales," Vol. I.). Montevideo, Uruguay: Editorial Alfa y Omega, 1946. 482 p.

This is not a dry law book as the title might suggest, but a living testament to the historic inequities of the Hispanic system of jurisprudence. In form the volume consists of the contemporary laws relating to women retained on the national books and the testimony of witnesses at hearings held by the Uruguayan Senate and House to consider changes.

Students of feminist subjects will find this helpful in understanding the bases for the centuries-old *ethos* against which some enlightened Hispanic women, along with their male defenders, rebelled (albeit unsuccessfully), with the encouragement of such men as the Spaniard Gregorio Martínez Sierra (see below) during the early years of the twentieth century.

Alzona, Encarnación. ***Rizal's Legacy to the Filipino Woman.*** 1956 [1953]. 22 p.

In 1889 José Rizal y Alonso, patriot and novelist exiled from the Philippines, sent an approving letter to the young women of Malalos when he heard that they had defied an ecclesiastic ruling forbidding them to study the Spanish language as an educational project. Calling uneducated women a "hindrance," he reminded them that "women are the first to influence the minds of men." He added, "If the Filipino woman does nothing to hurl off her fetters, she should not be entrusted with the education of her children!"[1]

During his years of exile in London, Rizal studied at the British Museum to continue his education and novel-writing.

---

[1] Rizal's influence among the Filipino people has been very great, for he was unremitting in his efforts to improve their lot. He was of Tagalong parentage, but he had a vision of a wider world for his people, which included becoming knowledgeable in the Spanish culture to which they were subject. Through his studies in Manila and European universities he accomplished this aim for himself and continued always to fight for freedom from this subjection. His day of execution, December 30, was made a national holiday in the Philippines.

His first fictional character, Maria Clara, became the idol of Filipino girls: she was "faithful, romantic, and idealistic." Unfortunately for the cause of women's advancement, Rizal's love of freedom, as well as his uninhibited literary portrayals of the clergy, cost him his life in 1896.

Anthony, Susan B. *An Account of the Proceedings on the Trial of Susan B. Anthony on the Charge of Illegal Voting at the Presidential Election in Nov., 1872.* (Women in America from Colonial Times to the Twentieth Century.) New York: Arno Press, 1974. 212 p. (Published first in 1874 by the Daily Democrat and Chronicle Book Print, Rochester, New York.)

Staunch feminist Anthony believed that the post-Civil War extensions of franchise to male blacks ought to have included all women as well. And so she illegally voted at a Rochester polling place to bring attention to her protest. After being fined, Anthony defiantly stated that she would never pay a dollar "of your unjust penalty" and in spite of Judge Hunt's order not to speak after sentencing, declared, "All of my sex is. . . doomed to political subjection under this so-called form of government." Her hopes of appealing her case in the Supreme Court for a definitive test, however, were frustrated when the lower court failed to enforce her sentence.

Appadorai, A., ed. *The Status of Women in South Asia.* Bombay: Orient Longmans, 1954; Washington: Zenger Publishing, 1978. 151 p.

The political and legal status of women in contemporary Vietnam, Thailand, India, Pakistan, Burma, Indonesia, the Philippines, Malaya, and Ceylon is the subject of this comprehensive appraisal, which took the form of a seminar held in

India. Ten experts contribute searching analyses of current problems: in addition, they offer as preliminaries to their discussions a consideration of the cultural and anthropological backgrounds relating to women. Matriarchal and patriarchal family patterns are discussed on pages 47-64.

Aranguren, José Luis. *Erotismo y liberación de la mujer.* Barcelona: Ediciones Ariel, 1982 [1972]. 151 p.

Four essays (the fourth being "La liberación de la mujer") address key problems of Spanish women as seen by this sympathetic author. Noting the progress in feminist causes made in other countries, he alludes frequently to ideas and books coming from abroad, especially the United States.

Astell, Mary. *An Essay in Defence of the Female Sex.* New York: Source Books Press, 1970. 133 p. (First published in England 1696.)

This edition of Astell's essay appears in its original format. Dedicated to Princess Anne of Denmark, it purposes, as Astell tells us, to "reduce the Sexes to a Level, and by Argument to raise Ours to an Equality at most with the Men." This Astell does by argument, comparing and contrasting physical attributes, intellectual abilities, and character traits, almost always to the favor of her own sex. Along with the argument she provides little preachments exhorting women to use their natural intelligence and not to allow discouragement lead them into slothfulness. The charms of feminine company are stressed by Astell, an outspoken precursor of the women's rights movement which flowered much later. (There is some question about the authorship of this essay. Did Mary Astell use the pseudonym of Judith Drake?)

Astell, Mary. *A Serious Proposal to the Ladies.* New York: Source Books Press, 1970. 162 p. (Originally published in 1691.)

Astell says that her proposal is "for the advancement of women's true and greatest interest" as she deplores the ignorance in which women were kept by their parents. It is her hope to be able to inspire in her fellowomen enthusiasm for education and for her iconoclastic proposal which is: To establish a community for religious retreat, where ladies will "suffer no other confinement but to be kept off the road of sin" and will drop the frivolities of the world to find wisdom in "such a Paradise as your Mother Eve forfeited, where men will not be able to hold the monopoly of the fruits of the tree of knowledge which they wish to keep from woman."

Astell, Mary. *Some Reflections upon Marriage.* New York: Source Books Press, 1970. 128 p. (Originally published in 1730.)

Chafing against the subjection of woman to man in marriage, Astell points out how the tables can be turned for a girl as soon as courtship is over and she must fawn over her husband, who may be her inferior, and be humiliated by his "indifference, neglect or perhaps aversion."

"But alas!" she writes, "what poor woman is ever taught that she should have a higher design than to get a husband?" and warns women against allowing themselves to get into a situation they once would have thought unendurable.

When Astell put her thoughts into words such ideas were indeed "subversive," but this did not prevent her from speaking out—"a lone voice crying in the wilderness" indeed.

Bainton, Roland H. **Women of the Reformation.** Minneapolis, Minnesota: Augsburg Publishing House, 1977 [1971]. 279 p.

Bainton gives as one of his reasons for writing this book the desire to bring attention to "those who have not had their due," which category includes women and heretics. Here he gives several women of Germany and Italy their due in a factual and well-documented account.

A short preface refers to the presence of misogyny in European history. Bainton shows disapproval of this injustice by pointing out the crucial part played by women of the Biblical and classical worlds, as well as later. As for the Reformation, he opines that if women had boycotted the movement it would have failed.

A unique feature of this study is that most of the biographical information gleaned from works in languages other than English has been translated, which enhances the research value for those who would not find the original sources accessible. Other features are the goodly number of illustrations and the bibliographies which follow each chapter.

Baldwin, Monica. *I Leap Over the Wall: Contrasts and Impressions after Twenty-Eight Years in a Convent*. New York: Rinehart and Company, 1950. 313 p.

Baldwin escapes from the confines of her traditional convent, but then in turn seeks escape from the real world which has passed her by. On the cliffs of Cornwall in southern England she finds a tiny cottage which reminds her joyously of a "cell of a medieval hermit," and she does not regret the convent which she has left behind, nor the real world with its lack of silence and privacy. [2]

---

[2] Monica Baldwin was a descendant of the sixteenth-century Thomas Baldwin

Bardèche, Maurois. *Histoire des femmes*. 2 vols. Paris: Stock, 1968.

In his introduction Bardèche declares that women prove themselves equal to men—or could if they had the opportunity—in all endeavors, as history proves many times over. Therefore, he believes, feminists were being too modest in their demands for equality, since they were already superior: "Les féministes qui revendiquent si âprement une égalité juridique se font de la femme une idée bien modeste. L'histoire des femmes prouve abondamment que la femelle n'est pas inférieure au mâle quand on lui confie des tâches viriles" (p. 11).

Historical support for his thesis may be found in such sections as "Les Femmes des chansons de geste et de l'amour courtois," "Du Quattrocento à la Renaissance," and "Les Femmes de la Renaissance et de l'Europe baroque." These three will be found in Volume II. Bardèche's style is readable, and notes accompany the test. Comparatists will find references to England, Russia, Germany, Italy, and Spain also.

Baritz, Loren, ed. *The Culture of the Twenties.* (The American Heritage Series.) Indianapolis: Bobbs, Merrill, 1970

Beatrice M. Hinkle's "Against the Double Standard" and Harold E. Stearns' "The American Mind" will be of interest for their contrasting analyses of this chaotic period in the wake of World War I. Both writers have in mind the fairly well-to-do middle class.

---

who leaped to freedom from the Tower of London, where he was held for assisting Mary, Queen of Scots to escape from Queen Elizabeth's guards.

Hinkle approves of "the new morality" growing out of revolt against the old *mores*, which she is convinced were inimical to woman's psychic development. Therefore she sees the change to be a therapeutic phenomenon, and although the new freedom has led to some troublesome social manifestations, she declares that it is long overdue.

Stearns, on the other hand, finds American women reprehensible because they have shirked their intellectual responsibilities. Hard-working pioneer men, he complains, entrusted culture to their women, who had more leisure, but women's lack of cultural interests caused the sterility which plagues American intellectual life. Apparently he was not aware that most women on the frontier were hard-working, too, and that opportunities for traditional cultural advantages were not readily at hand in the hinterlands.

Hinkle and Stearns illustrate two aspects of the controversy which inflamed public opinion in regard to women in the decade after World War I and during the Prohibition era (the "flapper" era), when it was believed that immorality and women's emancipation went hand in hand as the serious efforts of women to be heard in the political arena were largely ignored.

Barnard, H. C., ed. ***Fénelon on Education***. Cambridge: Cambridge University Press, 1962. 152 p.

To this collection of Fénelon's pedagogic works in translation Barnard supplies an introduction which sets the visionary French writer in historical and intellectual perspective, connecting him in thought with Montaigne (1533-1592), David Hume (1711-1766), and John Locke (1632-1704). Noteworthy is a translation of Fénelon's "Traité de L'Éducation des filles"

(1687), which begins, "Nothing is more neglected than the education of girls" and goes on to point out that since women constitute half the human race, their education should not be ignored. The enlightened "Advice to a Lady of Quality Concerning the Education of Her Daughter" (1715), is another of the translations found here, as is an essay by Bernard, "'Antiope'—Fénelon's Ideal of Womanhood, from *Télémaque*."

Although his recommendations are articulated within the traditional concepts of women's spheres (such as those prescribed by contemporary religion), Fénelon's ideas bespeak a genuine concern for the development of women's intellect, something which is not found in much of the advice given by his contemporaries in France and elsewhere. Yet he knew that French scholars were not ready to welcome a great number of "learned ladies" in their midst, as Molière's satirical drama attests.

Barnard's work is indexed, with notes and a chronological table of Fénelon's life.

Barros Vidal, Olmio. ***Precursoras brasileiras.*** Rio de Janeiro: A Nosti Editora, 1945(?). 277 p.

Women of Brazil eulogized for their achievements include a saintly woman, a warrior of pure Indian stock, and sixteen others outstanding in generally male-oriented occupations such as aviation, law, journalism, and medicine. A precursor of feminism, Nisia Floresta, is also praised for her concern for women. This work is annotated and well-illustrated but not indexed.

Batto, Bernard Frank. ***Studies on Women at Mari.*** (The Johns Hopkins Near Eastern Studies.) Baltimore: The Johns Hopkins University Press, 1974. 164 p.

Women in Retrospect: A Research Guide

"Viewed from the standpoint of ancient Mesopotamian society, the woman of Mari, like her counterpart in Babylonia, was already much 'liberated,'" writes Batto, citing as source of his information the publication of crucial new findings by archeologists.[3] Such discoveries, he avers, made a history of women of these areas more possible, and he points to works which, like his, could be helpful in future endeavors.

Batto's bibliography of works in English, French, and German orient the student to valuable materials in general history and specialized research.

Bay, J. Christian. *"Women Not Considered Human Beings,"* in ***The Fortune of Books: Essays, Memories, and Prophecies of a Librarian.*** Chicago: Walter M. Hill, 1941.

On pages 212-222 Bay considers a 1594 manuscript, *Disputatio nova qua probatur mulieres non esse homines nec salvari*, which "held the center of the academic stage, amidst impassioned debate, ten generations ago." Embroiled in this argument eventually were the highest theologians of the Protestant Church; yet it began as a semi-humorous experiment in dialectics to "prove" woman's inferiority. Set in motion, too was the legal apparatus of the church because the dispute involved the use of the Bible for facetious purposes.

---

[3] Excavations at Mari on the Euphrates at Nuzi and elsewhere yielded texts which shed light on customs in the first half of the second century B. C. For example, a clay map dating back to c. 2500 was found there. Mari was situated on the right back of the Euphrates about 7 miles NNW of Abu Kemal near the frontier with modern Iraq. The city was occupied from the second century B.C. through the seventh century A.D. During the time of Hammmurabi it enjoyed a period of great prosperity. Religion at Mari included the worship of the goddess Ishtar.

This valuable manuscript was obtained by Bay at the dissolution of the Cordes Library in Geneva.

Beach, John G. *Notable Women of Spirit: the Historical Role of Women in the Seventh Day Adventist Church.* Nashville, Tennessee: Southern Publishing Association., 1976. 125 p. Bibliography.

Beach reveals that women historically played a strong role in the Church up to this time, having held every administrative post except that of president and ordained minister. Chosen for special attention is Ellen G. White.

Beard, Mary Ritter. *On Understanding Women.* New York: Greenwood Press, 1968. 541 p. (First published in 1931.)

Historian Beard devotes herself to ferreting out neglected contributions made by women throughout the centuries, beginning with classical civilizations. Many allusions to women in early Christian times are here, as well as documentation of women's participation in the new age of science. Beard deplores the strength of sex antagonisms which have detracted from the accomplishments of women in all ages. A good bibliography will help her readers continue the fascinating work she so ably pioneered.

Beard, Mary Ritter. *Women as Force in History: a Study in Traditions and Realities.* New York: The Macmillan Company, 1946. 396 p.

This study serves as an excellent introduction to women's history, for it is objective, well-organized, wide in scope, readable, and replete with historical information. In it Beard traces historical reasons for women's subjection and shows its baleful effects clearly.

The dramatic impact of the first chapter, dealing as it does with the allegiance paid by women in Germany and Italy to Hitler and Mussolini in the 1930's and 1940's, reminds the reader that woman's influence can be used for evil as well as good.

Beard points to examples of social good accomplished by women in her critique of Henry Adams' work on medieval women wherein he uses the cathedrals Mont-Saint-Michel and Chartres as a background for his apotheosis of women.

Included is an important section devoted to English jurists William Blackstone (1723-1780) and Edward Coke (1552-1634), with an explanation of how their legal work affected both British and American systems of jurisprudence, to the detriment of women.[4] A useful comprehensive bibliography will be found on pages 333-345, and the work is indexed.

Beauvoir, Simone de. *Le deuxième sexe* (Collection Idées.) 2 vols. Paris: Gallimard, 1978. (First published in 1949.)

As one of her epigraphs to these volumes, which she intends as a definitive statement of woman's life, de Beauvoir quotes Poulain de la Barre, "Tout de qui a été écrit par les hommes sur les femmes doit être suspect, car ils sont à la fois juge et partie." ("Everything which has been written by men about women ought to be suspect, because they are at the same time judge and party.") Therefore from her vantage point of existen-

---

[4] Especially was this true of Blackstone, whose interpretations of the British common law Beard says, "fortified in the United States the doctrine of women's legal subjection to man." Beard attributes some of this veritable worship of Blackstone to sheer indolence on the part of lawyers in the early days of the Republic because Blackstone's interpretations were so easy to read and apply. See Chapter 5.

tial thought, de Beauvoir has seen woman's situation in a manner that is unique and which subsequently greatly influenced women writers grappling with the paradoxes (perhaps the Sartrian "absurdity" as well) of woman's life.

This work reflects de Beauvoir's wide acquaintance with many fields of learning, including anthropology, with special attention paid to the literatures of Europe and the United States. Many passages of fiction are considered in relation to the evocation of writers' concepts of essential femaleness.

Beauvoir, Simone de. *The Second Sex.* Translated and edited by M. Parshley. New York: Alfred A. Knopf, 1964. 732 p.

De Beauvoir's erudite and indispensable work on woman's "situation" is a classic which exists in a framework of existential thought, for the author has been satisfied with no less than an attempt at a definitive analysis of womanhood in essence and existence yesterday, today, and in the future.

The second part of *The Second Sex*, "Woman's Life Today," views women in various situations surrounding her biologic and social destiny. The conclusion, "Toward Liberation," encompasses de Beauvoir's thoughts on what women should expect of life.

Parshley has written a 14-page introduction and provided a comprehensive index.

Beaver, Robert Pierce. *All Loves Excelling: American Protestant Women in World Missions.* Grand Rapids, Michigan: Eerdmans, 1968. 227 p.

Beaver gives glimpses behind the churchly curtain as he considers the world-wide influence of the women who gathered money for missions and those who went out to do field work.

Chapter III on single women points out that their appointments so "grievously offended" public opinion about the "proprieties" that they were most often called to the American Indian missions, as being closer to home.

A bibliography of sources includes reports of the churches, religious journals, and books on relevant subjects.

Bedek, Evelyn B. *"Salonières and Bluestockings: Educated Obsolescence and Germinating Feminism,"* Feminist Studies, 3 (Spring-Summer, 1976).

Only in the *salon*, which was in effect an informal university held in private homes, could women ignore the general prejudice against the learned lady in England and France, says Bedek, as she pays tribute to women who brought their intellectual gifts into play as part of these conversational gatherings.

In sixteenth-century France Mme de Rambouillet (Catherine de Vivonne, 1588-1666) created an exclusive niche of tranquillity for both men and women after the turmoil of the wars of religion. Thus was established a tradition which lasted into the eighteenth century.

In England, where women felt less socially dependent because of the freer legal air, says Bedek, they were slower to adopt this means of social and intellectual interchange, but in the long run it was the English "bluestocking" (in French *bas bleu*) movement that made the greatest contribution to active feminism.[5]

---

[5] "Bluestocking" had already come to be a pejorative term to denote an intellectual woman who was humorless, pedantic, and probably only superficially intelligent, the object of satire by some dramatists, notably Molière in France. The term first came into vogue in Italy and France in Renaissance times to refer

Beirne, M. Francis (Sister). *L'Éducation des femmes du dix-septième siècle*. Irvington, New Jersey: Washington Irving Press, 1950. 78 p..

This short exposition begins with the ideas of St. François de Sales as expressed in his *L'Instruction à la vie dévote* (1609), considers the thought of St. Vincent de Paul and the pedagogy of the Jansenists and Port-Royal, then turns to secular education, with chapters on *les précieuses* and Molière's satire of them. The study closes with attention given to Mmes de Sévigné and de LaFayette, Fénélon, and l'abbé Claude Fleury. After this discerning bird's-eye view, a bibliography invites further study.

Bennett, Arnold. *Our Women: Chapters on the Sex Discord*. Plainview, New York: Books for Libraries Press, 1975. (Reprint of 1920 edition by George H. Doran.) 264 p.

It has been said that British novelist Bennett's opinion was that "any marriage is better than no marriage at all," and if this is true we cannot charge him with blatant prejudice, perhaps just a little myopia because of the tradition in which he was bred. In his rambling style he uses a hypothetical Jack and Jill to illustrate his views on the "war of the sexes." His solution is that each should exercise empathy: Jack should imagine himself in Jill's brain, and vice versa.[6] Bennett is convinced of the

---

to the blue stockings worn by the women (men were also in these intellectual gatherings) who formed groups for intellectual conversation. In England the term's origin is cloudy, but it may have referred to intellectually inclined, blue-stockinged women who were regular guests at a *salon* maintained by Elizabeth Montagu in London in the 1750's.

[6] Virginia Woolf uses a similar illustrative construct postulating a Shakespeare

inherent differences between male and female, seeing men as superior in intellect, women as superior in will-power (but, he qualifies, only for things of sentiment, not of reason). His putative evidence for male intellectual superiority can be found in Chapter 4, "Are Men Superior to Women?"

Bennett, Henry S. *Six Medieval Men and Women*. New York: Atheneum, 1981. (Cambridge University Press edition, 1955.) 176 p. Bibliography.

Two women figure in these pages, Margaret Paston and Margery Kempe. Looking at Margaret's life, Bennett notes what a burden was placed on the housewife to keep the wheels of domestic life humming smoothly. Bennett illustrates graphically one phase of these responsibilities by a detailed description of how much food was consumed in a month in the Paston household: all had to be prepared from its source—wheat, ale, meat, etc., and Margaret carried the main burden. The necessity for carrying out such labor, time-consuming and physically demanding as it was, was hardly conducive to intellectual accomplishment, no matter how gifted the women might be.

In his treatment of Margery Kempe Bennett remarks upon her frankness of self-revelation: no English writer, he believes, had hitherto committed to writing so "intimate, revealing, and human" an account of his or her life or thought—and in that account she expressed many times her great desire to be independent. Kempe's autobiography is the first one (extant) written in the English language.

with an imaginary sister.

Benson, Mary Sumner. *Women in Eighteenth-Century America: A Study of Opinion and Social Usage.* New York: Columbia University Press, 1935. 343 p.

The first part of this careful study deals with the influence of European theory on the nature and social status of women. The second half shows American practice.

Benson finds that in spite of the acceptance of European theory which relegated women to obedient submission and domesticity, American life and law tended to give women more freedom of movement and education. Moreover, she adds, some European theory actually encouraged the trend toward education for women, such as that body of thought articulated in the works of Samuel Richardson, with his *Pamela* and other novels. Benson mentions Mary Astell, Daniel Defoe, Mary Wollstonecraft, Jean-Jacques Rousseau and Fénelon, all of whom espoused the cause of women's education. This work is well-documented, and a bibliographical essay (pages 317-333) includes both primary and secondary sources..

Berkin, Carol R., and Clara M. Lovett, eds. *Women, War & Revolution.* New York: Holmes & Meier Publishers, 1980. 310 p. Index, notes, and bibliography.

The editors begin this well-documented anthology with an essay on the French Revolution, an occurrence which saw ordinary women of Paris using violence as men had done historically to achieve certain goals—not the usual goals of men, however, this time. The succeeding essays analyze how women fared in Nazi Germany as total war gripped the society, how women in the United States during World War II flocked to work in the shipyards to help the war effort, and how women lived as "comrades" under Russian, Cuban, and Chinese Communism. Moreover, the fate of women after the violence has ended becomes a preoccupation for certain of the authors as they look at the results, legal or social, of the wars or revolution notable for women's participation.

Bernard, Jessie. *"The Fourth Revolution,"* Journal of Social Issues, April, 1966, pp. 76-87.

The sexual revolution has joined the revolutions of automation, population growth, and race relations; it is one that has changed sex from procreation to both procreation and recreation, at least in the Western world, Bernard points out. Nevertheless, she maintains that the new freedom contains psychological hazards, especially for women, which should be taken into account before it can be decided whether these changes will bring great benefits to society. (Reprinted in *People as Partners*, edited by Jacqueline P. Wiseman [San Francisco: Canfield Press, 1971]).

Bertaut, Jules. *Madame Tallien*. Paris: Les Éditions de Paris, 1946. 245 p.

Bertaut presents a Spanish-born Parisienne who during a most remarkable life spanning the years 1773-1835 was known in turn as Thérésia Caburrus, la Marquise de Fontenay, citizen Tallien, financier Ouvard, and la Princesse de Caraman-Chinay. Never one to be outside the mainstream of events, Thérésia was involved with two leaders of the French Revolution active in the fall of Robespierre—as mistress of Paul Barras and as wife of Jean Tallien, who rescued her from prison where the so-called Committee of Public Safety had placed her.

In her dizzying career as a colorful, entirely free French Revolutionary figure Thérésia contrasts sharply with the women of the American Revolutionary period.

Bielenberg, Christabel. ***Ride Out the Dark.*** New York: W. W. Norton, 1971. 287 p. (Published in Great Britain as *The Past Is Myself* by Chatto & Windus, Ltd., 1968.)

Little did Christabel realize when she met and married a German citizen in England that she would become a prisoner in a prison state, Hitler's Germany. Far from being a Nazi, her husband Peter was with the doomed few who worked within Germany to rid their country of the "virus" of Nazism. Meanwhile Christobel was faced with the problems of finding food and safety for herself and two sons, at the same time plotting for the release of her husband who had been imprisoned at Ravensbrück for treason. She reveals in this extraordinary account how she, and the German women around her as well, survived in one of the most brutal societies history has ever known.

For male writers throughout the centuries who have either defended or doubted women's ability to cope with the world, stories such as this will prove, as some of the French male feminists have declared, that women are equal, even superior, to men when they are confronted with the harsh realities of life. And for those who have declared that women's deepest desires are attuned to home and family—stories like this prove that they are right, too.

Blackham, Robert J. ***Woman: In Honour and Dishonour.*** London: Sampson Low, Marston, and Company, n.d. 284 p.

Blackham dates the low political status of women from the rise of the Protestant Reformation in England, noting that before that time women had a greater measure of equality. To prove this he has chapters on women as law-makers, judges, and barristers.[7]

"In dishonour" refers to his section on women criminals. Since his background was law and as one-time under-sheriff of London he came into contact with both "honourable" and "dishonourable" women, we may wish to ponder his statement that in both areas women are often more ingenious than men.

Blanch, Lesley. *The Wilder Shores of Love*. London: John Murray, 1954. 323 p. Index. Bibliography.

Isabel Burton, Jane Digby El Mezrae, Aimée Dubucq de Rivery, and Isabella Everhardt all belonged to nineteenth-century Europe where, as is demonstrated by their adventures, the twentieth-century change in women's attitudes was already foreshadowed but where true freedom was not yet allowed. They are examples of women who resented the conventions that tried in vain to hold them; each found in the East, Blanch remarks, emotion and daring that were even then vanishing from the West with its deadening conformity.

Blashfield, Evangeline Wilbour. *Portraits and Backgrounds*. Freeport, New York: Books for Libraries Press, 1971. (Originally published in 1917.) 493 p.

---

[7] See Bainton (above), who declares that if women had boycotted the Reformation, it would not have succeeded.

These unusual biographies of unusual women include the scholarly tenth-century nun Hroswitha (spelled various ways), who wrote plays; Aphra Behn, who was the author of the first modern novel—she died in 1689 at the age of 49 "in harness, pen in hand"; Aïssé, an Oriental princess who was taken as a slave to become the *protégée* of French society; and Rosalba Carriera, a superlative artist in pastels who was a member of the famous Italian academies of Rome and Bologna.[8]

Blaze de Bury, Ange Henri. ***Dames de la Renaissance***. Paris: C. Lévy, 1886. 382 p.

Historical descriptions are woven into this interestingly presented text (in French) which emphasizes the role of women in the decades of the Italian Renaissance from its fourteenth-century manifestations to its decline. Here we find Laure de Noves (and Petrarch), La Fornarina (and Raphael), Vittoria Colonna (and Michelangelo), Lucrèce Borgia, and Bianca Capello.

Bofill, Maria, *et al.* ***La Mujer en España***. Barcelona: Ediciones de Cultura Popular, S.A., 1967. 159 p.

Four essays present a realistic appraisal of the Spanish culture's anachronistic ideas surrounding women: the concepts of *el pecado, la virtud, and la casa* (sin, virtue, and the home), as well as *el machismo*. The authors agree that in spite of social changes effected by their entrance into the work force, contemporary Spanish women had the same legal status as their grandmothers, "la eterna menor," even though the *Pacem in*

---

[8] The Boston Public Library has a copy of the first edition of Hroswitha's works, published in 1501 at Nuremberg.

Terris of Pope John XXIII explicitly allows the wife equality with the husband.

Bolton, Sarah (Knowles). ***Lives of Girls Who Became Famous.*** Revised edition. New York: Thomas Y. Crowell and Co., 1930 [1886]. 347 p.

Bolton gives perceptive attention to events in the lives of girls which prefigured their fame in later years, principally as feminists and authors. Some of these are Harriet Beecher Stowe, Helen Hunt Jackson, Lucretia Mott, Mary A. Andermore, Margaret Fuller, Mme de Staël, Rosa Bonheur, George Eliot, Elizabeth Barrett Browning, and Florence Nightingale.

A Portuguese translation, *Mulheres famosas de todos os tempos*, translated by Maria Rose Pazzanese, was published in 1944 by Editora Universitária, São Paulo, Brazil.

Booth-Tucker, F. de L. ***Memoirs of Catherine Booth, the Mother of the Salvation Army.*** 2 vols. New York: Fleming H. Rivell Company, 1980 [1892]. 692 p. Index in Volume II.

In 1870 Catherine Booth, wife of the founder of the Salvation Army, was forced by her husband's three-months' illness to take over the administration of the organization. This emergency called forth the latent energies and capacities for leadership of the woman who advanced the cause of the Army while she continued to carry out all her other duties, public and domestic. Booth kept up her missionary work for the next twenty years, until her death at the age of fifty-one. These volumes are a tribute to her genius and compassion.

The original of the 1892 edition is in the Princeton Theological Seminary Library, with the title *Memoirs of Catherine Booth.*.

Bordeau, Henry. *"Le procès de l'Impératrice,"* La Revue Universelle, XLII (15 décembre, 1931), pp. 723-741.

French journalist Bordeau reminisces about his encounter with a "liberated" female newspaper correspondent whom he met in Geneva in 1898 while covering the trial of Luchard, the assassin of Empress Elizabeth of Austria.

Bordeau tries to act gallant when his attractive fellow journalist agrees to have lunch with him, but he is nonplused when she insists upon paying her own way. At dinner when she does allow him to pay she finally justifies his cynicism about woman's capacity to succeed in a man's world by getting him to give her his story of the trial for her Milan newspaper. This proves to him that she was not competent to write a story of her own .

This little personal note reflects vividly the turn-of-the century attitudes toward women in journalism. Bordeau leaves Geneva satisfied that his ideas about "women's equality" are justified.

Bourdillon, Anne Frances Claudine. *The Order of the Minoresses in England.* Manchester, England: The University Press, 1926. 107 p.

Blanche de Navarre is especially to be noted in the history of the women who were connected with the Minoresses, Italian monasteries based on the gospel of St. Francis which found enthusiastic devotees among women as well as men. The first woman of this order was Clare, who in 1212 escaped from her well-to-do parents to take her vows from St. Francis himself. Subsequently the order spread to other countries besides Italy, and the first English order was founded in 1293.

Interesting are the disputes between the women and men followers: in general the men thought the women troublesome and believed that God was better pleased to be served by males than females. The struggle to maintain an independent order was a problem for the women from the beginning.

Bradford, Gamaliel. ***Daughters of Eve***. Boston and New York: Houghton Mifflin, 1930. 303 p.

Ninon de Lenclos, Mme de Maintenon, Mlle de Lespinasse, Catherine the Great, George Sand, and Sarah Bernhardt are the "Eves" whose entrancing histories are told by Bradford in Strachey-like style. Bibliographical notes are included, as well as an index.

Bradford, Gamaliel. ***Portraits of Women***. Boston and New York: Houghton Mifflin, 1916. 201 p.

Bradford looks at women from an unusual perspective as he declares that "woman already dominates our manners, our morals, our literature, our stage, our private finances" and at that time were effecting "the vastest social revolution since the appearance of Christianity." With this in mind, readers are free to formulate their own conclusions as to why he chose to concentrate on the "psychographs" (his term) of Lady Mary Wortley Montagu, Lady Holland, Jane Austen, Fanny Burney d'Arblay, Elizabeth Pepys, Eugénia de Guérin, and the Mmes du Deffand, de Choiseul, and de Sévigné.

Breisach, Ernst. ***Caterina Sforza, a Renaissance Virago***. Chicago: University of Chicago Press, 1965. 375 p.

Although Caterina began life as the illegitimate daughter of a duke of the house of Sforza, her vitality made her memorable in Renaissance history. Through her two marriages she acquired considerable power, yet Breisach sees her as "a pawn of Renaissance politics."

Profuse notes, which include many original sources such as letters, will please the most scholarly, those versed in Italian most of all. A very good index facilitates research.

Bridenthal, Renate, and Claudia Koonz, eds. *Becoming Visible: Women in European History.* Boston: Houghton Mifflin Company, 1977. 510 p. Index. Illustrated.

From an illuminating introduction through a series of scholarly essays by a variety of experts, this work looks at women in earliest societies (both primitive and classical), through the medieval ages, the Industrial Revolution, the awakening of the eighteenth and nineteenth centuries, up to the Nazi hegemony in Germany, the most perplexing example in the twentieth century, when amazing technological advances coincided with the greatest check to women's advancement.

Briffault, Robert. *The Mothers: A Study of the Origins of Sentiments and Institutions.* New York: Johnson Reprint Company, 1969. (Reprint of Macmillan Company 1927 edition.) 3 vols. Illustrated.

Briffault explains the inception of his massive work as being inspired by a desire to "draw up a list of the forms of the social instincts, and to investigate their origin." Early in his researches, he notes, he discovered that "the social characters of the human mind are, one and all, traceable to the operation of instincts that are related to the functions of the female and not to those of the male." Thus he was led to examine the matriarchal theory of social evolution, and these three volumes, comprehensive and erudite, are the fascinating result.

There is something good for everyone in this work, and careful searches are usually well-rewarded. Each volume is paginated separately, with the general index located at the back of Volume III, pages 721-841. The impressive bibliography found on pages 523-719 is of great value. The student should thank Briffault for his patience: the text alone runs to over 2000 pages. As a conclusion he apostrophizes "the eternal woman." In noting that love has been the prime mover in creating society, Briffault admonishes, "Men and women must view with sympathy, not with antagonism, one another's standpoint."

A personal note is interjected into the preface as Briffault brings his critics to task, remarking that he has worked practically alone, and explains that his method was that of allowing the facts to speak for themselves. In this way he subtly implies that his thesis was not entirely pleasing to a great number of his colleagues, for a touch of regret comes through when he admits that he lacked the support of those who disapproved of his unstinting praise of women.

An abridged Spanish version, *Las Madres,* translated by Martin Gerber was published in Buenos Aires by Ediciones Siglo Veinte in 1974.

Briffault, Robert. *The Mothers: The Matriarchal Theory of Social Origins.* Edited by Gordon R. Taylor. New York: H. Fertig, 1991. (Originally published by the Macmillan Company in 1931.) 319 p.

Briffault's abridgement of his longer work (above) contains a discussion of his main thesis, that patriarchal institutions are products of social evolution and not original biological constituents of human society; that patriarchal systems have always been preceded by the matriarchal familial form, which consists only of the mother and her offspring, a group of generations of women associated with their brothers and uncles.

In explication of this theory Briffault describes aspects of the matriarchal arrangements including, in Chapter VII, "The Position of Women in Matriarchal Societies," pages 179-210. In addition, patriarchy is considered at length. Although this work is conveniently indexed, it does not contain a bibliography. For this see the complete version (Volume III). This abridgement is a good introduction to the longer work.

Brittain, Vera Mary. *The Women at Oxford: A Fragment of History.* London: George G. Harrap and Company, 1960. 272 p.

"Oxford now opens its doors to a normal society drawn from both sexes," notes Brittain; however, things were not always that way, and it is only because of a few intrepid women that the right to be educated at Oxford became taken for granted.

The woman to whom most is owed is Anny Mary Anne Henley Rogers. Between the years of her birth and death "lies almost the whole story of women's acceptance by Oxford University," Brittain declares. therefore, the largest portion of this work is devoted to Rogers, with the struggles and successes of the determined pioneer well-told. As for the future, Brittain remarks that much more remained to be done to enable women to get true equality in education at Oxford., (See also entries on Vida Scudder and Virginia Woolf.)

Brittain, Alfred, and Mitchell Carroll. *Women of Early Christianity* (Woman in All Ages and in All Countries. Philadelphia: The Rittenhouse Press, 1908. 390 p.

Beginning with the earliest days when Christianity was a repressed "alternative" religion within the Roman Empire, women were notable for their strength of convictions. This book chronicles their destinies from their mention in the apostolic literature through the time of persecutions (two renowned martyrs were Blandina and Perpetua) and in the years after Christianity was accepted by Constantine the Great in 337 A. D. Following this came the rise of ascetic communities when women led lives of great austerity as nuns (and men as monks) and when women of religious fervor and administrative genius, such as St. Helena, became abbesses.

The narrative moves to the locus of Eastern Christianity, with Byzantine empresses the principal interest, and where Greek culture was more influential—"the story of the Christian women of the East is but a continuation of the story of Greek women." From this point on the number of notable women is surprising, as are their deeds. Featured are Eudoxia, Pulcheria, Eudocia, and most of all Empress Theodora. They were followed by the "Byzantine Empresses" of latter day notoriety— and the eventual fall of Byzantium.

Brooks, Geraldine. ***Dames and Daughters of Colonial Days***. New York: Arno Press, 1974. (Reprint of the 1900 edition.) 284 p.

Brooks calls attention to nine talented women who, in spite of society's efforts to handicap their intellectual development, managed to make their personal imprint upon the times. Her sources are mainly the researches of Alice Morse Earle and the archives of Boston libraries. Outstanding even in this select group are Anne Hutchinson, poet and founder of the first women's club in America (1636), Frances Mary Jacqueline La Tour, defender of Fort La Tour (1650), and a woman with an administrative gift, Margaret Brent, ruler of the Maryland colony (1650).

Brown, Charles Brockden. ***Alcuin: A Dialogue.*** Edited by Lee R. Edwards. (A Gehenna Facsimile.) New York: Grossman Publishers, 1971. 102 p. Illustrations.

This late eighteenth-century discourse in the cause of women's rights was composed by Brockden, an American novelist and pamphleteer, as a fictional dialogue and published in 1798 by T. & J. Swords at New York. The arguments in *Alcuin* are as relevant today as they were in the first days of the Republic when the idea that "all men are created equal" was revolutionary. It was literally taken by men (not reluctantly, it must be said—probably few analyzed the significance), so that women were not granted the vote, and the protests of certain women against being left out were generally ignored, something, which as Abigail Adams warned her husband John, presaged trouble for the future.

Brown, Dee. ***The Gentle Tamers: Women of the Old Wild West.*** Salem: Ayer Company, 1984. 317 p. (Reprint of the 1958 edition.)

"The sunbonnet myth" is one subject of Brown's attack as she follows pioneer women through their harrowing "unfeminine" experiences, showing how they made their indelible mark on education, politics, military affairs, recreation, and journalism.

The chapter "Male Viewpoint" ends the excitement on a dreary note, however: "It was the males. . . who brought about the destruction of [women's] lusty hegemony. . . . No male was willing to hew wood, draw water, cook meals or wash clothes for other males. . . . Faced with these inconveniences, the helpless men could think of no solution but to cry out for women."

Many short biographies can be found here, including those of Frances Grummond and Elizabeth Custer.

Buck, Pearl. *Of Men and Women.* New York: The John Day Company, 1971 [1941]. 203 p.

In this informal examination of the relationships of the sexes Buck, noted for her intimate knowledge of the Orient and her sensitivity to women's issues world-wide, makes cogent comparisons of the situation in the United States with those in China and prewar Nazi Germany, where women's freedoms were limited to an extent unknown in the United States. Buck asks the question, "Why do not American women use the independence that is available for the taking, and why do they feel that if they do their femininity will be jeopardized?"

Her assessment of the chances for a woman's using her education in the United States was negative, and she appears to reason for the *status quo* (although perhaps reluctantly): as she observes American women of that era, she saw them disinclined to be assertive intellectually for fear of disturbing that very *status quo* which hampered their development. As a result, they were likely to be harmed by an education which would make them dissatisfied with the *milieu* they had chosen, she surmised.[9]

---

[9] Buck had personal knowledge of anti-feminism in such an advanced country as the United States. When the Swedish Academy awarded her the Nobel Prize for Literature for her widely acclaimed novel about China, *The Good Earth*, many American critics denigrated her achievement (and the judgment of the Swedes)

Bui Tuong Chieu. *La Polygamie dans le droit Annamite.* (Thèse pour le doctorat en Droit, Université de Paris.) Paris: Librairie Arthur Rousseau, 1933.

An informative discussion of the institution of polygamy, with accent on the legal aspects in regard to the upper classes in Vietnamese society under the aegis of the French.

Burton, Jean. *Sir Richard Burton's Wife.* New York: Alfred A. Knopf, 1941. 378 p. Index. Bibliography.

"I wish I were a man," declared Isabell Arundell, "but being only a woman I would be Richard Burton's wife." She married him after ten years of trying—and it took her twenty-seven years more to become *Sir* Richard Burton's wife when he was knighted in 1886. Even though she envied her husband his freedom, she did not fail to make her own mark: her colorful travel books were published in 1875 and 1879; in addition she wrote a biography of her explorer-husband.

Butler, Pierce. *Women of Mediaeval France.* (Woman in All Ages and in All Countries.) Philadelphia: The Rittenhouse Press, 1908. 472p.

To begin his survey Butler describes the reign of the Capetian kings and details the intrigues of the women—here we learn of Bertrade, who had two husbands in a kind of *ménage à trois,* where they "hobnobbed most amicably." Under the head-

---

because she was a "popular" writer. Theodore Dreiser was so emboldened by this criticism that he committed the shocking *faux pas* of writing to her with the complaint that *he* should have won the award instead of her. Although she achieved much success, she was disheartened by how narrow-minded so many prestigious men of letters seemed to be.

ing, "Famous Lovers," he tells the story of Héloïse and Abélard, treating them as human beings, an overly romantic couple. Contrary to most historians Butler concentrates upon Héloïse, reminding us that "Paris, above all. . . . has kept the memory of the immortal daughter of the Cité with exceptional and unchanging fidelity"—a memory honored in the eighteenth century and during the Revolution.

Christine de Pisan and Jeanne d'Arc each deserves, Butler decides, her own chapter, and these, as well as all the other pages in this book, are worthy of careful perusal.

Camden, Carroll. *The Elizabethan Woman.* New York, London: The Elsevier Press, 1952. 333 p. Illustrated.

Camden's work is an excellent, well-documented study of all facets of women's life. The first chapter, "The Nature of Women," presents opinions about women current at that time, and the last chapter, "Certain Controversies over Women," shows how arguments grew out of those opinions. Contemporary literature is freely quoted, notes are detailed, and the bibliography includes both primary and secondary works. In addition, the style is readable.

Campo de Alange, Maria de Los Reyes Laffitte de Salamanca. *La mujer en España, cien años de su historia, 1860-1960.* Madrid: Aguilar, 1964. 389 p. Bibliography.

Spanish women, concludes Campo de Alange, must escape from the myths that have entrapped them before they can be looked upon as completely human, although she does signal "la espectacular transformación" visible at the end of the hundred years considered in this outline. In these pages the long road already traveled to achieve the changes are delineated in a well-presented text which is enhanced by numerous carefully chosen illustrations.

Capmany, Maria Aurelia, and Carmen Alcade. *El feminismo ibérico.* (Colección Libros Tau Ciencia y Cultura, 32.) Barcelona: Oikos-Tau, 1970. 150 p.

Centered upon the cities of Madrid and Barcelona where the consciousness of feminism was most alive, this study has an international flavor as it encourages Spanish women by referring to proponents of the movement and their successes. References are made to Virginia Woolf and George Bernard Shaw as well as their own compatriots Emilia Pardo Bazán and Margaret Nelken. Listed, too, are the feminist presses in Spain, and other sources of information and criticism appear in the appendix.

Casgrain, Thérèse. *Une Femme chez les hommes.* Montréal: Éditions du Jour, 1971. 296 p.

With this work Mme Casgrain has given the reading public an autobiography whose theme is the evolution of the Canadian woman's liberation movement. She reproaches the Canadian government for a discrimination which curtailed women's role in political life and scores as well the attitude of the Catholic clergy in lending its support, she avers, to the myth of the inferiority of women.

Castresana, Luis de. *Catalina de Erauso, la monja Alférez.* Madrid: Afrodisio Aguado, S A., 1968. 215 p.

Castresana declares that this is the first biography of Catalina, who was born in San Sebastián in 1592 and who at the age of thirteen, already in a convent, rebelled against tradition and escaped to go to sea dressed as a boy. Upon arriving in Mexico, she confessed her true identity to a bishop and returned to Spain in 1624, but 1630 saw her again in America, where she died at the age of 58. During the intervening years she found adventure in France and Italy as well, having received permission from Felipe IV and Pope Urbana VIII to continue dressing as a man.

Fortunately, Catalina took time to write her autobiography, *Historia de la monja Alférez, Doña Catalina de Erauso*, which should be absorbing reading for researchers in Hispanic or comparative studies.

Catalina, Severo. ***La Mujer.*** Buenos Aires: Espasa Calpe, 1968 [1954]. 212 p.

Catalina comments in regard to the nature of women and men: "Los hombres, por último, esclavisaron a la mujer por el gusto de declarse esclavos." Although he evidently looks upon this as exquisite gallantry, the rhetoric of "slavery" had become out-moded even in Latin America. According to him, women are, like Eve, responsible for the cataclysm in Eden (whether ancient or modern), which implies that Adam was, after all, only a slave to Eve as he catered to her propensity toward irretrievable mischief—and modern men share Adam's fate.

Catlin, George, E. G., ed. ***Mary Wollstonecraft, "A Vindication of the Rights of Women" and John Stuart Mill, "The Subjection of Women."*** (Everyman's Library.) London: J. M. Dent; New York: E. P. Dutton, 1929. 317 p.

These two classics of British feminist literature first appeared in 1792 and 1869 respectively. In a sympathetic introduction Catlin gives the philosophic backgrounds and fortunes of Wollstonecraft's impassioned work and calls her the persecuted pioneer of the woman's rights movement whose steadfastness still stands as a perpetual challenge against the interpretation of woman solely as "erotic being."

Mill's wife was active in the feminist cause when he wrote his influential essay, which Catlin describes as a lucidly reasoned and yet indignant exposition of the contemporary legal system under which a woman was not a person in her own right: Mill argues against endowing men with power without accountability, but he was realistic enough to believe that men would give up such power only very grudgingly.

Chandavarker, Ganesh L. ***Maharshi Karve.*** Bombay: Popular Books Depot, 1958. 233 p. Index.

The efforts of an enlightened Indian man to bring about social justice and educational opportunities for women are described in this biography. Karve, as a teacher in girls' schools, very early in his career espoused the cause of widow remarriage (religion forbade even girl widows to remarry) and started his own schools where he was freer to teach as he wished. Moreover, at the same time he joined the movement to eliminate caste barriers.

Chesteron, Ada. ***In Darkest London.*** London: S. Paul, 1930. Revised edition. 255 p. (1928 edition published in New York by The Macmillan Company.)

This adventuresome and compassionate author decided to find out what it was like to be a penniless, homeless woman in London. Disguised as such, she set out to confront whatever fate would bring her way—and this included spending a whole night in the streets because she could find no one who would take her in. Her daily life became a constant struggle to earn enough money for food and nightly shelter as she joined other derelicts who had even worse problems.

As a result of her experiences, Chesterton became a worker for the establishment of respectable refuges for migratory women.

Chinard, G. ***Les Amitiés américaines de Madame d'Houdetot, d'après sa correspondance inédite avec Benjamin Franklin et Thomas Jefferson.*** (Bibliothèque de la Revue de Littérature Comparée.)Paris: Librairie Ancien d'Édouard Champion, 1924. 63 p.

Mme d'Houdetot's correspondence with Franklin and Jefferson began when she was fifty and continued for ten years (1780-1790). During this decade she lived in retreat in the small village of Sauvois, and it was there that she received personages from many countries who came to Paris on missions of importance.

The death of Franklin in 1790 was a cause of much sorrow to her, for Jefferson was not able to replace Franklin in her heart, says Chinard, although she greatly admired Jefferson as the author of the Declaration of Independence at a time when Europe looked to the United States as the hope of the future. After Jefferson became Secretary of State he had less freedom to write directly, but he found ways to do so with discretion.

Chombart de Lauwe, M. J. *"The Status of Women in French Urban Society,"* International Social Science Journal, 14 (1962), pp. 26-65.

This survey, made among 460 working class and lower middle class women by the Groupe d'Ethnologie Sociale, concludes that changing attitudes toward the status of women are indicators of changes in the family and society at large. Women of varying ages with children were chosen from the newer districts of Paris. Two thirds of them said that society had not benefited from the changes, but that women themselves were happier, since they had become closer to equality with men.

The article appears also in *Comparative Social Problems,* edited by S. N. Eisenstadt (New York: The Free Press, 1964).

Chombart de Lauwe, Paul Henry, ed. ***Images de la femme dans la société; recherche internationale.*** (Collection L'Évolution de la Vie Sociale.) Paris: Les Éditions Ouvrières, 1964. 280 p.

Subjects of this group of studies, each presented by an expert from a different country, are: women in urban French society, women in Polish working class families, professional women in Morocco, legal attitudes in French Canada, attitudes in Côte d'Ivoire and in Togo, the Austrian woman, the Yugoslavian woman, and the changes occurring in French social life.

The approach of the work is factual and statistical, with ample documentation. The first chapter, "La nouvelle image de la femme dans la société," sets the international tone of the survey, states its principles and methods, and has some remarks on the future as the "woman problem" is seen as an integral part of the critical need for global social change. The emphases, it will be noted, relate to the "image," the concept women have of themselves, and, conversely, how others see them.

This was also printed in *La Revue des Sciences Sociales de L'UNESCO.*

Cintron, Felipe E. ***Notables mujeres españoles de la Antigüedad.*** New York: n.p., 1941. 47 p.

Cintron presents short sketches of the lives of women of antiquity about whom one hears little, but whom the author deems worthy of posterity's attention. These include: Helvia, mother of Seneca; Pola Argentaria, who lived in Spain during the first century A. D.; the wife of Sigeberto; Calsuinda, a princess of Toledo born in 532 A.D.; Princess Ingunda, a martyr for the Christian faith in 585 A.D.

Claridge, Mary. *Margaret Clitherow, 1556-1586.* New York: Fordham University Press, 1966. 196 p.

A Catholic martyr in York, England, at the time of the dissolution of the monasteries, Margaret was placed on a list with fifteen other recusant wives of tradesmen. Most of them, like her, were butchers' wives.[10] Although it stood to gain by the Protestant aversion to abstinence from meat, the butchers' trade produced more recusant wives in that period than any other trade in York. The women were condemned to prison, an experience which Claridge describes graphically on pages 67-86. In 1586 Margaret was crushed to death as her final punishment. An appendix sets forth genealogies, and the work is indexed.

Clark, Alice. *Working Life of Women in the Seventeenth Century.* New York: Harcourt, Brace and Howe, 1920. 320 p. Index. List of authorities.

---

[10] A recusant was a Roman Catholic who refused to attend the services of the Church of England from the reign of Henry VIII to that of George II. The dissolution of the monasteries occurred during Henry's reign. See Neville Williams, *Henry VIII and His Court* (New York: Macmillan, 1971), Chapter 4.

Clark characterizes the seventeenth century in England as one of crucial importance in the historic development of women as she analyzes this period between the Elizabethan era and the Industrial Revolution. According to her findings, in this period women were more actively engaged in industries than in the early twentieth century, while men were more involved in domestic affairs than in the 1920's.

Clark directs her attention to economic matters as they involved women, not to home and children. She considers separately capitalist ventures of women, agriculture, textiles, crafts and trades, and professions such as law, medicine, midwifery, teaching, and the clergy. It is her opinion that the rapid growth of capitalism was an unfavorable development for women because the change to a purely money economy made their contribution less necessary and even difficult to include in the advanced industrial system, a dilemma which would prove to be a perennial problem in centuries to come as well.

Clayton, Aileen. ***The Enemy is Listening.*** London: Hutchinson & Co., Ltd., 1980; New York: Ballantine, 1982. 404 p. Index. Maps, glossary and bibliography.

"A woman in a man's world" is how British Air Chief Marshal Sir Frederick Rosier termed Clayton. This man's world was RAF (Royal Air Force) air-ground communications, a decidedly male domain until the emergency of World War II claimed everyone, male or female, for the defense of the country. Because Clayton knew German, and the pilots of the RAF needed radio transmissions of attacking *Luftwaffe* crews translated instantaneously the "Y Service," staffed by women (from many nationalities eventually), came into being and soon proved itself indispensable.

Although the text of the book is often technical, Clayton has made it understandable; moreover, she writes of her personal experiences as a young girl at school in prewar Germany (her mother insisted that she learn German) and describes her feelings later at being a WAAF participant peripheral to the "kind and tolerant" RAF men who accepted having the women "inflicted" (her word) upon them. It would not be long before that tolerance would change to overwhelming respect and gratitude.

Clement, J., ed. ***Noble Deeds of American Women.*** Introduction by Mrs. L. H. Segourney. Williamstown, Massachusetts, 1975. (Reprint of 1851 edition.). 400 p.

These sketches of courageous yet all but forgotten women point up the amazing exploits of an earlier day. Clement tells the story of Deborah Samson, who when severely wounded while fighting in the Revolution disguised as a male, feared only that her gender would be discovered; of the mother who walked into an Indian camp amid warriors brandishing tomahawks to rescue her children; and of the Mohawk women who joined the temperance crusade to combat alcoholism among the Indian braves. Many others also deserve the attention Clement gives them in this enlightening book.

Coates, Mary Weld. ***"The Spanish Woman, the Spain of Today Repudiates Don Juan Tenorio,"*** *Hispania,* XIII (1930), pp. 213-217.

Coates defends Spanish women against the criticism that they lacked interest in their own progress toward equality. She calls attention to the growing strength of feminism since 1913 and lauds Blanca de Los Rios for having won a chair in the Spanish Royal Academy in 1928.

Cognet, Louis. ***Crépuscule des mystiques***. Tournai, Belgium: Desclée, 1958. 397 p.

Cognet's first chapter, "Le mysticisme en France au XVIIe siècle," has references to many women mystics, and three succeeding chapters emphasize the troubled life of Mme de Guyon (Jeanne-Marie Bouvier de la Motte) who lived from 1648 to 1717 and whose mysticism influenced Fénelon. From the age of five, Jeanne-Marie reported seeing visions and at the age of twelve was initiated into mysticism through her reading of François de Sales and Jeanne Chantal.

Cohart, Mary, ed. ***Unsung Champions of Women***. Albuquerque: University of New Mexico Press, 1975. 271 p.

Cohart's short introduction precedes essays from the pens of thirteen writers on the theory of women: Eliza Burt Gamble (1841-1920), Lester Frank Ward (1841-1913), Johann Jakob Bachofen (1815-1887) (whose ideas on motherright were revolutionary), Mathilde and Mathias Vaerting (authors of *The Dominant Sex),* Lydia Maria Child (1802-1880), Lady Sydney Morgan (1776?-1859), Otis Tufton Mason (1838-1908), Eugene A. Hecker (1880-1959), Plato, Condorcet (1743-1794), Herbert Spencer (1820-1903), and Elizabeth Robins (1862-1943). In addition Cohart sees philosopher Kant and the British writers Spenser, Tennyson, Meredith, and Browning within the feminist tradition.

Cohen, Rose. ***Out of the Shadow***. New York: George H. Doran Co., 1918. 313 p.

Cohen's viewpoint is distinctly attuned to women's feelings as she relates her experience as a Russian Jewess who with her family emigrated to the United States before World War I. Her account shows how strong were the ideas against which she had to struggle as her father, suspicious of the freedom women had in the New World, brought all the weight of Judaic tradition against her to tame her insubordinate spirit.

Collins, Marie, and Sylvie Weil Sayre,, eds. *Les Femmes en France.* (The Scribner French Series.) New York: Charles Scribner's Sons, 1974. 330 p. Illustrations. No index.

This anthology of short excerpts (in the originals, literary as well as historical or philosophical) from key writers offers a rewarding glimpse of the broad sweep of women's life in France from the seventeenth century to the mid-twentieth century. In bringing together these testaments to France's enduring feminism, Collins and Sayre do not concentrate upon the most notable writers, although they (both female and male) are well-represented; instead they bring forth from comparative obscurity some women whose writings are well-worth our attention and could lead to a desire to research them more thoroughly.

This volume contains, according to the editors, parts of documents not available in the United States, and thus this collection can be very useful to the researcher. Because of the very fact that it includes so many references to people, events, and places, a good index would have been more than helpful.

Cooper, Elizabeth. *My Lady of the Chinese Courtyard.* Illustrated. New York: Frederick A. Stokes Company, 1915. 262 p.

"One never thinks of Chinese women, except that they are mothers of Chinese men," said a Chinese writer when questioned as to why so little was known about women in China. Nevertheless, says Cooper, feminine influence has always been pervasive.

Now that China has changed so radically, this series of personal letters written by "Kivei-li" may evoke some of the essential nature of Chinese life for a woman of the upper class. Her intelligence shines through as she discusses Westernization and feminist ideas against the backdrop of her own repression by her husband's family.

Corcos, Fernand. *La Paix? Oui, si les femmes voulaient!* Paris: Éditions Montaigne, 1929. 294 p.

Feminist Corcos' purpose is to prove the existence of a women's pacifism and to encourage it, using as a touchstone the actions of French women in the First World War. As a feminist in the prewar years, he believed that mothers could prevent a holocaust, but as many women as men were in favor of the war when it came in 1914. Therefore, he says that women's attitudes are indiscernible from men's, for they worked in the war factories just as uncomplainingly as the men. Therefore in order to prevent future wars, he declares, it is necessary to mobilize women to enter combat with the men. Because they will not wish to undergo such sufferings they will bring their great influence to bear to outlaw war as a human activity. Corcos speaks to all women, not only French women, but his special appeal is to women writers, who should take up their pens in the cause of peace—*Guerre à la guerre!* ("War to war!") is his battle cry.

Cormack, Margaret Lawson. *The Hindu Woman.* New York: Teachers College, Columbia University Bureau of Publications, 1953. 207 p. Bibliography.

Through her travels and twenty-one year sojourn in India, Cormack hoped to resolve the paradox of Indian feminine life: utter subjection and yet the lofty idea of women with which Indian life is imbued. This work is based upon a study of ten Hindu female graduate students at Columbia, as a result of which Cormack concluded that the cultural emphasis in India was upon female passivity, conformity, self-control, the need for harmony, and the performance of socially prescribed duty. In return for their acceptance of this role, these Hindu students (of the privileged class) showed a psychological security rooted in the age old teachings of the Vedas. Cormack notes, too, that the Hindu woman's nature corresponded with the Freudian idea of the "feminine passive" type.

Cott, Nancy F., and Elizabeth H. Pleck, eds. *A Heritage of Her Own: Toward a New Social History of American Women.* (A Touchstone Book.) New York: Simon and Schuster, 1979. 608 p. Index and bibliographical notes.

The editors believe that "the investigation of women's history is necessarily comparative, and interdisciplinary." Following these guidelines, they trace women's life throughout the boisterous phases of the frontier, the Industrial Revolution, the immigrations of the nineteenth century, the Great Depression, wars, and sporadic feminist mutinies, all within the unavoidable Victorian-type female ambience which surrounded them. What is noticeable throughout this history is how much work women did and still do, as homemakers, pioneers, workers outside the home, wherever work is to be done, just as it happened in primitive tribes, according to anthropologists who have studied women's societal roles. Speaking of modern times, with all its technology, "for married women in full-time jobs the work day is probably longer than it was for their grandmothers."

Cotti, Colette. ***La Femme au seuil de l'an 2000.*** Paris, Tournai: Casterman, 1968 (?).

Cotti is highly optimistic for the future of the Frenchwoman, who, she asserts, by the turn of the century will be able to engage in a variety of activities which would seem amazing to women of the 1960's. If she so desired, she could go into politics, travel to the Inca country (or go to Texas), or enter the working world according to her talents. There is nothing apocalyptic in this presentation, but Cotti sees it as "la réalité" of everyday life. Illustrated with photographs.

Courtney, Janet Elizabeth (Hogarth). ***The Adventurous Thirties: A Chapter in the Woman's Movement.*** London: Oxford University Press, 1933. 279 p. (Reissued in *The Oxford Bookshelf,* October, 1937.)

Poets, "annualists," voyagers to India, critics of America, philanthropists, and *salons* in Great Britain are the categories chosen by Courtney to set forth the achievements of emancipated women of the 1830's in Britain, for this was a decade of comparative intellectual and physical freedom for women as the ideals of the French Revolution filtered in.

After this brief reprieve, however, reaction set in, and women writers felt the need to use male pseudonyms, such as George Eliot for Mary Ann Evans, Currer Bell for Charlotte Brontë, and Acton Bell for Anne Brontë.

Courtney, W. L. *"A Royal Blue-Stocking: Descartes and the Princess Elizabeth,"* pages 172-192 in *Studies New and Old.* London: Chapman and Hall, 1888.

Elisabeth, daughter of Elizabeth Stuart of England and Frederich V of Bohemia, and a sister of Charles I of England, was a *femme philosophe* who refused the hand and throne of Wladislas, King of Poland, to devote herself to philosophy and the friendship of Descartes.

In 1644, when Elizabeth was twenty-five, Descartes dedicated his *Principia philosophiae* to her because of her "incomparable" understanding of his system of thought. In 1667 Elizabeth became a Lutheran abbess in Westphalia, where she established a refuge for persons being persecuted for heretical opinions.

Cross, Barbara M., ed. *The Educated Woman in America: Selected Writings of Catharine Beecher, Margaret Fuller, and M. Carey Thomas.* (Classics in Education, No. 25. Teachers College, Columbia University.) New York: Teachers College Press, 1965. 175 p.

Cross' illuminating introduction paints the backgrounds and achievements of three women who found themselves "out of joint" with their times. Beecher appealed to women to make of homemaking an occupation which would utilize both their intelligence and their need for a sense of accomplishment by creating a "pink and white tyranny" in the home; Fuller's life was an example of a scholar who carried learning to its heights yet was never wholeheartedly accepted by even learned society (partly because of her unconventional sexual behavior); Thomas saw education as the key to woman's advancement and as president of Bryn Mawr College lavished her energies upon encouraging pure scholarship while asking society to give talented women a "sporting chance."

The readings themselves are sketchy, but the bibliography can lead interested readers into new paths.

Cunneen, Sally. *Sex: Female; Religion: Catholic.* New York: Holt, Rinehart and Winston, 1968. 171 p.

This survey concerns the re-evaluation of the role of women in the Roman Catholic Church attendant upon *Vatican II.* It is based upon revealing data supplied by thirty-five lay women and nuns. The questionnaire used is printed on pages 163-171.

Cunnington, C. Willett. *Feminine Attitudes in the Nineteenth Century.* New York: Haskell House, 1973. (The Macmillan Company, 1936.) 324 p. Illustrated.

The minutiae of the lives of "mute inglorious females" during the English Victorian age is the concern of this sprightly work. Cunnington sees Victorian women as creatures governed by "fashion, customs, habits, and instincts" as they more or less primly move through the decades from the 1830's to the 1890's. The impact of literature is noted, with such revolutionary novels as *Jane Eyre,* and the troubling question of education for women debated by Parliament is brought to the reader's attention.

Dall, Caroline H. *College, the Market, and the Court; or, Women's Relation to Education, Labor, and Law.* Boston: Lee and Shepard, 1868. 498 p.

Dedicated to Lucretia Mott, these lectures give a vivid picture of the deplorable nature of woman's relation to the three most crucial aspects of public life about which Dall is concerned. Her section on law considers women's position under the French law, the English common law, and the law of the United States. This work is minutely detailed and is indexed.

Daly, Mary. ***Beyond God the Father: Toward a Philosophy of Women's Liberation.*** Boston: Beacon Press, 1973. 225 p.

Daly takes an existentialist stance in her exhortative critique of patriarchal religion and calls for an end to the "looking glass society," referring to a mirror through which women are seen as victims of imponderable forces embedded in the omnipresent Judeo-Christian theology.

The last chapter is chaotic, but Daly's many allusions to existential thinkers throughout the work attest to the influence of that philosophy on the formulation of the aims of the twentieth-century women's movement. "At this point in history," Daly declares, "women are in a unique sense called to be the bearers of existential courage." Useful bibliographical notes accompany the text.

Dannett, Sylvia G. L., ed. ***Profiles of Negro Womanhood*** (Negro Heritage Library.) 2 vols. New York: Educational Heritage, 1964-1966. 704 p. Illustrations.

These useful volumes are designed to redress the imbalance in the availability of information about noteworthy black women. Volume I considers the years from 1619 through the nineteenth century, while Volume II is devoted to the twentieth century.

The work is illustrated by Horace Varela, and there are bibliographies to aid further research into the lives and accomplishments of the women.

Davies, Emily. ***Thoughts on Some Questions, Relating to Women, 1860-1908.*** New York: Kraus Reprints, 1971. (Cambridge, England: Bowes and Bowes, 1910.)

Reprinted from an original copy in the Kenneth Spencer Research Library at the University of Kansas, this volume contains thirteen essays by Davies, who was a pioneer in the British women's advancement cause. Published earlier in various British periodicals, they set forth Davies' arguments for increased opportunities for women, especially in higher education, which included the freedom to enter the medical profession. Her 1868 proposal for a college for women to provide an education similar to that given to men at Oxford and Cambridge underlines how deprived intellectual women could be in this Victorian age.

Davy, Marie-Magdelen. ***Simone Weil.*** (Témoins du XXe siècle.) Paris: Éditions Universitaires, 1956. 134 p.

In his preface to Davy's work Gabriel Marcel praises Weil as a testament to truth and to the absolute, an absolute related to her boundless compassion for human misery, about which she found most of the world unconcerned. In the section, "Quelques problèmes essentiels," Davy analyzes Weil's vision of social development directed toward the new humanity she so ardently hoped for.

Deiss, Joseph J. ***The Roman Years of Margaret Fuller: A Biography.*** New York: Thomas Y. Crowell, 1969. 338 p. Illustrations. Bibliography.

Deiss is the first among Fuller's biographers to use the correspondence between Margaret and her husband, the Marchese Ossoli. Other sources drawn upon are the diaries of

Mr. and Mrs. William Story, Fuller's friends throughout the last three years of her life. These three years are the "Roman years" which seemed so scandalous to her relatives that after her death in a shipwreck while returning from Italy to the United States, family members systematically destroyed all references to the marriage in their possession.

While in Italy Margaret Fuller espoused the cause of Italian liberty. Deiss sees that in having freed herself from the twin influences of Puritanism and Transcendentalism Fuller became almost wholly Italianized.

DeLeeuw, Hendrik. ***Woman, the Dominant Sex.*** New York: Thomas Yoseloff, 1957. 240 p.

DeLeeuw's theme is the "gradual dominance of woman over man and the birth and growth of what we have come to know as the 'American Matriarchate,'" in which woman is the boss and man the servant. To reverse this trend, he would keep women in the home for their own protection, for women who have forsaken the home, he concludes, find that "fame is bitter" and as a consequence are likely to become "neurotic."

When DeLeeuw turns to women in certain other countries he observes that Japanese women are breaking their bonds, Russian women are completely equal to men, while even Moslem women are joining the freedom movement. He notes approvingly, however, that French women never forget that they are female, and English women treat men better than American women, even though they, too, participate in the unprecedented drive for "liberation." DeLeeuw seems ambivalent in his approach toward this liberation. The attitudes of the 1950's, swerving from the strong advocacy of women's work during

World War II, and not yet cognizant of the dynamism of the 1960's, are illustrated in this work.

Demos, John. *"Witchcraft and Local Culture in Hampton, New Hampshire,"* pages 9-42 in *Uprooted Americans: Essays to Honor Oscar Handlin,* edited by Richard L. Bushman, *et al.* Boston: Little, Brown and Company, 1979.

Virginia Woolf wrote with discernment of the women of the past who were shunned by society because they were branded as "witches," enemies of society. Demos details the lives of some of the women in this small town in New England who were hounded by their neighbors, accused of fiendish knowledge and mischievous intent. Instead of their being an aberration in town life Demos reveals that witch trials were a *persistent* feature of life in early New England.

"Goodwife Eunice Cole" was one of the most feared of the "witches" noted in these pages: her sad story has come down as a legend. In fact, Demos shows as he ends this baleful chapter of women's history in colonial America, that traces of the legend survive even today in a children's game: one girl becomes Goody Cole, the other gives the "mean old witch" a whipping. But in 1938 the town of Hampton, on its 300th birthday, formally reinstated Eunice Cole, now deemed innocent, as a citizen.

Deutsch, Helene. *The Psychology of Women: A Psychoanalytic Interpretation*. 2 vols. New York: Greene and Stratton, 1954; London: Research Books, 1967.

Deutsch is a strict Freudian, having been one of Freud's disciples, so her bias is easy to identify. Woman's life is determined by her sexuality, she avers, and boldly divides women into types: feminine erotic, feminine passive, feminine masochist, and masculine active. There is no "feminine active," because "active" women have a "masculinity complex," she declares, and are thus outside the scope of her analysis.

The whole of Volume II concerns motherhood, with some attention paid to those older women who can no longer bear children. "Mothers" also encompasses stepmothers and adoptive mothers—motherhood is not tied to biology in this interpretation, although Freud is reputed to have declared, "Biology is destiny."

Deutsch's work can be useful as background reading if the student wishes to understand the rationale for the criticism of Freudian ideas which came with more realistic, less constricting theories about the psychology of women.

Diehl, Charles. ***Byzantine Empresses.*** Translated from the French by Harold Bell and Theresa de Kerpely. New York: Knopf, 1963. 308 p.

Because Athenais, Theodora, Irene, Thepano, Zoë, Bertha of Sulzbach, Agnes of France, Constance of Hohenstaufen, Yolanda of Montferrat, and Anne of Savoy lived in exotic splendor and knew how to use power, their lives have tantalized Diehl into describing them in this readable and informative group of biographies. There is no documentation, so the serious reader will need to delve into history further to verify facts (as far as is possible), which would probably disclose many other matters of interest.

Dirvin, Joseph I. ***Louise de Marillac.*** Preface by Cardinal Terence Cooke. New York: Farrar, Straus, and Giroux, 1970. 468 p.

"It is incredible that there has not been, since the death of Louise de Marillac in 1660, a fully documented biography of this great lady who is responsible for so much of the charity and social work and for legions of the dedicated workers of the past three centuries," writes Dirvin as he begins his thoroughly researched study of the woman who was the friend, guide, and co-worker of the better-known St. Vincent de Paul.

Pope Pius XI declared her a saint in 1934; Dirvin shows her to be worthy of sainthood not because she had no faults, but because her life was completely given over to the thought of her compatriots who endured hunger, illness, poverty, and the sorrows brought by war.

A copious index (pages 419-468) teems with names of people and places famous in French history and literature, suggesting the study of the seventeenth century from an unusual perspective.

Dodge, Norton T. *Women in the Soviet Economy, Their Role in Economic, Scientific, and Technical Development.* Westport, Connecticut: Greenwood Press, 1977. (Reprint of Johns Hopkins Press edition, 1966.) 331 p. Bibliography, 307-320.

Soviet Russian society, perhaps more than any other, says Dodge, "has developed and put to use both the strength and the genius of its women." Nevertheless, he cites the lower productivity of women, particularly in creative, scholarly work, as having adverse implications for them in the allocation of scarce educational resources—"women offer the nation a lower average return on investment than men." The reason for this is clarified in his conclusion, "Family *vs.* Work," which points up the most obvious reason for the disadvantageous situation for women, the burden of carrying the duties of both home and work, in spite of the legal espousal of equality throughout the society, for the government could not legislate changes in traditional male attitudes.

Dodge provides an excellent bibliography and the work is thoroughly documented. Even though at the end of the century the political situation changed drastically, there is little reason to assume, historically speaking, that the role of women would change quickly.[11]

Donaldson, James. *Woman: Her Position and Influence in Ancient Greece and Rome and among the Early Christians*. London: Longmans, Green and Co., 1970. (Reprint of 1907 edition.) 278 p.

Most of Donaldson's essays in this collection are reprints of his earlier articles in *Contemporary Review*. They are unusual for their unbiased treatment of women in antiquity; especially strong is his admiration of Sappho.[12]

A scholarly bibliography of works in French, German and Latin will be found on pages 256-260, and an index is included.

Dreier, Mary E. *Margaret Dreier Robins, Her Life, Letters, and Work*. Washington: Zenger, 1975 [1950]. Index.

The championing of industrial workers was the cause to which Margaret Robins devoted herself, and this cause brought her into the world of politics. She attended three conferences of

---

[11] With the breakup of the USSR in the 1980's, conditions for women were seen to be even worse, since certain benefits, such as government medical assistance programs for poor women, often became unavailable.

[12] Sappho's love poems are among the few extant writings of ancient Greek women. In spite of the fact that we have only fragments of her work, it is agreed that her poetic genius was of the highest order.

the International Congress of Working Women, campaigned to get Theodore Roosevelt elected, pushed for woman suffrage, and took part in activities connected with two world wars. Her forward-looking belief was that "industrial democracy must combine with political democracy."

Drinnon, Richard. ***Rebel in Paradise: A Biography of Emma Goldman***. Chicago: University of Chicago Press, 1982 [1961]. 349 p. Bibliography. Index.

Drinnon's well-documented study sees Goldman as indefatigable in pursuing her goals. From "her ghetto girlhood to her final breath" she waged an unrelenting fight—which included a term in prison—for the free individual in her rebellion against the established order. She was convinced that Communism offered greater social justice—until she was disillusioned when seeing it operating in real life after she was deported from the United States back to Russia. A good bibliographical essay as a guide to further studies on Goldman can be found on pages 313-333. (See also Goldman, Emma, below.)

Drury, Clifford Merrill, ed. ***First White Women over the Rockies***. (Northwest Historical Series, VI.) 3 vols. Glendale, California: Arthur H. Clark Company, 1963-1966.

This amazing work consists of diaries, letters, and biographical sketches of the six women who, accompanied by their husbands, made the overland journey across the Rocky Mountains in 1836 and 1838 for the purpose of bringing Christianity to the Northwest Indians.

Some of the manuscripts used to compile these accounts go back to 1833. Their abundance is typified by the writings of one couple, Elkanah and Mary Walker, which run to at least

300,000 words. Drury has done a service to American history by organizing this mass of data; his efforts were motivated by the conviction that the names of these women should be remembered with honor, and anyone reading their accounts will agree.

Evidently their example encouraged other women to dare to do the same, but with the purpose of establishing homesteads rather than proselyting. The church fathers, however, were not sure that they were wise in allowing the women to go, and some of the six original pioneers agreed with them.

Dunbar, Janet. *The Early Victorian Woman: Some Aspects of Her Life (1837-1852).* Westport, Connecticut: Hyperion Press, 1977. (Reprint of 1953 edition of George G. Harrap & Co. London.) 192 p.

Dunbar presents a comprehensive picture of English women's everyday life as reflected in diaries, letters, housekeeping account books, other private papers, and periodicals of the time. This period is seen as one of ferment beneath the prim appearance of acceptance and "respectability."

Women are viewed here from two broad perspectives: I. The Home Background, and II. The World Outside the Home. The latter includes women's literature, education, industrial employment, outstanding women, and the budding women's movement.

Dupont-Chatelain, Marguerite. *Les Encyclopédistes et les femmes: Diderot--d'Alembert--Grimm--Helvetius--d'Holbach--Rousseau--Voltaire.* Genève: Slatkine Reprints, 1970. (Reprint of Daragon [Paris] edition of 1946.)

As the title indicates, this work is an exposition of the influence exerted by women upon the men listed in the title.

These women include both wives and mistresses, and especially to be noted are Sophie Volland, Mlle de Lespinasse, Mme d'Épinay, Mme d'Houdetot, la Marquise du Châtelet, and Mme de Warens. The emphasis is upon the personal influence of the women, whereby these seemingly austere men became more human and understandable.

Dutt, G. S., trans. *A Woman of India*. New York: Macmillan, 1940. Introduction by Rabindranath Tagore. 144 p.

This biography of Saroj Nalina (1887-1927), founder of the Women's Institute Movement in India, was written by her husband, Rabindranath Tagore. In his introduction he writes that Saroj realized the ideal of life in which "the streams of intellect and emotion emanating from this vast universe" were not allowed to dry up in an outworn tradition which casts her sex in the role of the "woman who is only a housewife and nothing more."

This is an engrossing story which gives intimate glimpses into the daily life of contemporary Indian women and underlines the difficulty of their fight for recognition.

Effinger, John R. *Women of the Romance Countries.* (Woman in All Ages and in All Countries.) Philadelphia: The Rittenhouse Press, 1908. 401 p.

Effinger divides his work almost equally between Italian and Spanish women. Most unusual, perhaps, is the section on Spain, for books which treat of Italian women are plentiful, but those concentrating at length on Spanish women are not readily available, at least in the English language. Yet a constant theme in Spanish literature is Woman—usually about her foibles, failings or deceptiveness—and satire of her can be found in all eras. Of all the women in the Western countries, Spanish women seem to have had the least freedom, principally because of the deep-seated concept of *honra* (honor) within the minds of Spanish men.

Effinger begins with the period before the Moorish invasion and carries through to the nineteenth century, with one chapter devoted to Queen Isabella, whose support of Columbus' mission "gilds the reign of this queen with imperishble lustre." Even then he concludes that women enjoyed few social freedoms, nor did they organize aggressively to acquire them even though the political environment became less repressive, a situation which frustrated even the men who tried to help them (as the dramatist Gregorio Martínez Sierra).

Ellet, Elizabeth F. ***The Pioneer Women of the West***. (Essay Index Reprint Series.) Freeport, New York: Books for Libraries Press, 1973. 434 p. (Originally published in 1852.)

This is a supplement to Ellet's *Women of the American Revolution*, wherein Ellet gives credit to the "wives and mothers who ventured into the western wilds, and bore their part in the struggles and labors of the early pioneers."

Principal sources were the first-hand recollections of people still living, as well as the records of families who settled the areas from Tennessee to Michigan. Over sixty women figure in this minutely detailed work, which also gives vivid descriptions of the "hinterlands" from the viewpoint of women who had suffered the dislocations of the Revolution.

Ellet, Elizabeth F. ***The Queens of American Society***. 6th ed. Philadelphia: Porter and Coates, 1867. 464 p.

"Belles," or leaders of upper class society in nineteenth century United States, are given close attention by Ellet because it seems to her that "a comprehensive view of the best society would be a valuable part of the country's history." Her pages are replete with personal anecdotes describing the activities of women of wealth and station in an era when the adornment of society by "choice and cultivated flowers" was an end in itself and *noblesse oblige* a source of peer approval.

What gives Ellet's portraits deeper meaning is the fact that these seemingly frivolous activities took place in a tumultuous setting of events (including the Civil War) which have even more significance to researchers in American social history of our time. Ellet appears something of a prophet in the light of our present knowledge of the cataclysmic events which followed.

Ellet, Elizabeth F. ***Women Artists in All Ages and Countries***. New York: Harper and Brothers, 1859. 377 p.

Deploring the lack of a written history of female artists in the first half of the nineteenth century, Ellet endeavors to bring this segment of cultural history up-to-date. For sources of artists before that time she draws upon Ernst Gull's *Die Frauen in die Kunstgeschiche.* Her motive is "to show what woman has done, with the general conditions favorable or unfavorable to her efforts" and succeeds in creating an enlightening book which could have, as she hoped, inspired other women in their battle to surmount the many difficulties put in their way.

Ellet, Elizabeth F. ***The Women of the American Revolution.*** Introduction by Anne Hollingsworth Wharton. 2 vols. 2nd ed. Illustrations. Philadelphia: George W. Jacobs and Co., 1900. (Originally published in 1850.) 735 p.

Since Ellet's maternal grandfather was an officer in the Revolutionary Army, these accounts are often based upon oral communication and thus form a valuable documentary about women who had experienced the Revolution first-hand. Such a woman was Martha Wilson, a daughter of one of Washington's officers and the wife of another. Nor does Ellet neglect the contemporary pioneer women of Kentucky, Ohio, Virginia, and Wyoming who suffered from both British and Indian attacks. The stories of over one hundred women describe the incredible acts of heroism that belie the noxious *cliché,* "the weaker sex." (A photocopy of this volume is available Ann Arbor, University Microfilms International, 1980.)

Ellis, Havelock. ***Man and Woman: A Study of Secondary and Tertiary Sexual Characters.*** Boston and New York: Houghton Mifflin Company, 1929. 495 p. (Originally published in 1894.)

Ellis' premise is that the sexes are not equal, but instead are "equivalent." When his book appeared it was, in the author's own words, "a pioneering effort, not only in the sense of being the first attempt to view the totality of the phenomena involved, but in the sense that it tended to the conclusion that the sexes are equivalent in a way that excluded any note of superiority or inferiority on one side of the other."

In this volume Ellis includes both biological and psychological analyses. He sees women as basically more conservative than men, and he is convinced that women's special sphere is the bearing of children and their rearing in the home; he is convinced, too, that in the exploration of life outside the home, in industry and the arts, woman competes with man with less hope of success—a realistic conclusion which was based upon the prevailing situations faced by women.

Extremely influential when they were presented, Ellis' theories eventually came under severe criticism, but their value lies in the fact that he pioneered in the field of analysis.

Elyot, Sir Thomas. *The Defence of Good Women*. Edited by Edwin Johnston Howard. Oxford, Ohio: The Anchor Press, 1940. 85 p.

The only known copy of this famed work, which was published in England in 1560, is in the Henry E. Huntington Library. This edition is a reproduction of it.

Howard comments in his introduction that Elyot "strives to the best of his ability to present the actual virtues of good women, refraining from mere adulation." Elyot championed the cause of education for women, sharing the opinions of such prestigious Renaissance figures as Juan Luis Vives. Moreover, he practiced what he preached, for he made sure that his talented daughter, Margaret Roper, received the kind of classical training which at that time was the prerogative of upper class men.

Epstein, Louis M. *Sex Laws and Customs in Judaism.*. New York: KTAV Publishing House, 1948. 251 p.

Chapter I, pages 25-67, "Modesty in Dress," deals most specifically with women as it explains Judaic rules for dress and deportment while noting the rationale for historical taboos and regulations. Notes give the sources for them in religious books and provide background information for clarification. Other aspects of women's life as interpreted by the male-centered Judaic writers can be found in chapters on marriage, divorce, and other relevant subjects.

Eshleman, Lloyd W. *Moulders of Destiny.* New York: Covici Friede, 1938.

Chapter IX, pages 207-246, "Catherine de Medicis, Who Set a New Precedent for France" invites the reader to re-interpret the career of the "mother of kings," who has come down through history as an almost totally repellent figure.

Eshleman, however, using historical empathy, writes, "I recognized how unjust history had been to her," and goes on to set forth the details of her precarious position during wars at home and abroad that made it impossible for her to choose other than she did, unless she was willing to allow France and the Valois monarchy to fall to pieces because of the incompetence of the rest of her family, "a degenerate brood of Valois kings and princes," whom she, however, loved too much.

Espinosa, Juan de. *Diálogo en laude de las mujeres.* Edited by Angela Gonzales Simon. (Biblioteca de Antiguos Libros Hispánicos, serie A, Vol. VII.) Madrid: J. Garcia Morato, 1946. 355 p.

In her introduction Gonzalez warns readers not to be misled by the title of Espinosa's work, for it is merely a scholarly *tour de force* designed to impress other scholars by its erudition; therefore there is very little of substantive praise of women "A pesar de su título, tiene muy poco este libro de alabanza de las mujeres," she writes. "No es, como tantos otros de la época más que un pretexto para dar a conocer la cultura clásica del autor."

Fagniez, Gustave Charles. *La Femme et la société française dans la première moitié du XVIIe siècle.* Paris: Librairie Universitaire J. Gamber, 1929. 399 p.

With characteristic precision Fagniez goes into great detail concerning the kind of social world occupied by women in this period. The scope of his work is limited, since it is confined largely to consideration of the home, family, recreation, and religion. Some attention is given to the education of women, which he finds mainly directed toward forming "menagères" (homemakers) and "maîtresses de salon" rather than "femmes instruites."[13] Professional life for women was almost entirely related to skills for personal service to the upper classes, as Fagniez describes it. Chapter V, pages 204-266, however, details the *milieu* of the theater, which will be of especial interest for researchers on literary subjects.

The reader has no guide through the detailed pages of this work, for there is no index nor explanatory table of contents. Nevertheless, through diligent browsing one may find some worthwhile sidelights reflecting life in this rich period in French culture.

Fairchild, Johnson E., ed. **Women, Society, and Sex.** New York: Sheridan House, 1952. 255 p.

This series of thirteen lectures given by the Cooper Union begins with Margaret Mead's "One Aspect of Male and Female," while "The Lost Sex" by Marynia Farnham, and Harold Taylor's "Education for Women," spell out cogent problems for the educated and would-be-educated woman in America. The others deal with problems growing out of the

---

[13]Nevertheless, the French tradition could accept the presence of outstanding intellectual women in the *salons*, and a "maîtresse de salon" could be more than a charming hostess.

male-female dichotomy in human society which impinge upon such issues as family relations, psychological maturity, education, politics, and manners. No answers to the dilemmas are given, but the problems are stated succinctly, an advantage in promoting discussion.

Farber, Seymour, and Roger H. L. Wilson, eds. *The Potential of Women.* (Man and Civilization.) New York: McGraw-Hill Book Company, 1963. 328 p.

Farber and Wilson present in book form the record of the third symposium of *Man and Civilization* held at the University of California San Francisco Medical Center in January, 1963.

Five aspects of the subject are included, each one represented by three papers (with short bibliographies): (1) The Experimental Study of the Female; (2) The Spectrum of Femininity; (3) The Roles of Woman; (4) The Consequences of Equality; (5) The Male Revolt. The informal discussion which follows is characterized by spontaneity as the participants, both female and male, range from the scientific to the personal.

Fénelon, François de Salignac de la Mothe. *Traité de L'Éducation des filles* ("Treatise on the Education of Girls"). Introduction et notes par Albert Cherel. Paris: Librairie Hachette, 1920. 185 p. (Originally published in 1687.)

Far from advising the same liberal education for women that was given to men, Fénelon in 1687 proposed that female learning should be related to women's God-given duties—which at that time were encompassed by household management, child-rearing, and piety. Yet within this framework women were to be encouraged to learn to read, write, and figure, which was a moving away from the acceptance of illiteracy as the natural condition of most women, even in France.

This essay was not an isolated instance of interest in the development of women, for Thomas More, Juan Luis Vives, Rabelais, and Erasmus shared Fénelon's concern, as did Montaigne earlier. Moreover, Mme de Maintenon, as wife of Louis XIV, had already made her school for the daughters of impoverished nobles at St. Cyr justly famous. But Fénelon, who was a frequent visitor at St. Cyr, put his ideas into words so clearly and convincingly that his *Traité* influenced society's attitudes on the subject for centuries, both in France and elsewhere.

An appendix contains Fénelon's equally broad-minded (relative to his times) *Avis à une Dame de Qualité sur L'Éducation de Mademoiselle, sa Fille* (1715) ("Advice to a Lady of Quality Regarding the Education of Her Daughter"). (For English translations of these two works see H. C. Barnard [above].)

Feytaud, Jacques de. "De l'amour. I. Ni ange ni bête. II. La pelle et le fourgon," *Bulletin de la Société des Amis de Montaigne*, 5e série, no. 20 (oct.-déc., 1976), pp. 7-22; no. 21 (jan-mars, 1977), pp. 17-30.

Feytaud makes an intensive search through Montaigne's *Essais* to find his opinions on the education, formal and informal, of women. In general, he concludes, Montaigne found no real differences between women and men; they are made of the same mold, he believed, but women had the disadvantage that in marriage they found "peu de rafraîchissement, selon nos moeurs," ("very little mental stimulation, according to our social notions"). Well ahead of his times, Montaigne realized that to the detriment of their intellectual development, contemporary women were constrained by a social hypocrisy in a male-dominated society which he considered particularly "odieuse."

Montaigne encouraged both his wife, Françoise, and his adoptive daughter, Marie de Gournay, to become learned, but, as he knew, they would thereby gain in erudition but not necessarily in social acceptance. (See Mario Schiff, below.)

Finley, M. I. *Aspects of Antiquity: Discoveries and Controversies*. 2d ed. Harmondsworth, Middlesex: Penguin, 1981. (1968 edition published by The Viking Press, New York.)

In Chapter X, "The Silent Women of Rome," Finley observes that Roman women probably were not considered as individual human beings but as "fractions of the family." Regrettably, there is a complete lack of first-hand information on what these "silent women" thought. All we know of them—and this is remarkable and disappointing as well, considering how long the Roman civilization lasted—is only what has come down to us through men's writings, whether in literature or the arts, or through letters written by women—primarily mothers, wives, sisters, daughters—to soldiers in the farflung Roman provinces.

Finley sees some changes occurring in the latter days of the empire as a result of the introduction of the mystery cults, when total silence gave way to expression by means of religion. But this hardly makes up for the loss to posterity of documentation of great human interest. Naturally, we of that posterity wonder what happened to their writings. Could it be that they were purposely winnowed out by those to whom the preservation of literature was entrusted, or did women themselves destroy their own writings, as often happened in later centuries? The study of

Latin, so useful in spite of its antiquity, could have been made more interesting, less artificial, if a better balance, one that would reflect Roman society as it was, had been maintained.

Firestone, Shulamith. ***The Dialectic of Sex: The Case for Feminist Revolution.*** New York: William Morrow, 1970. 273 p.

Since the biologic differences between the sexes are becoming less relevant because of technology, Firestone argues, traditional prejudices which have kept women subservient in outmoded roles should be eradicated, but she admits that males will not willingly give up power.

An imaginative picture of how the world could be if the sexual class system should disappear and a "cybernetic socialism" should take its place is part of Firestone's argument for radical changes in social structures.

Seeing Freudianism as a disaster for women, Firestone brands it as "worse than useless," for it has, she declares, paralyzed the sexual revolution which had begun to improve women's lives. Freudian psychology's stigma is that it sought to socialize men and women to an artificial sex-role system, promoting the falsehood that biology should determine destiny and ignoring women's potential in other spheres. Israel and Russia are prime targets of her scathing indictments: she shows why the social changes brought about by the Russian Revolution and the concept of the *kibbutz* have failed for women.

A Spanish translation, *La dialéctica del sexo: en defensa de la revolución feminista,* was published in 1976 by Editorial Kairos, Barcelona.

Forsberg, Robert J., and H. C. Nixon. ***Madame de Staël and Freedom Today.*** (Twayne Series.) New York: Astra Books, 1963. 90 p.

Madame de Staël's thought is analyzed briefly in the light of her political opinions, which were based on her acquaintance with numerous contemporary thinkers and on her studies of ancient as well as modern writings.

Forsberg and Nixon credit de Staël with the acumen to perceive trends in political evolution as they point out how her encounters with such leaders as Gouverneur Morris and Thomas Jefferson reveal her unfailing devotion to the ideals of liberty and international cooperation. She also came into direct conflict with Napoleon because of his repressive measures and as a result spent many years in exile.

Abundant original quotations are provided, as well as a bibliography.

Forten (Grimké), Charlotte. *The Journal of Charlotte Forten: A Free Negro in the Slave Era.* Edited by Brenda Stevenson. (The Schomburg Library of Nineteenth-Century Black Women Writers.) Salem, New Hampshire: Ayer Company, 1990; New York: Oxford University Press, 1989. (An earlier edition edited by Ray Allen Billington was published in 1969 [London, Collier Macmillan].) 622 p.

Forten began her diary in 1854 when she was sixteen and continued it intermittently after her marriage to the Reverend Francis Grimké in 1892. A thread running through her narrative is a burning resentment against the rigid racial prejudice she experienced in Salem, Massachusetts, Port Royal, South Carolina, and Philadelphia.

This unusual document assists in the understanding of a sensitive, idealistic, and well-educated daughter of well-to-do Negro parents before and after the Civil War.

Fowler, W. Warde. *Social Life at Rome in the Age of Cicero.* London: Macmillan and Company, 1965. (Originally published in 1905.).

In Chapter V, pages 135-167, "Marriage and the Roman Lady," Fowler selects several Roman women who represent "types." He admits that we probably know less of the "ideal matron" than of the "one who forces herself into notice by violating the traditions of womanhood." It is not clear who interprets the actions as "violations," Fowler, or Roman writers themselves—notably the misogynist satirists such as Juvenal.

Franz, Nellie Alden. *English Women Enter the Professions.* Cincinnati, Ohio:Columbia University Press, 1965. 317 p.

Franz's purpose is to inform the reader of one of the "most remarkable events of modern times," English women's courageous effort to attain social and economic independence. She traces the background of inferior status and poor education accorded to women in England, then notes the gradual, hard-won changes which resulted in their entering the fields of teaching, medicine, civil service, architecture, engineering, the church, and law.

This work is well-documented and shows the author's keen understanding of her subject.

Frederich, Peter J. *"Vida Dutton Scudder: The Professor as Social Activist," New England Quarterly,* XLIII (September, 1970), pp. 407-433.

Frederich explores the early career of Vida Scudder, writer and professor of English literature at Wellesley College from the turn of the century to 1927. Scudder was the first woman to attend Oxford University, where in 1884 she sat in on John

Ruskin's last lectures.[14] Other influences on her thought were Tolstoy and European radical social prophets.

Scudder's feeling of guilt for her sheltered, comfortable existence in the midst of poverty and suffering motivated her to become a socialist who would act to bring about social justice by inspirational teaching instead of action in public affairs. Scudder's opinions prefigured many of the social currents of later days.

Friedan, Betty. ***The Feminine Mystique*** New York: W. W. Norton & Company, 1963. 410 p.

Attaining extreme popularity at once, this book helped spark renewed interest in American feminism in the 1960's and provided women with a "rhetoric" as a foil for the complacent attitudes of the 1950's. The book is documented by textual notes which also include pertinent quotations from the sources cited.

Friedan trained her sights on myth-makers who have contributed (and continued to contribute, she notes) to the "progressive dehumanization" of the American woman. Included in her indictments are Freud and his followers such as Helene Deutsch (see above), the functionalist sociologists represented by Mirra Komarovsky, Margaret Mead (see below), and the advertising industry with its co-conspirators, the marketing analysts.[15] Friedan tellingly dissects the destructive myth of the

---

[14] John Ruskin (1819-1900) belonged to the British Pre-Raphaelite movement, composed of artists and writers who rebelled against the materialistic values of the expanding industrialization and idealized those of the Middle Ages. His best-known work is *The Crown of Wild Olives* (1866).

[15] In connection with advertising, see Lee Rainwater's work (below) on consumerism.

"happy housewife" who delights in an obsessive consumerism, concluding that in fact countless housewives (especially those in suburbia) were suffering from "the problem that has no name."

Friedan offers hope and challenge in a call for a national education program similar to the post-World War II "GI Bill" legislated to assist returning male veterans who wished to take advantage of it. This new legislation for women would be directed toward the needs of women who seriously wanted to attend college, if only on a part-time basis. Theoretically, these deserving women would not drain family finances and would thus achieve educational goals without conflict with marriage, husband, and children, still the priorities to be reckoned with.

Friedländer, Ludwig. ***Roman Life and Manners***. 4 vols. Translated by Leonard A. Magnus from the original *Sittengeschichte* (1907). New York: Barnes and Noble, 1968.

Volume I, Chapter V, pages 228-267, considers the position of women in ancient Rome. Friedländer admits that his knowledge of Roman women encompasses very little that is not about the upper classes, and even then "history records from her conning-tower only those women who rise above the mass." The women whose fortunate fate gave them birth into the privileged classes are described as living their early years in seclusion and dependence upon parents but enjoying freedom to pursue their own ambitions after marriage—"often. . .the fate of the Roman world was decided by women."

As for education, Friedländer finds that for these women it was not limited. Martial, the Roman epigrammist, describes the "ideal woman" as rich, noble, erudite, and chaste, so this seems to point to a lack of prejudice against intelligent women. Nevertheless, philosophy proper was designated as a male province, and women were discouraged from studying it. There was no general consensus that women ought to be "equal to men," Friedänder finds. It is reasonable to assume that their social position alone encouraged society to accord them the privileges which men had as a matter of course.

Frois, Marcel. *La Santé et le travail des femmes pendant la guerre.* (Histoire économique et sociale de la Guerre Mondiale, série française.) Paris: Les Presses Universitaires de France, 1920 (?).

Prepared under the auspices of the Carnegie Fund for International Peace, this study considers all aspects of industrial work done by women during World War I, including the age of women workers and conditions in the factories or shops, as well as lodging and clothing. Frois underlines the importance of women's wartime contributions in time and labor, a factor in victory often overlooked when peace comes.

Fryer, Judith. *"American Eves in American Edens,"* American Scholar, 44, no. 1 (Winter, 1974-75), pp. 78-99.

The early nineteenth century saw the rise of utopian communities in the United States wherein participants hoped to find new modes of living that would free women from the constraints of their traditional roles, says Fryer. The Shakers, for example, objected that women were taxed without representation, for they were denied the vote; Mormon women saw in polygamy the elevation of their sex; the New Harmony community led by Robert Owen established the first public school which gave girls equality of education; and Brook Farm, most intellectual in emphasis, was guided by Bronson Alcott, who believed in the superiority of the female sex.[16] Basic to the philosophies of these experiments was the conviction that America could create a new Eden, a perfect society.

Fryer, Peter. ***Mrs. Grundy: Studies in English Prudery.*** New York: London House and Maxwell, 1963. 368 p.

This thorough overview of the taboos of "grundyism" is designed to "show how the prude in authority becomes a censor."[16] Fryer's design extends to the sociological and psychological effects of prudery, especially on children of the nineteenth century. War, revolution, and social class are considered as well in relation to this theme.

The linguistic portions of Fryer's work are extensive: the notes continue this analysis. Not all of his material, of course, concentrates on women, but since most taboos relate to the female sex, the researcher will have no trouble in finding relevant material. The index and bibliography will be found helpful.

Fuller, (Sarah) Margaret. ***Woman in the Nineteenth Century and Kindred Papers Relating to the Sphere, Condition, and Duties of Woman***. Edited by Arthur S. Fuller, with an introduction by Horace Greeley. New York: Greenwood Press, 1968. 420 p. (Originally published in 1874.)

The Margaret Fuller of Brook Farm fame is eulogized by Greeley as the most earnest and forceful spokeswoman of the

---

[16] The idea of "Mrs. Grundy" as an arbiter of manners is said to come from Tom Morson's *Speed the Plough* (1798): "They eat, and drink, and scheme, and plod,/They go to church on Sunday;/And many are afraid of God,/And more of Mrs. Grundy." A variant of this is that Mrs. Grundy was an American, a social martinet in Washington's highest circles, a personage whom no one could offend with impunity.

contemporary movement for equal legal rights for women. Included in this volume is Fuller's essay, "Woman," in which she exhorts women to carry on "the holy work that is to make the earth a part of heaven." Fuller's brilliance and erudition are evident in the wide-ranging allusions to historical figures, as well as to her contemporaries.

García Ortiz, Maria Guillermino. *Lo eterno femenimo.* Quito, Ecuador: Casa de la Cultura Ecuatoriana, 1969. 155 p.

Divided into two parts, this work of the feminist Ecuadoran professor of literature first confronts the woman question by seeing it in its contemporary aspects, with capital problems seen as poverty, lack of freedom and justice, and the death of spirituality.

The second part concerns women from Biblical and classic literature whose lives reflect their feeling of social responsibility at the community level, from Sarah to Antigone—"encarnaron la capacidad creadora y regeneradora de su pueblo."

Gautier, Paul. *Madame de Staël: dix années d'exil.* Paris: Plon-Nourrit, 1904. 427 p. Index.

Gautier bases this work upon a manuscript written by Mme de Staël during her exile in Switzerland. Although the manuscript is in fragments, Gautier sees it as having for posterity a more than passing interest, since it tells of her "duel" with Napoleon. [17]

---

[17] Napoleon was not the only one who had the distinction of exiling the freedom-loving de Staël: she had been exiled in 1789 after the Revolution and not allowed to return until 1795.

Gautier's work also includes an absorbing preface written by de Staël for the 1821 edition of her manuscript. In it are comments upon her bitter situation, forced upon her because she would not accept Napoleon's repression of her thought.

Gautier, Paul. ***Madame de Staël et Napoléon.*** Paris: Plon-Nourrit, 1933 (new edition). (First edition 1903.) 422 p.

At Napoleon's accession to power de Staël showed great enthusiasm for the new régime. In time, however, Napoleon tired of her "aggressiveness": she was more than a woman—she was a political thinker, and Napoleon hated women who were not "real women"—"vraiment femmes." She talked, she wrote, and she held a well-attended political *salon*, a troublesome person indeed. Even her books irritated him, for *Corinne* was pro-English in tone, and *De l'Allemagne* was pro-German—both countries were Napoleon's bitter enemies.

Although the Emperor was the victor in the duel, as was to be expected, Gautier declares that all the glory belongs to de Staël: for her the individual was all, for Napoleon the individual was nothing.

Gavron, Hannah. ***The Captive Wife: Conflicts of Housebound Mothers.*** (International Library of Sociology and Social Reconstruction.) London: Routledge & Kegan Paul; New York: The Humanities Press, 1970 [1966]. 176 p.

Stating that useful English sociological study should not ignore the past, Gavron delineates the historical backgrounds of the ideologies which prevail in contemporary society in regard to women especially. She determines from her survey that these ideologies conflict with present realities and thus create a host of problems for women in their search for ways to cope with their static role-playing. "What is needed above all," Gavron writes, "is some deliberate attempt to re-integrate women. . . with the central activities of society." Some suggestions for this are on pages 147-148.

This is a detailed study of a small sample of young women in both working classes and the middle classes in England.

George, Margaret. *One Woman's "Situation": A Study of Mary Wollstonecraft*. Urbana: University of Illinois Press, 1970. 174 p. Index.

Following existential analysis, George sees Wollstonecraft as fitting into a series of situations as her life unfolds from childhood to motherhood. It is her contention that women do not have a history, only a progression of situations. In this George acknowledges her debt to Simone de Beauvoir, the idea of a framework termed a "pre-historic document."

This may be a tenable theory, but if Mary Wollstonecraft did not have a history, history has created one for her now.

George, Walter L. *Intelligence of Women, The*. Boston: Little, Brown, and Company, 1917. 244 p.

In form this is a long, subjective, and easy to read essay on women, whom Britisher George thinks of as human beings who have intellects just as men do! His literary allusions give the flavor of studiousness which mixes well with the substance of his remarks.

In his empathetic and far-seeing musings on the "downfall of the home" he does not deplore it but thinks alternatives must be found to give women greater opportunity to escape isolation. One of his suggestions is for the construction of blocks of "clean flats" with centrally located restaurants to be run by the tenants themselves. During the economic and social dislocations suffered in England during World War I and its aftermath, however, such suggestions would have little chance of being implemented.

Gilman, Charlotte Perkins. ***The Living of Charlotte Perkins Gilman: An Autobiography.*** (Wisconsin Studies in American Autobiography.) Milwaukee: University of Wisconsin Press, 1991. (First published in 1935.)

Charlotte Gilman (1860-1935) achieved lasting fame for her prophetic *Women and Economics* which taught that the economic dependence of woman was the principal hindrance to living a full life and realizing her potential. In a series of lectures from 1890 on, "The Larger Feminism," Gilman reminded women of their power to change the world for the better and criticized them for their superficiality: "This is woman's century, the first chance for the mother of the world to rise to her full place, her transcendent power to remake humanity, to rebuild the suffering world—and the world waits while she powders her nose."

Gilman, Charlotte Perkins. ***Women and Economics.*** (Harper Torchbooks.) New York: Harper and Row, 1966. New York: Harper and Row, 1966. 356 p. (Originally published in 1899.)

Gilman's work is a classic in the history of the women's movement. Carl N. Degler's introduction to this edition sets Gilman and her writings in their sociological setting, late nineteenth-century United States, to emphasize the originality of *Women and Economics*, which is subtitled, *A Study of the Economic Relations between Men and Women as a Factor in Social Evolution.*

Gilman's guiding geniuses were Lester Frank Ward and Charles Darwin, but her work does not make strict scientific pretensions—it is expository and exhortatory, being directed toward the enlightenment of contemporary women, who were generally unaware of the economic forces of American capitalism directing their lives. In this effort the logic she uses goes skillfully to the core of the problem as she sees it.

So many of the suggestions in *Women and Economics* have been adopted that the revolutionary impact of this work may be lost upon modern women (and men as well), but through empathetic historical perspective the student can appreciate Gilman's contribution to the formulation of feminism as she calls upon the calm, slow, friendly forces of "social evolution" to effect what she sees to be just and right.

Ginzberg, Eli, and Alice M. Yohalem, eds. ***Educated American Women: Self-Portraits.*** New York and London: Columbia University Press, 1971 [1966]. 198 p.

This is the third and final volume included in a study of talented people begun in 1960 by the Conservation of Human Resources Project at Columbia University. Information was gathered by means of a carefully constructed questionnaire, from which came personal profiles of twenty-six women who were homemakers, career women, working women with children, and women in transition.

The editors summarize from time to time and append an afterword which notes that most of the women interviewed were not dissatisfied, but that "our society is still not sufficiently geared to permit women to realize fully their potentialities." The work emphasizes again and again the dilemma of the educated woman.

Glasgow, Maude. ***Problems of Sex.*** Boston: The Christopher Publishing House, 1949. 199 p.

Much of physician Glasgow's treatment is biologic in approach, as she puts forth evidence to support her thesis that in many ways the female is the superior sex but ruefully notes that for the most part men do not or will not recognize this. Marshalling a great number of topical facts to prove her point, Glasgow adds interest to her argument with facts not generally known. One of them is that Masika Lancaster made the models of the Normandy landings of World War II. Without researchers like Glasgow and Mary Ritter Beard (see above), many of these contributions would have been consigned to the dustbins of history.

Gloerfelt-Tarp, Kirsten, ed. ***Women in the Community***. London: Oxford University Press; Copenhagen; Oslo: Martin, n.d. Translated from the Danish. (Originally published in 1937 as *Kvinden i Samfundet*.)

The position of women in contemporary Denmark is set forth in a series of essays by Danes, except for one Swedish contributor, Alva Myrdal, who writes about the recent revolution in women's status. Covered are such subjects as demographics, trades and industry, education, politics, and law.

Goldberg, Harriet, ed. ***Jardín de nobles donzellas, Fray Martín de Córdoba: A Critical Edition and Study.*** (North Carolina Studies in the Romance Languages and Literatures, No. 137.) Chapel Hill: University of North Carolina Department of Romance Languages, 1974. 310 p.

Printed first in 1500 at Valladolid, Fray Martín's treatise was presented to Isabella, future queen of Castile, as a manual of instruction on how to be an excellent ruler and a perfect woman. It served a dual purpose, says Goldberg, having been designed also to convince Isabel's future subjects of the benefits of having a woman as their monarch. Therefore, with the general reader in mind Fray Martín balances pro-feminist and anti-feminist elements of current controversy, often enlivening his arguments with humor from *exemplae* which embodied the popular caricatures of woman's nature without identifying himself with them too clearly.

Goldberg's careful analysis in English runs from pages 17 to 126, while Fray Martín's text, copiously annotated in English, is in the original Castilian. An excellent bibliography is included, and the two indexes are especially useful for women's studies researchers.

Goldman, Emma. ***Living My Life***. New York: Alfred A Knopf, 1921. 2 vols. 993 p. Index. (An abridged edition, 754 pages, was published by New American Library, 1977.)

In 1885 Goldman, then sixteen, arrived in New York from Russia "with youth, good health, and a passionate ideal"—but with only five dollars in her purse and a sewing machine her only luggage. Her "passionate ideal" was anarchism, which developed into faith in Communism, and although her revolutionary activities led her into trouble with the authorities, she obstinately persisted in her rebellion. Finally she was forced to serve a two-year prison sentence, followed by deportation in 1919.

After viewing Communism in action in her native land, however, Goldman became disillusioned and sought a freer atmosphere in England, Spain, and at last Canada, where she died in 1940. *My Disillusionment with Russia* describes how she came to lose her faith in the humanitarian thrust of Communism. (See also Drinnon, Richard.)

Goode, William J. ***World Revolution and Family Patterns***. New York: The Free Press, 1963. Notes and index.

Goode undertakes "to describe and interpret the main changes in family patterns that have occurred over the past half-century in Japan, China, India, the West, Sub-Saharan Africa, and the Arab countries." Since the first part of the twentieth century had been noteworthy for its changes in woman's status, Goode can find much to report in almost every part of the globe. As a result of world revolution in human relationships, Goode sees an increased potential of greater fulfillment in the personal sphere for both women and men, even though some of the changes may be disturbing to the *status quo*.

Gornick, Vivian, and Barbara K. Moran, eds. ***Women in Sexist Society: Studies in Power and Powerlessness***. New York and London: Basic Books, Inc., 1971. 515 p. Index.

Thirty-three women have contributed to make this volume a realistic survey of American women's life in areas which they consider most crucial to the advancement of liberation. Each one writes in an area of her special interests, and the editors provide a bird's-eye view of the contents.

Graham, Gabriela Cunninghame. ***Santa Teresa: Her Life and Times***. 2 vols. London: Adam and Charles Black, 1894; Eveleigh Nash, 1907. 925 p.

Graham's readable account of one of the most famous religious figures in Spanish history is designed to show Santa Teresa (1515-1582) as the woman Teresa de Ahumada as well as

Teresa de Jésus the saint. Admiring of Teresa's pragmatic talents, Graham shows how it was that she "from nothing, and with nothing but her own energy, was able to rescue the whole order of Carmelites from the condition of apathy into which it had fallen." Santa Teresa's asceticism rather than her mysticism is stressed as she is described as a very human young girl and in maturity a talented administrator.

A Spanish translation by Isabel Alonso, *Santa Teresa: contiene la relación de su vida y su época: con algunas páginas de la historia de la última gran reforma de las órdenes religiosas,* was published in 1927 at Madrid by Revista de Occidente.

Gréard, Octavio. ***L'Éducation des femmes par les femmes: Études et portraits.*** Paris: Librairie Hachette, 1915. 360 p. (Originally published in 1886.)

After a preface in which he gives some historical anecdotes concerning pedagogy in the thought of French women, Gréard presents portraits of early proponents of women's education in France—Fénelon, Mmes de Maintenon, de Lambert, d'Épinay, Necker, Roland, and Jean-Jacques Rousseau. The student will enjoy the excellent discussions which provide detailed knowledge of the French position in the ancient (and modern) controversy on this subject, known as *la querelle des femmes,* to denote the ongoing controversy about the nature of women and their appropriate place in society.

Gregory, Chester W. ***Women in Defense Work During World War II: An Analysis of the Labor Problem and Women's Rights.*** New York: Exposition Press, 1974. 243 p.

Economic re-alignment in the United States was one of the results of the recruiting of great numbers of women workers while the country was at war. Social reorganization, too, took on a faster pace as training programs, child care and housing, supervision of wages, and legislation (notably a drive for the Equal Rights Amendment [ERA]) became part of the changes that needed to be made. Chapter XII, "The Black Woman in War Work, 1941-1945," describes how the drive for equality was hastened. A bibliography and textual notes document the work.

Grimal, Pierre, ed. *Histoire mondiale de la femme: Préhistoire et antiquité.* Paris: Nouvelle Librairie de France, 1956. 497 p.

This beautifully illustrated study is divided into five sections: women in prehistory (Louis-René Nougier); women in ancient Egypt in all three empires (Jean Vercoutter); women in Mesopotamia, Israel, and Hittite Anatolia (Jean Boltert and Jenny Danmanville); women in Crete and Greece (Robert Flacelière), and women in Rome (Pierre Grimal).

A useful bibliography on women in prehistory is included (pages 486-489).

Hahn, Emily. *The Soong Sisters.* Garden City, New York: Doubleday, Doran and Co., 1941. 349 p. Index.

Eling, Mayling, and Chingling Soong formed a trio whose activities during the Chinese Revolution of 1911 set in motion the transformation of woman's status. Hahn's knowledgeable presentation of the details of their lives makes this an important work for the understanding of how women lived in pre-revolutionary China.

An appendix gives the text of the sisters' broadcast to America from Chungking on April 18, 1940 during the time of the Japanese invasion when Chinese-American relations were very close.

Hahn, Lili. ***White Flags of Surrender.*** Translated by Sibyl Milton. New York: R. B. Luce, 1974. 354 p.

How women of the great city of Frankfurt, Germany, survived under Nazi repression and the shattering bombing raids of World War II is revealed in graphic detail in this unique account. Lili Hahn, daughter of a Jewish mother and German father, a respected physician, had chosen to pursue a career in journalism until the Nazi control of all media and the merciless strictures against the Jews forced her out of her profession to face a dark future. This book, in the form of journal entries running from January, 1933 to March, 1945, was written after the war.

Hale, Sarah Josepha (Buell). ***Woman's Record; or, Sketches of All Distinguished Women from the Creation to A.D. 1868.*** New York: Source Books Press, 1970. 912 p. (Reprint of 1855 edition by Harper and Brothers.)

In an evident effort to redress the neglect historically afforded to women, Hale undertook this ambitious project, which is preceded by an outstanding introduction. The work is divided into four eras, with selections from authors in each, and with 230 illustrations.

This remains a sourcebook of intriguing possibilities for the historian researching women before 1870. Hale's viewpoint is feminist—she would have had to be a woman with dedication to a cause to embark on such a formidable undertaking, which reflects her conviction that this compendium was long overdue.

Hall, Edward B. *Memoir of Mary L. Ware, Wife of Henry Ware, Jr.*. Boston: Crosby, Nichols, and Company, 1853. 434 p.

The modern reader will easily read between the lines of this detailed account which belies Hall's intention, which was, as he confides naïvely, to show that "the sphere of woman, even the most domestic and silent, is broad enough for the most active intellect." But Mary's letters, which form the true interest of the book, speak often of her "moral paralysis," which undoubtedly stemmed from a lack of intellectual challenge and boredom with so much unrelieved domesticity.

Finding herself a widow in 1823 at the age of twenty-five, Mary went to England to nurse her father's relatives, after which she returned to Boston to marry a clergyman, a widower with children. Henceforth she devoted herself to an intensely domestic existence. Her story is one of an effort to adjust to a Christian ideal of duty, but it appears that this adjustment was only outwardly successful.

Halle, Fannina W. *Woman in Soviet Russia.* Translated from the German by Margaret M. Green. New York: The Viking Press, 1975 [1933]. 409 p.

The 1930's were thought to be the dawn of a new age under the Communist regime, and Halle regards her work "as a report upon the momentary position of an experiment of world-wide historical significance," especially in regard to the changes in relations between the sexes. A survey of the status of women in earlier periods in Russian history precedes her account of the Revolutionary era. Lenin's "glass of water" theory in regard to the free love controversy is treated at length.

An index is furnished, as well as a bibliography which cites relevant works in Russian.

Hammond, Harriet Milton. *Aunt Bet, the Story of a Long Life: A Memoir of Elizabeth S. W. Taylor*. Winchester, Virginia: The Handley Library, 1900. 155 p.

Hammond presents a closely-written biography of the daily life of Elizabeth Taylor, who lived from 1800 to 1883 in Clark County, Virginia. This is an excellent study for the researcher in American civilization who would capture the flavor of the prosperous domestic world of a slow-paced society that has now all but disappeared.

Harding, Esther M. *Women's Mysteries, Ancient and Modern.* New York: Putnam's, 1971. 256 p.

This work was published under the auspices of the C. G. Foundation for Analytic Psychology, and as the subtitle indicates, is "a psychological interpretation of the feminine principle as portrayed in mythology, story, and dreams."

Carl Jung, (once a disciple of Freud), remarks in his introduction that Harding "has devoted herself to compiling...the archetypal material of the feminine compensation." Archetypes, according to Jung, reach back to the deepest layers of racial history, and, it is assumed, relate to woman's essential nature.

Much of Harding's analysis deals with the legends surrounding moon imagery as conceived by primitive peoples, both because of night mystery and the moon's cyclical progressions as are seen, for example, in the worship of Ishtar, Isis, and Osiris, especially in ancient Egypt. Harding gives more credence to the intuitions, wisdom, and customs of ancient peoples in all parts of the world than to modern rationalists. She predicts a return to respect for primitive concepts, to be sparked by modern interest in analytical psychology.

Harris, Sara. ***The Sisters: The Changing World of the American Nun.*** Indianapolis: Bobbs-Merrill, 1971. 333 p.

The revolutionary *Vatican II* revealed, says Harris, "the openness and warmth that lay hidden" in the personalities of Catholic women who had chosen the religious life. Here she puts into print their frank opinions of the issues and perplexities that confronted them in a new era, such as mode of dress, marriage, changes in the mass, and the espousal of social causes. Treated at length is the work of white nuns in black ghettos in American cities. Expressed, too, is the resentment felt by many nuns against the male-dominated decisions of the Church.

Harwell, Richard Barksdale, ed. ***Kate: The Journal of a Confederate Nurse by Kate Cumming***. Baton Rouge: Louisiana State University Press, 1959. 320 p.

Kate Cumming served as a nurse from 1862 to 1865 with the Army of Tennessee, working in mobile hospitals. Like Florence Nightingale, she was highly critical of the male administrators and sympathetic to the soldiers, both Confederate and Union. Moreover, she was slightly disdainful of the Southern women who she thought were failing in their duty to the fighting men. Kate's journal is insightful and valuable for its realistic pictures of war and its references to contemporary women.

Haskell, Molly. ***From Reverence to Rape: The Treatment of Women in the Movies.*** 2d ed. Chicago: University of Chicago Press, 1987. 425 p.

Within a chronological structure Haskell sees the movies as reflective of deep-seated social attitudes which appeared to change from the concept of woman as feminine ideal to a less reverent presentation of her as the "flapper" of the 1920's and as a sex object in the 1960's and 1970's. Paralleling the earlier characterization, however, was the emergence of the independent woman, a concept which tended to fade, perhaps because it was less compatible with audience appeal.

The work is illustrated and an index cites the specific films and persons highlighted in the text.

Haté, Chandrakala, A. *The Changing Status of Woman in Posence India.* Bombay, London: Allied Publishers Private, 1969. 284 p.

Based mainly upon statistical data, this study concerns the way in which India was developing in regard to women and the way women were adjusting as traditional and revolutionary influences seemed to be converging to create a new social climate.

Middle class urban women from Maharashtra—Bombay, Poona, Nagpur, and Sholapur—are the focus of the survey. Haté shows that only slow advances were being made in education, careers, health, and religious attitudes. This is attributed to the fact that women were a demographic minority: the 1967 census revealed that there were 941 females to 1000 males, mostly because of the neglect of girl children and the risks of child-bearing.

Hays, Elinor. *Those Extraordinary Blackwells: The Story of A Journey to a Better World.* New York: Harcourt, Brace & World, 1967. 349 p. Bibliography and index.

In this highly detailed history of an unusual family Hays shows that one part of the "better world" in the eyes of the Blackwell sisters was improvement in the position of women in nineteenth century America. Elizabeth led the way, becoming the first *bona fide* woman physician, Hays asserts, in the modern world. Other causes in which they fought in concert were slavery, temperance, women's rights, education—in fact, every cause that was blown their way by the winds of change (and they caused some of the changes). The men of their family were similarly inclined. One brother married Lucy Stone, who became famous for her audacious speeches against women's inferior status.

Healy, Emma Thérèse (Sister). ***Women According to Saint Bonaventure.*** Erie, Pennsylvania: Villa Maria College, 1956. 275 p. Index.

"Woman in Nature" (according to Biblical accounts), and "Woman in Grace" (married or virginal) are the two aspects of woman's existence, leaving only woman as divine ideal to be truly revered (Mary is the ideal). Bonaventure, says Healy, "entertained a great mistrust of worldly, beautiful women" as "the first cause of evil on earth." Therefore he cautiously advised a strategy of "successful retreat" before their onslaughts.

Healy's analysis presents an authoritative statement on early, ascetic Christian misogyny and the transmutation of woman into a mystic ideal, sexless and unattainable. These concepts with their narrow focus permeated Western culture through the spread of Christianity.

Hecker, Eugene A. ***A Short History of Women's Rights from the Days of Augustus to the Present Time with Special Reference*** *to England and the United States.* 2d ed., revised. Westport, Connecticut: Greenwood Press, 1971. 331 p. (Originally published in 1924.)

In this carefully-prepared compendium which deals with legal matters up to 1924 Hecker works from primary sources and makes constant references to them, which proves to be of great assistance to the student seeking information concerning Roman law, Catholic law, and the law of the Germanic peoples. On pages 174-235 are set forth the laws relating to women of each state of the United States as they stood in 1914.

Heinrich, Mary Pia (Sister). ***The Canonesses and Education in the Early Middle Ages.*** Washington, D.C.: Catholic University of America, 1960 [1924]. 218 p. (Also available on microtext from Notre Dame University.)

This volume, which deals with France, Belgium, Germany, Ireland, and England, has as its subject the quality and extent of education imparted to girls of the nobility from the sixth to the twelfth centuries. Surprisingly, Heinrich remarks that these girls "enjoyed the advantages of a literary education more frequently than their brothers."

A wealth of detail can be found in this work, which includes information on contemporary legislation, such as Charlemagne's efforts at educational reform, an outline of the curricula offered in the convents, and references to a great number of women students who were outstanding. An excellent bibliography lists relevant French, German, and English works.

Héricourt, Jenny d'. ***A Woman's Philosophy of Woman; or, Woman Affranchised.*** Westport, Connecticut: Hyperion Press, 1981. (First English publication, 1864.) 317 p.

This is a translation of Mme d'Héricourt's message to her critics—Michelet, Proudhon, Girardin, Legouvé, Comte, and others "who think they have the last word about women." This pioneer French feminist saw woman "in marriage a serf, in public a sacrifice, in labor an inferior, in civil law a minor, in political life a being with no existence."

This is also good reading for those who are studying in disciplines where the author's "adversaries" (her term) are being highlighted, for these men were influential figures whose works were admired in their own time and are still consulted for their social commentary.

Herold, J. Christopher. *Love in Five Temperaments.* New York: Atheneum, 1961. 337 p. Illustrations.

Five *Parisiennes* of varying attitudes toward love—and their *amours* and political intrigues made famous in history—are presented by Herold as worthy of special attention: Mme de Tencin, who at an early age as an unwilling nun aspired to move from powerlessness to unlimited political power; Aïssé, who was sold in Turkey as a four-year-old slave to the French ambassador, M. de Ferriol; Mlle Delaunay de Staal, lady's maid to the machiavellian Duchesse du Maine; Mlle de Lespinasse (Julie), who "became a power in the world," as she outshone Mme du Deffand in that lady's own *salon*, usurped the affections of Mme du Deffand's favorite, d'Alembert, and had a definite influence on the *Académie Française*; and Mlle Clarion, who as an incomparable actress at the *Comédie Française* was praised by both Diderot and Voltaire, as well as other notables of the day, including Mme de Staël.

Herold includes separate bibliographies of French works on the subject of each woman, and a good index follows.

Hewitt, Margaret. ***Wives and Mothers in Victorian Industry.*** Westport, Connecticut: Greenwood Press, 1975. (Originally published in London in 1950.) 245 p.

Hewitt's purpose is to study the effects of the nineteenth-century growth of the factory system on homes and families. Noting that although the work of women in such activities as agriculture and textiles had always been an important factor in human life, she points out that with the advent of the Industrial Revolution the disruption of families became an overwhelming problem.

Chapter V, "Cotton Mill Morality," and Chapter VI, "The Married Operator as a Home-Maker" reflect Victorian concern with the increasing severity of this societal dilemma. Hewitt makes references to Elizabeth Gaskell's novels which served to bring attention to the shocking conditions of the proletariat.

A good bibliography on pages 226-236 will prove valuable for further study.

Hillesum, Etty. ***An Interrupted Life: The Diaries of Etty Hillesum, 1941-1943.*** Introduction by J. G. Gaarlandt. Translated from the Dutch by Arno Pomerans. New York: Pantheon Books, 1983. 226 p.

Etty Hillesum was a gifted writer, a lover of literature, a deeply religious thinker. Nevertheless, as a Jew her life was snuffed out in the Nazi camp of Auschwitz in 1943. Etty's emotional and at the same time realistic account of her attenuated days, one by one, expresses her resignation, yet her love of life and empathy for others.

Toward the end of the book Etty writes of a group of Jewish women, many with small children, who were waiting in the cold to be deported from Holland. They suffered "as if spun in a web of sorrow."

Hobbs, Lisa. ***Love and Liberation: Up Front with the Feminists.*** New York and London: McGraw-Hill Book Company, 1970. 159 p.

In form this is a polemical essay which argues that since the biologic value of women (traditionally the only value) has disappeared because of over-population, it is imperative to reconstruct society on lines that will include women as equal participants in all facets of life (as well as save the environment from destruction). Yet ruefully Hobbs finds both sexes (as reflected in the advertising media) holding on to anachronistic stereotypes of male-formed roles. Her answer seems to be more dedication on the part of women to join the front lines of feminism.

Hohman, Daisy Lucie. ***Go Spin, You Jade: Studies in the Emancipation of Women.*** London: Watts, 1967. 152 p. Index.

Historically oriented, this account of the feminist movement in England begins with the influences of Renaissance ideas. Its accent is upon the personal actions of women who caused the movement to carry momentum from the eighteenth to the twentieth century.

Holcombe, Lee. ***Victorian Ladies at Work: Middle Class Working Women in England and Wales, 1850-1914.*** Hamden, Connecticut: Archon Books, 1973. 253 p.

Tying the evolution of women's paid employment to the advances in the women's movement in England and Wales, Holcombe describes conditions in teaching, nursing, clerking in shops and offices, and government service. In summary, she finds that the women's movement, though it may now be called women's liberation or the sexual revolution, is an ongoing struggle which has by no means been won, partly because of women's failure to fight for equal rights.

Abundant textual notes are provided, and the index serves as a means of identifying special areas of concern.

Holloway, Laura C. *The Ladies of the White House, or In the Homes of the Presidents*. New York: Ams Press, 1976. (Reprint of the 1882 edition.) Illustrations.

The women who graced the White House from 1789 to 1880 are described in detail in these portraits because, Holloway explains, they had up to now no biographers, in spite of the fact that many had been of outstanding intellect.

Taking a feminist perspective, Holloway is aware throughout of the constrictions of the feminine domain and the disadvantages felt by these women in their girlhood as well as in adult life.

Horner, Matina B. *"Fail, Bright Women,"* Psychology Today, 3 (November, 1969), pp. 36-38; 62.

Quoting Samuel Johnson's truism, "A man is in general better pleased when he has a good dinner upon his table, than when his wife talks Greek." Horner comments, "So she doesn't learn Greek." This article considers the phenomenon of a culturally-induced will-to-fail among women in academic life and in careers later on, the causes of which seem to be guilt and despair about achieving. Horner notes that 65% of the females in her study avoided success, while only 10% of the males did.

Hottel, Althea E., ed. ***"Women Around the World,"*** in *Annals of the American Academy of Political and Social Sciences,* 375 (January 1968), pp. 1-175.

The current status of women in the United States, Canada, Europe (west and east), Africa, the Middle East, Southeast Asia, Japan, and the South Pacific is the subject of this helpful overview. Conspicuous by their absence are the women of the Hispanic world.

Huber, Joan, ed. ***Changing Women in a Changing Society.*** Chicago: University of Chicago Press, 1973. 295 p.

Twenty-one topical essays include, among others, ones about professional women in France; women in the armed forces, women publishers, African-American women, and gynecologists. The bibliographies which follow some of the essays are easily the most helpful part of this compilation.

A Spanish translation, *La nueva mujer,* was published by Editores Asociados at Mexico City in 1976.

Hughes, Muriel Joy. ***Women Healers in Medieval Life and Literature.*** Freeport, New York: Books for Libraries Press, 1968 [1943]. 180 p.

Universal curiosity exists concerning the healing lore of bygone days now that modern science has widened the gap between people and Nature. Hughes satisfies this curiosity in a scholarly way as she searches contemporary writings to cite examples from medieval sources—legends, church records, and writers such as Chaucer. She finds that "history and literature alike pay tribute" to women's practical wisdom in herbal medicine and nursing procedures.

Even then, as now, women were excluded from the front ranks of medicine as men struggled for a monopoly in the field, using recourse to the "scientific method" as the starting point of effective treatment. This professional rivalry did not prevent sufferers, however, from expressing gratitude, says Hughes, as she points out the contribution of the nuns and mentions such women as Christine de Pisan, the Paston women, Princess Anna Comnana, Héloïse, and Trotula of Salerno. Trotula was possibly the author of *De passionibus mulierum,* which presents the viewpoint of medieval women themselves on the subject of women's ailments and their treatment.

This book encompasses much: it contains a bibliography (pages 153-171), an index, an appendix, "Women Practitioners of the Later Middle Ages," and a glossary of widely-used herbs.

Hunt, Morton M. ***The Natural History of Love.*** New York: Alfred A. Knopf, 1959. 429 p.

The plan of Hunt's book rests on chronology, but this formal framework is softened by the imaginative style, and the scholarship, though satisfyingly evident, does not lie heavily on the pages.

We are carried from ancient times to the twentieth century, entertained at every turn and made to conclude at the end that if it is possible to become an expert on love by reading a book, this is the book. Besides that, it is indexed and has a copious bibliography.

Huntington, Annie Oakes. ***Testament of Happiness; Letters of Annie Oakes Huntington.*** Edited by Nancy Byrd Turner. Portland, Maine: The Anthoensen Press, 1947. 235 p.

Letters written over a period of fifty years, from 1885 to her death in 1940 describe this American woman's childhood in China in the American colony at Hong Kong and her subsequent years in New England and the American South. All the letters but one are addressed to women.

Hutton, J. Bernard. ***Women in Espionage***. New York: The Macmillan Company, 1971. 192 p. (First printed in Britain as *Women Spies*.)

"The intelligent and skillful women spies described in this book are genuine spies, who do difficult and dangerous jobs efficiently," writes Hutton in the prologue which sets the stage for a description of the much maligned Mata Hari. This book has a sharp international flavor, for spies of all nations are "as busy as beavers in every quarter of the globe." Hutton's detailed stories of little-known women who have succeeded in the spy world are startling vignettes written in a casual, journalistic style.

Inguanti, Maria. ***Le Donne della Riforma in Italia***. Rome: Casa Editrice Battista, 1968. 53 p.

Vittoria Colonna, Gicelia Gonzaga, Renata di Francia, and Olimpis Morato are the principal subjects of this study, preceded by an introduction briefly describing the sixteenth-century *milieu* in which they endeavored to live self-assertively. Inguanti praises their courage.

International Congress of Women. ***Our Common Cause: Civilization: Report of Congress of July 16-22, 1933.*** New York: National Council of Women of the United States, 1933. 974 p.

This voluminous report contains the text of a series of round table discussions which covered a variety of subjects under two main headings: "Security" and "Opportunity"—security from disease, crime, prejudice, war, and employment; opportunity for education, leisure, improvement of the environment, and to raise the level of the communication media. All these goals are as pertinent today as when they were formulated at the time of the world-wide Great Depression. Gratifying improvements had been made in certain areas, such as medicine and education, but the goal of pacifism so hoped for after World War I would not be achieved, for, ironically, this was the year of Adolf Hitler's ascent to power, and World War II was just over the horizon.

James, Bartlett Burleigh. ***Women of England.*** (Woman in All Ages and in All Countries.) Philadelphia: The Rittenhouse, 1908. 425 p.

James moves from the women of ancient Britain to the improvement in the conditions of their lives under the Roman occupation which, however, afforded only a veneer of civilization. Even this disappeared when the occupiers were ordered away to defend embattled Rome. Subsequently Britain suffered invasion from Teutonic tribes, the Angles, Jutes, and Saxons, and it was their ideas of women which were of primary influence.

Of great interest is the chapter "Women of the Monasteries," pages 153-169, which describes the organization of the cloisters during Anglo-Saxon times and notes, too, that the nuns were versed in Latin and were often charged with the education of children in schools established by Theodorus and Hadrian. Moreover—something which is not generally known, because monks have historically been given the credit—in addition to the reading of theological and classical literature, they had the duty of copying and embellishing manuscripts. "It was not unusual for a nun to become proficient in Latin versificiation and to correspond in that language with others of a similar literary taste and training." The convents were also centers of medical treatment.

This productive era, howevr, was not to last forever. The suppression of the monasteries by Henry VIII was a disaster for English nuns and women for whom convent schools had been the only schools available for girls. After their suppression, female education was virtually extinguished and not until the days of the *salons* and bluestockings did English women effectively rebel against their disadvantaged position.

James ends his most illuminating survey with a chapter on the women of Scotland and Ireland, pages 383-425.

Jordan, Ruth. *Sophie Dorothea*. New York: George Braziller, 1972. 292 p.

The life of the German prince who became George I of England forms the background of Jordan's study. The heroine is Sophie Dorothea, the prince's unhappy divorced wife who, Jordan avers, has been consistently neglected by historians.

For twenty years Sophie Dorothea was a political prisoner in the castle of Ahlden, and although Jordan does not hold her completely blameless, she finds that Sophie's victimization was due to the conspiracies of men who needed her out of the way. When he became king of England, George was already in possession of his wife's considerable fortune, Jordan reveals, and neither he nor his father wanted her to be at liberty to try to reclaim it, nor to investigate other unsavory acts of theirs which had ruined the life of this unfortunate princess.

Jourda, Pierre. *Marguerite d'Angoulême, Duchesse d'Alençon, Reine de Navarre (1492-1549): étude biographique et littéraire.* 2 vols. (Bibliothèque Littéraire de la Renaissance, nouvelle série, tomes XIX et XX.) Genève: Slatkine Reprints, 1978. (Paris: Librairie Ancien Honoré Champion, n.d.) Illustrated.

Jourda has endeavored to make this study of the intriguing Queen Marguerite a definitive one and so has spared no pains to make it reflect his great respect for her life and writings. While basing his work upon contemporary documents and her correspondence, he also allows her to speak for herself through her poetry.

The footnotes are particularly helpful for researchers who might wish to continue further in this field. An exhaustive bibliography is listed on pages 1139-1162.

Joyce, T. Athol, and N. W. Thomas, eds. *Women of All Nations: A Record of Their Characteristics, Habits, Manners, Customs, and Influence.* Genève: Slatkine Reprints, 1978. 2 vols. (A 1942 edition in 1 volume was published by Funk & Wagnalls, New York, 1942. First published at London by Cassell and Company, 1909, 2 vols.) Available on microfilm from Research Publications, New Haven, Connecticut, 1975. (History of Women, Reel 739, no. 5918.1.)

These beautifully illustrated volumes by two scientists of the British Royal Anthropological Institute take a broad view of history to relate the story of "how woman has ceased to be the slave of man . . . and has become his help-meet." Even though this evolution has paralleled the advance of civilization, they conclude, many women in so-called progressive countries are in a worse situation than their "savage sisters"

This is a good sourcebook (over 700 pages long) for the description of contemporary native customs and attitudes before industrialization had its impact upon them. Every part of the globe is covered, and a bibliography and an index (at the back of Volume II) are convenient guides to the geographical areas.

Jung, Leo, ed. *The Jewish Library*. Volume III: *Woman*. London: The Soncino Press, 1970. 239 p.

For Jung's collection fifteen women and men bring their opinions to bear on a variety of subjects relating to Western European Jewish women such as education, rules for conjugal relations, divorce, health, and social activities. Most of these writings are permeated with an idealism that convinces the reader that they are prescriptive rather than descriptive. A section of the Jewish woman in Germany (pages 174-200) considers trends toward feminist thinking.

Justin, Dena. *"The Downfall of Women,"* Intellectual Digest, IV (October, 1973), pp. 90-91.

Digging back into mythology, Justin finds that once upon a time the ancient world knelt at the altars of the great Mother Goddess, but a successful male rebellion deposed her, and the precept of the new masculine order became Apollo's dictum: "Keep women down."

Kardiner, Abram. *Sex and Morality*. Indianapolis: Bobbs-Merrill, 1954.

Chapter VIII, "The Modern Family," has a section entitled, "Effects of Feminism" that presents an unbiased view of the central dilemma in the modern woman's life. Kardiner considers the crucial question of how a modern woman can be a person of dignity (and even prestige) and be a happy home-maker as well. Since he considers the consequences of an either/or decision ultimately undesirable, he leans toward the doubtful expedient of asking society to "restore" prestige to homemaking, and to realize that the economic goals men are trained to revere are not necessarily the best for women or, in the final analysis, for men either.

Kaur, Manmohan. *The Role of Women in the Freedom Movement (1857-1947)*. Delhi, India: Sterling Publishers Private, 1968. 287 p.

Indian women's fight for freedom took on the character of a double struggle, Kaur reveals in this first-of-a-kind account. First it was for freedom from Britain, for which Kaur fought side by side with men. Then it was freedom from the centuries-long enslavement to the bonds and even the horrors of Indian culture. The British were forced to leave, but the latter struggle continued.

Through this book Kaur, who was born in what is now West Pakistan and attended schools in the Punjab, Delhi, and Holland, hoped to bring the Indian woman's plight to the attention of the world. It is based upon government records for the pre-1917 period, newspaper reports, periodical articles, and numerous first-hand accounts. Much of the text is devoted to biographical information on individual women, including Annie Besant, an Englishwoman who in 1803 at the age of 46 left England to embrace Indian culture (including theosophy) and join the struggle for India's freedom from British rule.

This work is well-annotated and has an appendix, "Details on the Custom of Widow Burning, or Satisuttee (sati or suttee)," which graphically illustrates the ordeals to which women were subjected. A bibliography, pages 265-278, rounds out this unique contribution to women's history.

Keddie, Nikke R., ed. ***Scholars, Saints, and Sufis: Muslim Religious Institutions in the Middle East since 1950.*** Berkeley: University of California Press, 1972.

"Variation of Religious Observance among Islamic Women," by Robert A. Fernea and Elizabeth W. Fernea, points out that religious observances are not shared jointly by men and women under Islam, and this gives the women a certain amount of personal autonomy, for they have had "freedom to develop meaningful rituals that reflect their own needs and concerns."

Kelso, Ruth. ***Doctrine for the Lady of the Renaissance.*** Urbana: University of Illinois Press, 1981 [1956]. 475 p..

Kelso's excellent study of the years between 1400 and 1600 begins with Christine de Pisan's remark that even the wisest of male writers generally somewhere along the way find occasion to belittle women, if not on grounds of their "evil nature," then certainly because of their imputed "inferiority." Nevertheless, Kelso bases her work on her own observation that such misogynist generalities are proved false by the countless accomplishments of women explicated in the texts she delves into, which are listed on pages 326-462.

Kendall, Elaine. ***"Beyond Mother's Knee,"*** *American Heritage*, XXIV: 4 (June, 1973), pp. 12-16; 73-78.

In this valuable article Kendall points out the narrowness of educational opportunities available for girls and women in the United States before the twentieth century, noting that "long before the Revolution American males had already entered Harvard, Yale, and Princeton, as well as a full range of other educational institutions," while very often girls were actually proscribed from learning even to read and write, except at "mother's knee." A revealing commentary on the oft-noted misogyny of American culture, this essay documents the struggles of women to attain even a modicum of opportunity for intellectual development.

Key, Ellen. *The Morality of Women and Other Essays.* Translated from the Swedish by Mamah Bouton Borthwick. Chicago: The Ralph Fletcher Seymour Company, 1911. 78 p. (Available from NYT Microfilming Corporation, Glen Rock, New Jersey, 1975 ed., Gerritsen Collection of Women's History.)

Key's ideas on the "woman question" have become so much a part of modern thinking that her work is often forgotten. Her formula for the new concept of morality, "Love is moral without legal marriage but marriage is immoral without love," has been accepted by many, rejected by others, but very few have not heard of this romantic and idealistic concept. Nevertheless, Key interprets freedom as requiring extremely stringent rules of conduct.

In her two essays, "The Woman of the Future" and "The Conventional Women" she expresses her hope that women of the twentieth century would be able to create a "new woman," one who will be equal to men, but also chaste, reserved, soulful, proud, and true. "The woman of the future exists already in man's dreams of women, and woman fashions herself according to the dreams of men." The "eternal feminine," Key believes, can be found in such women as Heloïse, Mlle Lespinasse, Elizabeth Barrett Browning, Eleanor Duse—and Mona Lisa.

Key, Ellen. ***The Renaissance of Motherhood.*** Translated from the Swedish by Anna E. B. Fries. New York: Source Books Press, 1970. (Reprint of the 1914 edition by G. P. Putnam's Sons.) 171p.

Motherhood, declares feminist Key, should be viewed as an educative vocation to which women will bring qualities of the "new woman," accepting of their own freedom and proud of their mission as shapers of the souls of their children.

Key, Ellen. ***The Woman Movement.*** Translated from the Swedish by Mamah Bouton Borthwick. Introduction by Havelock Ellis. New York: G. P. Putnam's Sons, 1922 [1900]. (Available on microfiche from Washington Microcards, 1974 ed.) 224 p.

Noting the success of the first Swedish feminist novel, *Hertha*, Key predicts a demand for "vital air for woman's soul and a share in life's riches," a chance to aspire, to fulfill herself, even though most women will be led by their nature to seek home and motherhood. Her attitude toward the feminist Norwegian playwright Henrik Ibsen is ambivalent: although his intentions were to free women, he also put unrealistic "fancies" into their heads, Key opines.

Key's work, characterized by Ellis as a reasonable and temperate exposition of feminist claims, is a pioneer effort which expresses many of the ideas that are still being debated. Not only does Key mark the events of the movement, but she considers its psychological effects upon both women and men. Prescient, she notes the new problems being created for marriage and motherhood by remarking, "The marriage is absolutely wrecked when the wife brings to it all the new demands of woman, but the husband [brings to it] all the primeval instincts of his sex."

Kiddle, Margaret. *Caroline Chisholm*. Melbourne: Melbourne University Press, 1990 [1969]. 208 p.

Chisholm, called the most remarkable woman in early Australian history, believed that women could find unlimited opportunities in this new land. Her ardent efforts to encourage female emigration, however, were met with apathy on the part of some people and active opposition, official and unofficial, on the part of others. Here again an idealistic woman pioneer found that the way to possible independence for her sex was a thorny one, some of the thorns being stereotypes embedded deep in European culture.

Kiefer, Otto. *Sexual Life in Ancient Rome.* Translated from the German *Kulturgeschichte Rome under Besonderer Berücksichtigung der romischen Sitten* by Gilbert and Helen Highet. New York: Barnes and Noble, 1953. 379 p.

Although the entire book may be considered related to the subject of woman, Chapter I, "Woman in Roman Life," and Chapter VI, "Men and Women of the Imperial Age," will be of most interest. The latter chapter includes material on Augustus' daughter Julia, wife of Tiberius, and on Julia's own daughter, "the younger Julia."

In his conclusion Kiefer declares that his own philosophy of life is an integral part of his work. Therefore, perhaps the reader might want to read the conclusion (pages 365-370) first, in order to winnow out the subjective from the objective as reading proceeds.

Kirkpatrick, Clifford. ***Nazi Germany: Its Women and Family Life.*** New York: Ams Press, 1981. (Reprint of 1938 publication by Bobbs-Merrill, Indianapolis.) 353 p.

An excellent bibliography, pages 303-333, is one of the features of this work (many entries are in German). Another which will interest historians especially is the perspective of the author as he studies Germany at a time when the Nazis had not yet been branded as aggressors and criminals but rather as possible "re-organizers" of the chaotic German state, the hope of the German people.

Kirkpatrick concludes that certain psychological satisfactions accrued to many women as they came to identify with "a great tribal in-group" headed by Adolf Hitler, seen by them as "father, lover, savior, protector, and leader." He shows, however, that for intellectual and feminist women who opposed Nazi ideology there was a total annihilation of the women's movement following the repression of their leader, Gertrud Bäumer, in 1933.

The title of Kirkpatrick's work was changed in 1939 to *Women in Nazi Germany,* for publication by Jarrolds, Ltd., in London.

Klein, Viola. ***The Feminine Character: History of an Ideology.*** Introduction by Janet Sayers. New York: Routledge, 1989 [1946]. 202 p.

The object of this much-discussed study is to "discover whether there are traits which can be called typically feminine, and if so, what they are. Klein calls her work exploratory and not definitive, which is understandable, considering the amorphous nature of the subject. One of the areas of "loose ends" which she hopes will be investigated by other researchers is the effects of discouragement in shaping the female psyche.

Adjunct to her own work Klein offers a survey of what some of her precursors have done—Havelock Ellis, Otto Weininger, Freud, Helen B. Thompson, L. M. Terman, C. C. Miles, Mathias and Mathilde Vaerting, Margaret Mead, and W. I. Thomas

An analysis of the novel, *The Rebel Generation* by Jo V. Amers-Küller is appended.

A Spanish translation of Klein's work by Gino Germani (with a preface by Karl Mannheim), *El carácter femenino: historia de una ideología,* was published in 1990 by Ediciones Paidós, Barcelona.

Komarovsky, Mirra. **Women in the Modern World.** Dubuque, Iowa: Brown Reprints, 1972. (Published by Little, Brown, and Company, 1953.) 319 p.

The central question around which Komarovsky's work revolves is "How and for what are we educating our daughters?" Far from being an academic question, it is one involving the whole society, and society, thinks the author, is a "patient" for whom a cure must be sought.

Age-old dilemmas are considered: anti-feminism, feminism, home and/or career, romance *vs.* reality, dependence *vs.* independence, as well as the problems created by theories of women that give rise to myths, such as those of Freud and Helene Deutsch.

Four case studies round out the social analysis: a happy career wife, a woman with a problem-ridden pattern of career plus home, a new-style feminist mother, and a professional woman with a conflict in roles. (See Betty Friedan, *The Feminine Mystique,* for a critique of Komarovsky's stance.)

Koren, Else Elisabeth (Hysing). ***Diary, 1853-1855.*** Translated and edited by David T. Nelson. Eden Prairie, Minnesota, 1985. (Published by the Norwegian-American Historical Society, 1955.) 381 p.

Leaving a sheltered home-life in Norway in 1853, Koren came as a bride to a life devoid of comforts in the wide expanse of unsettled Iowa. As a pioneer her life encompassed almost the whole of the sweep of the Norwegian immigrant story, to which this diary forms a prologue, Nelson points out. Koren's two-year diary is significant not only because it gives an intimate glimpse into one woman's feelings about her situation, but also because it is one of the few accounts we have of the Norwegian women pioneers. One speculates about why her diary was so short-lived: that, of course, is probably a story in itself.

Koyama, Takashi. ***The Changing Social Position of Women in Japan.*** Paris: UNESCO, 1961 [1959].

A sociological survey of changes made in the position of Japanese women after World War II, using published and unpublished material, is here presented through the efforts of five women and two men, all Japanese. A public opinion survey is included, in which women give their opinions; these are incorporated into the general conclusions found on pages 145-152.

Lackey, Walter K. ***The Family in Classical Greece.*** Ithaca, N.Y.: Cornell University Press, 1983 [1968]. 342 p.

In Chapter VII, "Women in Democratic Athens," Lackey rejects the often-held idea that all Athenian women were sequestered and denigrated, claiming that it depends upon what social class is being considered. Middle-class women he shows as having greater freedom than is generally supposed, but then, he adds, so did middle-class men, since the aristocratic class had to live by narrowly-defined rules.

References to women in other Greek states can be found in the index. Lackey refers often to Greek dramatists and to Plato as evidence for his conclusions.

Laigle, Mathilde. *"Le Livre de trois vertus" de Christine de Pisan et son milieu historique et littéraire.* (Bibliothèque du XVe siècle, tome VI.) Paris: Honoré Champion, 1912. 375 p. (Available on microfilm from the New York Public Library—22-16588.)

Laigle argues that Christine de Pisan can hardly be seen as a champion of female emancipation, in spite of her espousal of education for women, because rather than advising independence, Christine goes as far as to advise patience and gentle resignation even in an unhappy marriage. What she does favor, Laigle believes, is for a woman to put her personal energies to work in combating evil. Even the education she argues for is that which would enable women to master the practical techniques necessary to the management of estates when men are absent travelling or at war. Thus for her time Christine is both conservative and radical. It is necessary to view her work from the perspective of the France of her times.

"Chacun à sa tâche"—each one to her own task—is Christine's rule as she praises moderation, modesty, and acceptance of one's place in life, declares Laigle in "Le prétendu féminisme de Christine de Pisan," on pages 120-123.

Laird, Donald, and Eleanor C. Laird. ***The Psychology of Supervising the Working Woman.*** New York and London: McGraw-Hill Book Company, 1942. 202 p. Index.

In 1942 the United States was at war and needed manpower in the defense factories, in offices, in government work, even in the armed forces. A problem appeared, however: should women be treated differently, since most women were not used to a out-of-the home work environment. As a result, the Lairds came up with this guide, both to inform male supervisors and to placate them, for not all men were happy about this social change. This work, now something of a museum-piece, is enlightening as a reflection of the wrenching caused by the emergency and as such can be useful as retrospective sociological study.

The Lairds' purpose was to provide a handbook for male supervisors who had to learn to get along with women workers, like it or not. They profess to have the secret of making women work more diligently: tell them that they are doing better than the men. The Lairds add a little sugar-coating for the disgruntled (we assume) supervisors, however: "Today woman can vote, but until Nature makes it possible for her to be a father, she will continue to feel that she has been shortchanged." The Lairds' perception of the necessity for this soothing statement is in itself is a reflection of the obstinacy of the old ideas, even in face of such an emergency as World War II, when the nation was fighting on two fronts and factories were working day and night.

It is difficult nowadays to believe that this book with its underlying premises had considerable currency when it was published. One must conclude that the psychology of women was a closed book to male executives—and perhaps they could have remained indifferent to it if they had not had such an overwhelming need for womanpower "for the duration"— which is as long as the need would last and the trouble of dealing with women would dissipate, so it was believed, when women went back into the home "where they belonged."

Langston-Davies, John. *A Short History of Women.* New Delhi: Vanity Books, 1990. New York: The Viking Press, 1927.

As the author states, this little book "tries to explain the forces and the elements which combined to produce the myth of the Female Character which so obsessed our immediate ancestors. It is still hard for the average man, and woman also, to see . . .women free from all preconceptions as to what they ought to be as feminine females."

First of all Langston-Davies considers the basics, beginning with biology. From there he takes the historical approach with sections on primitive society, ancient civilizations (Asia, Greece, Egypt, Rome), the early Christian era, the Middle Ages, and thence to a section with the title, "Modern Times: From Womanly Woman to Intelligent Being." Then he dares peep optimistically into a future which, he hopes, will flow along the seemingly logical progression from prejudice to enlightenment.

Larsen, Anna Astrup. *"Four Scandinavian Feminists,"* Yale Review, IV (January, 1916), pp. 347-362.

Larsen points to the achievements of Camille Collect, Frederika Brewer, Selma Lagerlöf, and Ellen Key, who in their work "have complemented one another and together. . . have created a harmoniously-developed and well-balanced form of feminism" in the Scandinavian countries.

Laumonier, Paul. *"Madame de Montaigne, d'après les Essais,"* pages 393-407 in *Mélanges offerts à M. Abel Lefranc.* Paris: Librairie E. Droz, 1936.

Françoise de Lachassiagne was thirty-two when she married Michel de Montaigne, and all indications lead us to believe that she was worthy of him intellectually, for she had received a strict education consonant with her family's high social position.

Laumonier judges that Montaigne was devoted to his wife, since he dedicated his *Essais* to her, but it his opinion, too, that Françoise was not happy. Although Montaigne had a high regard for the intelligence and potential of women, he was not always supported in this by others in the society, as is attested to by his adoptive daughter, Marie de Gournay.

Lebedun, Jean. *"Harriet Beecher Stowe's Interest in Sojourner Truth, Black Feminist,"* *American Literature,* 46 (November, 1974), pp. 359-363..

Noting that Stowe has sometimes been characterized as anti-feminist, Lebedun cites her evident admiration for a freed slave, "Isabella," who became a feminist orator. Too, he points to certain evidence of pro-feminist leanings in Stowe's writings, especially in *My Wife and I,* where she considers the woman question as it was debated at that time. [18]

---

[18] Harriet Beecher Stowe is the author of the myth-shattering novel *Uncle Tom's Cabin* (1851) which became important in stirring popular opinion against slavery before the Civil War.

Lee, Helene R. *Bittersweet Decision: The War Brides Forty Years Later.* Lockport, New York: Roselee Publications, 1985. 382 p. Photographs.

Of perennial interest are the "war brides" who leave their native lands to settle in a foreign land, usually bereft of friends and family to ease their transition from one culture to another. In the case of English war brides of Americans who were stationed in Britain or its colonies during World War II, the culture shock, it was believed, would not be insurmountable, since language and traditions were similar. Problems there were aplenty, and great were the illusions about the United States, some which were shattered, some not.

In this compendium of personal histories based upon correspondence and interviews, the women look back upon their experiences and describe them candidly in their own words. A reproduction of the questionnaire used is included.

Leonard, Eugenia Andruss. *The Dear-Bought Heritage.* Philadelphia: University of Pennsylvania Press, 1965. 658 p.

Leonard's work, as Margaret Chase Smith writes in the foreword, is an exposition of "what the American colonial women brought with them from the seventeen lands of their origin; what they found when they arrived in the new land; and what they did to help in building a nation."

Leonard finds that colonial women shared the basic function of women which had been theirs throughout the 6000 years of recorded history, and like women everywhere, their consistent aim was to improve the conditions which their children would have to face as they grew up.

Women's political and economic rights in colonial days are treated in Chapters 10 and 11. An excellent bibliography is included.

Leonard, Eugenia Andruss. *"St. Paul on the Status of Women,"* Catholic Biblical Quarterly, 12 (January, 1950), pp. 311-320.

"Probably no writer in the Christian era has been more frequently quoted on the status of women than St. Paul," writes Leonard, but she criticizes the narrow base from which his interpreters have worked, pointing out that evidence for Paul's respect and acceptance of women has been ignored in favor of his words that reflect the usual misogynist bias in Roman and Jewish cultures.

Each facet of Paul's comments on women is briefly examined here.

Lewis, Oscar. *"Husbands and Wives in a Mexican Village: A Study of Role Conflict,"* American Anthropologist, 51 (1949), pp. 602-610.

The village is Tepoztlan, and it was there that researchers found the husband the supreme "boss" of the family—that is, according to tradition. But, observes Lewis, "actually there are few homes in which the husband truly controls his family." He finds women more in conflict with the traditional pattern than men, even though they wish a man to be *macho* (manly). Women prefer to work outside the home and are not enthusiastic about having children, it appears to him.

Lewis concludes that Tepoztlan's personal relations are not less conflict-ridden than those in urban society.

Licht, Hans. *Sexual Life in Ancient Greece.* Translated from the German by H. Freese. (Loeb Library.) New York: Barnes and Noble, 1963. 556 p.

Of greatest interest in this work are the following sections: Introduction—Greek ideas of life; Part I, Chapter I—"Marriage and the Life of Woman"; and Part II, Chapter I, "The Love of the Man for Woman." This scholarly tome by an eminent German classicist is a standard in the field for those researching the history of ancient cultures as it was known. An edition was published by the American Anthropoligcal Society in 1934.

Lifton, Robert Jay, ed. *The Woman in America.* (The Daedalus Library.) Boston: Houghton Mifflin Company, 1965. 293 p. (Reprint by Greenwood Press, 1977.)

Represented here are several dedicated researchers in the field of women's studies in the 1960's: Erik H. Erikson, Diana Trilling, David Reisman, Alice S. Rossi, Esther Peterson, David C. McClelland, Carl N. Degler, Edna G. Rostow, Lotte Bailyn, Jill Conway, and Joan M. Erikson. They cover subjects as discrete as work, psychology, images of women, equality of the sexes, and adjustment to a changing world. Added are two biographies—of Eleanor Roosevelt and Jane Addams.

Lillo Catalán, Victorian. *La influencia de la mujer.* Buenos Aires: La Vista Americana de Buenos Aires, 1940 [1931]. 109 p.

Seeing woman as a truly human being—"un ser humano"— Lillo argues that progress can be achieved only if woman is given all the freedom she needs, contrary to her present situation. Cited under "Pensamiento" are most historians' anti-feminist ideas, including sources as discrete as Hippolyte Taine and Lan-Ta-Ka to complete this interesting survey.

Livermore, Maria A. ***The Story of My Life, or The Sunshine and Shadow of Seventy Years.*** (Women in America from Colonial Times to the 20th Century.) New York: Arno Press, 1974. Illustrations. 736 p. (This is a reprint of the 1897 edition published by A. D. Worthington, Hartford, Connecticut.)

Born in a Boston which was still a pretty country town of between thirty and forty thousand inhabitants, strong-minded Maria Livermore grew up to observe her country during storms of the Civil War, the pioneering movement, the temperance crusade, as well as turbulent events in Europe and England.

Always a champion of women's rights, Maria lectured untiringly to speak out for higher education, business and industrial training, and other "privileges" for her sex. Some of her lectures are reprinted here, including one entitled, "What Shall We Do with Our Daughters?"

Log-Cabin Lady, The: An Anonymous Autobiography. Boston: Little, Brown, and Company, 1922. 108 p.

This self-revealing portrait shows vividly how a young girl, having passed her childhood in freedom in a Wisconsin pioneer log cabin, becomes "broken" to the harness of social conformity as the wife of a diplomat in England. The poignant descriptions of her unhappiness and humiliations under her husband's often irascible tutelage give perspective on what was considered important and acceptable in the contemporary social environment and emphasize the difficulties the writer experienced in trying to adjust.

Lombroso-Ferrer, Gina. ***The Soul of Woman: Reflections on Life.*** Translated from the Italian, *L'Animo della Donna.* New York: E. P. Dutton, 1953 [1923]. 269 p. (The 1922 edition is available on microfilm from the University of Pittsburgh.)

Using as an epigraph, "I write for those who suffer," Lombroso-Ferrer calls Book I, *Woman's Tragic Position,* the main thought of which is that "the key to woman's nature is her alterocentrism, a need to love which makes her dependent and causes all her unhappiness." Man, on the contrary, she sees as dependent on himself alone.

In Book II she considers woman's soul, intellect, moral feeling, love, and desire for justice, presenting a candid and practical analysis of woman's character which will enable men to understand women, but the mystical quality in Lombroso-Ferrer's work is too pronounced to be "practical" in the everyday sense of the word. Her analysis ends on a note of despair when she concludes, "It is of no use for women to protest or try to change things. Things are as they are. When God created woman out of Adam's rib she became. . . nothing else." In spite of this, her work can be seen as a measure of how much Italian women have progressed, albeit slowly, since the 1920's.

Longmore, Laura. ***The Dispossessed.*** London: Jonathan Cape, 1959. 334 p.

The author characterizes her work as a study of the sex-life of Bantu women in urban areas in and around Johannesburg. It deals with the conflict between the tribal *ethos* and that of the European middle class culture, underlining the temptations which beset Africans who moved to Johannesburg to work. As the people moved to the city, they formed a proletariat which was poorly amalgamated into the more sophisticated way of life. The distress caused by the maladjustments is well-documented in this serious study.

Ludovici, Anthony M. *Lysistrata, or Woman's Future and Future Woman.* New York: Gordon Press, 1977 [1921]. (Reprint of edition published by E. P. Dutton and Company, 1925. First published in 1921 in London.) 110 p.

Ludovici sees feminism in Great Britain a threat to the harmonious relations of the sexes because of its exacerbation of hostility which will lead to the annihilation of love.[19] Thus he predicts a bleak future for "these islands," even though he declares that he is "pro-feminist."

He proposes that many of society's values be recast to "put woman back in her place" in order to save the world. Unfortunately, he complains, only a "manly man" as a leader for the "masculine renaissance" can do this, and the pity of it is that for a century or more, England has failed to produce such a man. (Evidently he did not feel suited for leadership.) He is so desperate that he recommends the eugenics movement as a way out—for men.

Luppé, Albert Marie Pierre de. *Les Jeunes Filles à la fin du XVIIIe siècle.* Paris: Librairie Ancienne Édouard Champion, 1925. 256 p.

---

[19] In 1927 Ludovici was a participant in a symposium of women about women's changing roles. His contribution was, "Woman's Encroachment on Man's Domain," which must have struck a discordant note. See "The New Woman " (below).

One of the first chapters, "Couvent ou Famille?" and the last, "Mariage ou Cloître?" demonstrate the range of choices available to Frenchwomen of the eighteenth century, many of whom De Luppé shows to be unhappy because of these limitations—and because girls were married so young, often at the command of ambitious or tyrannical parents.

This scholarly work is full of fascinating insights into the lives of contemporary women such as Mme de Genlis, Mme d'Épinay, and Mme de Saint Laurent, whose letter regarding the search for a suitable husband for her daughter is printed in an appendix.

Textual notes are abundant, and a good bibliography (pages 227-242) gives valuable clues to further research into this period.

Lynd, Robert S., and Helen Merrell Lynd. *Middletown: A Study in American Culture.* New York: Harcourt, Brace, and World, 1957 [1929].

Based upon the study of 30,000 inhabitants of a Midwest U.S. city, this long-term work pioneered in the objective sociological method of acquiring detailed knowledge about "what is American." Three chapters (pages 110-178) give insight into attitudes about the nature of women and roles determined by the society to be compatible with this nature. These findings were valuable in understanding the slow progress of women's emancipation in the early twentieth century.

Lynd, Robert S., and Helen Merrell Lynd. *Middletown in Transition: A Study in Cultural Conflicts.* New York: Harcourt, Brace and World, Inc., 1982 [1937].

This is a continuation of the Lynds' study of a "typical" American city, produced eight years after *Middletown*. For women's concerns, see Chapter V, pages 144-203, "Making a Home." Some coverage will be found in Chapter II, "Getting a Living," also, and the index can be used to track down other leads. It appears that Middletown had seen very little change in attitudes about women's life and expectations during the eight years that had elapsed since the first investigation.

McAleavy, Henry. *That Chinese Woman: The Life of Sai-chin-hua*. London: George Allen and Unwin, 1959. 208 p.

Last survivor of the Boxer Rebellion of 1900-01, Sai-chin-hua died unnoticed in 1936. But in 1887 she had begun an adventure which became a national legend as she sailed to Europe, met the German Count Waldersee, and finally married him in Peking. Her story gives fascinating perspective on Chinese-European relations and also touches upon how World War I affected these relations.[20]

McAleavy's translation is from the first biography of Sai-chin-hua, which was printed in China in 1935.

Machann, Virginia Sue Brown. *"American Perspectives on Women's Initiations: The Mythic and Realistic Coming to Consciousness."* Unpublished Ph.D. dissertation, University of Texas at Austin, 1977. 553 p. (Available in photocopy [1981] from University Microfilms, Ann Arbor, Michigan.)

---

[20]The "Boxers" organized a secret society in 1900 to mount a rebellion against the European economic hold on China, but it was severely repressed by the European nations acting jointly. Economic benefits to the invaders included the opium trade, which the Chinese government tried in vain to eliminate.

Machann finds great interest in the "coming to consciousness" of six American women as revealed in their autobiographies: Anne Bradstreet, Elizabeth Ashbridge, Margaret Fuller, Margaret Mead, Anne Morrow Lindbergh, and Mary McCarthy. In addition, she makes a detailed assessment of heroines in the novels of Hawthorne and Henry James in relation to this theme.

Magne, Émile. ***Madame de LaFayette en ménage, d'après des documents inédits.*** Paris: Éditions Émile-Paul Frères, 1926. 293 p.

Scholarly, informative, but also eminently readable, Magne's account of Mme de LaFayette's family dates from 1601, with many pages devoted to her father and much fewer to her mother. A genealogical table details her three families: les Pioches, les Péna, and les LaFayette.

Mair, Lucy. ***African Marriage and Social Change.*** London: Frank Tass and Company, 1969. 191 p.

Mair presents contrasts between the older modes of life led by African women in accordance with tribal customs and the contemporary ways which have been touched by industrialization. She notes that these changes are not always in the interest of harmonious adjustment in marriage. Her research sheds light upon the lives of tribes in all parts of Africa. An accompanying map shows their location on the continent, and a table (pages 160-166) has descriptive listings of the tribes, a useful feature.

Maistriaux, Robert. ***La Femme et le destin de l'Afrique: les sources, psychologiques de la mentalité dite primitive.*** Preface by Edouard Morot-Sir. Elisabethville: CEPSI, 1964. 534 p. Bibliography.

The fate of developing nations, says Miastriaux, is in the hands of women—or, rather, of mothers. Therefore no solution to problems in Africa can ignore women's liberation from ignorance, for the black woman is highly intelligent, able to reason well and judge competently. She is in no wise inferior to African men, but she, as mother, has many handicaps, such as a lack of education related to her own situation—and this education must be directed by people of her own race. The analysis of the psychology of the "primitive" mind is especially relevant in this regard.

Martin, Marie-Madeleine. *Le Génie des femmes*. Paris: Éditions du Conquistador, 1950. 200 p.

The 36-page foreword of Martin's work contains a valuable historical survey of the changing position of women as it notes a number of almost forgotten women of cultural attainments in France. The author sees the changes as a series of advances and set-backs which resemble the rock of Sisyphus: for example, women in ancient Egypt enjoyed a liberty that was unknown to the Greek women five hundred years later; the women of the twelfth and thirteen centuries fared better than their sisters in France during the Wars of Religion, and, worst of all, the nineteenth century saw women so intellectually subjected as to make them comparable to the Athenian women in their *gynécée*. As for the twentieth century, Martin sees the woman freer to follow in the ways of men, but she objects to this, for she believes that women have a unique genius and should not deny it by copying masculine ways to which she will never be able to accommodate herself.

To round out her study Martin has chosen a number of women whom she sees as having possessed this unique female genius, including Mme de Sévigné, la Marquise de Rambouillet, Mlle de Lespinasse, Christine de Pisan, Santa Teresa of Spain, George Sand, and Katherine Mansfield.

Martín de Córdoba, Fray. *Jardín de nobles doncellas.* (Colección Joyas Bibliográficas, v. 10.) N.p.: Madrid, 1953 [1532]. 115 p.

P. Felix García's introduction to this fifteenth-century courtesy book is excellent for its clear exposition of the historical and social *milieu* in which Fray Martín composed his work for the Infanta Isabella, who later became Queen of Spain.

Fray Martín writes with calm reason to show why women should be submissive, pious, and (especially) chaste. The student of Spanish culture will be well paid for a careful perusal of this book, since it contains the kernel of the Spanish tradition in regard to the nature and position of women.

Martínez Sierra, Gregorio. *Cartas a las mujeres de España.* Madrid: Estrella, 1926. (First published in 1916.) 299 p.

In this refreshingly different collection of encouraging essays from the pen of a male Spaniard, noted dramatist Martínez Sierra tells women that they are definitely equal to men, and they ought to be *international* feminists, they ought to go to school (especially to study law), and furthermore, he counsels, contrary to traditional teachings, that they must not supinely suffer but must work energetically to create their own destiny: "No hay que sufrir con resignation el destino: hay que crear con energía el destino." To illustrate his counsel, he relates aspirations to the ideals of freedom espoused by the American poet Walt Whitman outlined on pages 239-244.

Martínez Sierra, Gregorio. *Feminism, feminidad, y españolismo.* Madrid: Editorial Saturnine College, S. A., 1920. 277 p.

Much of the material in this book is related to the First World War as it affected women in Spain in their thought and actions.

Martínez Sierra is generous in his praise of women's contributions in all spheres of civilization. In one section, "Lo que hacen las mujeres de Europa mientras los hombres se están matando" ("What the women of Europe do while men are killing themselves," pages 211-228), he looks at England, Belgium, Austria, France, Germany, and Hungary, seeing women as having little patience with destruction. Another essay deals with the feminist views of Britisher H. G. Wells (pages 65-76). This era was one of optimism for world peace, along with concern for the improvement in women's status. With the coming of the Depression and World War II, belief in peace and support for women's causes waned.

Martínez Sierra, Gregorio, ed. *La Mujer moderna.* Madrid: Editorial Saturnine Calleja, 1920. 198 p.

Writing to encourage feminism in Spanish women, Martínez Sierra notes that the word *mujer* represents a long history of subordination from which contemporary women were just being liberated. In this collection he presents opinions about woman suffrage held by Spanish men. Most of the contributors agree that the future of their country would be brighter if Spain, like England and the new Communist régime in Russia, would give women equality and opportunity.

Martínez Sierra, Maria. *La Mujer española ante la república.* Madrid: Ateneo de Madrid, 1931. 184 p.

Martínez Sierra offers this selection of lectures given in May, 1931, as homage to Gregorio Martínez Sierra, the pro-feminist dramatist (see above). The lectures, addressed to women specifically, also pay honor to Marina Pineda.

Mason, Amelia Gere. ***Women in the Golden Ages.*** New York: The Century Co., 1901. 396 p.

Mason refers to what she considers the "golden ages" of intellectual accomplishment by women, including Greek women, Roman women, Christian nuns, Renaissance learned ladies, and women of the *salons* in France. They are depicted sympathetically by Mason in her effort to show women at the turn of the twentieth century that intellect has never been the sole province of men, even though, she observes, society has been slow to recognize it.

Mason, Otis Tufton. ***Women's Share in Primitive Culture.*** New York: D. Appleton & Company, 1900. 295 p. (Available on microfilm from the University Microfilms International, Ann Arbor, Michigan.)

In savage societies, says Mason "nothing is more common than to see the sexes lending a helping hand in bearing the burdens of life," and he goes on to describe in detail the important role of women in setting in motion the multiplicity of industries that have enabled humankind to prosper. By keen observation and acquired knowledge of nature's ways women became food bringer, weaver, skin dresser, potter, artist, linguist, founder of society, and patron of religion. She was also "Jack-of-all-trades" and beast of burden, he notes realistically. Sources for this illustrated work are found in history, linguistics, archeology, folklore, and the living peoples studied by anthropologists up to this time.

Mathews, Winifred. ***Dauntless Women: Stories of Pioneer Wives.*** (Biography Index Reprint Series.) Freeport, New York: Books for Libraries Press, 1970. 164 p. (Originally published in 1947.)

The pioneers in these narratives are Christian women who became missionaries in India, South Africa, the South Sea Islands, and Korea. One of the most pervasive themes is the nostalgia of the women for their Western homelands.

Matulka, Barbara. ***An Anti-Feminist Treatise of Fifteenth-Century Spain: Lucena's "Repetición de Amores."*** (Comparative Literature Series.) New York: Institute of French Studies, 1931. 24 p.

Noting that "treatises against women are rarer in fifteenth-century Spain than one would surmise," Matulka explains that we know of these mainly because of the impetus they gave to defenders of women to put their views into words.

In her thorough and scholarly manner Matulka gives the background and content of the work of Lucena, who was then a student at Salamanca and was eager to exhibit his scholarship to impress and support Pedro Torrellas, Catalan poet and notorious woman-hater. One of Torrellas' poems, "Maldezir de las Mugeres," became, Matulka notes, "the *casus belli* of a veritable courtiers' war" on the subject of women.[21] Torrellas appears as a champion of men in Juan de Flores' novelette, *Grisel y Mirabella* (c. 1485)..

---

[21]This was part of an international debate, known in France as *la querelle des femmes*, wherein male savants took delight in displaying their sophistry and supposed expertness on the subject.

Matulka's pamphlet contains facsimiles of the beginning of the "Maldezir" and of the title page of *Grisel y Mirabella* (edition of 1524).

Maulde la Clavière, R. de. ***The Women of the Renaissance: A Study of Feminism.*** Translated by George H. Ely. London: G. Allen, 1911. New York: G. P. Putman's Sons, 1905 [1900]. 510 p. Index.

This is an excellent, readable, insightful book which makes individual Renaissance women understandable as it shows how they felt about their lives and what they tried to do to improve their situation. In spite of these efforts, authoritarian tendencies of the Church nipped feminism in the bud, and highly influential male satirists used their pen to cut down all that had given women faith, enthusiasm, and meaning to their lives, the author declares. An excellent index makes this long work easy to use for research.

Mead, Margaret. ***Male and Female: A Study of the Sexes in a Changing World.*** New York: William Morrow and Company, 1950. 477 p.

American anthropologist Mead analyzes the relationships of the sexes from the perspective of various primitive cultures she has studied: the Samoan, the Manus, the Arapesh, the Mundugamor and Iatmul of New Guinea, the Tschambuli people, and the people of Bali—all in the South Pacific area. Then turning to the more complicated field of modern United States, she attempts to analyze the results of the prevailing ideas of sex differentiation. In this endeavor, the approach is less precise, unavoidably so.

Mead's conclusions lead her to argue for a greater acceptance of the neglected gifts women could bring to the overly male-oriented society. A useful feature of this work is an appendix which describes each South Pacific culture studied, with a short bibliography following each section. Two other appendices, "The Ethics of Insight Giving" and "Sources and Experience in Our American Culture," are added.

The value of Mead's work has been recognized internationally and translations are found in several languages. The French edition, *L'Un et l'autre sexe,* published in 1988 by Denoel/Gonthier (Paris), was translated by Claudia Ancelot and Henriette Étienne. The Italian version, *Maschio e femmina,* published in 1966 by Casa Editrice Il Saggiatore of Milan was translated by Maria Epifani and Roberto Bosi.

Mead, Margaret. *"What Women Want."* Fortune, XXXIV, no. 6 (December, 1946), pp. 172-174; 218.

A frustrated Freud is supposed to have asked the question, "What *do* women want?" Anthropologist Mead tries to answer it from her specific observations of what American women seem to want. This is not so easy as it appears to be, she finds, because women's true wants are often compromised by circumstances and emotions which confront them at home, at work, and in society at large. One of her pleas was for men to share more of the home-making activities (not necessarily the dreaded "housework"). She saw as a palliative the increased application of technological advances to take over some of the drudgery that makes lonely housework unbearable for many women.

Meissner, Hans-Otto. ***Magda Goebbels: The First Lady of the Third Reich.*** Translated by Gwendolen Mary Keeble. New

York: Dial Press, 1980. 288 p. Bibliography. Index. Photographs.

Women were not featured in the Third Reich as active participants in the government. The Nazis, as soon as they were in power, took steps to kill the woman's movement by repressing its leader, Gertrud Bäumer. The underlying assumption was that women should be concerned only with church, kitchen, and children. In no sense of the word could Magda Goebbels, wife of Joseph Goebbels, the all-powerful Propaganda Minister, be considered a feminist—just the opposite indeed. But this book is fascinating, for her exciting yet doomed life illuminates the role of women in the almost inexplicable years in Nazi Germany. The cult of Adolf Hitler, with its antipathetic attitude toward women, held Magda so firmly in its grasp that when Hitler committed suicide, she and her husband, formerly second in power to Hitler, poisoned their six children before they ended their own lives.

Mencken, H. L. *In Defense of Women.* Alexandria, Virginia: Time-Life, 1982. New York: Garden City Publishing Company, 1918. 210 p.

Writing in 1918 at the close of the First World War, journalist Mencken takes note of the "war between the sexes" and relates it to the social changes brought about by the war. He predicted that a characteristic of the immediate future would be a shortage of men in the Western world which would, he thought, make more logical the approval of woman suffrage, reform of marriage laws, and other relaxation of controls within the traditional *mores.*

Two of women's greatest burdens, according to feminist Mencken, are "the stupid masculine disinclination to admit [women's] intellectual superiority, or even their equality ... and the equally stupid doctrine that [men] constitute a special and ineffable species" which is "too bright and good for earthly food."

Mencken's book was influential in the cause of feminism. A French translation by Jean Jardin was published by Gallimard in 1934 as *Défense des femmes*.

Mermaz, Louis. ***Madame de Maintenon, ou l'amour dévot***. (Ces Femmes qui ont fait l'histoire: Collection dirigée par Joël Schmidt.) Lausanne: Éditions Rencontre, 1985 [1965]. Illustrations. 223 p.

Françoise de Maintenon arrived in Paris in 1648, the same year as the Fronde triumph.[22] In 1652 she was married to the noted writer Paul Scarron, who died in 1660. In 1683 Françoise and Louis XIV were secretly married, and from this alliance stems her position in history: as his uncrowned wife she exerted a strong influence over him, especially in religious matters, and earned fame as one of the most influential women in French history. In 1715 she retired to the convent of St. Cyr, which she had founded, and died there in the same year.

These are the personal events in a woman's life against a backdrop of wars, the rise and fall of statesmen, and the struggle of conflicting ideologies. Françoise had an enduring interest in the education of women (of the upper class), which was the motivation for the founding of the convent of St. Cyr.[23]

---

[22]The Fronde was a political party when Cardinal Mazarin was minister during Louis' minority (1648-1653); its adherents rebelled against the despotism which characterized the government.

[23]St. Cyr is best known now as the principal French military school. The

Mermaz's biography is factually written in a simple, interesting style, but without reference to documents.

Meyer, Johann Jakob. ***Sexual Life in Ancient India, a Study in the Comparative History of Indian Culture.*** New York: Barnes and Noble, 1953. 591 p.

This well-documented work makes use of literature (the epics, the *Mahabharata* and the *Ramayana*), scripture, and historical records to set forth the ideas of ancient India in regard to love, marriage, the legal status of women, religious precepts for interpersonal relations, and other subjects. Woman is seen in contradictions: a chattel, a power, a curse, a revered one (mother), a source of evil, and a creature of beauty.

Meyer's work is an extremely complex one, not easy to read, but valuable for gaining knowledge of a culture so different from that of the West. A copious index simplifies searching for detailed research.

Michelet, M. J. ***Woman.*** Translated from the French *Les Femmes* by J. W. Palmer. New York: Carleton, Publisher, 1866. 283 p. (Originally published in 1859.)

"The worst destiny of a woman is to live alone," avers Michelet, as he adds, "There is no life for woman without man." This appears to be a sincere statement, for Michelet does not strike a vainglorious attitude. In fact, he has a myopic compassion (or pity) for the women of his time who, needing men for their very existence (unless they were wealthy, perhaps), must suffer so much from men's actions. Nevertheless,

changeover came in 1806.

he does not argue for a change in the *status quo* but rather would caution accommodation by women.

Michelet, one of France's noted historians, is also a man of his time and place, for he goes on to call woman a goddess to be worshipped. Along with this he remarks naïvely that the woman in mundane life ideally is "loving, humble, and anxious to obey"—hardly the role for a goddess, however!

In regard to the future, Michelet the idealist sees the intermingling of races through marriage, by which woman's force for peace and unity will cause her angelic, civilizing virtues to become tangible in society at large.

Middleton, Dorothy. ***Victorian Lady Travellers***. Chicago: Academy Chicago, 1982. 182 p. (Reprint of the 1965 edition of E. P. Dutton.) Index.

The astonishing adventures of such intrepid women as Isabella Bird Bishop, Marianne North, Fanny Bullock Workman, May French Sheldon, Annie Taylor, Kate Marsden, and Mary Kingsley form the substance of this absorbing little volume. Their forays into unknown territory were not for discovery *per se*, opines Middleton, but were individual gestures of "housebound, male-dominated Victorian women" who found boredom intolerable and went to amazing lengths to escape it.

Mill, John Stuart. ***The Subjection of Women***. Introduction by Wendell Robert Carr. Cambridge, Massachusetts, and London: MIT Press, 1978 [1970]; Cambridge University Press, 1978.[24] 101 p.

---

[24]There are innumerable editions of this work (with a variety of introductions), which has enjoyed a revival in the late twentieth century.

Mill was called by Lydia E. Becker, leading pioneer of the English women's rights movement, the person "who dealt the first effectual blow at the political slavery of woman." Carr, however, believes that Mill's influence has been overstated, since the chief attraction of his essay was the appeal of his name, so well-connected with philosophy. Nevertheless, Carr also considers this influence crucial, since it endowed the women's cause with a uniqueness as a reform movement by giving it "so exalted a statement of its aims." Carr seems not to stress that Mill's wife was an ardent feminist and thus had much to do with Mill's conviction that women needed to strive for legal rights and dignity.

Millett, Kate. *Sexual Politics.* New York: Simon and Schuster, 1990 [1970]. 393 p. Bibliography.

In this now classic work of contemporary feminist literature Millett endeavors to unseat the false gods created by men through history to maintain woman's subjection, keeping her unaware that patriarchal institutions are not grounded in nature but merely in long-standing custom and law.

Undergirding their efforts to prevent woman's attaining freedom, she argues, are the all-pervasive teachings about woman's "place" which are found in religion, social theory, literature, and psychology (especially Freudian), all of which tend to an inexorable possession and use of power by males.

Millett points out, too, that the difficult advances toward emancipation made by women in the years 1830-1930 were overtaken by a counterrevolution sparked by Hitler's principles of National Socialism in Germany, and Soviet repressions inherent in Stalinism. Much of her exegesis consists of excerpts from the works of D. H. Lawrence, Norman Mailer, Henry

Miller, and Jean Genet to illustrate how "sexual politics" have permeated literature and distorted the perception of women.

This work, which has contributed much to the creation of a "feminist rhetoric," is documented and has a good bibliography.

Moore, Doris Langley. *The Woman in Fashion.* London: B. T. Botsford, Ltd., 1949. 184 p.

Two introductory chapters, "Fashion in Theory" and "Fashion in Practice," consider psychological and historical reasons for interest in dress, as well as the desire for fashion changes. Moore rejects the theory of such writers as J. C. Flugel who in his *Psychology of Clothes* asserts that sexual motivations are paramount.

Interest is added to the book by illustrations of representative apparel modeled by famous women in the arts from 1800 to 1927, with a generous explanation of each.

Morais, Vamberto. *A Emancipaçao da mulher: as raíses do preconceito antifeminino e seu declínio.* Rio de Janeiro: Gráfica e Editora Cital, 1968. 229 p.

Morais considers the rationale which lies behind the modern woman's desire for improvement of her position in society. In doing so he analyzes reasons for her generally inferior status in historical, psychological, theological, literary, and social perspectives, and the result is a scholarly, thorough study which is designed to promote understanding.

Although Morais pays special attention to Brazilian women and their situation, his analysis is directed toward the whole of Western culture.

Morena, Amparo. *Mujeres en lucha: el movimiento feminista en España.* (La Educación sentimental, 3.) Barcelona: Anagrama, 1977. 221 p.

During the nineteenth century it was difficult for the woman's movement to gain momentum, even with the encouragement of certain male feminists such as Gregorio Martínez Sierra who wrote to stress the urgency of mounting a struggle so that Spanish women could enter the world of the future as women in other nations were doing.

Here we have fundamental documents which trace the history of the feminist movement in Spain which were basic to the struggle and gave continuity to its progress. Bibliographical references and an index are included.

Morgan, David. *Suffragists and Democrats: The Politics of Woman Suffrage in America.* East Lansing: Michigan State University Press, 1975 [1972]. 225 p.

Morgan, a British political scientist, declares that his purpose is to elucidate the practical politics surrounding the passage of the Nineteenth Amendment of the United States Constitution. He does a creditable job of analyzing how conflict between Southerners and Westerners in Congress created many troublesome times for President Woodrow Wilson. The fear of the Southerners was that black women, once enfranchised, would seriously weaken the *status quo*; on their side, many Western Congressmen were acutely aware of the pressure from their female constituents to vote for the amendment.

Morgan attempts to show, too, how various kinds of social change from 1850 onward have affected woman's political power. Louis Young, reviewing this work in the *American*

Historical Review of June, 1973, points out that Morgan is less than precise in his use of certain names and dates and cites, for example, his unfortunate confusing of Lucretia Mott with Elizabeth Cady Stanton. Therefore the reader should keep the possibility of error of detail in mind. A good bibliography is a useful feature of this work.

Morris, Jean. ***Against Nature and God: The History of Women with Clerical Ordination and the Jurisdiction of Bishops.*** London: Mowbrays, 1973. 192 p.

"History may be hidden in many ways," observes Morris, citing even an "evasion of facts through prejudice" as a reason for the dimming of the fame once enjoyed by such eminent religious women of the early Christian Church such as Brigid of Kildare, Hilda of Whitby, Julie-Sophie Gilette, Teresa of Avila, as well as female Bible figures. In later days she finds both Renaissance and Reformation detrimental to the status of women.

Morris' work gives many neglected women of Italy, Spain, France, Germany, Poland, Austria, England, and Ireland, deserved attention. A valuable pioneer study, well-written and containing a good bibliography, this volume contains many fascinating clues for further research.

Muraro, Rose Marie. ***A Mulher no construçao do mundo futuro.*** Petrópolis, R. J.: Editora Vozes, 1972 [1967]. 207 p.

The life of Brazilian women past and future is considered in this work, which also contains a group of poems to women, pages 193-202. An appendix, "A nova estrutura da familia," considers change in the traditional family patterns. A bibliography is also included. Abundant original quotations are provided, as well as a bibliography.[25]

Myrdal, Jan. *Report from a Chinese Village.* Translated from the Swedish by Maurice Michael. New York: Random House, 1965. (Pantheon paperback, 1981.)

Part VI, pages 203-239, "Women," contains stories of Chinese village women in their own words transcribed by anthropologist Myrdal and his wife in 1962 while living in a village of North China. For this project they were given special permission of the revolutionary government.

Some of the stories found here are those of a 53-year-old woman who had been sold, another whose feet had been bound, a woman Communist pioneer, and a housewife-farmer. Included, too, are one woman's work schedule as she manages home and farm, and a week's menu for her family.

Neff, Wanda Fraiken. *Victorian Working Women, An Historical and Literary Study of Women in British Industries and Professions, 1832-1850.* London: Tass, 1966. 288 p. (Reprint of 1929 edition, George Allen and Unwin, with added bibliography.)

In her list of occupations Neff includes the textile worker, the non-textile worker (agriculture, trades, crafts), the dressmaker, the governess. Also considered is the familiar Victorian stereotype, the leisured lady heroine without occupation.

Most of the material is factual, with descriptions of legislation designed to improve women's industrial conditions. Refer-

---

[25] Señora Muraro's 1992 publication on the future of Brazilian women is *A mulher no Terceiro Milênio: uma história da mulher através dos tempos e suas perspectivas para o futuro.*

ences to British novels which reflected society's preoccupation with issues relating to women are manifold, especially those of the Brontë sisters, Charles Dickens, George Eliot, Elizabeth Gaskell, and William Makepeace Thackeray.

Nehru, Rameshwari. *Ghandi is My Star.* Patna: Acharya Ramlochan Saran, 1950. 201 p.

Deploring the fact that women freedom fighters of India had not yet had their due in acclaim, Nehru notes that Raja Narendra Nath began the Indian National Congress and edited for sixteen years the *Mirror of Womanhood.* Moreover in her foreword she cites others who are outstanding.

Explicated here is the philosophy, inspired by Ghandi, which gave momentum to changes for the betterment of women's place in Indian society.

"New Woman, The," *Current History,* XXVII: 1 (October, 1927), pp. 1-48.

This symposium is excellent reading for an overview of the conflicting ideas about women being bruited about in the 1920's just after women in the United States had won the right to vote. Gathered here are Carrie Chapman Catt writing on the benefits of woman's suffrage, while Charlotte Perkins enumerates women's achievements because of it. Leta S. Hollingsworth muses on "The New Woman in the Making," while Anthony M. Ludovici complains about "Woman's Encroachment on Man's Domain." Martha Bensley Brière describes "The Highway to Woman's Happiness," and Joseph Collins, a physician, considers "Woman's Morality in Transition" (he is a pro-feminist). Magdaleine Marx closes the session with a lament about "The Frenchwoman's Lack of Political Progress," thus dimming the optimism a bit, but in general the tone is one of hope for the future in this truly transitional era.

It is especially enlightening to read of these views held by futurists, who, naturally enough, were unable to forecast the Great Depression of the thirties and World War II of the forties, with their ineluctable changes, few of which carried on the benefits to women which these writers had envisaged.

New York City Commission on Human Rights. ***Women's Role in Contemporary Society: The Report of the New York City Commission on Human Rights, September 21-25, 1970.*** New York: Avon Books, 1972. 800 p.

The mountains of testimony at this hearing on women's issues were edited to make this readable, though still voluminous, version of the transcript. Participants included persons of both sexes prominent in the women's liberation movement, as well as authorities in many fields: economics, banking, labor, the professions, politics, and others. Included are forewords by Commissioner Eleanor Holmes Norton and Mayor John V. Lindsay.

Nouacer, Khadidja. ***"The Changing Status of Women and the Employment of Women in Morocco,"*** *International Social Science Journal,* 14 (1962), pp. 124-129.

The education of Moroccan girls is carefully outlined as Nouacer shows how this education relates to changes in opportunities for women. The accent is upon society's approval or disapproval for certain modes of employment; teaching is approved, while office work meets less approval because it necessitates the mingling of the sexes. Factory work for women is held in low esteem unless the place of work is a textile or carpet industry. Emancipation is slow, Nouacer observes, partly because even among young people there is apprehension about change.

Noun, Louise R. *Strong-Minded Women: The Emergence of the Woman Suffrage Movement.* Ames: Iowa State University Press, 1986 [1969]. 222 p. Index.

Noun's focus is upon the years 1866-1872, when Iowa women were encouraged by the 1868 adoption of suffrage for Negro males to press for women's political rights for themselves, in spite of bitter opposition. She tells of the crucial role of organizers and lecturers who, more aware of the issues than the majority of women, had the active support of suffragists from the Eastern states.

Nystrom-Hamilton, Louise. *Ellen Key, Her Life and Her Work.* Translated by A. E. B. Fries. Introduction by Havelock Ellis. New York: G. P. Putman's Sons, 1913. 187 p.

The accent here is upon the life of Key, internationally famous Swedish feminist known for her moderate approach to feminist concerns. Her desire was to reconcile the concepts of woman as mother and woman as equal partner with men in the world's activities.

This biography was written from first-hand information, since the author was a friend of the family. An appendix, pages 179-187, gives quotations from newspaper stories about Key on her sixtieth birthday.

O'Connor, Lillian. *Pioneer Women Orators: Rhetoric in the Antebellum Reform Movements.* New York: Columbia University Press, 1954. 264 p.

With the spread of democracy in American life, women's voices were much more readily heard, for they were fired by such humanitarian issues as slavery, women's rights, and temperance, and lecturing was one of the most effective ways to bring their messages to the voters.

O'Connor introduces the leading female speakers of the nineteenth century and offers criticism of their oratory in light of the traditional rhetorical criteria. An excellent bibliography will be found on pages 232-246.

O'Malley, I. B. *Women in Subjection: A Study of the Lives of English Women before 1822.* London: Duckwith, 1933. 365 p.

Subjected by law, religion, custom, and lack of education, English women nevertheless found inner resources and so vindicated themselves, says O'Malley. In effect, her work is a history of their vindication in life and letters which climaxes in the "springs of the women's movement."

Here Jane Austen is seen as her "own woman," as are Mary Wollstonecraft and many of the working women who are described graphically in Chapter IX. O'Malley also includes with this indexed work a list of crucial dates extending from c. 657 (time of St. Hilda's stay at Whitby) to 1832 (the enactment of the Great Reform bill). This study is well-documented.

O'Neill, William L. *Everyone Was Brave: A History of Feminism in America.* Chicago: Quadrangle Books, 1971. 379 p.

O'Neill suggests that feminism might best be understood as a reaction to the pressures accompanying the emergence of the nuclear family instead of a "rebellion" born of ancient slavery. Otherwise, he asks naïvely, why did not American women ask to be included in the Declaration of Independence?

Although this book includes much detail on the suffragette activities, it is shallow historically and should not be relied upon for background. Periodical sources are given.

O'Neill, William L., ed. ***The Woman Movement: Feminism in the United States and England.*** (Historical Problems, Studies and Documents.) Chicago: Quadrangle Books, 1971. 208 p.

The first five chapters of O'Neill's work orient the reader to the history of the feminist movement and form an introduction to the documents which follow. He addresses Anglo-Americans in the main, noting the failure of the feminist efforts in England and the United States, in contrast to their success in Sweden. Document 22, Ethel Puffer Howe's "The Meaning of Progress in the Woman Movement" (1929), is a stock taking appraisal which cuts to the heart of the matter regarding progress, or lack of it, in the feminist realm.[26]

Osborne, Duffield. ***"Antigone on Woman Suffrage,"*** *Yale Review,* IV (April, 1915), pp. 590-607.

The reader looks in on imaginary encounter between Socrates and his wife Xantippe regarding the Athenian assembly's coming debate on suffrage for the women of Athens. When Socrates tells Xantippe that he wishes to consult her on the subject, she immediately declares that she is for granting suffrage. But after she has been subjected at length to the brilliances of the Socratic method, she ends up by directing him to oppose the change in order to preserve all the privileges Athe-

---

[26]Howe's article was first published in *Annals of the American Academy of Political and Social Sciences,* 143 (May, 1929).

nian women were supposedly enjoying. Aspasia, Socrates' female friend, is also there to chime in occasionally, and he out-reasons her as well, deftly getting the women to agree to all the traditional hypotheses. Open to question is whether Socrates would really have defended these ideas.

This article's interest today lies in how well it reveals the reasoning of some of the most educated men in the pre-woman suffrage days in the United States (and elsewhere), when it was common to hear it said (by males), "If a woman wants her rights, she will have to give up her privileges." Socrates makes it palatable for her to do so—or does he?—the question is apropos, since Plato, his favorite pupil, has been shown to be a pro-feminist, something which Osborne ignores (or doesn't believe).

O'Sullivan-Beare, Nancy. *Las Mujeres de los Conquistadores: la mujer española en los comienzos de la colonación americana.* (Aportación para el Estudio de la Transculturación.) Madrid: Compañia Bibliografica Española, 1956. 383 p.

It is not generally known that Spanish women often crossed the Atlantic to take their places beside their husbands, regardless of the difficulties of settling in unknown lands. O'Sullivan-Beare shows us women in Las Antillas, where a woman founded the hospital of San Nicolas; women in Peru, where they intervened politically (five are named here); in Chile, where they travelled with Cortés; in short, they went wherever Spanish men dared to go.

Source documents are listed on pages 307-372, and a chronological table (1492-1580) clarifies the record of events. Since the work is indexed, it is possible to trace references to specific women.

Ouellette, Lucien. *"Woman's Doom in Genesis 3:16, Catholic Biblical Quarterly*, 12 (1950), 389-399.

The Vatican's *Divino Afflante Spiritu* (1943) raised some knotty problems for Catholic theologians concerning traditional theory on the justification for woman's subjection. This essay, though rather esoteric for non-theologians, gives insight into the circuitous path historically taken and is therefore of interest to those who wish to trace the evolution of both religious and secular thought on woman's destiny, from early Christian times to the present, regardless.

Parton, James, *et al,* eds. ***Eminent Women of the Age; Being the Narratives of the Lives and Deeds of the Most Prominent Women of the Present Generation.*** New York: Arno Press, 1974. (Reprinted from the 1869 original published at Hartford, Connecticut by S. M. Betlo.) 628 p.

Fanny Fern, Grace Greenwood, Elizabeth Cady Stanton, and Horace Greeley, among others, join Parton in amassing this wealth of information about American and British women. Many of them are still keenly remembered, but many others have suffered a dimming of their fame and deserve a revived interest.

Categories such as education, women's rights, drama, and medicine divide the work. Eighteen biographees from other nations are included also.

Patai, Raphael, ed. ***Women in the Modern World.*** New York: The Free Press; London: Collier-Macmillan, 1967. 519 p.

Patai introduces this collection of factual essays to present a worthwhile survey of women's status all over the contemporary world. Many "worlds" are considered, among them the Indian

(Asia), the Muslim, the Latin-Mediterranean (including South American), the Afro-Asian, the Communist (former USSR and China), and the Western (United States, Britain, and Scandinavia). The approach is sociological. Short bibliographies follow each section, and biographies of the contributors are furnished on pages 511-519.

Paulme, Denise, ed. ***Women of Tropical Africa.*** Translated by H. M. Wright from *Femmes d'Afrique Noir.* Berkeley: University of California Press, 1971 [1963]. 308 p. Index.

This is an important collection of studies, translated from the originals of French women anthropologists, concerning contemporary women in Guinea, the Niger, Central African Republic, Burundi, and Dakar and environs. The varied subjects include: family structures and customs, woman's position in a nomadic society, the legal position of women, and others.

The work is illustrated and contains an extensive analytical bibliography on pages 231-293.

Perkins, A. J. G., and Theresa Wolfson. ***Frances Wright, Free Enquirer: The Story of a Temperament***. New York and London: Harper and Brothers, 1939. 393 p. Index.

This is the fascinating story of a rebel, Frances Wright D'Arusmont, born in Scotland in 1795. Part of her rebellion took the form of uncompromising truth-seeking: she learned early that "truth still had to be found . . . and men were afraid of it."

The truth Frances sought was related to social justice, and it was the problem of slavery which most engaged her energies as she traveled on frequent and extended visits to the United States and Haiti.

The authors make generous use of personal letters, diaries, and contemporary newspaper articles.

Pernoud, Régine. ***La Reine Blanche***. Paris Éditions Albin Michel, 1972. 366 p. Bibliography.

Pernoud provides the reader with glimpses into the life and times of Blanche of Castile, mother of Louis IX (1215-1271), as she acted as regent of France during Louis IV's minority and in his absence while he traveled on his first Crusade. Attempting to dispel some of the unfavorable legends which have tarnished Blanche's name by painting her as a self-seeking and crafty woman, Pernoud justifies her by pointing out that Louis, beloved as he was by his people, owed much to his mother's guidance in the ways of justice and sympathy for the underprivileged. Moreover, Blanche comes through as a stateswoman holding her own against an antagonistic aristocracy.

Phillips, Margaret, and W. S. Tomkinson. ***English Women in Life and Letters.*** London: Oxford University Press, 1926. 403 p. New York: McCann and Geohegan, 1975. 319 p. Illustrations.

The seventeenth and eighteenth centuries are the focus of this generously illustrated book which sympathetically and with scholarly care documents the status and activities of women. The lives of Margaret Paston, Dorothy Osborne, Elizabeth Pepys, Fanny Burney, and Elizabeth Gaskell are a few of the "in-life" heroines portrayed here, while such well-known fictional heroines as Pamela (Samuel Richardson), Moll Flanders (Daniel Defoe), and Evelina (Frances Burney) are shown as reflections of social conditions, usually extremely constraining ones for women of "respectability."

Woman's education in this period is treated at length, a chapter deals with the plight of women workers in early factories, and "The Woman Criminal" gives a graphic picture of the London Defoe knew. (At that time "criminal" might refer to a great number of misdeeds besides violent crime. These could range from a failure to pay debts [poverty was no excuse] to charges of prostitution.)

Pierre, André. *Les Femmes en Union Soviétique: leur rôle dans la vie nationale.* (Bibliothèque de la Recherche Sociale, Institut Catholique de Paris.) Paris: Spes, 1960. 324 p. No index.

Pierre's sources can be found on pages 307-308: he has depended upon Russian newspapers, journals, and some Russian or French books for data and background, but evidently little documentation originating from women themselves.

This work begins with Lenin's declaration that the Soviet revolutionary sweep had left not a trace of woman's inequality, because of Article 122 of the new Constitution. Nevertheless, it was necessary later on to take "reactionary" steps to protect the health of women when equality had forced them to undertake the work of men in mines and other hazardous work situations, since World War I had caused the loss of so many men.[27] Pierre sees the Russian women themselves endeavoring to restore the idea of romantic love in the "automaton society of equality," where women do not long for equality—which he seems to believe would have a chilling effect upon the relations between

---

[27] Losses were so heavy that Russia had made a separate peace with Germany in 1917.

the sexes. Article 122 turned out to be a mixed blessing, but not because its intent was at fault.

Pinchon, Jerome, ed. ***Le Ménagier de Paris: traité de morale et d'économie domestique, composé vers 1393 par un bourgeois parisien.*** Paris: Société des Bibliophiles Français, 1846.

A sixty year old husband wrote this manual to instruct his fifteen year old bride in the arts of domestic economy. He informs the reader that it was at the bride's request, since she felt ill-informed, having been an orphan with little opportunity to learn how to manage a house in Paris and a country estate, as she was expected to do.

The girl's willing mentor leaves nothing to chance: she is instructed in everything, from religious duties to cookery, from housecleaning to tending sick animals. The goal is to mold a perfect lady (and a hard-working one), who would be a shrewd *menagère* and a pious, submissive wife. (See Pichon, above.)

Pinkham, Mildreth Worth. ***Women in the Sacred Scriptures of Hinduism.*** New York: Ams Press, 1967. 239 p. Index. (Reprint of the Columbia University Press edition of 1941.)

The Hindu scriptures prescribe behavior in all phases of a female's life, and the noble ideals incorporated in these writings have fostered the qualities of nurture in women but have not recognized their need for freedom, since they have been instructed to revere their husbands as their god, asserts Pinkham.

Being subjected to child-marriage, suttee, easy divorce by males, and other customs inimical to women, they have accepted passivity as a way of life. Pinkham's study analyzes pertinent quotations from the *Vedas, Brahmanas, Upanishads, Laws of Manu, Puraras, Mahabharata, Bhagavad Gita,* and the

Ramayana. The useful bibliography has a section on "Indian Womanhood."

Pivar, David J. **Purity Crusade: Sexual Morality and Social Control, 1868-1900.** (Contributions in American History, No. 23.) Westport, Connecticut: Greenwood Press, 1973. 308 p.

The "purity movement" in the United States paralleled the woman's movement, and some suffragettes belonged to purity organizations, since the issue of prostitution (the target of the purity crusade) meshed with feminist objectives. By the 1880's the woman's movement had identified itself with this crusade.

Pivar weaves threads of social thought into the factual fabric of his narrative to give it historical depth, and bibliographical notes document the work.

Potter, David M. **"American Women and the American Character,"** pages 65-84 in *American Character and Culture: Some Twentieth Century Perspectives,* edited by John A. Hague. DeLand, Florida: Everett Edwards Press, 1964.

The tendency to think in male terms even when speaking of the historical shaping of American character is scored by Potter in this readable essay, but he continues the error by considering American women only in relation to contemporary urban conditions, ignoring history's dynamic changes on the female American character because he believes homemaking to be a homogeneous occupation in all times and places. He ignores, too, women who were not strictly homemakers—the nineteenth century, for example, was noted for its exceptional women.

Evidently convinced that woman's character cannot be related to purely American developments as man's can, Potter recommends Simone de Beauvoir's *The Second Sex* and Mirra

Komarovsky's *Women in the Modern World*, perhaps as clues to how women should accommodate within an existential "situation" which can be viewed apart from history.

Powell, Chilton Latham. ***English Domestic Relations, 1487-1653.*** (Studies in English and Comparative Literature.) New York: Columbia University Press, 1914. 274 p. Bibliography and index.

The perspective from which this subject is seen is documentary, with Powell making careful use of primary sources to achieve a scholarly and readable overview of women's place in the society, especially in Chapter II, "Contemporary Attitudes towards Women."

Four informative appendices appear on the subjects of Henry VIII's first divorce, which brought about far-reaching changes in the attitudes of society; John Milton's first divorce tract, prompted by his wife's leaving him just after their marriage; Harringon's book on marriage (1528); and a listing of typical domestic books designed to inform wives and husbands of their duties.

Proudhon, P.-J. ***La Pornocratie, ou Les Femmes dans les temps modernes.*** Paris: A. Lacroix, 1875. 268 p.

Proudhon, a social philosopher widely praised among contemporaries in France for his work, *La Justice,* directs this diatribe at two feminists whom he prudently designates as "Mmes J*** et Jenny d'H***." He denounces their espousal of greater freedom for women as subversive of all he reveres: "nos anciennes institutions," which are the incarnation of the pure justice to which he has dedicated himself in life and work.

A section, "Notes et Pensées," contains anti-feminist epigrams which are likened to the aphorisms of Goethe by "C. E.," who has written an admiring preface to Proudhon's strictures. Proudhon himself ends what he considers a superb work of logic (with kindly intention toward "normal" women, not feminists) by declaring that woman "est toujours idéale quand elle n'est pas mauvaise"—the ideal woman can never be immoral (or perhaps intransigent).

The two feminists are, of course, Juliette Lambert and Jenny d'Héricourt (see below). Instead of seeming out-dated nowadays, Proudhon's exposition contains ideas which are still alive and well.

Putnam, Emily James. *The Lady.* Chicago: University of Chicago Press, 1970. 323 p. (Reprint of the 1921 edition of G. P. Putnam's Sons.)

In her introduction Putnam tries to find an answer to the question, "What is a 'lady'?" She decides that as a *genre* a lady is a product of leisure, and that although this kind of being was disappearing on the eve of the 1920's, she will never be forgotten. Therefore Putnam's main work is designed to fit into a historical framework as she considers the ladies of Greece and Rome, the medieval ladies of the castle and abbey, the ladies of the Renaissance, and the *grandes dames* of the *salons* in France. Moving to England we learn of the "bluestockings" and Hester Thrale's circle, about which James Boswell wrote in his *Life of Samuel Johnson*.[28] Of special interest to American

---

[28] In spite of Hester Thrale's popularity as long as she was married to a man of means and station, when she became a widow and married her children's Italian

readers might be Putnam's section on the aristocratic Southern women during the period before the Civil War (or "War Between the States," as they would have called it).

Queen, Stuart A., and Robert W. Habenstein. *The Family in Various Cultures.* 3rd edition. Philadelphia: J. P. Lippincott Company, 1967. 346 p.

The authors give a comprehensive and readable description of marriage in various cultures, with emphasis on the status of wives in such societies as the American Indian (Toda and Hopi tribes), African (Baganda), classical Chinese, Israeli, ancient Hebrew, Roman, early Christian, English (Anglo-Saxon and medieval), American (colonial and modern), and African-American. The work's value as a useful sourcebook is enhanced by bibliographies which follow each chapter.

Rainwater, Lee, *et al. Workingman's Wife.* (Perennial Works in Sociology.) New York: Arno Press, 1979 [1958]. 238 p. (Reprint of the Oceana Press edition.)

A preface by W. Lloyd Warner of the University of Chicago characterizes this marketing study by Social Research, Inc. as "a tool to use in applying social science to the practical affairs of everyday life"—which here means how to convince, through advertising, the workingman's wife to spend her money as desired by marketing strategists on behalf of large corporations. As such it has a cynical, paternalistic tone—and one might also say, annoying.

music teacher, she was cut off from "polite society" by her erstwhile friends.

The findings of this "scientific" study are based upon data gathered from 600 women in Chicago, Louisville, Trenton (New Jersey), and Tacoma, representing four main sections of the United States. Part I deals with the psychology of the women—their "psychosocial world" wherein their personal values are bounded by the home and family.

Part II, "Consumer Behavior," considers the way psychologic configurations artfully influence the women to buy the "right" things. Here we see faith in the power of advertising as the authors remark, "The working class housewife's taste levels are still in the process of change—and will continue to change in conformity with what the advertisers suggest to her is correct." This was post World War II era when women were not needed in defense work, so it became socially and economically desirable for them to concentrate upon homemaking and child rearing to vacate the workplace to make way for returning veterans.

In general, the concept of the female consumer presented here is that of a passive, repressed, not too intelligent creature, full of good will but unsure of herself, waiting for business to tell her what she wants to select on her shopping trips. This study is the natural subject of unfavorable comment by Betty Friedan in *The Feminine Mystique* (see above) in her chapter on "The Sexual Sell."

Ramabai Sarasvati, Pundita. ***High-Caste Hindu Woman, The.*** 2d edition. Philadelphia: Jas B. Rodgers, 1888. 119 p. (German edition published in Halle by J. Fricke, 1895.)

In an introduction to this seemingly unpretentious little book Rachel L. Bodley informs the reader that in writing it Pundita Sarasvati broke "the silence of a thousand years." For the first time it became possible for the world to hear Indian women complain of their harsh lot, which forced them to endure chattel law, childhood marriage, suttee, female infanticide, untreated diseases, and other inhumanities sanctified by the laws of Manu which preach, "Women are as impure as falsehood itself."

In this landmark volume the author asks her readers to encourage Indian women in their struggle for freedom and education. To this end she suggests practical ways of assisting them.[29]

Ramos, Maria. ***Mulheres da América.*** Rio de Janeiro: José Alvaro, Editora S.A., 1964. 180 p.

Gathered together are laudatory sketches of forty-two women from Argentina, Brazil, Columbia, Cuba, El Salvador, Guatamela, Honduras, Mexico, Paraguay, Peru, and Uruguay. Included is one woman from the United States—Jacqueline Kennedy. A poem composed in her honor is found here as well.

Ravenal, Florence Leftwick. ***Women and the French Tradition.*** New York: The Macmillan Company, 1918. 234 p.

Ravenal's work reflects the era when the emotions stirred by World War I and the movement for women's rights were animating the sympathy of the American public for the French people.[30]

Here Ravenal is sharing her enthusiasm for several French women whom she has come to admire through her own studies. Many are the paths she points out for her readers to follow in

---

[29] This work is part of the Gerritsen Women's History collection, no. 2308.

[30] At this time President Woodrow Wilson was the object of admiration, even love, in France, which made for close ties between the two nations.

their own study of such women as Arvède Barine, George Sand, Mme de Staël, Mme de Sévigné, and Mme de La-Fayette.

Reed, Evelyn. *Problems of Women's Liberation: A Marxist Approach.* New York: J. Norton, 1972 [1969]. 96 p.

The two great revolutions of prehistory, the Agricultural, made by women, and the Metal, made by men, are the focus of Reed's discussion. The downfall of matriarchy and the rise of patriarchy, she believes, precipitated a 4000-year slide to the brink of annihilation of humanity by increasingly destructive wars.

Reed sees anthropology as the most fruitful field of learning for a deep understanding of woman's liberation. Nevertheless, she admits, its insights have alarmed those who would bolster the *status quo.* While agreeing with Betty Friedan (see above) to some extent in her analysis of the "feminine mystique," Reed is not convinced that education alone will accomplish the desired goals: women must become active politically, she contends.

A 1964 translation of Reed's work was published in Mexico D.F. by Fontamara under the title of *Sexo contra sexo, o clase contra clase,* with Helga Pawlowsky and Rosa Cañadel, the translators.

Rees, Richard. *Simone Weil: A Sketch for a Portrait.* Carbondale: Southern Illinois Press, 1966. 205 p. Index.

Harry T. Moore, in his preface to this work, asserts that Rees "views Simone Weil as a saint, taking the term from T. S. Eliot's reference to her." Moore agrees that Simone's death by self-imposed starvation in England as a protest against the starvation of the people in France by the Nazis was a "strange but important martyrdom."

Rees' emphasis, however, is on the humanity of Simone Weil, on her gifts as philosopher, social critic, and woman of letters. Her message Rees puts into poet William Blake's words, "Go, love without the help of anything on earth."

Reich, Emil. ***Women Through the Ages.*** 2 vols. London: Methuen & Co., 1908. 538 p. Index and illustrations.

This overview of women from ancient Egypt to modern times is arranged according to nationalities. Reich's traditional bias when dealing with the feminism of the nineteenth century is visible, but it can be overlooked, since he includes so many women who did not share his prejudices. Moreover, his scholarship makes the book very useful, especially when he is concerned with women in ages farther removed from him chronologically, perhaps because they posed no threat.

Renard, Marie-Thérèse. ***La Participation des femmes à la vie civique.*** (Collection L'Évolution de la Vie Sociale.) Paris: Les Éditions Ouvrières, 1965. 175 p.

The evolution of the rights of women and feminist movements in France are traced in the first part of this social analysis, with a listing of four current organizations devoted to the promulgation of feminist causes. The second part scrutinizes how well French women were accepting their political responsibilities and offers statistical evidence to support the conclusion that not enough women were acting in the civic sphere.

Reuther, Rosemary Radford, ed. *Religion and Sexism: Images of Women in the Jewish and Christian Traditions.* New York: Simon and Schuster, 1974.

This is a scholarly work which traces the backgrounds of Hebrew and Christian influences on women, showing how they have been shaped by the concepts inherent in these religions.

Thirteen scholars of both faiths have contributed to make this a valuable resource book. Twelve of the thirteen are women.

Reynier, Gustave. *La Femme au XVIIe siècle, ses ennemis et ses défenseurs.* Paris: Librairie Plon, 1933. 276 p.

Reynier opens his work with a quotation from Alexandre Dumas *fils,* "Dieu a créé la femelle; l'homme en a fait la femme." ("God created the female; man made a woman out of her.") But Reynier objects to this, saying "Il serait probablement plus juste de dire que la femme s'est faite elle-même." ("Probably it would be truer to say that woman has made herself.")

Reynier's principal interest is the education of women in the seventeenth century. After explaining the earlier resurgence of the "querelle des femmes," he discusses how women were able to educate themselves and explicates how men regarded these efforts, becoming either "ennemis" or "défenseurs." Especial attention is paid to the ideas of Molière, who trained his brilliant wit upon "les femmes savantes."

This is a valuable historical work, and since so many persons are mentioned, an index would have been most helpful.

Reynolds, E. E. *Margaret Roper, Eldest Daughter of Sir Thomas More.* New York: P. J. Kenedy & Sons, 1960. 149 p.

The main sources for this biography, the first published about Margaret Roper, are the accounts of the life of Thomas More and his own *English Works*, because of the scarcity of primary materials concerning Margaret. All her letters, however, are found here in full.

Chapter II deals with Margaret's humanistic education, which corresponded to the strict contemporary theories on women's education (for women of the upper class only), such as those of Erasmus and Juan Luis Vives, the Spaniard whose *Instruction of a Christian Woman* was extremely influential. Margaret's most important mentor was her father, who encouraged her scholarship as well as her writing of poetry. On page 35, for example, can be found a letter from him which clearly shows the esteem in which some men held educated women in that time and place.

Reynolds, Myra. *The Learned Lady in England, 1650-1760.* (Vassar Semi-Centennial Series.) Gloucester, Massachusetts: Peter Smith, 1964. 489 p. Bibliography. (First published at Boston by the Houghton Mifflin Company, 1920.)

Before launching into her highly detailed account of "learned ladies," how they became learned, and what results came from their learning, Reynolds sketches the state of feminine learning in England before 1650. Her last two chapters discuss books written about women and describe satiric representations of women in contemporary drama. A summary ties together the author's findings: although there was a "lavish sowing of seed," the actual fruits of learning were few because "the world listens unconvinced and in the actual affairs of life apparently applies the old standards."

This book is a pleasure to use, for it provides much material in a well-organized presentation. It is indexed and has a general bibliography as well as a listing of books written by women before 1760.

Rheingold, Joseph C. *Fear of Being a Woman: A Theory of Maternal Destructiveness.* New York and London: Grune and Stratton, 1964. 756 p. Index.

Rheingold inform his readers of his stance in an introduction which criticizes existentialist Simone de Beauvoir (to whom he says he is "in debt," however) and Freudian Helene Deutsch for not interpreting women completely, as he does. This may sound as if he is sympathetic toward women, but at the end of his "complete" interpretation he finds himself back with the well-worn myths (as far back as Eve and Pandora) by concluding that women, especially mothers, are to blame for most of the troubles in human relationships. A capacious bibliography, pages 715-741, is worthy of the student's perusal.

Richards, Samuel Alfred. *Feminist Writers of the Seventeenth Century.* London: D. Nutt, 1914. 146 p.

Calling the Renaissance "the cradle of the feminist movement," Richards considers the works of France's Poulain de la Barre, Marie de Gournay, Jacques du Bose, Louis Machon, Anne de Schurman, Jacquette Guillaume, G. de Bertron (Marquis of Halifax), C. M D. Noel, G. S. Aristophile. In addition, he refers to fictional works of the period.

It is to France of the seventeenth century that we must look if we are to trace the women's movement, Richards declares, noting that *les précieuses* paved the way for the serious advocates of the equality of the sexes, those who acknowledged the learned ladies' social and literary supremacy. In England, he notes, 1832 was a turning point in the emancipation movement, but he gives credit to Mary Wollenstonecraft for her courageous pioneering work in bringing the deplorable situation of intellectual women to public attention.

Richardson, Bertha Jane. *The Woman Who Spends, A Study of Her Economic Function.* Introduction by Ellen H. Richards. 2nd edition, revised. Boston: Whitcomb and Barrows, 1913. 161 p.

Social economics is primarily a woman's problem, asserts Richardson, since women have the leisure and education to direct the development of social conditions. In light of this concept, her writing deals with choice, responsibility, and independence of thought in regard to the temptations of the emerging affluent society.

Such a work as this can give perspective on what was projected and hoped for just before the outbreak of World War I, and one can compare it with what has actually resulted from this new-found affluence.

Rico, Heidi K. de. *Páginas intimas de la mujer boliviano.* Tupiza, Bolivia: Ediciones Rico, 1970. 280 p.

Feminist de Rico, a native of Switzerland but by marriage Bolivian, presents her book as "un guía de preparación de la nueva mujer boliviana . . . para hacer los cambios sociales que necesita la mujer." From her vantage point as a European who had lived five years she shares her observations concerning the lack of education and the few cultural opportunities available to women, as well as the great economic disadvantages they suffered. By writing her book to help "prepare" such women, de Rico underlines how great she felt would be the psychological difficulties confronting women who wished to begin the fight for change.

Riegel, Robert. *American Feminists.* Lawrence: University of Kansas Press, 1963. (Greenwood Press Reprint, 1980.) 223 p.

Riegel presents in a readable style vignettes of leading feminists, ending with a chapter, "Why a Feminist?" in which he analyzes their motivations. Here are found perspectives on Frances Wright, Elizabeth Cady Stanton, Martha Wright, Charlotte Gilman, Susan B. Anthony, Amelia Bloomer, Lucy Stone, and others. Riegel sees Wollstonecraft's *A Vindication of the Rights of Women* (1795) as a source from which many American feminists derived their ideas.

Rigaud, Louis. *L'Évolution du droit de la femme de Rome à nos jours.* Paris: Éditions Spes, 1930. 54 p.

Written by a lawyer, this compendium traces laws in France in regard to women as they were affected by Roman law, ancient law, laws during the Revolution, the Napoleonic *Code Civile*, and contemporary law. This makes enlightening reading for anyone concerned about the disadvantages of women in any country whose legal system reflects similar influences.

Rodocanachi, Emmanuel Pierre. *La Femme italienne avant, pendant et après la Renaissance.* Paris: Hachette, 1922 [1907]. 439 p.

This well-illustrated volume is replete with information concerning the daily life of the famous women (and men) of the period—Isabella d'Este and Catherine Sforza are featured. There are readable descriptions of the sumptuous life enjoyed by the élite, but one also finds here the subterranean aspects as in the section "Condition civile de la femme," which sets forth the laws governing women (most are in Latin), and added is a section on woman slavery.

A good index, pages 407-436, enhances the accessibility of the information, and a bibliography is included.

Roe, Frances M. A. ***Army Letters from an Officer's Wife.*** New York: Arno Press, 1979. 389 p. Illustrated. (First published in New York and London by D. Appleton and Company, 1909.)

In 1871 Frances Roe wrote her first letter to her family from a stagecoach stop in Colorado territory, the only woman traveling with "many dreadful-looking men." But on the way to her husband's station she saw houses that were more dreadful-looking yet: even the hotel was made of dirt and a few dry goods boxes.

The personality of an intrepid, good-humored woman shines through these letters to her family back home, written as she traveled as far north as wild Montana and Utah (where she observed Mormon customs), longing for the day when she could return to Washington for the 1888 presidential inauguration.

These letters are well worth reading, not only for their detailed descriptions of places and people of that day, but also for an understanding of how women thought of themselves and their place in society. Frances quotes her grandmother as saying cryptically, "It is a dreadful thing not to become a woman when one ceases to be a girl"—that is, not to be able to resign oneself to the roles designated for women in the society.

Rogers, Cameron. ***Gallant Ladies***. New York: Harcourt Brace and Co., 1928. 363 p. (Available on photocopy, 1988, LBS Archival Products, Des Moines, Iowa.)

Finding unconventional women exciting, Rogers paints some pictures of women who in their own times brought retribution and persecution down on their adventurous heads. Among those found here are Mata Hari (Gertrude Margarete Zelle), a dancer renowned as the World War I spy who was executed by the French; Mary Read and Anne Bonny, who flirted with danger as pirates; Belle Starr, an outlaw of the American West; Lola Montez, who through intrigues became fabulously wealthy but died in poverty, and Marie de Rohan, "queen of cabals."

Ronhaar, J. H. ***Women in Primitive Motherright Societies.*** The Hague: Gronigen; London: David Nutt, 1941. 541 p.

Although Ronhaar states that this ethnological study is not directed to the lay person, much of it is fascinating reading for any serious student, and especially informative for those concentrating upon the evolution of human family patterns. Areas studied are: Australia, Micronesia, Dutch East Indies, Malaysia, India, America (including the Indians of Canada and the Arctic), Engano, Timor, Kisar, Leti, and others. A bibliography is included.

Rossi, Alice S., ed. ***Essays on Sex Equality: John Stuart Mill and Harriet Taylor Mill.*** Chicago: University of Chicago Press, 1970. 242 p.

Rossi introduces the Mills with an essay, "Sentiment and Intellect" (pages 3-63), to answer the question, "How did this man come to write a book on women?" She gives credit mainly to Harriet Taylor and their friendship of twenty-eight years before their marriage, which took place when she became a widow. Harriet, then, was the inspirer and sharer in the production of *The Subjection of Women* (1864) and two essays on the franchise and marriage, which are reprinted here. These writings appeared between 1831 and 1869.

Rousselot, Paul. *Histoire de l'éducation des femmes en France.* (Burt Franklin Research and Source Works Series, 875.) 2 vols. New York: B. Franklin, 1971. 472 p. (First published in Paris by Didier in 1883.)

Rousselot has amassed a wealth of detailed information concerning the historical aspects of the education of Frenchwomen. Especially interesting are his accounts of female education in the crucial seventeenth century, when attention was being drawn to this controversial subject by the sympathetic theorizing of such prominent social critics as Fénelon and Montaigne (and the unsympathetic satires of Molière). At this time Mme de Maintenon was earning praise for her academy at St. Cyr, which she had founded for the enlightened training of girls of the impecunious nobility.

Rousselot makes great use of primary sources, such as diaries and theoretical writings, and literature figures prominently in the work as well.[31]

Rover, Constance. *Love, Morals, and the Feminists.* London: Routledge & Kegan Paul, 1970. 183 p. Index and bibliography. Illustrations.

What early feminists wanted, avers Rover, quoting G. E. Mowry, was "equality based upon. . . a standard of feminine virtue, not masculine sin." Observing that the idea of "free

---

[31]This is available also on microfiche (New Haven, Connecticut: Research Publications, History of Women.)

love" was concomitant with French Revolutionary thought which touched off Saint Simonianism and early feminism, Rover notes that British and American overtones of prudery prevented newly independent women from leading full lives, hampered as they were by fear of public opinion.

Rover draws together the diverse currents of concerns among feminists as they worked for the vote and social changes that would eliminate some of the worst abuses in regard to women. A chapter on the Pankhursts is included.

Ryan, Mary P. *Womanhood in America: From Colonial Times to the Present.* New York: Franklin Watts, 1975. 496 p. Index.

Ryan purposes to give as complete as possible (in one volume) of the kaleidoscope of American women's lives from one century to the next: thus she finds herself describing a paradox—women who in early centuries helped found a nation and were respected as "mothers of civilization," but who by the twentieth century had been trivialized by advertising and popular culture into consumers and "sex objects"—while continuing to carry the responsibilities of home and family and more— and, even more paradoxically, having much more political power than women throughout American history.

Developments leading to this dilemma have not been unnoticed by women: Ryan comments upon the "cages" from which they continue to try to pry themselves free in order to have a serious influence upon history. "Woman's rage against her imprisonment is in fact a fixture of womanhood. It records the high cost of imprisonment. . . ."

Sartin, Pierrette. *La Femme libérée?* Paris: Stock, 1968. 286 p.

Sartin, writer, professor, and sociologist, brings attention to the injustices suffered by women in contemporary French society. This book is not a *cri de guerre,* she asserts, but it does ask Frenchmen to work toward the betterment of their feminine compatriots as they would for any human being.

Schiff, Mario. ***La Fille d'alliance de Montaigne: Marie de Gournay.*** (Bibliothèque de la Renaissance, no. X.) Genève: Slatkine Reprints, 1978. 146 p. (First published in Paris by Librairie Honoré Champion, 1910.)

Marie de Gournay's essay, "Égalité des hommes et des femmes," written in 1622, and the 1626 edition of "Grief des dames" will be found on pages 61-77. Schiff adds material on variants of the manuscripts as well as useful bibliographical information and facts on this early feminist's reception in Italy and her friendship with Anne-Marie de Schurman.

Schirmacher, Kaethe. ***The Modern Woman's Rights Movement: A Historical Survey.*** Translated from the 2nd German edition by Carl Conrad Eckhardt. New York: The Macmillan Co., 1912 [1905]. (New York: Kraus Reprints, 1971.)

Although this pre-World War I survey deals primarily with woman's situation in the Germanic countries, all English-speaking geographic areas, the Romance countries, and the Near and Far East also receive attention.

In this readable reportage about conditions at the turn of the century Schirmacher's concludes, "In the greater part of the world woman is a slave and a beast of burden. If she rules, she rules through cunning. In the European countries she exists merely as a sexual being under conditions that dwarf her humanity even if she lives in luxury and adulation."

Schoenfeld, Hermann. ***Women of the Teutonic Nations.*** (Woman in All Ages and in All Countries.) Philadelphia: The Rittenhouse Press, 1908. 412 p.

From the early centuries of the Teutonic race to the present, German women appear to have had less encouragement and opportunity to influence the development of a humane society than women in such societies as France and Britain. Schoenfeld traces these years with careful scholarship (including short chapters on Polish and Russian women), detailing some outstanding literary flowerings along the way, as in the days of the Minnesingers and the "New Learning" during the Renaissance. Later, with the Reformation , bonds tightened upon German women (notably Jewish women): the case of Sophie Dorothea, the imprisoned princess, epitomizes this repression.

Schoenfeld writes hopefully of the emancipation of the German woman at the end of the nineteenth century, with a notable women's literary output a good sign for the future. Since he wrote at the turn of the twentieth century, he could not know what German history had in store for women. "To do all things vehemently has always been a German trait," he remarks.

Schreiner, Olive. ***Women and Labour.*** London: Virago Press, 1985. (Original publication in New York by Frederick A. Stokes Company, 1911.) 299 p.

Noting the great advances in technology which released humans from the heavy labors of the past, even in the home, Schreiner is concerned that women will have too little to do to challenge them if alternative occupations are not opened up to them, whereby they can use their gifts. A problem which she foresaw was an incipient parasitism as modern inventions freed them from three-fourths of the traditional tasks of society through which they had experienced a feeling of participation. Without this, a sense of isolation could become overwhelming. Therefore Schreiner argued for women's right to enter new fields of work already being opened up for men.

This was written just before World War I, when her argument received an unexpected answer: manpower became crucial to the war effort—but, as it turned out, this was only for the emergency. For the most part, women were expected to go back to their prewar existence.

Scott, Anne Firor. ***The Southern Lady: from Pedestal to Politics, 1830-1930.*** Chicago: University of Chicago Press, 1970. 247 p.

Scott looks for the reality under the mythical romance attached to the days of life in the American South and finds many women discontented with the patriarchal, paternalistic institutions of that slave-holding society. She sees the Civil War as having an emancipating effect on women as the dearth of men forced them to take up hitherto forbidden occupations. This was a time of increased interest in women's organizations—missionary societies, clubs, and groups crusading against child labor and for woman suffrage.

Scott, Anne Firor Scott. ***"Self-Portraits: Three Women,"*** pages 43-76 in *Uprooted Americans: Essays to Honor Oscar Handlin,* edited by Richard L. Bushman, *et al.* Boston: Little, Brown and Company, 1979.

The lives of the three women who figure here—Jane Franklin Mecom, sister of Bejamin Franklin; Elizabeth Sandwich Drinker, and Eliza Lucas Pinckney—spanned the years from

1712 to 1807. Their social and economic situations differed, but their destinies held many similarities: instead of accomplishments posterity would acclaim, regardless of their obvious intellectual gifts, each one's small place in history was embodied by her ability, determination, and devotion to work to create a cohesive family which grew to include several generations. They were truly "founding mothers" who deserve our admiring attention.

Scott presents three women as a "microcosm" of colonial America in contradistinction to the macrocosm described by traditional historians. In their view the colonial period was a time of the Revolution, the Constitution as conceived by the "founding fathers," and a subsequent phenomenal economic development—a world looked at solely in male terms. In reality, she asserts, this broad sweep of history was hardly noticed by women, whose history continued apart from men's as they tried to cope in a new country, resigning themselves to frequent pregnancies, childbirth, illnesses and deaths of family members, and the frequent absence of husbands or other males (who could be at war, at sea or traveling for business) to assist them." ("God's sacred will be done.")

All the while, too, these three uncommon women found time to read and write: books and diaries or letters were part and parcel of their daily existence. Jane, of course, had already been noted for her letters, but only because they were written to her famous brother Ben. Through her voracious reading she had become aware of the "woman question" and had read Mary Wollstonecraft's *Vindication of the Rights of Women,* but it had little relevance for a woman immersed in the duties of a large and not prosperous household.

Seltman, Charles. ***Women in Antiquity.*** New York: Westport, Connecticut: Hyperion Press, 1989. 191 p. (Reprint of 1956 edition by Thames and Hudson, London.) 191 p.

A lively sympathy for women permeates this little volume written by the eminent classicist, whose style is both informal and based on sure scholarship.

Of all the women he has studied, Seltman finds that the ancient Spartans are most to be envied by women in other places and times (including our own).[32] "It has yet to be shown," he writes, "that any women in history led such well-adjusted lives as the women of ancient Sparta." Seltman is ready with his proof in case he should be challenged in this opinion, which he expected.

Shorter, Edward. ***"Female Emancipation, Birth Control, and Fertility in European History,"*** *American Historical Review,* 78, no. 3 (June, 1973), pp. 605-640.

In this well-documented article Shorter points out that demographers have been unable to explain many phenomena related to population rise and fall because they have paid insufficient attention to the history of that group of the population most closely involved with fertility—women. He states that his purpose here is to present an argument linking the history of women to this "parabolic rise and fall of fertility." He also finds

---

[32]Sparta was a totalitarian society based upon strict militaristic principles which included taking boys from their mothers at an early age to live in barracks with the men in order to develop hardy soldiers. Usual historians do not include much, if any, material on the life of Spartan women, but it appears that the women were independent and athletically inclined.

fault with "belletristic" evidence used by writers of women's history who have been "loath to employ either solid demographic data or to borrow arguments and techniques from the social sciences in general." Included in this criticism are such works as Kate Millett's *Sexual Politics* (above).

After identifying the crucial elements in new attitudes among women, Shorter traces historical, political, and psychological factors present from the nineteenth century on in Western society to substantiate his thesis. His many bibliographical notes could form an excellent way to continue the serious pursuit of the subject. If Shorter's claim to originality is valid, the myopia of demographers is nothing short of amazing.

Silva, Carmen da. *A Arte de ser mulher.* (Biblioteca da Mulher Modern.) Rio de Janeiro: Editora Civilizaço Brasileira, S. A., 1966. 251 p.

Modern Brazilian women have the choice now of "living or vegetating," says da Silva, admitting, however, that tradition has made the art of truly living difficult for women. She suggests some ways of breaking out of the hold: the last section has as title, "Para os Moços."

Simkins, Francis Butler, and James Welch Patton. *The Women of the Confederacy.* St. Clair Shores, Michigan: Scholarly Press. Index and bibliography (pp. 291-98). 406 p. (Reprint of 1936 edition by Garrett and Massie, New York 1936.)

It is to be assumed, say the authors, that the outstanding personalities of the Confederacy were men, for only men were political and military leaders. The subject of this book, however, is the traditional role of Southern women which precluded them during the war from engaging in many types of activities that were not part of their "feminine duty." This meant, too, that their contributions were overlooked at that time. Nevertheless, their newfound freedom brought them fame later, notably for their devoted work as nurses and their ability to withstand privation after their first flush of enthusiasm for the war had turned to shocked realization of the cruel realities confronting them.

This book is replete with accounts of women's efforts to cope with war and its aftermath. Letters, diaries, newspaper and travelers' accounts, reminiscences, and memoirs, as well as numerous secondary works, are drawn upon as Simkins and Patton endeavor to "eliminate exaggeration and folklore" and clear away some of the romantic illusions usually associated with Southern womanhood. Copious notes accompany each chapter, and a bibliography of sources is appended. This is a worthwhile survey of an aspect of American history which is often overlooked by the usual historian of the "War Between the States."

Simpson, Lesley Byrd, ed. ***Little Sermons on Sin: The Archpriest of Talavera, by Alfonso Martínez de Toledo.*** Berkeley: University of California Press, 1969. 200 p.

"Women are wicked, no doubt about it, declares the fifteenth-century Archpriest, although he discovers some excuse for the young and beautiful," writes Simpson as she introduces her translation of this famous (and infamous) expression of Spanish asceticism and anti-feminism. Unfortunately, this document has been carefully preserved, not only because it was considered useful as a carrier of the traditional misogyny, but also because it was considered to have literary merit.

Sinclair, Andrew. ***The Better Half: The Emancipation of the American Woman.*** Westport, Connecticut: Greenwood Press, 1981. Bibliography and index. 401 p. (First published in New York by Harper and Row, 1965.)

Sinclair takes a chronological approach to the evolution of feminism, writing realistically about such topics as nineteenth century medicine, religion, the factory system, and the trek westward, remarking that "virgin land usually spelt to a woman isolation, disease, and hopelessness."

Each fact-filled chapter is accompanied by bibliographical notes, and an index makes the facts accessible. This is very useful as a an unvarnished introduction to the American woman's bitter struggle for equality.

Skrjabina, Elena. ***Siege and Survival: The Odyssey of a Leningrader.*** Translated and edited by Norman Luxenburg. Foreword by Harrison E. Salisbury. Carbondale: Southern Illinois University Press, 1971. 171 p. Index.

The twentieth century is unique in the demands it has made upon women to cope with war, and they had often to face it alone, without men beside them. World War I brought unparalleled hardships to women in France where they were the only women in war zones. But World War II made almost all of Europe, and Britain as well, into battle zones for women, areas full of privations, dangers, and emotional trauma.

Leningrad, whose 900-day siege by the Nazi army and air force has been documented by Harrison E. Salisbury, was one of the cities that suffered the most. Elena's account, written in the form of a journal from June 22, 1941 to February 6, 1942, lays bare the hunger, terrors and despair of women. Elena escaped from the city, where over 3,000,000 starving people were trapped, by crossing the frozen Lake Ladoga, taking her mother (who died shortly after), two children, and their old nurse ("nana") with her, a superhuman act of endurance. This was only the beginning of a journey of hunger and heartache which did not end until the war was over.

Smith, Frank. ***The Authorship of 'An Occasional Letter on the Female Sex,'*** " *American Literature,* II (1930-31), pp. 277-280.

Smith calls attention to an anonymous letter published in August, 1775, in the *Pennsylvania Magazine,* which he designates as "perhaps the first plea for the emancipation of women published in America."

Tradition has assigned this letter to Thomas Paine, but Smith brings evidence to refute this, thus taking from Paine his reputation as being the first champion of American women. He shows that the letter in question is an excerpt from an article by Antoine Léonard Thomas which was translated from the French version specifically for American readers of the above-mentioned magazine.

Societàs Umanitaria. ***L'Emancipazione femminile in Italia, un secolo di discussioni, 1861-1961.*** Firenze: La Nuova Italia Editrice, 1962 (?). 238 p.

Celebrating a century of unification, this report grew out of a convention at Turin in 1961 under the auspices of women's associations, with Dr. Teresita Sandeschi Schelba the head. The emphasis is upon the contributions to Italian culture made by women throughout the centuries, especially during the Renaissance (pages 45-59), and women writers are given their share of attention (pages 285-300). Ideologies which determined the status of women in Italy are analyzed as well.

Spencer, Anna Garlin. ***Woman's Share in Social Culture.*** (American Women: Images and Reality.) New York: Arno Press, 1972. 413 p. (First published in 1912.).

Dedicated to the memory of Lucretia Mott, this cultural history looks at primitive, ancient, and modern women, surveying education, work, and marital status. Spencer includes an unusual treatment of marriage and divorce in the section, "Social Use of the Post-Graduate Mother."

Spruill, Julia Cherry. ***Women's Life and Work in the Southern Colonies.*** New York: Norton, 1972. 426 p. (Reprint of 1938 edition of University of North Carolina Press, 1938, with new introduction by Anne Firor Scott.)

Every aspect of women's life in the American colonies of the South before the Revolution is treated in this scholarly work. Chapter I, "Women Wanted," shows how the need was met for men to obtain wives to establish homes while they tamed (or annihilated) the Indians and made the wilds habitable.

Contemporary ladies' magazines are used freely to illustrate women's interests and the kinds of advice they were given to help them adjust to their lot, personal or public. Even under the rude conditions of life, the emphasis for all but the lowest classes was upon femininity, gentility, and docility, just as it was in England.

Stanton, Elizabeth Cady, *et al.* ***History of Woman Suffrage.*** 6 vols. New York: Source Book Press, 1970. (Originally published in 1882-1922.)

Stanton is joined by sister suffragettes Susan B. Anthony, Ida Husted Harper, and Matilda Joslin Gage to create this monumental history of the United States' women rights movement. This is a work that was once lost from view as the ferment of the equal suffrage cause faded with the coming of the Great Depression when political freedom seemed less significant than economic survival. In that time of emergency and political confusion woman's desire for change was seen as a threat to male breadwinners. During those years, for example, it was not unusual in a school system for all married women teachers to be dismissed on the assumption that they were taking away men's jobs—and that they had husbands to support them.

Stebbins, Lucy Poate. *London Ladies: True Tales of the Eighteenth Century*. New York: Columbia University Press, 1952. 208 p.

Stebbins' choice of ladies was dictated by her own interest in them, so here one can find Martha Ray (Lord Sandwich's mistress), Elizabeth Simpson Inchbald (actress and writer), Sally and Maria Siddons (daughters of Sarah Siddons), Amelia Alderson Opie (novelist), Dorothea Lieven (who held a *salon* in the Hôtel Talleyrand), and Jane Welsh (the scholarly wife of Thomas Carlyle, the historian). A good bibliography is appended.

Steffen, Christine Cecelia. *"Women in* Las siete partidas *of Alfonso X de Castilla y Leon."* Unpublished dissertation, University of Texas at Austin, 1979. 240 p.

The thirteenth-century legal code, "Las siete partidas," is "an invaluable source of information concerning all aspects of Castilian and Leonese society of that period," declares Steffen. Her analysis illustrates the code's influence on the lives of women within the society, an influence which was almost entirely repressive.

Stendahl, Kristen. *The Bible and the Role of Women: A Case Study in Hermeneutics.* Translated by Emilie T. Sander. (Pacet Books, Biblical Series, 15.) Philadelphia: Fortress Press, 1966. 48 p.

Biblical interpreter Stendahl of Sweden declares, "It seems to be almost impossible to assent—be it reluctantly or gladly—to the political emancipation of women while arguing on biblical grounds against ordination of women. This is a reconsideration of the traditional base for women's subordination as found in Genesis and the apostle Paul's writings.

Stenton, Doris Mary. *The English Woman in History.* London: George Allen and Unwin; New York: The Macmillan Company, 1957 [1929]. 363 p. Index.

Stenton states her purpose as being "to display the place women have held and the influence they have exerted within the changing patterns of English society from the earliest down to modern times." Thus she begins with Tacitus, the Roman historian, and ends with John Stuart Mill, author of *The Subjection of Women* (1869).

In choosing sources Stenton has relied on contemporary documents—legal, historical and personal (including the Paston letters); medieval literature, and novels of later times.

Many examples and descriptions of strong-minded women are included, and Chapters VII and VIII deal with the beginnings of English feminism and the "new scholarship," respectively.

Stern, Madeleine B. *We, the Women: Career Firsts of Nineteenth-Century American Women.* New York: B. Franklin, 1974. 403

p. Bibliography and index. (Reprint of the 1962 edition published by Schulte Publishing Co.)

Based upon intensive researches, these biographical essays introduce Mary Ann Lee, Ann S. Stephens, Harriet Irwin, Louise Bethune, and Sophie G. Hayden as pioneers in the arts; Sarah G. Bagley, Lucy Hobbs Taylor, Ellen H. Richards in science and technology; Rebecca Pennell Dean, Isabel C. Barrows, and Belva Ann Lockwood, trail-blazers in the professions; Rebecca W. Lukens, Victoria C. Woodhull, and Candace Wheeler, in the vanguard of business and industry.

Stevens, Doris. *Jailed for Freedom.* New York: Boni and Liveright, 1920. 388 p. (1990 reprint of this edition made by Ayer Company, Publishers, of Salem, New Hampshire.)

This dismal story, parallel to that of the British women's experience, is told by one of the participants who adopted militant strategies to dramatize women's right to vote in the United States. As they descended upon Washington when Congress was debating the Nineteenth Amendment, they were arrested on President Woodrow Wilson's orders. [33]

The band of protestors were jailed under horrifying conditions, their civil rights completely ignored as they were force-fed and subjected to other humiliating treatments. This event, remarks Stevens, has the "elements of both ruthlessness and martyrdom."

---

[33] Wilson was the architect of the plan for the League of Nations, along with being the chief exponent of political freedom for European nationalities after World War I. Politically, however, women everywhere were non-persons.

Short *vitae* of all the martyrs are appended to this volume, which should be on every American's reading list.

Strachey, Lytton. *Eminent Victorians.* New York and London: Harcourt Brace Johanovich, 1979 [1918].

Florence Nightingale is the highlight of pages 129-196, wherein Strachey tells us that she was not that saintly, self-sacrificing, delicate maiden of popular legend, but an administrative genius with a "demonic frenzy" for action, a woman who rebelled against the emptiness of a well-to-do home and decided to make herself useful to society by entering nursing. At the age of 34, however, she shocked the British military caste by turning upside down all the established rules of procedure, unfraid of the flaming hatred to come out of the "smouldering hostilities" of the medical authorities. Her aim was to reform military hospitals, and that is what she did.

Straelen, H. J. J. M. *The Japanese Woman Looking Forward.* Tokyo: Kyo Bun Kwan, 1940. 191 p. Bibliography.

Straelen states that the Japanese wife's problem directly stemmed from religion, which permeated the homogeneous society. For this reason we have chapters on how Confucianism and Buddhism relate to womanhood. These were oppressive forms of thought, but a break came in 1853 when Japan's isolation came to an end. Over the years which followed Japanese women became exposed to Western ideas and in the 1930's began to demand their rights as human beings, thus precipitating a long struggle.

Strickland, Agnes. *Lives of the Queens of England from the Norman Conquest.* 8 vols. London: George Bell and Sons, 1882. Index.

Sixteen years in the writing, these eight volumes encompass the lives of Britain's female monarchs from Matilda of Flanders to Anne Stuart, who died in 1714. (The whole of Volume VIII is devoted to Anne.) Of the thirty-four queens considered, thirty wore the "crown matrimonial," while four wore the regal diadem, notes Strickland.[34]

In describing her methodology Strickland assures the reader that she is unbiased, not fearing to "reveal the base metal" which may be "hidden beneath a meretricious gilding." "The duty of historians," she declares, "is to keep to the facts."

This massive work is rich in resources happily made especially accessible by the comprehensive index which is in Volume VIII, pages 557-666.

Sullerot, Évelyne. ***Woman, Change, and Society.*** Translated by Margaret Scotford Archer. (World University Library.) New York: McGraw-Hill Book Company, 1971. 254 p.

"It is clear that women are dissatisfied almost throughout the world," writes Sullerot and goes on to seek out the roots of this universal discontent. Significantly the first chapter deals with the patriarchal system, after which are considered the demographic, educational, legal, and religious aspects of woman's role, as well as the conditions of employment women must contend with. The approach of the book is multi-national: the student of comparative sociology will find much useful data in it.

---

[34] Anne, the daughter of James II by his first wife, Anne Hyde, married a Danish prince, George, in 1683. During her reign so many writers in many branches of learning flourished that this time is known as the "Augustan age of English literature."

Summerskill, Edith Clara (Baroness). *A Woman's World.* London: Heinemann, 1967. 258 p. Index.

The example of her physician father inspired Summerskill to aspire to a career in medicine. This book, however, is not devoted to that field but is a vehicle for her keen observations on all that concerned women: politics, World War II, national health insurance, anti-feminism, divorce, abortion, and the international scene (especially in regard to Russia, China, and Japan).

In summing up Summerskill hopes her book will encourage modern women to take advantage of the opportunities open to them in fields which were not always accessible to women. In her chosen field "Dr. Edith," as she preferred to be called in spite of the title which was granted in 1961, was encouraged by her father and husband.

Sutch, W. B. *Women with a Cause.* Wellington: New Zealand University Press, 1974. 248 p. Index.

Having been brought up in an unusually egalitarian home in Lancaster, England, Sutch was horrified at the treatment of women as inferior beings in the "real" world. Here she presents a case against the educational systems of New Zealand and Australia which conditioned girls from earliest school years through the universities to accept British customs and laws which gave a lower status to women.

Comparisons of economic opportunities for women in various countries such as Sweden, Russia, Canada, and the United States with those in New Zealand and Australia are a valuable part of Sutch's study.

Talbot, D. Amaury. *Woman's Mysteries of a Primitive People: The Ibibios of Southern Nigeria.* (Tass Studies, General Studies, No. 57.) London: Tass, 1968. 252 p. (Originally published 1915.)

A woman's viewpoint on the life of women among this "strange race" inhabiting the southeastern part of Nigeria is given here as a result of research by two sisters, both anthropologists.

Male anthropologists and sociologists in England encouraged the Talbots' efforts, being aware that the status of primitive women was known to English-speaking countries only through what had been said and written by men, Nigerians or otherwise, and that information, they realized, was not unbiased—or was fraught with ignorance of the real situation, since lack of communication between the sexes in the Ibo tribe seemed endemic.

The Talbots elicited the cooperation of the Ibo women: the result is an amazing account of the hardships and even outrages encountered by females from childhood through the period of the "fatting-houses" before marriage. They learned, too, of the existence of secret societies for wealthy women.

This pioneering work contains many revealing anecdotes; it also notes the "latent power" of the feminist movement stirring in Africa as the cruel lot of such women as these was coming to the attention of the West.

Tallentyre, S. J. *The Women of the Salons and Other French Portraits.* New York and London: G. P. Putnam's Sons, 1926 [1901]. 235 p.

Tallentyre introduces in a relaxed manner the *grandes dames* who through the innovation of the *salon* made an irradicable impression on French life and letters, as well as on European culture in general in the seventeenth and eighteenth century. Through these intermediaries, both sexes of the upper classes were able to engage in both serious and light-hearted conversation as in no other place. Their influence was not simply cultural, however: many political issues were discussed, and social changes of significance to women were germinated within the sanctuary of these private gatherings.

Tallentyre offers as well portraits of Letizia Bonaparte, mother of Napoleon, and Dr. Theodore Tronchis, who treated most of the "butterflies" of Paris in his Geneva sanitarium and who "began to exercise upon the habits and hygiene of women an influence far greater than Rousseau's" with his exhortations to drop artificiality and drugs and embrace a more healthful way of life.

Tavris, Carol. *"Women in China: The Speak-Bitterness Revolution" and "A Plague of Meetings: In China, Everybody is a Psychologist,"* Psychology Today, 7, no. 12 (May, 1974), pp. 43-49, 92, 97-98.

In Communist China, writes Tavris, "the contrast between past and present is so striking that many women feel that they already have attained their half of heaven, that they have reached the goal of full equality with men." China must be judged on its own terms, she warns, however, for in many instances old stereotypes still are strong, as, for example, in sexual matters, where the society seems only to have moved "from ninth century feudalism to nineteenth century Victorianism," speaking within the Western framework.

Tavris' well-illustrated field report is based upon a month-long observation of China on a trip sponsored by the United States-China Friendship Association.

Taylor, G. R. Stirling. *Mary Wollstonecraft: A Study in Economics and Romance*. New York: Greenwood Press, 1969. 209 p. (Originally published in 1911.) Index.

A Vindication of the Rights of Women (1791) remains as "a call which has not yet been heeded" except by the "few who think," wrote Taylor in 1911, praising it as "a monument of thought."

This perceptive study of Wollstonecraft concludes that she was "a being who stood alone, a singularly detached part of her surroundings, who possessed a touch of calm indifference beneath her passionate energy.

Thieme, Hugh P. *Women of Modern France.* (Woman in All Ages and in All Countries.) Philadelphia; The Rittenhouse Press, 1908.

In Chapters III through IX, pages 71-275, Thieme provides a detailed panorama of France in the seventeenth century, where woman, "at their best," shine as never before and never since. In these closely detailed pages he tries to include each woman of influence in letters, religion, (Port-Royalism especially), and *salon* life. The last two chapters in this section are devoted to "*salon* leaders and their unique contribution to the development of French culture.

Thompson, Roger. *Women in Stuart England and America: A Comparative Study.* London: Routledge and Kegan Paul, 1978 [1974].

Britisher Thompson uses oft-discussed ideas of Alexis de Tocqueville and Frederick Jackson Turner as the framework for his social analysis of American life as he applies them to women. One specific idea, promulgated by Turner, was that the "closing" (disappearance of "free" land) of the American western frontier in 1898 had a crucial influence upon the American character. Thompson views this "shaping" as being a male phenomenon, rather than seeing it as a factor in molding women's character as well. Women are seen as a generic counterfoil to raw Nature: their role was to "civilize" the men while the men tamed the West. "Morals are the work of women," he declares and notes the deplorable values in societies in which women are held in low esteem.

Thompson has used for source material mainly British novels of the seventeenth century to compare English women and their counterparts in America, with literature about London as a focus for one and documents of early life in Massachusetts and Virginia for his knowledge of the other. This disparity has given him some trouble, since they are not comparable vehicles.

The conclusion is that frontier women, as was to be expected, exerted a civilizing effect upon men (unless, of course, they were derelict women who shirked their duties, narrowly defined by Thompson himself according to traditional stereotypes).

Because of women's laudable contribution to American life, Thompson maintains, American men "rewarded" them with the vote. (See Stevens, *Jailed for Freedom* on this point.) He does not explain, however, why the franchise was delayed until 1919, twenty one years after the "closing" of the frontier—nor does he explain why British women were not granted the vote until centuries after their men had become "civilized."

In spite of Thompson's naïve social criticism, founded in part on a strict dichotomy of roles of "good" and "bad" women, one can find here a good bibliography and useful documentary notes. (See Potter, above.)

Titmuss, R. *"The Position of Women in the Welfare State: Some Vital Statistics,"* pages 83-102 in *Essays on the Welfare State.* London: George Allen and Unwin, 1958.

Titmuss recounts some achievements of the woman's suffrage movement in Britain within the eighty years since its inception. Presented are vital statistics to chart the changes in woman's position since 1900, and delineate the pressing new problems thereby created for makers of social policy, since women are living longer, with a consequent increasing pressure on social services.

Titmuss points out that women past forty, for example, are able to contribute much more than society's opportunities make possible and scores prejudices and moral platitudes surrounding them. Changes in marital customs are also revealed, as the study focuses upon divorce rates and the lessening number of marriages broken by death before the age of sixty.

Tornius, Valerian. *The Salon, Its Rise and Fall: Pictures of Society through Five Centuries.* Translated by Agnes Platt. New York: B. Blom, 1971; London: Thornton Butterworth Ltd., 1929. 320 p. Index and bibliography. Illustrations.

Here we can find the familiar names of French *salonières* and many who are not so familiar, beginning with the Renaissance in Naples, which an admiring Tornius calls "the cradle of the Salon." In Florence Dante thundered misogynist epithets; in Naples Boccaccio and Castiglione good-humoredly countered with their admiration of women's intelligence and charm. Within the span of centuries Germany is represented by Karoline Flachsland, Luise von Ziegler, and Henriette von Roussillon of Darmstadt, among others.

It was Napoleon with his repressive régime who rang the death knell of the slow-paced, intellectual *salon*. His strictures against Mme de Staël, whom he drove into exile, were repeated for *salonière par excellence,* Mme de Récamier, de Staël's friend. Tornius regrets its passing, with little hope of its revival because of the materialism of modern society. "This continual preoccupation with material things, this incessant greed, give life a mechanical rhythm which can only find relief in sensationalism." Ruefully he asks women, (for men will never be able to recreate the delights of those conversational feasts), "When will women again be ready to act as leaders of social distinction and tradition, taking their place once more in the centre of all that is of greatest interest in their times?"

Short bibliographies of works in English, French, Italian, and German accompany each chapter.

Toth, Karl. ***Woman and Rococo in France.*** Translated by Roger Abington from *Weib und Rokoko in Frankreich; aus dem Erleben eines Zeitgenossen.*. Philadelphia: J. B. Lippincott, 1931 [1924]. 399 p.

Asserting that the eighteenth century in France was, contrary to general opinion, an age of mediocrity, Toth proposes to write its history around the figure of a mediocre man, Charles-Pinot Duclos, who is a "manly representative of this most feminine of epochs . . .who with a firm hand suppressed in himself the womanish neurosis of his time." It is apparent throughout the book that Toth approves neither of France nor women.

Nevertheless, the book makes fascinating reading because of the author's relaxed use of his vast scholarship, even though he often reaches out into vague and biased generalities to prove the superiority of German culture over the French, smarting because "the Frenchman has outdone [the German] in the world's affection." Thus Toth's work occasionally becomes a political diatribe.

Trotsky, Leon. *"Hands Off Rosa Luxembourg,"* in *Writings of Leon Trotsky* pages 131-142. English translations edited by George Breitman *et al.* New York: Pathfinder Press, 1973.

Trotsky dared defend Luxembourg (also spelled Luxemburg) against Stalin's "vile and barefaced calumny," saying how important it was to preserve a "beautiful, heroic, and tragic image to the young generation of the proletariat." Luxembourg, a Jewess (1871-1919), was a founder of the Polish Social Democratic Party and the most intelligent leader of the Marxists in Germany's post-World War I civil war. She was assassinated in 1919 in Berlin.

Turner, Justin G., and Linda Levitt Turner. *Mary Todd Lincoln: Her Life and Letters*. New York: From International, 1987. 750 p. (Reprint of Alfred A. Knopf 1972 edition.)

The 609 letters of Mary Lincoln, wife of President Abraham Lincoln, form a valuable part of this scholarly work, the reading of which will give an understanding of the unfortunate First Lady who suffered so much at the hands of the myth-makers, past and present. The Turners redress the uneven balance with a well-documented interpretation that is both sympathetic and honest.

Vaerting, Mathilde, and Mathias Vaerting. ***The Dominant Sex: A Study in the Sociology of Sex Differentiation.*** Translated from the German by Eden and Cedar Paul. Westport, Connecticut: Hyperion Press, 1980 [1923]. 289 p. Index. Bibliography.

The epigraph to this work, a pioneer in the field, is Spinoza's "Truth is the name we give to errors grown hoary with the centuries," and, as this implies, the authors are concerned with evaluating old concepts and adumbrating new ones. One new idea, the one around which the book revolves, is the theory that what we call "masculine" qualities today are merely the qualities of a dominant sex, and that what we call "feminine" qualities are merely the qualities of a subordinate sex. These qualities, they aver, are not congenital but are re-acquired from generation to generation. Men, however, are also seen as "oppressed" because they are forced into roles not necessarily related to their true personalities.

This, "a detailed study of the sociologic factors of sex differentiation," is a pioneer in its field. It has its historical aspects, too, for an analysis of the matriarchal era is used to emphasize the points the authors are making.

Van Doren, Carl. ***Jane Mecom, the Favorite Sister of Benjamin Franklin.*** New York: The Viking Press, 1960. 255 p.

Van Doren deserves applause for his belated act of justice to the "talented and long-suffering" Jane Mecom as he studies her personality through the letters she wrote to Franklin over a period of sixty years.

Most critics have viewed Van Doren's work as a contribution to further the understanding of the more famous brother, but J. H. Powell in the *Saturday Review of Literature* (October 21, 1950) calls it "a history of a private world into which, when he could, Franklin stepped," and terms this biography "an illuminated book, whose little beam reflects upon a diamond."

Vicinus, Martha, ed. ***Suffer and Be Still: Women in the Victorian Age.*** Bloomington: Indiana University Press, 1973. London: Methuen, 1980. 239 p.

Varied subjects pertinent to the Victorian *ethos* in regard to British women make this an appealing collection, in spite of the dismal title. Within the *potpourri* are overviews of the governess, Gilbert and Sullivan's characterizations, superstitions regarding health, painting (with illustrations), prostitution, working class women, the ideas of John Stuart Mill *vs* those of John Ruskin (with protests by Kate Millett), stereotypes of "femininity," and unconscious repression according to Freud.

Vicinus' observations concerning the "perfect Victorian lady" precede these essays, all by different authors. Added to this is a bibliographical essay of 500 entries on the effects of social change. Notes and an index enhance the research potential.

Vigman, Fred K. ***Beauty's Triumph, or The Superiority of the Fair Sex Invincibly Proved.*** Boston: Christopher Publishing House, 1966. 202 p. Bibliography.

The title of this polemic refers ironically to a bluestocking work published in 1739, for Vigman sees no "triumph" for the liberated woman, only the burden of neuroticism and a deep *malaise* in society as women are released from domesticity and its attendant values, mistakenly rejecting the "norm of feminine behavior" as formulated by patriarchal authority.

What Vigman has undertaken with such extravagant bias is "a social history of the rise of sex egalitarianism, gentility, feminism, and hedonist ideas of modern women and the consequences thereof, from the Renaissance to modern times." Henrik Ibsen's Hedda Gabler is seen as one of the symbols of modern female neuroticism. Vigman suggests that the task of the next fifty years should be to resolve the contradictions inherent in the "historical impasse" in order to rescue the American husband from his confusion and frustration.

Virey, Julien-Joseph. *De la femme sous ses rapports physiologique, moral et littéraire.* Paris: Chez Crochard, 1825.

Although many of the scientific ideas of this physician have been supplanted, his book is enlightening in that it enables the reader to become acquainted with the thought of the day and perhaps to sympathize with novelists in their desire to stand back from their own society to portray their heroines as real people.

Dr. Virey sees climate and race as crucial factors in the "varieties" of women; his approach is partly anthropological. In society he sees the "virtuous" woman as being a greatly-needed asset to a people, and his concluding section, "Dissertation sur le libertinage et ses dangers," is his contribution to the advancement of this idea, a contribution which displays well his intimate knowledge of Greek and Roman classical culture and demonstrates his far-sightedness.

Wagenhein, Leah. *"A Chat with Armando Palacio Valdès on Feminism."* Hispania, XII (November 1929), pp. 439-446.

Declaring himself "más feminista que las mismas señoras sufragistas de Inglaterra," Valdès tells interviewer Wagenheim the reason: English women want only the vote, but he wants for women the whole area of politics, including the administration of the judicial system. Men, he counsels, should devote themselves to business and the arts and sciences while women are wielding the scepter in the political world, certainly an iconoclastic new plan for the historical division of labor!

Waldeck, Rosie Goldschmidt. *Prelude to the Past: The Autobiography of a Woman*. New York: William Morrow, 1934. 375 p.

Insight into the effects of the First World War on the private lives of several women in Germany, Austria, and France is provided by this book, first published anonymously. Many harrowing truths are revealed from the standpoint of women as they suffer dislocation from their homes, the loss of the men they love, even in one case denunciation by the authorities on the charge of spying (of which this woman was acquitted). Speaking from a personal perspective Waldeck considers herself similar to most women in that her energies are directed toward finding happiness in love, but at the same time she is highly critical of marriage as a contemporary institution.

Watson, Foster, ed. *Vives and the Renascence Education of Women.* New York: Longmans, Green & Co.; London: Edward Arnold, 1912. 259 p. Index. (Available in photocopy from Ann Arbor University Microfilms, 1989. ["Out of Print Books on Demand."])

Watson presents excerpts from the writings of several influential sixteenth-century educators in Britain such as Richard Hyrde, Sir Thomas More, Sir Thomas Elyot, in addition to

Juan Luis Vives (1492-1540). Vives, a Spaniard, resided at the English court until 1528, during the time when the Spanish Catherine of Aragon, as Henry VIII's first wife, was queen.[35] In his introduction Watson praises Catherine, who had received a classical education in Spain, for initiating the interest in women's education which Vives did so much to encourage.

A feature of this work is the bibliography that lists early editions of the original writings, which were published in Latin, Castilian, German, and French, in addition to English. A Spanish translation of Watson's work entitled *Vives* was published in 1923 by Ediciones de la Lectura, Madrid.

Watson, Paul Barron. *Some Women of France.* Freeport, New York: Books for Libraries Press, 1969. (First publication in 1936 by Coward McCann, New York.) 269 p.

Watson's choice of the following seven women is based upon his belief that they had not so far received adequate scholarly attention: Héloïse, Isabeau de Bavière, Mme du Deffand, Mme de Staël, Delphine Gay, Marie d'Agoult, and Juliette Lambert.

Marie d'Agoult is known chiefly by her effort to arouse the French public to a more liberal attitude towards women's rights with her *Essai sur la liberté* (1847). Juliette Lambert, too, had strong feminist leanings and thus found herself target of the verbal attacks of such eminent misogynist figures as Proudhon.

Wedd, A. F., ed. *The Love Letters of Mary Hays (1779-1789).* London: Methuen, 1925. 250 p. Index.

---

[35] Vives' most noted work on the subject of women's education is *Instruction of a Christian Woman; A Plan of Studies for Girls, and The Duties of Husbands,* written around 1520. Available in translation by Foster Watson.

Wedd, a great-grandniece of Mary Hays, rescued these letters from oblivion, letters written to a lover who died before their marriage could take place. Mary's ten years of mourning were broken when she joined a circle of feminists and became acquainted with Mary Wollstonecraft and William Godwin. Mary's letters are interesting in themselves as they show the feelings of a woman who was "a strange mixture of prudery and boldness" in her time.

Included in this volume are some letters from Wollstonecraft in which she gives advice on being an independent woman: "It requires a great resolution to try rather to be useful than to please." She adds warningly that in spite of everything, "Your male friends still treat you like a woman," which meant, in their circles, like a Victorian lady.

Wellington, Amy. **Women Have Told: Studies in the Feminist Tradition.** Boston: Little, Brown and Company, 1930. 204 p.

Mary Wollstonecraft leads the short procession of "unfeminine" women. Others who join are Margaret Fuller, the Brontë sisters, Olive Schreiner, Charlotte Gilman, May Sinclair, Ellen Glasgow, and Rebecca West. "The feminist writers *are* the feminist tradition, declares Wellington.

Whitham, J. Mills. **Men and Women of the French Revolution.** (Essay Index Reprint Series.) Freeport, New York: Books for Libraries Press, 1968. 419 p. Index. Illustrated. (Originally published in 1933.)

Three chapters of this book are devoted to women: Chapter IV, "Mme Roland and the Salons," Chapter V, "Charlotte Corday and Liberalism," and Chapter VI, "Mme Tallien and the Thermidorean Reaction."

Whitham seeks to show how certain outstanding individuals helped to determine their own fate by their actions relative to their belief in the Rights of Man. He gives these seventeen rights on pages 398-400, provides a chronological table of events occurring during 1789 and 1799, and adds a bibliography.

Willard, Frances Elizabeth, and Mary A. Livermore, eds. *American Women: Fifteen Hundred Biographies.* 2 vols. Detroit, Michigan: Gale Research, 1973. 812 p. Index. (First published in New York in 1897 by Mast, Crowell, and Kirkpatrick, 1897.) Assisted by many able contributors, the editors produced a valuable encyclopedia of nineteenth-century women as a memorial to their lives and achievements which otherwise, considering the neglect of women by most historians, would have been lost to posterity.

Over 1400 word-portraits of the biographees grace the pages, providing countless sources of information for the researcher in women's studies—or the browser in any discipline related to history.

Woodsmall, Ruth Frances. *Moslem Women Enter a New World.* (Publications of the American University of Beirut, Social Science Series, no. 14.) New York: Ams Press, 1975. 432 p. Index. Illustrations. (Reprint of edition published by Round Table Press, New York, in 1936.)

The institution of *purdah* has always stirred the Western woman's imagination.[36] Woodsmall gives us the story of the

---

[36]The practice of *purdah* is the ancient custom of concealing women from men or

Moslem woman from a Western woman's point of view, for Woodsmall recounts her experiences in Iraq, Iran, India, Egypt, Palestine, Jordan, Syria, and Turkey to show how women in these nations were slowly becoming aware of themselves with a new vision (which, however, was later dimmed under some governments). Concomitant with this new awareness was their re-interpretation of religious teachings in regard to woman's status in the home and society. In an appendix Woodsmall sets forth the principal Koranic teachings about women.

Wright, Louis B. *Middle Class Culture in Elizabethan England.* (Huntington Library Publications.) Chapel Hill: University of North Carolina Press, 1935. Bibliography.

Chapter XIII, "The Popular Controversy over Women" (pages 465-507), gives a scholarly account of Renaissance England's version of the old *querelle des femmes.* The book is well worth reading for its exhaustive treatment of a middle class culture in which women shared, for even though woman's public life was restricted, she was beginning to make her influence felt in such areas as literature keenly felt.

Wright, Thomas. *Womankind in All Ages of Western Europe, from the Earliest Times to the Seventeenth century.* Boston: Longmans Press, 1978. (Originally published in London by Groombridge and Sons, 1870[?]). 340 p. Illustrations.

---

strangers by curtains at home or a veil and long coverings in public. In certain countries the requirement for observing this practice has been intensified as governments turned toward theocracy.

The major part of this work (pages 100-290) is devoted to the life of women in feudal society, especially in the French castle. The narrative moves informally and is livened by quotations from the courtly poetry of the day, while illustrations show costumes then worn by women, principally of the upper classes.

Other chapters feature women in ancient Gaul and Celtic Britain, and those in Teutonic nations (including the Anglo-Saxon), as well as Renaissance times.

Zassenhaus, Hiltgunt. ***Walls: Resisting the Third Reich--One Woman's Story.*** Boston: Beacon Press, 1993 [1974]. 247 p.

The twentieth century was the age of "total war" when women were as intimately involved in military affairs—except for actual combat ordered by governments—as men. Espionage and resistance activities, therefore, became ways in which women could bolster men's efforts (since war has historically almost entirely a male enterprise), work for peace, and give the word "heroine" a new meaning.

In her informally-written autobiography, *Baum bluht im November,* Zassenhaus, a German brought up in a family which dared to reject Nazism, reveals how she became a supposed member of the Gestapo and how she outwitted them, how she assisted foreign prisoners at great personal risk, including keeping track of all Scandinavian prisoners for Count Folke-Bernadotte's Swedish Red Cross rescue mission. After the war Zassenhaus received honors from Norway, Denmark, and West Germany. In 1974 she was nominated for the Swedish Nobel Peace Prize.

Women in Literature and the Arts

Women in Literature

Aldington, Richard, trans. *The Fifteen Joys of Marriage.* New York: Halcyon House, 1933 [1926]. 241 p.

Traditionally this fifteenth-century satire on women has been ascribed to Antoine de la Sale, although Aldington doubts his authorship. Taken from the French *Quinze joies de mariage* written in the 1760's, the subtitle reads: "with an addition of three comforts more, Wherein the various miscarriages of the wedded state, and the miserable consequences of rash and inconsiderate marriages are laid open and detected."

Naïvely, Aldington notes that it is "an innocent sort of book for all its malice. Its satire is not cruel, for it is far too obvious," as in Chaucer's "The Miller's Tale." Nevertheless, he does object to its sweeping generalizations about the "feminine mind," calling it over-simplification—the feminine mind is too complex to be constrained into de la Sale's narrow confines, he believes.

Anderson, James Edward. *Strange, Sad Voices: The Portraits of Germanic Women in the Old English "Exeter Book."*[1] Unpublished Ph.D. dissertation, University of Kansas, 1978. 244 p.

Anderson notes that the *Exeter Book* (*Codex Exoniensis*) contains all the important German "women's poems" in Old

---

[1] The *Exeter Book* is a collection of MMS given by Bishop Leofric to Exeter Cathedral, where it still remains in the library. They date from the eighth century.

English. In this unique poetry may be found brief observations on woman's place in Germanic society, a place which was rigidly defined, much more so than in Hebrew society, for example.

The legal status of a woman (a chattel) Anderson sees as the determining factor of her destiny among Germanic peoples: here he confirms this by showing how extensive is legal diction in the works he has chosen to study as reflections of Germanic society.

Appignanesi, Lisa. *Femininity and the Creative Imagination.* London: Vision Press, 1973. 320 p.

Femininity is defined on pages 1-19 in relation to the approach of this book, which is purely literary in scope and should not be looked upon as a "sociological mine for the pillaging of half-truths." Henry James, Robert Musil, and Marcel Proust serve here as "mines" to search for moral sensibility, completeness, and creativity respectively, according to Appignanesi's concept. Quotations from Proust and Musil are in English. A short bibliography and an index of names are included.

Balderston, Katharine L., ed. *Thraliana, or The Diary of Mrs. H. L. Thrale, 1776-1809.* 2 vols. Oxford: Clarendon Press, 1950 [1942].

Hester Thrale's diary is an unsurpassed sourcebook for English manners and letters in the late eighteenth century, for as a lady of means, charm, and intelligence Hester presided over a *salon* frequented by such imposing personalities as Dr. Samuel Johnson, James Boswell (her rival), Fanny Burney and Fanny's father, Charles Burney, the renowned music historian.

Hester knew everybody who was "anybody" in London society during the years of her heyday. Unfortunately, when after being widowed she married Signor Piozzi, her daughter's Italian music master, she became *déclassée* in the eyes of polite society, and all her erstwhile friends deserted her for marrying beneath her. Personal happiness was of little consequence in that rigid society.

Balderston's notes are helpful in clarifying the references in the text, as is the extensive index at the end of Volume II. This study was published in cooperation with the Huntington Library.

Bali, Om Prakash. ***The Treatment of Marriage in the Plays of Rachel Crothers.*** Unpublished doctoral dissertation, Miami University, 1979. 151 p.

Bali sees Crothers as fully aware of the ambiguities in women's struggle for self-fulfillment and their search for identity. Yet Crotherss seems unwilling to insist that radical change is needed, for the emotional needs of her characters reveal that they (and women in general, she seems to say) are dependent upon upon male attitudes which preclude their true independence of spirit.

Barish, Jonas A. *"Ovid, Juvenal, and The Silent Woman," PMLA,* 71 (1956), pp. 213-224.

According to Barish, Jonson is attempting to achieve the courtly effect when he tries to combine Ovid's worldliness with his own rather Juvenalian moralizing. As a result, this leads the playwright into a dilemma which prevents him from realizing the harmony he seeks in the creation of *The Silent Woman.*

Barreno, Maria Isabel, *et al. **The Three Marias: New Portuguese Letters.*** Translated by Helen R. Lane. Garden City, New York: Doubleday, 1975. 432 p.

Translated from the Portuguese, this is the "mutinous" book that so shocked the 1972 Lisbon government that they precipitated a *cause célèbre* by arresting and banning the authors. Fortunately, that government was replaced by a more liberal one before the three Marias (the other two are Maria Teresa Horta and Maria Fatima Velho da Costa) could be sentenced, and the case was dismissed.

The book itself consists of letters, poems, essays, and stories which the three Marias exchanged weekly, voicing their strong protest against the cruelty of the repression and exploitation of women in Portugal.

Basch, Françoise. ***Relative Creatures: Victorian Women in Society and the Novel.*** New York: Schocken Books, 1974. 360 p. Index and bibliography.

Basch combines social history and literary criticism to make a readable and thoughtful assessment of the well-trod ground of Victorian feminism, offering much detail that serves as a backdrop for her original interpretations. Attention is given to often-forgotten heroines in novels of both women and men writers, heroines whom Basch sees as reflections of the society.

Baudin, Maurice. ***The Profession of King in Seventeenth Century French Drama.*** (The Johns Hopkins Studies in Romance Literatures and Languages, Vol. XXXVIII.) Baltimore, Maryland: The Johns Hopkins Press, 1941.

In Chapter III, pages 51-63, "The Stateswoman," Baudin sees the politically-minded woman portrayed in drama as a "woman who, confronted by a tradition denying to women the capacity to rule, was usually content to advise, or to rule from behind the throne," but who occasionally showed a remarkable skill in the art of reigning.

To illustrate this, Baudin surveys the rationale for this denial of equal authority in the wielding of power, bolstering his remarks with copious references to such authorities as Aeschylus (as in *Agamemnon*), Erasmus, Calvin, Rabelais, and Montaigne, who are not willing, he concludes, to grant women full power. Nevertheless, he also points out that writers like Corneille (in *Livée*) and Racine (in *Athalie*) show the reverse—that women have the ability if given the opportunity (for weal or woe).

Baumal, Francis. *Le Féminism au temps de Molière.* (Bibliothèque International de Critique.) Paris: Renaissance du Livre, 1923. 162 p.

Baumal sees the aspirations of the women of the *bourgeoisie* set upon the greater freedom accorded to women of the aristocracy in France. Molière's dramatic treatment of the social tensions created by *bourgeois* feminism is reviewed in the light of this evolutionary tendency which the aristocracy wanted to to check.

Bayerschmidt, Carl F. *Sidgrid Undset.* (Twayne World Author Series.) New York: Twayne Publishers, Inc., 1970. 176 p. Bibliography and index.

A strong sense of the importance of the individual is part the Norwegian temperament: this made it natural that the Norwegians were the first to grant the suffrage to women. But had that changed life for women? For Undset there had to be another dimension for women than political rights; there also had to be religious faith to give meaning. For her that faith was found in Catholicism, says Bayerschmidt.

Undset's absorbing novel, *Kristin Lavransdatter*, which won for her a Nobel Prize, is a well-researched saga in three volumes appearing from 1920 to 1922, *The Bridal Wreath*, *The Mistress of Husaby*, and *Korset (The Cross)*. It is set in Norway of the Middle Ages (Undset had a keen interest in Old Icelandic and Celtic literatures as well).

As a devoted Catholic in her social novels Undset sets forth high ideals for women (and men as well). But her method is not to present strictly moral heroines: they have to make their mistakes and suffer for them. Almost always Undset's writings revolved around the concerns of a woman—how could she blend both regard for self and need, or even craving, for love (which most of them seem never to attain), how could she develop autonomy and at the same time fulfill others' expectations of her (so that she would be loved)? Will her decisions compromise one or the other of these—or even both? But over all, can these needs be melded into a happy marriage? A procession of Undset's heroines grapple with these questions.

Beaty, Jerome. *"Middlemarch" from Notebook to Novel: A Study of George Eliot's Creative Methods*. (Illinois Studies in Language and Literature, Vol. 47.) Urbana: University of Illinois Press, 1960. 134 p. Bibliography.

Though not written with an eye to identifying methods of creation peculiar to female writers, this work may be of interest to those who care to study the ways of the imagination in order to determine whether the female intellect differs essentially in kind or in use of energy.

Bedford, Herbert. *The Heroines of George Meredith.* Port Washington, New York: Kennikat Press, 1972. 166 p. (Originally published in 1914.)

George Meredith is generally known as a champion of women, as he uses novels to impart ideas which were iconoclastic in his time. He proved himself to be more in tune with the growing woman's movement than with more timid novelists who shrank from being "outsiders" as Meredith was. Here Bedford has mined twelve of Meredith's works for female characterizations. One might assume that these heroines have strong feminist opinions, but Bedford points out that this is not necessarily the case: they are not women fighting for freedom or spokeswomen for a cause; the heroines represent women as they are in general. But such women as Diana of *Diana of the Crossways* show by their words that they are conscious of the disadvantages of being a woman in Victorian society, even though they may have position and connections. Bedford uses examples from the novels as illustrations to support his findings.

Bettelheim, Bruno. *The Uses of Enchantment: The Meaning and Importance of Fairy Tales.* London: Thames and Hudson, 1976. New York: Alfred A. Knopf, 1977. 323 p. Index and bibliography.

Much of the wisdom that has been handed down to us orally is called "old wives' tales", but who has heard of "old husbands' tales" as possible keys to the understanding of life? Even the folk tales which feature men (such as the "Three Wishes" and "The Fisherman and His Wife") revolve around women's wishes. (The only lesson to be learned from these is that women are never satisfied in their desire for material goods, an unimaginative conclusion.) The figures of females are pivotal in most of the tales. The "Sleeping Beauty" is a girl, of course, and in "Hansel and Gretel" the stepmother plays a crucial role, while the witch, too, is female. The story of Cinderella and her troubles (with a stepmother and two sisters) and eventual triumph teach traditional social values to girls even before they can read. We are not sure of the gender of the wolf, but certainly Little Red Riding Hood and her grandmother were female.

Bettelheim's book does not use womanhood *per se* as a theme, for he looks upon fairy tales as characteristic of the culture as a whole, but one can hardly miss the implications as he presents his interpretations, which he leans toward Freudian and Jungian psychology. Seven out of the eight famous tales he chooses for extensive analysis in Part Two deal with females, only one, "Jack and the Beanstalk," about males. Within Part One the "*The Goose Girl:* Achieving Autonomy" is of especial interest.

Since Bettelheim is convinced that the reading of fairy tales assists children in divining the meaning of life, and since most such stories are of keener interest to girls, one wonders if these can be partly responsible for the female's greater interest in the psychological concerns of interpersonal relationships, while males are so often criticized for their lack of interest or insensitivity to them. Bettelheim's work is provocative of further research for those interested in a combination of women's studies, psychoanalysis, and folklore. The book has been translated into Italian as *Il mondo incantato* (Milan, 1978) and German as *Kinder brauchen Marchen* (Stuttgart, 1977).

Bloch, R. Howard. *"The Arthurian Fabliau and the Poetics of Virginity,"* pages 231-249 in *Continuations: Essays on Medieval French Literature and Language, in Honor of John L. Grigsby,* edited by Norris J. Lacy and Gloria Torrini-Goblin. Birmingham, Alabama: Summa Publications, 1989.

Bloch begins by describing the chastity testing *motif* found in certain courtly romances: supposedly, the test reveals the impossibility of finding a woman who can pass the test. Instead of further analysis of the *fabliaux,* however, Bloch turns to the biblical story of Creation to analyze the situation in which the first human couple find themselves—what does it mean that Eve is created after Adam? From this scene he travels to misogynist patristic writers who confounded themselves to the point of desperation by trying to define a virgin, or even virginity as a quality. As Bloch comments, "A certain inescapable logic of virginity, most evident in medieval hagiography, leads syllogistically to the conclusion that the only good virgin—that is, the only true virgin—is a dead virgin."

Thus very early the apologetics of misogyny stained Western thought, with its legacy of anti-feminist writings. These concepts, combined with the comic spirit of the medieval poets and singers, gave rise to the earthy *fabliau,* the farce, and other types which perpetuated the symbolisms marking woman's inferiority and deceitfulness derived from Genesis. Chaucer, Boccaccio, Jean de Meung, and Antoine de la Sale figure here also.

Block, Toni, "Shaw's Women." *Modern Drama,* II, no. 2 (1959), pp. 133-138.

Bernard Shaw had a predilection for strong women, says Block, and here she presents a few of them who figured in his life: Jenny Patterson, May Morris, Ellen Terry, Stella Campbell, Charlotte Payne-Townsend, and two family members, Grandmother Shaw and Shaw's own mother, Bessie Gurley Shaw, who was called "the worst of all possible mothers."

Shaw's feminist leanings encouraged him to call upon such women as these as prototypes for his often iconoclastic plays and their frank portrayals of "unfeminine women."

Bluestone, George. *Novels into Film.* Berkeley: University of California Press, 1966. 237 p. Bibliography and index.

Bluestone compares the two vehicles of novel and cinema for their adequacy in conveying to the reader/viewer certain ideas and situations for which some novels have become classics. After his theoretical analyses, he uses a number of movies to show how successful the transfer from book to motion picture has been. Of these three have focused on women or the novels by women: Jane Austen's *Pride and Prejudice,* Emily Brontë's *Wuthering Heights,* and Flaubert's *Madame Bovary.* Least successful, he believes, was the screening of the last.

Interestingly written, Bluestone's work is made more useful by the frequent use of footnotes which point to topical criticism of other films.

Boccaccio, Giovanni. *Concerning Famous Women.* Translated with an introduction and notes by Guido A. Guarino. New Brunswick, New Jersey: Rutgers University, 1987 [1963]. 257 p. Illustrations.

Guarino's work is a translation of *De claribus mulieribus* (1355-59), based on the edition of Mathias Apiarus (Berne, 1539), which reproduces all the biographies of women written by Boccaccio.

The purpose of this edition, says Guarino, is "to render Boccaccio's work accurately into readable English" with a style compatible with a "quaint air." He succeeds in producing a clear and entertaining work, one that has added importance in that it makes more accessible the ideas of a writer whose literary influence on the subject of women was almost without parallel in western Europe and Britain. (Boccaccio has a mixed reputation: he is often called a pro-feminist.)

Bolster, Richard. *Stendahl, Balzac, et le féminisme romantique.* Paris: Menard, 1970. 226 p.

Bolster perceives the rising expression of feminine discontent in the early years of the nineteenth century as "one of the great social movements of those revolutionary times, in which the French Revolution and the rise of romanticism were outstanding phenomena."[2] To show how woman's concerns were reflected in contemporary writings, Bolster examines what he considers feminist leanings in the works of novelists like Stendahl and Balzac, along with other male writers such as Sénacour, Laclos, Fourier, and Saint-Simon.

Although the author's effort is worthwhile, his evidence is often less than convincing. Nevertheless, it can be useful for the critical reading of these Frenchmen. Were romanticism and feminist thought compatible?

Bomli, P. W. *La Femme dans l'Espagne du siècle d'or.* La Haye: Martin Nijhoff, 1950. 390 p. Index and bibliography.

---

[2] Stendahl was the pseudonym for Henri Beyle.

Bomli acknowledges that one of the problems in writing a book on this subject is that primary sources are often lacking, since the women of Golden Age Spain were rarely articulate concerning themselves and their lifestyle, or if they were, posterity does not have the benefit of the record.[3] Therefore, he decides, it is necessary to rely upon literature written by men and the accounts of a few travelers, principally Mme d'Aulnoy's *Relation du voyage d'Espagne* (1691) for a good part of the testimony. Unfortunately, the authenticity of Mme d'Aulnoy's accounts has been questioned. (See R. Foulché-Delbosc.)

Quotations from contemporary Spanish literature abound in this work. Lope de Vega, well-known for his capricious treatment of women, is especially evident. Lope, like France's Molière, satirized the learned women of his day, but Bomli carefully identifies many of these neglected Spanish *sabias* (*femmes savantes*), who have not often received attention from literary historians.

This is a valuable and fascinating work, and Bomli has provided an index and bibliography for the researcher.

Bonne, Rena Barbara. **"The Female Presence in the Novels of Virginia Woolf and Colette."** Unpublished Ph.D. dissertation, Case Western Reserve University, 1979. 214 p.

The maternal figure is Bonne's first preoccupation as she studies these writers' works to discover their concepts of feminine sexuality. Her findings lead her to stress that both Woolf and Colette find almost insuperable difficulties in the woman-

---

[3] Compare the similar situation regarding women in other places, as brought out by Finley and Brée (*q.v.*).

man relationship, and therefore they imply that the androgynous mind may bring escape or balance to a woman's life.

Bourciez, Edouard Eugène Joseph. *Les Moeurs et la littérature de cour sous Henry II.* Genève: Slatkine Reprints, 1967. 437 p. (Originally published at Paris, 1886, as a doctoral dissertation.)

Since the court of Henry II (1547-1559) was dominated by his wife, Catherine de Medicis, and his mistress, Diane de Poitiers, it is natural that Bourciez's book is replete with comments about the ladies at the court.

Henri's court is noted for its revival of the manners and customs of chivalry. On pages 89-100 Bourciez considers the heroines of the popular romances of chivalry, especially the *Amadis de Gaule,* including a detailed contrast between the Spanish and French characterizations of Oriane (pp. 363-373), who in the legends is the lady love of the hero Amadis.

Bowman, Frank Paul. *"Suffering, Madness, and Literary Creation in Seventeenth Century Spiritual Autobiography," French Forum,* I (1976), pp. 24-48.

The "spiritual autobiographies" of seventeenth century mystics reveal "a personality in a crisis bordering on madness, which crisis is transformed into coherence by the autobiographical act," says Bowman. Thus we can glean valuable insights not only from contemporary mysticism but also we may learn about the relation between language and being.

Four women mystics are considered here: Saint Marguerite (Marie Alacoque), Mme de Guyon, Antoinette Bourignon, and Jean des Anges.

Bradford, Gamaliel. *Elizabethan Women.* Edited by Harold Ogden White. (Select Bibliographies Reprint Series.) New York: Books for Libraries Press, 1969. 243 p. (First published in 1936.) Index.

This collection consists of essays written by Bradford, the Elizabethan scholar, between 1890 and 1910 as guides to the appreciation of women's role in Elizabethan life and their representation in literature.

Singled out for extended discussion are the characters created by playwrights Dekker, Heywood, Middleton, Webster, Beaumont and Fletcher, Massinger, Ford, Shirley, and Spenser. Meriting Bradford's especial attention is the portrayal of Cleopatra in its varied ways in contemporary drama.

Brater, Enoch, ed. *Feminine Focus: The New Women Playrights.* New York: Oxford University Press, 1989. 283 p. Index.

Brater has gathered together essays by fifteen writer-critics who present detailed analyses of the work of innovative dramatists who in their resistance to "marginalization" find drama a "forum for the exploration of the full dimension of that greatest collection of all—our own humanity." To enhance the written word and stress the idea of a forum, oral interviews are used also.

Some of the writers featured here are Caryl Churchill, Ariane Mnouchkine,, Elin Diamond, Susan Glaspell, Helene Keyssar, and Leslie Kane.

Braun, Sidney D. *The "Courtisane" in the French Theatre from Hugo to Becque (1831-1885).* (The Johns Hopkins Studies in Romance Literatures and Languages, Extra Volume, XXII.) Baltimore, Maryland: The Johns Hopkins Press, 1947. Index and bibliography (pp. 145-159).

Braun's purpose is to identify French attitudes toward the *courtisane* as a recognized type which attained prominence first in Greece, where the word *hetaira* ("companion") was an honorable appellation. With La Fontaine the *courtisane* became a literary type in France.

Braun explicates terms used to describe *courtisane*-like women and illustrates these concepts more clearly by literary examples to show the changes in social attitudes toward such problems as marriage customs and divorce. Becque and Dumas *fils* especially encouraged a growing tendency to de-typify women and portray them as human beings.

Bravo-Villasante, Carmen. *La Mujer vestida de hombre en el teatro español (siglos XVI-XVII)*. Madrid: Revista de Occidente, 1955. 238 p. Index.

An excellent survey of the reasons for women's concealing their identity in the Spanish plays of this era: the wish to follow one's lover, to go to war for adventure, to avenge the death of a male relative, to seize power for herself or another, and other excuses. Illuminating examples from the plays are included, the textual notes are invaluable, and a bibliography is provided on pages 7-16.

Bravo-Villasante, Carmen. *La Vida y obra de Emilia Pardo Bazán.* Madrid: Revista de Occidente, 1962. 392 p. Index and illustrations.

Bazán was a prolific writer in the naturalistic tradition who was also an astute champion of feminism—probably the outstanding one of her place and time, nineteenth century Spain. Here Bravo-Villasante presents a biography of Bazán, along with a bibliography of her works, on pages 309-351.

Braybrooke, Patrick. *Some Goddesses of the Pen.* London: C. W. Daniel Company, 1927. 156 p

    Braybrooke's guiding principle was "to select those who are most diverse one from the other." Therefore he eschews comparisons and considers on their own merits Sheila Kaye-Smith, Rose Macaulay, Ethel H. Dell, Baroness Orczy, Mrs. Alfred Sidgewick, Mrs. Henry de la Pasture, and Mrs. Baillie-Reynolds. Plentiful quotations from the works of all the women lend fascination to the re-visiting of these writers, some of them whose fame has faded, some who have gained in attention.

Brée, Germaine. *Women Writers in France: Variations on a Theme.* New Brunswick, New York: Rutgers University Press, 1973. 90 p.

    The theme of this Brown and Haley lecture is the ancient and still vital *querelle des femmes*. Brée sees the French literary tradition, even that now in the making, as "obviously unfavorable to women writers," as she points out how literary historians, through selection, determine that women will not be remembered—assuming that literary criticism remains in the hands of men. Her pessimistic appraisal scores the courtly tradition for having made of woman an *objet d'art*.

Brenier de Montmorand, Antoine François. *Une femme poète du XVIIe siècle: Anne de Graville, sa vie, son oeuvre, sa posterité*. Paris: Auguste Picard, 1917. 328 p.

    Anne de Graville is placed in her *milieu*, the late fifteenth and early sixteenth centuries, as the author emphasizes both her erudition and her sympathy for the Reformation. Anne was an ancestor of the writer Honor d'Urfé, de Montmorand tells us, but he insists that she should be admired for her own merits, which have not generally been acknowledged.

An appendix, pp. 273-285, gives a list of books in Anne's personal library. Copious page notes accompany the text of this valuable study.

Brewer, Pat Bryan. *"Females, Fiction, and the Negro Image: The Negro as Reflected in the Work of Southern Female Writers of Fiction."* Unpublished master's thesis, Vanderbilt University, 1969. 205 p. Bibliography.

In the first section of this study, representative works by Ellen Glasgow, Elizabeth Madox Roberts, Caroline Gordon, Katherine Anne Porter, Eudora Welty, and Carson McCullers are examined to trace the development of the Negro image in their writings. The second section delves more deeply into the fiction of younger writers Flannery O'Conner, Elizabeth Spencer, and Shirley Ann Grau to discern any differences between their concepts and those of earlier writers.

Brewer sees the "humanizing interpretation of the Negro character" being carried on by the younger generation in an effort to find ways of dealing with the race problem in the South. (Also see Putnam's *The Lady* for a chapter on upper class women in the states where slavery existed.)

Broe, Mary Lynn, and Angela Ingram, eds. *Women's Writing in Exile.* Chapel Hill, University of North Carolina Press, 1989. 442 p.

Metaphorical as well as physical exile is explored in this collection of studies by women of various backgrounds. Virginia Woolf is an example of the former, for in *A Room of One's*

Own she describes graphically the sensation of being "alien" while walking in home territories.

Bryan, Margaret B. *"Volumnia—Roman Matron or Elizabethan Huswife?" Renaissance Papers,* 1972, pp. 43-58.

Instead of portraying Coriolanus' mother as the classic Roman matron, Shakespeare gives her a double identity which veers sharply from the expected, writes Bryan. At the beginning of *Coriolanus* Volumnia is seen as a dignified Renaissance lady, but by the time the play ends she appears as an ordinary violent Elizabethan woman who reflects the theme of the play, "disorder is the microcosm."

Bulliet, Clarence J. *Venus Castina: Famous Female Impersonators, Celestial and Human.* New York: Covici, Friede, 1928. 308 p. Illustrations.

The Venus Castina was the understanding goddess of "feminine souls locked up in male bodies"—gods, demi-gods, princes, heroes, priests, mystics, degenerates, rogues, souls of all kinds.

Bulliet searches history and dramatic literature for devotees of this goddess, beginning with Achilles, Hercules, and Samson of mythical fame, and running the gamut to the nineteenth century, with Rimbaud, Swinburne, and Walt Whitman seen as acolytes of the unconventional goddess.

Burney, Fanny. *Diary and Letters of Madame d'Arblay.* Edited by Charlotte Barrett. 4 vols. (English Gentleman's Library.) London: Bickers and Son, 1876[?].

Fanny Burney (1742-1840) has left us a diary that is unsurpassed as a sourcebook for the details of a young woman's life in her epoch and social station. Highly intelligent, she looked with a critical (and dismayed) eye at the differences with which females and males were treated, whether in private life, in society or in literature.

Although her rebellion found expression only in her diary (which she addressed as "Nobody"), very little escaped her scrutiny. In later years she probably would have been called a feminist for such entries as: "Why, permit me to ask, must a female be made Nobody? Ah, my dear, what were this world good for, *were* Nobody a female?" Although for many years the idea of marriage was repugnant to her ("O how short a time does it take to put an eternal end to a woman's liberty!"), late in life she was fortunate enough to meet and marry the Frenchman Alexandre d'Arblay, who not only "allowed" her to write but actively helped her.

Although for a time she was inhibited by the fear that she would be criticized and scorned for unladylike "scribbling," Fanny's first novel, *Evelina,* (published before anyone knew the author was a woman), was a hit of the literary season, praised even by the usually dour Dr. Samuel Johnson, who welcomed her into his select coterie where he held court at Mrs. Thrale's *salon.* Not bad for a young girl whose father had affectionately called her his "little dunce" because she, the slowest of the family, did not learn to read and write until she was eleven.[4]

Cameron, Edith. *"Women in Don Quijote,"* Hispania, IX (1926), pp. 137-157.

---

[4] Mrs. Burney taught her children to read and write. This was the only formal schooling Fanny had. She was offered the opportunity to go to school in France with her sisters, but she declined, preferring to educate herself in the extensive family library.

In this useful article Cameron gives a list of female characters in *Don Quijote*, with comments from Cervantes regarding them. She classifies them in relation to their social and civil position, along with their philosophic attitudes toward life (realistic, romantic, idealistic).

Cameron sums up Cervantes' attitudes under the rubrics that bear upon marriage, love, home, beauty, chastity, and so forth, concluding that these attitudes are "democratic and reverent."

Camproux, Charles. *Le Joy d'amor des troubadours.* Montpellier: Causse et Castelnau, 1965. 209 p.

The tone of the book is set by the first chapter, "Amour et civilisation," after which Camproux leads us in a scholarly way through the stages of love to that *joie d'amour* which is the pure love of others described as *amour parfait* in Marguerite de Navarre's *Heptameron* and as found in the utopian atmosphere of Rabelais' *Abbey de Thélème.*

Chapter VI, "La Femme," pages 98-111, considers female troubadours and comments upon the idea of the equality of the sexes implicit in the world of courtly love. In this chapter Camproux returns to the theme of liberty which he has touched upon earlier.

Carroll, Mitchell. *Greek Women.* (Woman in All Ages and in All Countries.) Philadelphia: The Rittenhouse Press, 1908.

Greek literature in which women's influence is central is given close attention by Carroll (pages 41-129). His discerning interpretations add new distinction to the women of the heroic age as he downplays the wars and warriors who are usually featured in discussions of Homer's epics. One finds an unusual way of looking at events in Chapter III, "The Women of the *Iliad,*" and in Chapter IV, "The Women of the *Odyssey.*"

Chapter V, "The Lyric Age," comments about the epic poet Hesiod (c. 800 B.C.), unhappily responsible for the myth of Pandora who, like Eve, supposedly caused all the misery mankind must suffer. Carroll points out that in this new age the idea of woman shows a marked decline from the respect accorded her in the Homeric sagas.

In Chapter VI, "Sappho," Carroll joins the many poets and scholars—even among her contemporaries—who have praised the exquisite poetry of the "first great historical woman of Greece" (c. 700 B.C.)—and speaking from the perspective of our own age we may call her the first feminist, a woman who never wore the mask of hypocrisy and who, highly educated, had devoted her poetic gift to Aphrodite.

Unfortunately, only fragments of Sappho's work exist. Carroll has quoted from them to illustrate her thought. An intriguing part of Carroll's work for literary historians is his reference to the nineteenth-century discovery of more of Sappho's poetry, such as a 20-line fragment within the Oxyrhynchus papyri, discovered by English archeologists in a dig in Middle Egypt in the years 1896-1909.

Castiglione, Baldesar. ***The Book of the Courtier.*** Translated by Charles E. Singleton. Garden City, New York: Doubleday & Company, 1959. 387 p. Index. Illustrations.

Il Cortegiano (*The Courtier*), written in 1528, has been regarded as the "courtesy book" *par excellence,* and as such it has been of incomparable influence upon the manners and literature of Europe as it became a code book for the upper classes.

In form the *The Courtier* is a record of sprightly conversations held by a group of courtiers, women and well as men, on subjects ranging from events and personages of classical times to the conduct of their contemporaries. Of special interest are the exchanges featured in Book Three, where the focus of the discussion is determining what is the perfect woman, for the *querelle des femmes* fascinates them all. One will find arguments on both sides. The ideas of such speakers as Magnifico Giuliano became a guide for the "perfect lady" for many years to come.

Cazamian, Louis. *Le roman social en Angleterre (1830-1850)*. New York: Russell and Russell, 1967.

Chapter III, pages 110-160, are of interest, as it deals with Eleanor Gaskell (1810-1865) and her "interventionisme chrétien,"the moral tone of her writings. Cazamian points out while other women writers touch on industrial questions lightly, Gaskell's theme is that of social responsibility in an age of widening capitalism, with increasing misery the lot of the working classes. She shows her characters trying to find ways of adjusting to the new, less human environment confronting them. One of the ways she suggests is that of religion, which Cazamian identifies as the crucial social force of the period he analyzes.

Cazaux, Yves, ed. *Mémoires et autres écrits de Marguerite Valois.* Paris: Mercure de France, 1971. 333 p.

The indomitable and gifted Marguerite (1586-1615) wrote her *mémoires* at the age of forty while imprisoned in the castle of Usson by order of her brother, Henry III, because of her participation in conspiracies against him. After gaining her freedom in 1605, she lost her royal husband, Henry IV, to Marie de Médicis because of her childlessness. Thereafter she lived in independent magnificence in Paris till her death, having retained her queenly title after the divorce.

In preparing this copiously annotated work with the collaboration of Henry Barbiche, Cazeau uses the first edition of Marguerite's writings as his source.

Chabrol, Claude. *Le Récit feminine.* (Approaches to Semiotics, no. 15.) The Hague; Paris: Mouton, 1971. 142 p.

The Frenchwoman as mirrored in the periodical *Elle* and others of its kind is the focus of this study. Chabrol asserts that to read these magazines is to gain glimpses of the state of relationships between women and men within the society. But the question is, he asks, can one rely on them for a true picture, or only a flawed reflection?

Charles, Edwin. *Some Dickens Women.* London: T. Werner Laurie, 1926. 350 p. Index.

Characters of the "softer sex" (Charles' term) from Dickens' novels are introduced here in the persons of Sairey Gamp, Dora, Mrs. Nickleby, Madame Defarge, Betsy Trotwood, and others. Abundant passages from the novels highlight Charles' belief that Dickens had a high regard for women, admiring especially their acumen and their capacity for self-sacrifice, often a necessary quality in Victorian times.

Charrier, Charlotte. *Héloïse dans l'histoire et dans la légende.* (Bibliothèque de la Littérature Comparée, tome 102.) Paris: Librairie Ancien Honor Champion, 1933.

Charrier divides her work into two parts: Part I,"L'histoire d'Héloïse," considers the sources of our knowledge of Héloïse and Abélard's love affair with its happiness, subsequent troubles, separation, then the death of both lovers. Charrier's work is tradition-shattering, for she argues that Abélard changed the wording of their love-letters for his own glory and other unworthy reasons; and she gives proof for her statements by citing the unique extant letter which is known to have been written by Héloïse.

Part II—"La légende d'Héloïse," notes that the medieval period showed indifference to the story of the lovers after its initial popularity had waned. After the medieval period, however, came accounts by Jean de Meung, François Villon, Petrarch, Bussy-Rabutin, Dom Gervaise, Alexander Pope, Colardeau, Rousseau, Remusat, and other lesser known writers in all ages, some sympathetic, some definitely not. The period of the greatest enthusiasm for this story was from 1675 to 1875.

The bibliography (pages 597-655) includes editions of the original Latin of the correspondence, as well as editions in other languages with Latin translations. Many scholarly notes encourage more research on this intriguing subject.

Collis, Louise. *The Apprentice Saint: Memoirs of a Medieval Woman.* London: Michael Joseph; New York: Perennial Library, 1983. 269 p. Index, bibliographical references.

Collis tells the heartening story of Margery Burnham Kempe, who was born ca. 1373 in Bishop's Lynn (King's Lynn) in Norfolk, also the birthplace of Fanny Burney. At an advanced age Margery felt impelled to write her memoirs, but she could not read. Undiscouraged, she learned to read for that purpose and subsequently produced the first extant autobiography written in English, *The Book of Margery Kempe.*

Chapter XXV, "St. Bridget's Example," describes one of Kempe's inspirations—a woman who was born in 1303, had eight children, and achieved sainthood.

Cornillon, Susan Koppelman, ed. *Images of Women in Fiction: Feminist Perspectives.* Bowling Green, Ohio: Bowling Green University Popular Press, 1972. 399 p. Index.

Cornillon has brought together a group of thoughtful essays which speak to the concerns of women: "The Woman as Heroine," "The Invisible Woman," "The Woman as Hero," and "Feminine Aesthetics." A useful bibliography can be found on pages 355-391.

Couch, John Philip. *George Eliot in France: A French Appraisal of George Eliot's Writings, 1858-1960.* (University of North Carolina Studies in Comparative Literature, No. 41.) Chapel Hill: University of North Carolina Press, 1967. 199 p.

Couch offers a conscientious study that traces the fortunes of Eliot's novels and sets her in perspective with other English writers within the intellectual pattern of the times. The mystery of why Eliot was not accepted by contemporary French critics, except for Montégut and Scherer, until after her death is explained in part by the label "morally unsafe" attached to her works at a time when "respectability" was at its height.

Copious bibliographical notes giving sources of French criticism are included, and the index indicates subjects as well as persons.

Crandall, Coryl, ed. *Swetnam the Woman Hater: The Controversy and the Play.* Lafayette, Indiana: Purdue University Press, 1969. 164 p.

Along with providing a modern edition of the 1620 play by Joseph Swetnam, Crandall sets forth the backgrounds of the feminist/anti-feminist controversy that was vivid in the minds of the popular reading public. Also included here are some feminist responses to Swetnam's misogynist drama.

Crane, Thomas Frederick. *Italian Social Customs of the Sixteenth Century and Their Influences upon the Literatures of Europe.* New Haven: Yale University Press, 1920. 689 p.

Because the subject of women was of such moment to sixteenth century Italians of the upper classes, numerous references to love, beauty, and the role of women (including *la querelle des femmes*) can be found in this scholarly and well-written work. Bibliographical notes assist the reader further in locating pertinent primary material, especially in the Italian literature of this period, and the detailed table of contents, as well as a good index enhance the work's value.

Crocenti, Lelia. *Narratrici d'oggi.* Cremona: Gianni Mangiarotti, 1966. 126 p.

Alba de Cespedes, Fausta Cialente, Elsa Morante, Natalia Ginzburg, Beatrice Solinas Donghi, and Leda Muccini are the subjects of Crocenti's critical essays which have comparative accents in references to Jane Austen, Baudelaire, Freud, Kafka, Proust, and Verlaine.

Cruppi, Louise. *Femmes écrivains d'aujourd'hui, I: Suède.* Paris: A. Fayard, 1912. 487 p.

Cruppi approaches her substantial study of Swedish literature by beginning with the year 1845, progresses through the naturalist school of writers to the feminist Ellen Key, and closes with a study of Selma Lagerlöf, the novelist. An appendix gives the principal works of each writer considered and lists the French translations of her work. Cruppi's choice of chronology brings her well into the twentieth century.

Cruz Rueda, Angel. *Mujeres de Azorín.* Madrid: Biblioteca Nueva, 1953. 296 p. Index.

This sympathetic analysis is intended to penetrate the soul of the "lovely women" who inhabit the many volumes of Azorín, portrayed as "lovely" whether they are *viejas, criadas, esposas, religiosas, pecadoras, comediantas,* or others possessed of a unique *persona.* This is evidently a subject which fascinates Cruz Rueda, as can be noted in his "Despedido," pages 289-292, which lacks the arrogant, judicial tone of many other Spanish works about women. (Azorín is the pseudonym of José Martínez Ruiz)

Debower, Lore Loftfield, ed. *"Le Livre de trois vertus of Christine de Pisan."* Unpublished Ph.D. dissertation, University of Massachusetts, 1979. 426 p.

Here is presented the text of Christine's best-known work, composed in 1415 and hitherto unedited, as it appears in the Boston Public Library manuscript (Medieval French MS 101). This is preceded by an introduction which gives a valuable overview of Christine's life and work. Unique in her time, Christine earned money by her pen and at the same time set forth well-reasoned ideas directed toward women, ideas that are still fresh and relevant today.

Dédéyan, Charles. *Madame de LaFayette.* Paris: Société d'Éditions d'Enseignement Supérieur, 1965. 301 p.

Mme de LaFayette's *La Princesse de Clèves* (1678) has been called the first psychological novel for its minute revelations of the nuances of her characters' emotions.[5] Here Dédéyan looks at this masterpiece from the perspective of the court life upon which she trained her keen powers of observation and interpretation. Dédéyan divides his analysis of her life and art into two parts, "La vie, l'entourage et les collaborateurs" and "La romancière et le peintre de la cour," and adds a generous bibliography on pages 283-297.

Defourneaux, Marcelin. *L'Inquisition espagnole et les livres français au XVIIIe siècle.* Paris: Presses Universitaires de France, 1963. 214 p.

The rationale of the Catholic *Index* regarding books for or about women is evident in the *Catalogue des livres français condamnés (1747-1807),* pages 169-205, when the undermining of the traditional attitudes was feared and repression seemed efficacious. Rousseau's *Émile,* De Morveau's *Législation du divorce,* Sante-Pallaye's *Histoire littéraire des troubadours* (1775), Vanel's *Galanteries des rois de France,* (1794?), Jean de La Fontaine's *L'art d'aimer* and *L'Art de connaître les femmes,* La Marquise de Pompadour's *L'Académie des dames* (1680), Monvel's *Les victimes cloîtrées,* and Agrippa's *De L'Excellence et superiorité des femmes* were all placed in the subversive class. These do not exhaust the list.

Dejob, Charles. *Les Femmes dans la comédie française et italienne au 18e siècle.* Genève: Slatkine Reprints, 1970. 418 p. (Originally published in 1899.)

---

[5] Mme de LaFayette published several works with women-related themes, including *Mlle de Montpensier* (1662) and *Zaïde* (1670), under the pseudonym of Segrais.

Women with faults, women who know what they want, imprudent women, mothers who envy their daughters, all kinds of courtesans, deceived women, and good women (who resist seduction and forgive husbands)—these and many more types figure in this versatile survey of women characters in the plays of a great number of notable writers, including Émile Augier, Carmontelle, Goldoni, Molière, Goethe, Schiller, and Alexandre Dumas.

Delafield, Edmee M. ***Ladies and Gentlemen in Victorian Fiction.*** New York and London: Harper Brothers, 1937. 294 p.

A Victorian enthusiast, Delafield shares her delight in the outmoded niceties and pomposities so characteristic of this era, whether the setting is Britain or the United States. This book recreates the vanished world she admires by contrasting the "then" and the "now" and accenting the "then" with excerpts from such writers as Charlotte Yonge, Harriet Martineau, Elizabeth M. Sewell, Elizabeth Wetherell, and Louisa May Alcott.

Delany, Paul. ***British Autobiography in the Seventeenth Century.*** London: Routledge and Kegan Paul; New York: Columbia University Press, 1969.

Chapter X, pages 158-166, is devoted to "Female Autobiographers," who because they were isolated in real life "merit separate treatment." He goes on to say that in their writing women show "a deeper revelation of sentiments . . . and more subtle analyses than one finds in comparable works by men." Pointing to the rise of a special "feminine sensibility" that was usually ignored by the dominant literary male, he comments that this neglect was encouraged by traditional stereotypes.

Mary Penington, the Duchess of Newcastle; Lady Ann Fanshaw; Ann, Lady Halkett; Mary, Countess of Warwick, and Lucy Hutchinson are treated at length. These, along with other references, provide starting points for fruitful research.

Deschamps, Nicole. *Sigrid Undset, ou La morale de la passion.* Montréal: Les Presses de l'Université de Montréal, 1966. 193 p. Bibliography.

Deschamps perceives Undset as sharing with other Norwegian literary giants a preoccupation with the question of morality, but instead of illustrating her principles in *romans à thèse* as others have done, Undset uses love as her lodestar, creating situations in which women of varying personalities strive for fulfillment as human beings as well as lovers.

In her novels Undset underscores women's difficulties in their search for identity in a realistic world. She visualizes for them, as she did for herself, an ideal society in which "l'amour-passion" could survive marriage, and survive the modern drive for female liberation as well. [6]

Deschamps traces the evolution of Undset's themes in the novels, showing how they parallel the writer's own real life transformations as she moves from scenes of medieval life with *Kristin Lavrandsdatter* (for which she won a Nobel Prize) to contemporary environments and modes of thought, including existentialism and Catholicism.

---

[6] Undset lived through World War II, but she was forced into exile by the Nazis during their occupation of Norway. She traveled in the United States, speaking about Norway and her writings.

A valuable bibliography in several languages (pages 181-192) completes the volume.

Doubleday, Neal Frank. *"Hawthorne's Hester and Feminism,"* PMLA, 54 (1939), pp. 825-828.

Doubleday writes this to warn those who would read into Hester's use of "consecration" in *The Scarlet Letter* as an advocacy of a new standard of sex morality on Hawthorne's part. To the contrary, he believes that, given the presence of feminist ideas in his era, Hawthorne could be using Hester's dilemma to point out the error of being "estranged from the normal existence of woman." Those "norms," however, were those from which many contemporary women were striving to be free.

Doubleday uses as cogent illustrations Chapter XIII of this novel and parts of *The Blithedale Romance,* where the character of Zenobia exhibits "feminist" qualities.

Driver, Sam N. *Anna Akhmatova.* (Twayne's World Author Series.) New York: Twayne Publishers, 1972. 162 p.

Akhmatova, who lived from 1880 to 1966, became an established lyric poet in Russia before World War I. Driver analyzes the poetry she wrote from 1912 to 1922 (with excerpts in English translation) delineating themes of love, war, the city, and the Communist culture against which she rebelled.

Dronke, Peter. *: A Critical Study of Texts from Perpetua (203) to Marguerite Porete (1310).* New York: Cambridge University Press, 1984. Bibliography and index.

A book about women writers from the pen of a devoted medievalist can be looked upon as a welcome treat. Except for a few almost forgotten scholars, almost no one has devoted his/her pen to reviving the memory of medieval women, unless, perhaps, they had scandalous reputations which have survived them.[7] Even less likely was it to find a book on medieval women *writers*. Christine de Pisan has been discovered; we now know something of Hroswitha, who was neglected for centuries; Hildegard's works (twelfth century abbess of Bingen) remain to be translated from Latin. Professor Dronke can lead the way to a renewed interest in medieval women which was a part of scholarship earlier.[8]

Dronke's work has been translated into Italian as *Donne e cultura nel Medioevo: scrittrici medievali del II al XIV secolo* by Saggiaatore, Milano, 1986.

Duckett, Eleanor Shipley. ***Women and Their Letters in the Early Middle Ages.*** Northampton, Massachusetts: Smith College, 1965. 28 p.

In this Katharine Asher lecture Duckett points out that scribes in ancient and early medieval times, being busy with papal and imperial epistles, had no time for the writings of "mere women," and therefore women's letters have in most cases been lost. Yet because of a myriad of allusions to them in

---

[7] Exceptional scholars are the writers of the series *Woman in All Ages and in All Countries*, published in the United States in 1907-1908 (and cited in this bibliography).

[8] Theologians are ones we should expect to know about Perpetua, a lady of Carthage who was martyred for her Christian faith during the reign of the Roman emperor Septimius Severus (193-211 A. D.). She was one of the countless women so persecuted before Christianity became the state religion. Women proved themselves to be as courageous in martyrdom as men, but yet the early church did not allow women to speak in assembly. Christianity had already adopted its patriarchal practices.

Roman and later literatures we know that women were persistent letter-writers, and many of them are enumerated here.

Dunbar, Janet. ***Peg Woffington and Her World.*** Boston: Houghton Mifflin, 1969. 245 p. Bibliography and index. Illustrations (including portraits).

Margaret (Peg) Woffington had her own philosophy of life: ". . . if she served the public as a stage-player—and she was a superlative actress—that was as much as they had a right to expect. What she did with her private life was no conern of theirs." In her narrative Dunbar combines descriptions of both: Peg had an Irish *joie de vivre* which served her well in the eighteenth century Dublin, London, and Paris which became her chief *milieux*. Students of the theater will enjoy this carefully done history, for at the close of the book they will feel as if they have really made a friend of Peg. On pages 234-237 is a list of parts played by Peg during her career, including plays by Joseph Addison, Aphra Behn, Colley Cibber, William Congreve, Henry Fielding, and—most especially—William Shakespeare .

Dunbar, Olivia Howard. *A House in Chicago*. Chicago: University of Chicago Press, 1947. 288 p.

This is the story of Harriet Converse Tilden Moody, wife of the poet William Vaughn Moody. After his death Harriet, with her special talent for inspiration, made a summer retreat in her Massachusetts home for musicians, painters, and poets, forming a coterie that included scores among the intellectual and artistic figures of the day. Harriet, too, wrote a play, *Enter Women* (1939).

Durning, Russel E. *Margaret Fuller, Citizen of the World, an Intermediary between European and American Literatures.* (Beihefte zum Jahrbuch für Amerikastudien, 26.) Heidelberg: Carl Winter-Universitätsverlag, 1969. 144 p.

Emerson is said to have remarked about Margaret Fuller that America did not know what to do with its most gifted woman, and perhaps she did not know what to do with America. Evidently its breadth of vision was too narrow for her, for she spent much of her time in Italy, where she married Count Ossoli.

Fuller's love of the international in literature led her to study several languages (including Latin) and, as Durning shows here, she applied her own criticism to such notables as Dante, George Sand, and Goethe, with her interpretations of works in French, Italian, Spanish, and German literatures still valid today. Her sensitivity to the ambiguous and difficult role of women, especially those with intellectual interests, is expressed in her *Woman in the Nineteenth Century* (see below).

Edgeworth, Maria. *Letters from England, 1813-1844.* Edited by Christina Colvin. Oxford: Clarendon Press, 1971. 649 p.

Colvin's introduction orients the reader to Maria Edgeworth's worlds, the Ireland where she was born in 1768 and the England where she was educated for a short time before returning to her family. This thoroughly researched edition of her correspondence includes plentiful explanatory notes and indexes of place names and persons to whom Edgeworth alludes. It makes good background study for the novels.

A biographical index gives added information for those wishing to know more about Edgeworth's family and friends.

Edwards, Lee R. *"Women, Energy and "Middlemarch,"* Massachusetts Review, 13 (Winter-Spring, 1972), pp. 223-238.

Although women have looked to the character of Dorothea as a symbol of female rebellion, Edwards sees only disappointment for readers who had hoped to find in the novel solutions to the problem of how a woman can transmute her essential energy into self-directed channels. Eliot (Mary Ann Evans) shows herself to be a proponent of the values of patriarchal society and gives women no real hope of achieving transcendence, according to Edwards' analysis.

Ellet, Elizabeth. **Women Artists in All Ages and Countries.** New York: Harper & Brothers, 1859. 377 p. (A microfilm of this work is available at New Haven, Connecticut: Research Publications, 1975. [History of Women, Reel 256, no. 1716].)

Ellet cites the lack of a written history on female artists that includes the nineteenth century and wrote this to fill that gap, with her major source of biographies Ernst Gull's *Die Frauen in die Kunstgeschiche.* Her aim is not criticism *per se,* but "simply to show what woman has done, with the general conditions favorable or unfavorable to her efforts." She adds that she "hopes to inspire with courage and resolution" other artists to overcome difficulties that would surely be put in their way. This is excellent reading for the serious student of art history.

Elson, Arthur. **Women's Work in Music.** Boston: The Page Company, 1904. 269 p.

Elson traces women's musical accomplishments from ancient times through the medieval period, and onward. One chapter is devoted to Clara Schumann, and featured also is

Theresa von Paradies (b. 1759) who became blind at the age of three but still became a pianist and a composer who could dictate her compositions note by note with no alterations. She was admired by many of the male musicians of her day, including Mozart. An appendix, pages 235-260, lists women composers of Britain, Germany, France, and the United States.

Epton, Nina Consuelo. *Love and the English.* London: Cassell, 1960. 389 p. Index and illustrations.

Epton's fascinating style within a literary framework makes it easy to read her book thoroughly without realizing that a great deal of scholarship is being absorbed at the same time. Her approach is chronological, from Anglo-Saxon to modern times.

Chapter VI, "The Twentieth Century: The Age of Sex," in which Epton strays into sociological analysis, lacks the piquancy represented by Monsieur Morall's gallant but myopic comment in the seventeenth century: "Most Englishmen prefer wine and gaming to women; in this they are the more to blame as women are much better than the wine in England."

Espina de Serna, Concha. *Mujeres del "Quijote."* Madrid: Renacimiento, 1930. 208 p.

Eight essays consider the many women characters created by Cervantes to grace the pages of his masterpiece, from "La dama de los altos pensamientos" (Dulcinea) to "Violetas de la paz y de la muerto." Espina de Serna's style is unhurried, in keeping with the rhythm of Cervantes' descriptions of the circuitous adventures of Don Quijote.

Evans, Oliver. *Anaïs Nin.* Carbondale: Southern Illinois University Press, 1968. 221 p.

Evans' critique forms the first comprehensive study of Nin's novels and other writings in which Nin combines symbolist and surrealist trends, explores the "cities of the interior," and in so doing calls upon her training in psychiatry. Evans compares Nin's work to that of D. H. Lawrence who also uses basic symbols to form a system of analogies through which to interpret the human mind and emotions.

Faillie, Marie. *La Femme et le code civile dans la "Comédie Humaine" d'Honoré de Balzac.* Paris: M. Didier, 1968. 224 p. Bibliography.

This well-documented study delves into Balzac's novels to show his portrayal of women in the roles by which they were defined in society: unmarried, married, and women with children.

Set in the context of the French *code civile,* Balzac's novels reflect the basic laws, and Faillie clarifies those most relevant to women—specifically those dealing with persons and marriage. In addition, she contrasts the 1828 laws with those of 1960.

Fauchery, Pierre. *La Destinée féminine dans le roman européen du dix-huitième siècle: essai de gynéconythie romanesque.* Paris: Librairie Armand Colin, 1972. 900 p.

This massive and fascinating work concerns itself with the sad procession of victims of this period who are seen imprisoned in the myths of feminine nature and destiny.

Fauchery uses religious symbolism to dramatize the myth of self-sacrificing duty in "Prélude," "Offertoire," "Sacrifice," three parts of Section I. "Quels moyens le roman offre-t-il au *moi* féminin de se rejoindre lui-même?" he asks as he intensively analyzes the literature of many European countries with an approach that is "féminophile" enough for the most ardent literary feminists who also demand sound scholarship.

A perusal of the copious index will show which authors one should be familiar with in order to derive the most benefit from this painstaking work.

Febvre, Lucien. *Autour de "l'Heptaméron."* Paris: Gallimard, 1944. 299 p. Bibliography.

Febvre uses as epigraph Marguerite de Navarre's own words, "Deux coeurs en ung, et chascun content" ("Two hearts in one, and each one happy") and appropriately divides this study into two parts: "Marguerite La Chrétienne," and "Marguerite qui fit *L'Heptaméron.*" To conclude he asks the question, "Marguerite simple, Marguerite double?" and decides that one must search for the deep unity underneath the appearance.

Feininger, Andreas. *Maids, Madonnas, and Witches: Women in Sculpture from Prehistoric Times to Picasso.* Translated from the German by Joan Bradley. New York: Harry N. Abrams, 1961. 194 p.

The text to accompany Feininger's photographs was written by J. Bon, and Henry Miller is responsible for a rather confused introduction which seems to do little to clarify the subject. The main body of the work, however, forms a fascinating panorama of the development of sculpture in a variety of cultures. The work deals with women as seen by male sculptors, not with women sculptors.

Ferrante, Joan M. *Woman as Image in Medieval Literature from the Twelfth Century to Dante.* New York: Columbia University Press, 1975. 166 p.

Women in twelfth-century literature, although important, are not life-like characters but are merely symbols of problems, philosophical or psychological, that trouble men, according to Ferrante. They can represent cosmic forces—as in Latin allegories—or they can embody male ideals. Thus they dominate man because they are so vividly tied to his own concerns; therefore he implants this symbolism within literature and religious exegesis. This latter is of crucial importance, Ferrante points out, because the cult of the Virgin Mary had the effect of giving value to women, with power going to strong women who could wield it. Arthurian literature, with its mystical ideals of women, is also considered in this study, which is indexed and includes bibliographical references.

Feugère, Léon. *Les Femmes poètes au XVIe siècle.* Paris: Didier et Cie, 1860. 393 p.

Feugère's studies of women are found on pages 1-232, the remainder being devoted to other famous sixteenth-century figures. Included among the women are Marguerite de Navarre and Marie de Gournay, both of whose works are carefully analyzed.

Feugère tells of the crucial part played by Montaigne's *Essais* in inspiring Marie when she was fifteen to become self-educated. After she became his adoptive daughter, his encouragement of her achievements was in direct contrast to the attitude of most other men of the time whose misogynist beliefs harbored "une rancune . . . contre l'esprit des femmes."

The other women writers considered here are not well-known, but each vignette is interestingly written, inviting the reader to delve further to rediscover such women as: Louise Labé, Marie de Romieu, Catherine des Roches, Madeleine

Neveu, Marie Stuart, Jeanne d'Albert, and others. Quotations from some of their works are found here.

Fisher, Marvin. *"Melville's 'Tartarus': The Deflowering of New England,"* American Quarterly, XXIII, no. 1 (Spring, 1971), pp. 79-100.

Fisher interprets Melville's short story, "The Tartarus of Maids," as an indictment of American industrial society which destroys the feminine values (love, feeling, nurture) in favor of the aggressive, impersonal force of the machine which bids to make love meaningless.

Seeing the woman as having lost the power she had in the Old World, Fisher echoes the thought of Henry Adams who commented ruefully that in the America of his day a Virgin could not command nor a Venus exist.

Fletcher, Jefferson Butler. *The Religion of Beauty in Women; and Other Essays on Platonic Love in Poetry and Society.* New York: Haskell House, 1966. 205 p.

A description of the "religion of beauty" that was so influential in medieval times and has reached even to modern literature will be found on pages 1-28, where Fletcher identifies Cardinal Pietro Bembo as the first exponent of this religion. Following Bembo were Castiglione, with *The Courtier* (1528), Michelangelo, Vittoria Colonna, Marguerite de Navarre, and in England Sir Philip Sidney and other poets. Dante's ideal, Beatrice, is considered on pages 30-52, where the religious aspect is stressed.

Foulché-Delbosc, R. *"Mme d'Aulnoy et l'Espagne,"* Revue Hispanique, LXXVIII (1926), pages 1-151.

Mme d'Aulnoy (1651-1705) is known for her admiration of Spanish literature, which she brought to the attention of the public in France through her writings. Her most influential works were *Mémoires de la cour d'Espagne* (1690) and *Relation du voyage d'Espagne* (1691), which were considered authentic travel accounts up to the nineteenth century.

In this well-documented article Foulché-Delbosc gives reasons for doubting that Mme d'Aulnoy was writing from her own experience. It is true, however, that she lived abroad for many years, being a *persona non grata* in France after her plot against her husband, whom she had accused of high treason, miscarried. (See also F. W. Bomli.)

Fowler, Lois Josepha. *"Diana of the Crossways: A Prophecy for Feminism,"* pages 20-26 in *In Honor of Austin Wright*, edited by Joseph Baim *et al.* (Carnegie Series in English, no. 12) Pittsburg: Carnegie-Mellon University, 1972.

Fowler points out that the twentieth century owes a debt to a number of Victorian writers for early perceptions of women's emerging psychological dilemmas as unprecedented freedom threatened to create tensions between the drive for self-fulfillment in the wider world and the need to maintain femininity. Diana in Meredith's novel is a woman who symbolizes these conflicts as she achieves a measure of self-determination which, however, does not always bring the happiness she expects.

Frazer, James George. ***Garnered Sheaves: Essays, Addresses, and Reviews.*** London: Macmillan and Company, 1931.

"A Suggestion as to the Origin of Gender in Language," pages 183-197, takes a look at a perplexing linguistic phenomenon. Frazer propounds his hypothesis to explain the seemingly arbitrary designation of words in certain languages as masculine or feminine, calling upon his own and other anthropologists' knowledge of primitive tribes. He points out the frequent occurrence of "men's language" and "women's language" in the same tribe, relating this in part to the custom of stealing women from other tribes. In the long process of evolution in language Frazer sees certain words of the languages being discarded and others kept, according to a logical pattern.

Most of Frazer's allusions are to the tribes found in South American areas, especially the Carib, Guatemala, and Paraguay. Quoting from *L'Homme Américain* (Paris, 1939), he also includes information concerning the speech of the two sexes in the words of the French ethnologist, Alcide d'Orbigny, who studied South American tribes, and a list of words from each language is provided.

Fulbright, James Stephen. *"William Blake and the Emancipation of Women."* Unpublished Ph.D. dissertation, University of Mississippi, Columbia, 1973. 118 p.

Covering the period from 1778 to 1793, this study includes chapters on the women in Blake's family, his historical paintings featuring women, and his relations with the bluestocking *salon* of Harriet Mathew, as well as material about his friendship with feminists Mary Wollstonecraft, James Barry, and Henry Fuseli.

Gardiner, Judith Kegan. *"Psychoanalytic Criticism and the Female Reader,"* Literature and Psychology, XXVI, no 3 (1976), pages 100-107.

Female readers' confusion began in 1879 with Freud's remark on *Hamlet*: "Every member of the audience was once a budding Oedipus in fantasy." Gardiner, noting the male orientation of such a statement imagines women asking themselves, "Am I, too, part of 'every member of the audience'?" Thereby she exposes the weakness of psychoanalytic interpretation: it sees literature almost wholly from a male perspective even while analyzing female characters. Chaucer's "Wife of Bath" figures here, too, as Gardiner notes Norman H. Holland's treatment of her characterization.

Gasiorowska, Xenia. ***Women in Soviet Fiction, 1917-1964.*** Madison and London: University of Wisconsin Press, 1968. 288 p.

World interest was aroused in the 1920's when after the Revolution it became known that the Soviet Union's new constitution had granted full political equality to women, including relaxed rules for marriage and divorce. The reality, however, did not match the hopeful action, for it was soon believed that "equality" in marriage was a threat to the stability of the family.

The granting of freedom, both political and social, to women seemed to be a dangerous road to travel, with unknown consequences at the end.

As a result, Gasiorowska sees Soviet women in contemporary fiction facing dilemmas common to women in other countries, with the added perplexity for writers faced with the problem of showing them living (more or less contentedly) in an even more repressive society as a fast-paced industrialism (to try to catch up with the West), Stalinism, and World War II came to be the overwhelming facts of life.

Gasiorowska's description of women as "soulful and moderate in their demands for personal happiness and emotionally involved in their professional work" also contains the *caveat* for readers that "the world of Soviet fiction is governed by the laws of Socialist Realism." The heroines, therefore, come across as rather stereotyped. Nevertheless, one can believe that they are indeed approximations of actual Russian women, since, Gasiorowska reminds us, "types" are based upon social realities.

Many specific novels are discussed fully within a chronological framework, and a bibliography of English translations of Russian novels is provided. Valuable additions, too, are a glossary of Russian terms and acronyms found in the text, and an excellent index.

Gaskell, Elizabeth C. *Letters.* Edited by J. A. V. Chapple and Arthur Pollard. Cambridge: Harvard University Press, 1967. 1010 p.

The authors justify the publication of this voluminous correspondence because of the unique revelations it affords, as well as the intrinsic interest of Gaskell's *milieu* and the great influence of her novels. They note that Gaskell wrote her biography of Charlotte Brontë using Brontë's letters as her chief source.

Useful features of this unusual work are the indexes of people and the many literary references with which Gaskell dots her writings.

Genlis, Mme de. *Dernières lettres d'amour, publiées par André Castelot.* Avant-propos par M. le Duc de la Force. Paris: Bernard Grasset, 1954. 303 p. Index.

This unusual volume presents the intriguing "correspondance inédits de la Comtesse de Genlis et du Comte Anatole de Montesquiou," but the tenor of the letters is not as it appears. Far from being "romantic"—the *amour* is strictly friendship. The exchange was initiated when Mme de Genlis was 79 and Comte Anatole de Montesquiou was 39: they were to write "tous les jours des folies et des bêtises" for each other's amusement. As it turned out, Instead of frivolous daily records of amusing gossip and such nonsense, however, the missives became serious exchanges of opinions, wide-ranging in subject but with much humor and candor. Their disagreement over Napoleon's merits is especially interesting, as it highlighted how the two, opposite in sex and age, differed in regard to the social changes which were coming about.

The considerable preface, pages 7-62, gives an excellent account of Mme de Genlis' eventful life.

Gerber, Philip. *"The Alabaster Protégée: Dreiser and Berenice Fleming,"* American Literature, 43, no. 3 (May, 1971), pp. 217-230.

Gerber shows how Dreiser metamorphosed an actual person into the heroine of his novel, *The Stoic.* Drawing from contemporary newspaper reports of the appearance and activities of Emilie Grigsby, Dreiser created the fictional Berenice in ways that are illustrated by Gerber with samples of the reports and the comparable finished excerpts from the novel.

Gérin, Winifred. *Charlotte Brontë: The Evolution of Genius.* Oxford: Clarendon Press, 1968. 617 p.

Gérin justifies the appearance of "yet another work" on Charlotte Brontë by citing her own ten years' sojourn in Haworth and her intimate acquaintance with the scenes of Charlotte's life. In addition, Gérin was the first biographer to have access to information, given by the Heger family, concerning Charlotte's Belgian experience. Included in an appendix are the French texts of her letter to M. Heger (with English translations).

Gérin's definitive work is copiously annotated, contains bibliographies, and is well-indexed.

Ghinger, Carol Fay. *"Alienation and the Quest for Self: The Powerful Heroine in Fiction."* Unpublished Ph.D. dissertation, University of Colorado at Boulder, 1978. 305 p.

Remarking that the quest for selfhood has been traditionally defined in male terms in literature, Ghinger uses several well-known novels to illustrate her theme of women's two options: to be masculine or to be feminine. On the basis of the novels she has studied Ghinger concludes that male literary figures usually achieve integration at the end of their quest, but she does not see the same dénouement for most female characters.

Gibbs-Smith, Charles H. *The Fashionable Lady in the Nineteenth Century.* London: Her Majesty's Stationery Office, 1960.

Gibbs-Smith limits his work to the styles worn by women of fashion who served as the ideals for other women to strive for, as well as the inspiration for dress designers. This book is an excellent one for the student who is interested in the nineteenth-century novel: it makes it simpler to imagine the heroines of Austen, Thackeray, Balzac, Stendahl, Tolstoy, and other writers who portrayed women of fashion so carefully.

Gilbert, Miriam Anne. *"The Shrew and the Disguised Girl in Shakespeare's Comedies."* Unpublished dissertation, Indiana University, 1969. 245 p.

Shrewishness and disguise, says Gilbert, are ways in which certain female characters in nine of Shakespeare's plays pretend to be men, physically or psychologically, and thus they try out "the possibilities of a man's world" that would otherwise be unavailable to them. She believes that Shakespeare shows shrewish behavior to be both an expression of independence and a cover for fear, while disguise as a male offers opportunity for freedom and a way of sensing the difference between true and false ways of living. This is an intriguing thesis interestingly presented.

Gill-Mark, Grace. *Une Femme de lettres au XVIIIe siècle: Anne-Marie du Boccage*. (Bibliothèque de la Revue de Littérature Comparée, tome XLI.) Paris: Librairie Ancienne Honoré Champion, 1927. 182 p. Index. Bibliography.

A much-admired woman of the intellectually vibrant eighteenth century, Anne-Marie was born in Rouen in 1710, where in later years she was to preside over a *salon* frequented by friends from England and Italy as well as France.

Even Voltaire is said to have praised her by saying that of all the women in the world she was the most worthy of having friends—and she counted among them such figures in France as Condillac, Marmontel, Mably, Montesquieu, and notables from other countries—Benjamin Franklin of the budding democracy in America, as well as Edward Gibbon, Lord Stanhope (the younger), and Lord Chesterfield from England. These notables seemed to be compatible, even though at that time, France and England were not on the best of terms politically, being rivals in North America—which indicates again that intellectual society is international in interests.

Anne-Marie herself was an assiduous traveler. Sojourns in England, Holland, and Italy whenever possible and devotion to her writing as a serious pursuit added variety to her stimulating personal relations and made it possible for her to maintain the intellectual versatility so admired in women or men in French society.

Godbold, E. Stanly. *Ellen Glasgow and the Woman Within.* Baton Rouge: Louisiana State University Press, 1972. 322 p.

Gorbold's accent is upon biography: Glasgow's art and her intellectual life are not clearly defined. But this work is rich in documentation, since access to all manuscript sources were available, as well as a good collection of letters and other scarce materials.

Goddard, Eunice Rathbone. *Women's Costume in French Texts of the Eleventh and Twelfth Centuries.* (The Johns Hopkins Studies in Romance Literatures and Languages, volume VII.) Baltimore: The Johns Hopkins Press. 265 p. (Originally published at Paris by Les Presses Universitaires in 1927.)

This is a highly specialized contribution to medieval studies in that its purpose is "to discuss . . . thoroughly . . . the terminology of words relating to women's costume" in old French texts. In doing this Goddard is revising prior works: Godefroy's *Old French Dictionary* (Paris, 1880-1902); M. Winters' monograph, *Kleidung und Putz der frau nach altfranzösischen chans de geste* (Marburg, 1886), and V. Gay's *Glossaire archéologique* (Paris, 1887). She comments that aside from Marie de France "we know of no poets in our period that were not of the male sex."

The present work consists of an introduction, a glossary, and bibliographies of texts read: works on archeological aspects, philology, and on costume. Some general descriptions are included which will be of interest to readers whose interest is medieval dress but not in Old French. Among the illustrations are seven plates taken from contemporary art and sculpture.

(See also Thomas Wright, *Womankind in All Ages of Western Europe* [above] for additional illustrations.)

Golenistcheff-Koutouzoff, Elie Nikolaevich. *L'Histoire de Griselda en France au XIVe et au XVe siècles.* Paris: E. Droz, 1933. 291 p.

The story of "patient Griselda" achieved popularity through works as disparate as Boccaccio's *Decameron* and Chaucer's *Canterbury Tales,* among others. The theme is the testing of a wife's patience under her husband's cruelties, which are accepted as reasonable by the culture—in fact, "l'humilité de Griselda ne ressemble point à la patience servile" because the theme of the persecuted wife is so pervasive in culture.[9]

The second chapter underscores the widespread vogue of the Griselda legend in France in this period as its ideas became incorporated into such influential books as *Le Ménagier de Paris* (1393) and Christine de Pisan's *Livre de la Cité de Dames* (1405).

González, Manuel Pedro. *Rosalia de Castro en inglés: glosa del centario.* Habana: Dirección de Cultura, 1938. 21 p.

A constant "dolor de la vida" pervades the poetry of Rosalia de Castro, says González, a sadness springing from the ever-present consciousness of the social stigma of her illegitimacy.

---

[9] That is to say, Griselda's humility is not at all akin to servility because the concept of the persecuted wife is based upon a fact of human nature and is one which is found everywhere among all peoples. Ergo, the prevalence of cruelty, physical or mental, toward wives makes it acceptable.

Selections from her poetry are presented here in English, including "En las orillas del Sar" (1884), translated in 1937 by Griswold Morley as "Beside the River Sar."

Gordan, John D. *"A Legend Revisited: Eleanor Wylie, "* American Scholar, XXXVIII (Summer, 1969), pp. 459-468.

The legend which Gordan wishes to revisit and interpret is the one perpetrated by an unfavorable press, which characterized American poet Wylie (1885-1928) as a notorious figure who, for one thing, had had four husbands—a symbol of independent thinking unusual for her time.

Gordan believed that Eleanor (or Elinor) Wylie's true literary merits would bring her back to public attention, especially because of her volumes of poetry, *Angels and Earthly Creatures,* as deserving of a reappraisal to match the critical praise of many of her contemporaries, who deemed them the best written by a woman in the first quarter of the century.

Goulianos, Joan, ed. *By a Woman Writ: Literature from Six Centuries by and about Women.* Baltimore, Maryland: Penguin Books, 1974. 379 p.

Twenty women are represented in this attention-holding anthology made up of excerpts from less-known poetical, fictional, and non-fictional works, preceded by a short introduction in which Goulianos explains the incentive for compiling this book: "If there was one phrase that women writers had passed on to each other throughout the centuries—from Margery Kempe to Margaret Cavendish to Virginia Woolf—it was this—that what mattered was to attempt to tell one's truth, to write 'what you wish to write.'"

Goulianos, Ruth. *"Women and the Avant-Garde Theatre,"* Massachusetts Review, 13 (Winter-Spring, 1972), pp. 257-267.

This article takes the form of an interview with playwrights Rochelle Owens and Rosalyn Drexler and director-actress Crystal Field. Discussion centers around how being a woman has been a determining factor in the careers of the three women.

Grandgent, Charles H. *The Ladies of Dante's Lyrics.* (The McBride Lecture Fund, Western Reserve University.) Cambridge: Harvard University Press, 1917. 181 p.

Violetta, Matelda, Pietra, Beatrice, and Lisetta are the ladies whose trail, "however vague and vanishing," Grandgent follows as he speculates upon whether these characters are based upon real women or, most probably, ghosts of damsels admired and sung by Dante in his early youth. His wife Gemma, Grandgent notes, is never mentioned by the poet.

The text is enlivened and clarified by many excerpts from the Dantean lyrics in English translation.

Graves, Robert. *Wife to Mr. Milton: The Story of Marie Powell.* New York: Noonday Press, 1966 [1943], 380 p.

Graves, an eminent British poet and novelist, wrote this sympathetic portrayal in the form of an autobiography of the oft-maligned Marie (or Mary) Powell, John Milton's first wife who married him in 1643 when she was seventeen and he was thirty-five.[10] A month later she took the scandalous step of leaving him which, it is thought, impelled him to write his

---

[10] Graves' own autobiography is *Goodbye to All That* (1929). He is known for his poetry on World War I and such works as *I, Claudius*.

ponderous treatise on divorce. Milton argued that love and compatibility must be the basis of marriage; otherwise there is no true marriage at all. He came to understand that the meager education given to girls could hardly prepare them to be compatible mates for highly educated men (and his father had provided him with a superb education, followed by Continental travel). When Marie returned to him, he made great efforts to make her life happier. Perhaps it was their differences that attracted him: he was a scholarly introvert, she an extroverted member of a large, noisy family. Unfortunately, Marie died giving birth to her fourth child. [11]

Gravier, Maurice. *Le Féminisme et l'amour dans la littérature norvégienne, 1850-1950.* (Bibliothèque Nordique, nouvelle série.) Paris: Lettres Modernes, 1968. 331 p.

Ibsen is known as the first modern literary apostle of feminism, reflects Gravier as he asks, "How have women fared in Norway because [Ibsen] wrote so tellingly of their dilemma?" He sees Norwegian feminism "in search of a program" as he traces its development since the mid-nineteenth century and decides that what is needed is a new Sigrid Undset, with her soulful understanding of the grandeur of woman.

Gravier's study is well-done, interesting, and informative. An index would have been helpful.

---

[11] Serious researchers might want to read Milton's insightful *The Doctrine and Discipline of Divorce, Restored to the Good of Both Sexes,* and other writings on the subject, which seem very modern in their open-minded approach.

Gregory, Allene. *The French Revolution and the English Novel.* Port Washington, New York: Kennikat Press, 1965. (Originally published in 1915.)

Of interest are Chapter VI, "Some Typical Lady Novelists of the Revolution," and Chapter VII, "The French Revolution and the Rights of Women." The novelists include Elizabeth Inchbald, Amelia Alderson Opie, Charlotte Smith, while a later chapter concentrates on Mary Wollstonecraft, with some background material on the feminist movement.

Griffith, Dudley David. *The Origin of the Griselda Story.* (University of Washington Publications in Language and Literature, Vol. 8, no. 1.) Seattle: University of Washington Press, 1931 [1916]; Folcroft, Pennsylvania: Folcroft Library edition (reprint), 1973. 120 p. Index.

Though not a study of woman *per se,* this could be a useful resource for the assessment of attitudes implicit in centuries-old interpretations of women and their place in the scheme of life. Griffith shows that the Griselda legend has been approached in many scholarly ways while the woman herself has been ignored, even though her actions are the key to the "testing" that takes place in this intensely male-oriented situation.

Grigson, Geoffrey. *The Goddess of Love: The Birth, Triumph, Death and Return of Aphrodite.* New York: Stein and Day, 1977 [1976]. 256 p. Bibliography and index. Illustrations.

Grigon's enthusiasm for his subject is evident in the text, generously illustrated with photographs of sculpture, and enhanced by quotations from poetry, ancient and recent, in homage to Aphrodite, or Venus. He takes a chronological approach, chronicling her "birth" as a goddess who remains immortal in the hearts of mankind, as is colorfully expressed in Swinburne's "Hymn to Proserpine."

It took until the end of the twentieth century, maintains Grigson, for the true Aphrodite to be "reborn," since masks are no longer needed: the demise of *bourgeois* prudery allows us to admire her, and what she represented to the ancient Greeks, without censure. Of especial interest for the study of literature is the section, "Sappho's Aphrodite," which quotes the only complete poem by Sappho which has come down to us.

Grisay, August, et al. *Les Dénominations de la femme dans les anciens textes littéraires français.* (Publication de l'Institut de Lexicologue française de l'Université de Liège.) Gembloux: J. Duculot, 1969. 259 p.

This erudite book is full of interest for those with a general command of French. The authors consider, for example, the various Latin words to denote the female of the human species: *mulier, femina, matrona, domina, puella.* They do the same for Old French in greater detail, using much original literature as illustration. These various denominations have important social implications, for they refer to woman's functions and status and therefore to her "value."

An index is provided, as is a bibliography of Latin, French, and German works.

Grundy, Isabel. *"Ovid and Eighteenth Century Divorce: An Unpublished Poem by Lady Mary Wortley Montagu,"* Review of English Studies, 23, no. 92 (November, 1972), pp. 417-428.

This article contains the text of Lady Montagu's "Epistle from Mrs. Y—— to Her Husband, Occasioned by the Divorce Case of Wm. Yonge against his Wife Mary." Grundy refers to the influence of other contemporary women writers as well as to that of Ovid and Alexander Pope.

Guiguet, Jean. *Virginia Woolf and Her Works.* New York: Harcourt, Brace and World, Inc., 1965. 487 p. Translated by Jean Stewart. (Originally published in France in 1962.)

Guiguet's emphasis is upon the novels and Woolf's methods and problems as she wrote against the vivid background of her personal life. Certain of her non-fiction works "pamphlets"), especially *A Room of One's Own,* can be seen as indicators of irrepressible contradictions also found in such works as *Orlando* and *The Years,* contradictions which threatened to undermine her health.

Says Guiguet, "If the interpretation of life which [Woolf] offers cannot be matched with universally valid and practically useful rules of conduct, there emerges from it, nonetheless, a lesson whose significance exceeds that of any formula. It can be summed up in a single word, for which the whole of her work is the explanation . . . Being."

This work is interesting as well for its many references to other writers. It has an index and good bibliography.

Gutwirth, Madelyn. *"Madame de Staël, Rousseau, and the Woman Question," Publications of the Modern Language Association (PMLA),* 86, no. 1 (January, 1971), pp. 100-109.

Lifelong ambivalences toward her role as a writer caused by the disapproval of men, especially her father and mentor Rousseau, are mirrored in Mme de Staël's works, notably *De la Littérature* (1800) and *De l'Allemagne* (1810-1814), Gutwirth points out. In addition, she suffered repression from Napoleon, who went as far as to exile her from France.

Mme de Staël, however, was nothing if not a determined person. Finally, she wrote the second preface to her *Lettres sur J.-J. Rousseau* three years before her death at the age of forty-eight (the first was written in 1788). This shows a more distinct leaning toward feminist ideas: she argues that women should be allowed to develop their talent for writing to the fullest, in spite of male detractors like Rousseau who, "étonnés de rencontrer des rivaux parmi les femmes . . . ne suivent ni les lois d'honneur ni celles de la bonté."— "amazed at finding rivals among women . . . follow neither the laws of honor nor good will."

To illustrate her findings Gutwirth makes good use of relevant passages from both writers. Although they are in the original French, she paraphrases them in English.

Haig, Stirling. ***Madame de LaFayette.*** (Twayne World Authors Series.) New York: Twayne Publishers, 1970. 164 p.

Written in English, this is a good introduction to the understanding of Mme de LaFayette as a woman living in an age of civil war, when, nevertheless, *salons* and literature saw a brilliance hardly outshone later. Her works, of which *La Princesse de Clèves* (1678) is the best known, is permeated with a pessimistic attitude concerning love, probably influenced by her own unhappiness in marriage. It has been called the first French psychological novel because it reveals with candor the moral dilemma faced by a married woman in conflict because of her love for her husband and her passion for another man.

Mme de LaFayette, too, adopted a male pseudonym when penning her earlier works—that of "Segrais."

Haight, Anne Lyon, ed. ***Hroswitha of Gandersheim; Her Life, Times, and Works.*** New York: Hroswitha Club, 1965. 129 p.

Haight has drawn from libraries in Europe and the United States for her study of the tenth century environment in which Hroswitha lived, and where she wrote the dramatic works which were to lie neglected for centuries, waiting for their rediscovery in modern times. This drama, says Haight, "benefited from the cultural and educational excellence of the splendid Ottonian era reflected in contemporary monasteries."[12]

A comprehensive bibliography adds to the interest of this book, as does the good index.

Hamilton, Arthur. *A Study of Spanish Manners (1750-1800) from the Plays of Ramón de la Cruz.* (University of Illinois Studies in Language and Literature, Vol. XI, no. 3.) Urbana: University of Illinois Press, 1926. 72 p.

The importance of women in setting the tone of society is abundantly illustrated by Hamilton as he isolates characterizations from the plays of de la Cruz. Among some of the more interesting of these are the *petimetra*, the bourgeois woman of fashion, and the *maja*, a colorful working class girl with liberated ideas on marriage.

Hanrahan, Thomas S. J. *La Mujer en la novela picaresca española.* (Biblioteca Tenanitla: Libros españoles y hispanoamericanos, vols. 9, 10.) Madrid: Ediciones José Porrua Turanzas, 1967. 384 p. Bibliography.

Emphasizing the theme of asceticism as part of the Spanish attitude toward women, Hanrahan presenta a commendable

---

[12]"Ottonian" refers to that brief period in German history when under Otto III (983-1003) comparatively peaceful conditions, political and religious, favored art and learning.

survey of the works of such writers as Mateo Alemán, Cervantes, Quevedo, and Vincente Espinel, along with detailed studies of selected women characters from their works.

In Chapter V, "Ascetismo y feminismo," pages 85-98, Hanrahan comments upon the relation of the picaresque to the asceticism of the teachings directed toward the Spanish woman in order to mold her into "la perfecta casada" ("the perfect wife"), as illustrated earlier in works like Fray Martín de Córdoba's *El Jardín de nobles donzellas*.

Haraszti, Zoltan. *"The Works of Hroswitha,"* More Books: The Bulletin of the Boston Public Library, 20 (1945), pp. 87-119; 139-173.

Hroswitha, who is now regarded as the earliest German poet and her poems some of the greatest in the Middle Ages, lived in the Benedictine abbey of Gandersheim as the Carolingian Renaissance was making its influence known. After six centuries of neglect, her plays and other works, written in Latin, were brought to light by humanist Conrad Celtes, first poet laureate of Germany, who discovered her manuscripts at St. Emmeram. Even afterward, however, Hroswitha's accomplishments were slow to receive recognition.

Haraszti asserts that her plays "present an entirely isolated phenomenon," for they date back two hundred years earlier than the generally accepted date for the origin of the medieval drama. Apparently the neglect was intentional.

Hartley, Susan Rebecca. *"The Later Novels of George Meredith: Woman's Struggle for Emancipation."* Unpublished Ph.D. dissertation, Florida State University, 1973. 163 p.

Meredith welcomed the Victorian agitation for the reform of women's legal and social position, says Hartley, not only for the sake of women but for society as a whole. Such novels as *The Egoist* and *Diana of the Crossways* are analyzed here to demonstrate Meredith's understanding of the personal struggles involved for women who wished to assert their selfhood and move toward social involvement. Meredith also considered alternatives to indissoluble marriage ties to allow women to escape from often intolerable iron clad relationships.

Haskell, Molly. ***From Reverence to Rape: The Treatment of Women in the Movies.*** New York: Holt, Rinehart & Winston, 1974. 388 p. Illustrations.

Within a chronological structure Haskell sees the movies as reflective of deep-seated social attitudes which appeared to change from the concept of woman as feminine ideal embodied in Mary Pickford, "America's sweetheart," to a less reverent presentation of her as the "flapper" of the 1920's and as a sex object in the 1960's and 1970's. Paralleling the early characterizations, however, was the emergence of the independent woman, such as Kathryn Hepburn and Joan Crawford, a concept which tended to fade, perhaps because it was less compatible with the *mores* favored by the typical audiences. The index of this work cites the specific films and persons highlighted in the text, a helpful feature..

Hatzfeld, Helmut. ***Estudios literarios sobre mística española.*** (Biblioteca Románica Hispánica.) Madrid: Editorial Gredos, 1955.

Chapter V, pages 263-290, "Mística femenina clásica en España y Francia," is of interest. Hatzfeld also adds the explication, "Experiencia religiosa y aportación lingüistica de Santa Teresa de Jesús y de la Venerable Marie de l'Incarnation." These two saintly women are compared in regard to their social and psychological influences as well as to their use of language in expressing metaphysical concepts. Hatzfeld sees Santa Teresa as "dueña absolute del lenguaje," while Marie de l'Incarnation is "su humilde servidora."[13]

Hawkins, Richmond Laurin, ed. *Newly Discovered French Letters of the Seventeenth, Eighteenth and Nineteenth Centuries.* Cambridge: Harvard University Press, 1933.

One of the letters of interest discovered by Hawkins is a short one which Mme de Genlis wrote to the literary critic François-Benoît on May 8, 1815 (pages 122-124). He had unfavorably reviewed her recent book, *Histoire de Henri le Grand*, calling it a historical novel instead of true history, an account which seemed designed to flatter the Bourbons, and thus to win the favor of Louis XVIII. Mme de Genlis' polite but firm letter intends to refute that charge. (Her book appeared in 1815 during Napoleon's One Hundred Days, but he was too busy then to concern himself with repressing books, as he had earlier with Mme de Staël.)

Hawkins also includes some nineteenth century letters from "Rachel," who was a Jewish girl of humble parentage who became a renowned singer, appearing at the *Théâtre Molière* and later at the *Comédie Française*, where she made her début

---

[13] Santa Teresa was an inveterate reader of popular novels of chivalry, like most of the readers of her time. She excelled as a writer as well. Her letters are judged the best in Spanish literature.

as Camille in Corneille's *Horace*. Most of her letters, on pages 161-175, are to her parents. To round out the letters by women, on pages 176-179 is printed an April 4, 1846 letter from George Sand to George Sumner, the younger brother of American statesman Charles Sumner, in which she expresses opinions on world peace and the dispute between Britain and the United States over the Oregon Territory. All the letters mentioned above are in French. Hawkins' instructive, detailed comments are in English.

Healy, Elliott D. *"Louise Labé and the Contessa de Dia,"* in *Studies in Comparative Literature*. Edited by Waldo F. NcNeir. Baton Rouge: University of Louisiana Press, 1962.

Healy finds spiritual kinship between the two women in spite of the three and a half centuries separating the countess, a Provençal poet, and Labé, about whom we know little except that she wrote one book of poetry in 1555 and that she was both erudite and athletic.

Heilbrun, Carolyn. *"The Masculine Wilderness of the American Novel,"* *Saturday Review*, 55 (January 29, 1972), pp. 41-44.

According to Heilbrun, most American novelists fail to portray "fully human women" in their celebration of physical power and violence, and in their implicit rejection of feminine values set themselves apart from the mainstream of the writings of novelists in other parts of the world.

Heller, Otto. *Studies in Modern German Literature*. Boston: Ginn and Company, 1905.

The value of Heller's presentation of contemporary female writers in Germany, found on pages 231-295, lies chiefly in his bringing attention to them, since his criticism is based upon a certain prudery (he upbraids Maria Janitschek, for example, for her lack of "maidenly modesty" and "unbridled candor") as well as an evident belief in the inviolability of limitations imposed by "Nature" on the creativity of women authors.

Even while he commends them for their enormous output, which justifies including them in a separate section, Heller deplores their "startling absence of freshness and originality" in contrast to women such as George Eliot (Mary Ann Evans) and George Sand. Among those cited are feminists Gabriele Reuter and Helen Böhlen (who was guided by Nietzsche), as well as anti-feminists Clara Viebig and Ricarda Huch. Huch had written nine novels before she was thirty-eight, in addition to critical works, plays and poetry. Calling her *Erinnerungen von Ludolf Ursleu dem Jungeren* her best work, Heller compares her to William Makepeace Thackeray, the British novelist. This novel has been translated by W. A. Drake as *Unconquered Love* (London: Eyre & Spottiswoode, 1931).

Henderson, Nancy L. *"Virginia Woolf's Search for Woman's Place in Scholarship and Art."* Unpublished master's thesis, Florida State University, 1964. 96 p. Bibliography.

Woman's intelligence, postulates Woolf, is intuitive, while man's is factual, and the question of superiority-inferiority is irrelevant. Nevertheless, says Henderson in this careful study, Woolf deplores the effects of sex bias, or the consciousness of sex bias turned against oneself, for it arrests a woman's full development as an artist. Even to her final work, *Between the Acts,* Woolf continued to try to work out a solution to this perennial problem.

Henriot, Émile. *Portraits de femmes d'Héloïse à Katherine Mansfield*. Paris: Michel, 1950. 465 p.

More than fifty famous women (and some of lesser renown) are included in this carefully presented text which quotes generously from original sources. Henriot chooses women of several nations who are considered in the light of their personal accomplishments and/or in relation to well-known men such as Liszt, Flaubert, Constant, and Stendahl.

Henríquez-Ureña, Pedro. ***Literary Currents in Hispanic-America.*** Cambridge: Harvard University Press, 1946.

On pages 75-82 Henríquez-Ureña mentions women who were among the noteworthy writers in the South American colonial period. Outstanding among them was Sor Juana Inés de la Cruz (1651-1695) of Mexico, whose life story is a "prodigious tale of devotion to knowledge," but whose search for it was for the most part thwarted.

On pages 186-189 and 275-276 are listed women writers of modern times from Uruguay, Argentina, China, Peru, Cuba, Santo Domingo, Venezuela, and Brazil. Of Gabriela Mistral of Chile Henríquez writes, "Her work, both in prose and in verse, is one of the noblest of our times." He admits, however, that she, like Sor Juana and her female contemporaries, came to write often on the themes of "disillusion and thwarted lives."

Hentsch, Alice Adèle. ***De la littérature didactique du moyen âge s'addressant specialement aux femmes.*** Halle: Couesland, 1903. 239 p.

After an enlightening introduction which views the varied authors who wrote these didactic books, Hentsch lists and criticizes 114 of them, not only works in French but also some in German, Italian, and Latin. She notes that many of the books were addressed to princesses from whom the writers hoped to receive "un secours pécuniaire" (monetary assistance).

In spite of the many preachments directed at women in an effort to make them pious and unworldly, Hentsch points out that women were probably more literate than men at this time and they, at least those belonging to the privileged classes, enjoyed more liberty than is generally thought. A list of books published after 1550 will be found on pages 235-238. (On page 184 there is a reference to the "danse macabre.")

Hinkley, Laura L. *Ladies of Literature.* New York: Hastings House, 1946. 374 p. Index.

Hinkley's method is to let writers explain themselves through their diaries, letters, recorded conversations, and certain autobiographical portions of their works. The result is a readable and enlightening series of essays on Fanny Burney, Jane Austen, the Brontës, Elizabeth Barrett Browning, and George Eliot. Each essay is accompanied by a useful bibliography.

Holbrook, David. *The Quest for Love.* London: Methuen & Co., 1964. 376 p.

Poet Holbrook reveals his interest in the connection between psychoanalytic theory about love and the human confrontation with reality. Chapter 2, "Chaucer's Debate on Marriage," and Chapter 4, "The Fiery Hill—*Lady Chatterley's Lover,*" are insightful. Characteristically, Holbrook finds Lawrence's portrayal of a sexual relationship actually antithetical to love.

The index provides many intriguing clues to other comments about women, such as men's "fear of women."

Horwitz, Barbara Joan. *"Jane Austen and the Writers on Women's Education."* Unpublished Ph.D. dissertation, State University of New York at Stony Brook, 1979. 337 p.

Horwitz finds Austen innovative in her approach to women's education, for not only did she espouse schools outside the home for them, but she asserted that women could educate their husbands as well as the other way around. Too, since Austen declared that the goal of education is self-knowledge, her novels are free from the didacticism that marred the novels of writers who narrowly defined what women should learn in the interest of conforming to society's "norms."

Huas, Jeanine. *Les femmes chez Proust.* Paris: Hachette, 1971. 286 p. Bibliography, pp. 277-286.

In *La Recherche* Huas finds female characters seemingly based upon actual women in Proust's life, whom she lists on pages 11-12, using their contrasts as a framework for her study.

Through his sufferings, often caused by women, Proust achieved that "sérénité scientifique" through which he created a universe of his own, Huas remarks. She wonders too, however, if as a result of his own deficiencies Proust purposely transmuted some of these women into asexual, minimally human beings, thus assuaging his own pain but nonetheless leaving himself open to criticism because of the deficiencies in these characterizations.

Huguès, Micheline. *"Le sommeil d'Adam et la création d'Eve dans la littérature hexamérale des XVIe et XVIIe siècles,"* Revue de Littérature Comparée, 49 (1975), pp. 179-203.

Centuries-long controversy has flowed around the two accounts of the creation of Eve, each one in the biblical Genesis.

Huguès points out here that Genesis 2:18-25 has been chosen by poets rather than 1:27 because the former is "riche de suggestions esthétiques et idéologiques."[14] In illustration of this, Huguès cites the works of Maurice Scève (*Microme,* 1562), Guillaume Du Bartas (*Semaine,* 1578), John Milton (*Paradise Lost* 1672), and Charles Perrault (*Adam, ou La Création de l'homme*).

Ihrig, Grace Pauline. ***Heroines in French Drama of the Romantic Period.*** New York: King's Crown Press; London: Oxford University, 1950. 240 p. Bibliography, index.

Ihrig purposes to show by quotations (in French) and examples how the selected heroines illustrate Romantic social problems, manners, and philosophy. She dips into the eighteenth century for background, conventions, and idealization, and then brings the reader to an awareness of nineteenth century themes which impinge upon women's life, such as religion. Ihrig concludes that women were portrayed as victims of the repressions of society and opines that change for them was seen to be necessary, at least by sensitive writers.

A chronological list of plays under scrutiny, from Voltaire's *Zaïre* (1732) to *André del Sarto* (1848) by Alfred de Musset.

---

[14] Genesis I:27—So God created man in his own image, in the image of God created he him; male and female created he them. Genesis 2:18—And the Lord God said, It is not good that the man should be alone; I will make him an helpmeet for him. Genesis 2:21-23—And the Lord God caused a deep sleep to fall upon Adam, and he slept; and he took one of his ribs, and closed up the flesh instead thereof; And the rib, which the Lord God had taken from man, made he a woman, and brought her unto the man. And Adam said, This is now bone of my bones and flesh of my flesh; she shall be called Woman, because she was taken out of man. (Verses are from the King James version.)

Jameson, Anna M. *Characteristics of Women, Moral, Poetical, and Historical.* New York: Ams Press, 1967. (Originally published in 1846, with many subsequent editions.) 340 p.

Jameson's introduction consists of a dialogue between a woman and a man regarding the comparative merits of the sexes, with the woman defending the admirable qualities of her own sex. (Compare Mary Astell's similar comparisons (below). The text itself illustrates the woman's defense through a lengthy consideration of the female characters in Shakespeare's dramas. The original London edition is illustrated with 50 vignettes.

Jameson, Anna M. *Memoirs of the Loves of the Poets: Biographical Sketches of Women Celebrated in Ancient and Modern Poetry.* (Essay Index Reprint Series.) Freeport, New York: Books for Libraries Press, 1972. (Originally published in 1857.) 517 p.

This is a goodly selection of women and their *inamorati* who were inspired to create poetry in their honor. Jameson begins with classic times and meanders through the age of the troubadours, the Renaissance in Italy and England, and neo-classical times in England and France. Some attention is given to nineteenth century poetry. The text is enhanced by illustrations from the poetry.

No index in provided and since the arrangement is not strictly chronological, the assiduous researcher will depend upon the table of contents for guidance.

Jayal, Shaakambari. *The Status of Woman in the Epics.* Delhi: Motilal Banarsiass, 1966. 340 p. Bibliography and index.

Jayal notices the difference between the depiction of women in the earliest epics of India, where women are shown discussing deep metaphysical subjects and enjoying freedom of thought, movement, and action, and their portrayal with women in later epics, where they have lost these freedoms and a confining didacticism has become embedded in the text.

As time passed, Jayal explains, the Indian woman suffered a decline in prestige which is reflected in the epics. This caused her finally to be visible only in relation to sexual functions—as wife, mother, widow or seductress.

J. J. Meyer's *Sexual Life in Ancient India* (below) is cited by Jayal as a unique and valuable portrayal of women in the ancient literature. Meyer, he asserts, first called attention to the historical importance of these characterizations in the epics, for they continue to exert strong influences over the women of not only India but all of southeast Asia.

Jeffers, A. Norman. *"Women in Yeats' Poetry,"* in *Homage to Yeats, 1865-1965*, by Walter Starkie and A. Norman Jeffers. (Papers read at a Clark Library Seminar October 16, 1965.) Los Angeles: University of California, 1966.

In his youth, says Jeffers, Yeats was bemused by Rossetti's dream women, with ideals of a "perfect love." These ideals were woven into the poetry Yeats wrote under the inspiration of his love for Maud Gonne. When Maud married another man, Yeats' trauma was so agonizing that he called it a "withering into truth."

Jessup, Josephine Luril. *The Faith of Our Feminists: A Study in the Novels of Edith Wharton, Ellen Glasgow, Willa Cather.* New York: Richard R. Smith, 1950. 128 p.

Separate biographies , followed by bibliographies, of the three writers are tied together by their treatment of the theme of woman's desire "to be herself . . . to measure attainment irrespective of a sexual function." Jessup's critique assesses how well each writer succeeded in creating realistic characters, both women and men.

Johnson, R. Brimley. *Some Contemporary Novelists (Women).* (Essay Index Reprint Series.) Freeport, New York: Books for Libraries Press, 1967. 220 p. (First published in 1920.)

Trends in the writings of the post-World War I "new" women are delineated by Johnson in the introduction to this collection of fourteen essays dealing with as many writers. Most of them—the exception is Virginia Woolf—have not achieved the lasting remembrance they deserve, he says, for although their depictions are true to life, they may have been in search of a deeper reality than the literal—and this deeper reality was related to the continuing conflict about women's place that had changed dramatically since the war.

The lesser-known writers whom he brings to attention are: May Sinclair, Eleanor Mordaunt, Rose Macaulay, Sheila Kaye-Smith, Ethel Sidgwick, Amber Reeves, Dorothy Richardson, Stella Benson, E. M. Delafield, Clemence Dane, Mary Fulton, and Hope Mirrlees.

Jones, Howard Mumford. *"American Comment on George Sand, 1837-1848," American Literature,* III (January, 1932), pp. 389-407.

Jones calls these comments on the French writer some of the "curiosities of comparative literature," for the evaluations of Sand's work reveal the prejudices of the critics; anyone French probably was immoral; as a woman Sand's flouting of convention was especially shocking; and, furthermore, she wrote *novels* (the American reading public still thought novels rather sinful). Therefore Jones decides that in the face of such deep-seated biases we should be skeptical about the extent of the influence of French romanticism on American literary thought.

Jones, Margaret. *"Dialectical Movement as Feminist Technique in the Works of Carmen Laforet,"* pages 109-120 in *Studies in Honor of Gerald E. Wade.* (Studia Humanitatis, directed by Bruno M. Damiani.) Madrid: Ediciones José Turanzas, S. A., 1979.

Jones addresses the question of whether Laforet can be called a feminist, even though she writes almost exclusively about women. The old conflict between repression and independence becomes "feminine *vs.* feminist." In Laforet's work we often find female characters who struggle with this problem (such as Andrea in *Nada* [Barcelona, 1945]).

The goal of the characters is self-assertiveness, but the pull of society, represented by relatives' opinion, male *machismo,* and the messages of the contemporary media (the cinema especially), is overwhelming, for "the myth of the happy ending," or "the Cinderella goal," must lead to home and family. What if the character does not conform? Jones addresses this, too, by considering some of Laforet's other novels.

Jonin, Pierre. *Les personnages féminins dans les romans français de Tristan au XIIe siècle; Étude des influences contemporains.* (Publications des Annales de la Faculté des Lettres.) Aix-en-Provence: Gap, 1958. 528 p.

Dedicated to Jean Frappier, the noted medievalist, this thorough study seeks to shed light on its subject from all perspectives, historical, literary, and religious.

Jonin explains his choice of theme, the role of women in setting events in motion, by pointing out that, after all, "c'est un geste de femme qui crée véritablement le drame du roman." This is his rationale for the careful analysis of the personalities of Iseut la Blonde, Iseut aux Mains Blanches, and Brangien, which becomes the volume's principal focus. The literary-minded will find most assistance in the third part of the work (pages 141-338), with "Les courants littéraires."

A generous bibliography is provided, along with indices of subjects and authors.

Kaplan, Sydney Janet. *The Feminine Consciousness in the Novels of Five Twentieth Century British Women.* Urbana: University of Illinois Press, 1975. 182 p. Bibliography and index.

Dorothy M. Richardson, Virginia Woolf, May Sinclair, Rosamund Lehman, and Doris Lessing are the five who impress Kaplan by the "ingenuity" with which they define themselves as "feminine" according to men's concepts, at the same time rebelling against the implications of these concepts. This rebellion is reflected in the characters in their novels.

Kapp, Julius. *The Women in Wagner's Life.* Translated from the German by Hamah Waller. New York: Alfred Knopf, 1931. 285 p. Index.

According to Kapp, the four most important women in Richard Wagner's life were Minna Planer Wagner, his unhappy wife; Mathilde Wesendouk, Cosima von Bülow, and his mother, to whom he was always "tenderly devoted."

Kavanaugh, Julie. *French Women of Letters: Biographical Sketches.* (Collection of British Authors, Vol. 582.) Leipzig: Bernhard Tauchnitz, 1862. 344 p.

Noting the durability of the "ideal history" created by the imagination, Kavanaugh states her purpose as being to explicate the role of women writers in transmitting this history from generation to generation. In a carefully written series of sketches she turns her attention to many of the most brilliant lights of French literature: Mlles de Gournay and de Scudéry, and Mmes de Tencin, Riccoboni, de Genlis, de Charrière, de Krüdener, Cottin, and de Staël (who receives more detailed treatment).

Although this work is more than a century and a half old, it has many intriguing insights to offer the literary researcher.

Knight, Alan E. *"The Farce Wife: Myth, Parody, and Caricature,"* in *A Medieval French Miscellany,* pages 15-25, edited by Norris J. Lacy. (Humanistic Studies, 42.) University of Kansas Publications, 1972.

Knight sees the medieval farce and other myth-making vehicles as powerfully conservative forces in society as they identify a wife as the source of all marital troubles. This idea, Knight explains, furnishes weak husbands with imaginary sanctions. If this rationale is not enough, excuses may be found in the myth that women are sometimes possessed of the devil (or were demons themselves), a not inconsiderable charge in medieval times.[15]

Kooiman-Van Middendorp, Gerarda Maria. *The Hero in the Feminine NoveL* New York: Haskell House, 1973. 174 p. Bibliog-

---

[15]Virginia Woolf in *A Room of One's Own* touches on these superstitions.

raphy. (Originally published in 1931 at Middelburg by Den Boer.)

After reviewing the characterizations of heroes in the novels of twelve English women from Aphra Behn to Mrs. Humphrey Ward (Mary Augusta Ward), and including the "greats"—Jane Austen, the Brontës, and George Eliot— Kooiman-Van Middendorp concludes that their deficiency in creating strong male characters arose from their diffidence in the face of public opinion. This opinion, which forced them to be "ladies" in a restricted sphere, also deprived them of the social experience that would enable them to be more realistic.

Lafitte-Houssat, Jacques. *Troubadours et cours d'amour.* ("Que sais-je?" numéro 422.) 3e éd. Paris: Presses Universitaires de France, 1979 [1950]. 126 p.

Chapter I, pages 11-23, "La Condition des femmes au moyen-âge," introduces the reader to the ideas of the "courts of love" which in the twelfth century were codified into a system of commandments and judgments described in Chapter IV, "Le Code d'amour" and Chapter V, "Les Jugements d'amour."

The rest of the book is devoted to the literary manifestations of *l'amour courtois* in the poetry of the troubadours and the *romans* of Chrétien de Troyes, who blended the two currents of chivalric romance, that of the Midi of France, where Eleanor d'Aquitaine and Marie de Champagne were its protectors, and the Celtic legends of the Round Table.

Lahy-Hollebecque, Marie. *Anatole France et la femme.* Paris: Éditions Baudinière, 1924. 252 p.

Laly-Hollebecque approaches this fascinating investigation into France's attitude toward women as shown in his literary works by contrasting his ideas on love with his concept of reality. In his *Garden of Epicurus* France seems to adhere to a traditional French interpretation tinged with tolerant cynicism. She concludes that France actually shows neither pity nor justice for women, even though in other respects he was the most advanced writer of his time.

Laiglesia, Edward de. *La Mujer en los libros de caballerías.* Madrid: [Fortenet], 1914. 45 p.

As we read in *Don Quijote,* the good don's head was turned by his obsession with reading books of chivalry—they were not of the "real world," and Cervantes with rollicking humor showed how Don Quijote could mistake a real woman—a rough peasant maid, Aldonza Lorenzo—for the dainty "Dulcinea" of his dreams. In this lecture, however, Laiglesia defends the books of chivalry—Carolingian and Arthurian—for the best that is in them, "las mujeres." Thus he takes a new approach to the romances that Cervantes seemed to disapprove of so heartily.[16]

Lewis, C. S. *The Allegory of Love: A Study in Medieval Tradition.* Oxford: University Press, 1936. 378 p.

Lewis' work has attained the status of a classic in the interpretation of the medieval *ethos,* one important feature of which was the conception of woman's role as more of an ideal to inspire man rather than a person in her own right. The emphasis Lewis makes is literary, with the *Romance of the*

---

[16] But when Don Quijote's library was "purged" by his solicitous friends who thought that romances had affected his mind, he was allowed to keep *Amadís de Gaula,* the most popular of all.

*Rose, The Faerie Queen*e, and Chaucer's and other works the objects of intensive scrutiny within the concepts of erotic allegory. As medievalism declined, a more realistic approach can be seen in the works of Renaissance writers.

An Italian translation, *L'Allegoria d'amore: saggio tradizione medievale* (Turin, 1969) and a Spanish translation, *La Alegoría del amor: estudio sobre la tradición medieval (Buenos Aires, 1969) are available.*

Lida de Malkiel, María Rosa. **Dido en la literatura española: su retrato y defensa.** (Coleccióon Tamesis, serie A, monografía XXXVII.) London: Tamesis Books, 1974 [1944]. 166 p. Index.

"Virgil cantó la pena de una mujer enamorado con los acentos ante los cuales han palidecido las glorias del héroe y de sus armas"—("Virgil sang of the sufferings of a woman in love with a poignancy which made the glories of the armed exploits of the hero pale"), writes Lida de Malkiel as she defends the oft-maligned heroine of the *Aeneid.*

Citing the literature of Spain for its anti-feminism (in Cervantes, Tirso de Molina, Alarcón, Calderón, and others) and Chaucer in England (with his "House of Law") she notes in contrast that San Jerónimo played a large role in the defense of women in medieval times and favored their education, as did Petrarch in Italy.

In his prologue to this edition Yakov gives a short survey of Lida de Malkiel's literary career, stressing the value of this scholarly work which had been published thirty years earlier.

Lilja, Saara. **The Roman Elegists' Attitude toward Women.** (Annales Academiae Scientiarum Fennicae, Series B, Humaniora, Vol. 135.) Helsinki: Suomalainen Tiedeakatemia, 1965. 288 p.

In this study of the poetry of Ovid, Propertius, and Tibullius, Lilja finds that they are generally in favor of a monogamous, free love relationship, but within the context of society's conventions. Men, they lament, are slaves of women, love is a disease, but feminine beauty is to be adored.

Ovid, Lilja decides, is the most sensitive to women's point of view, since he seems to think that their happiness should be considered.[17] A good bibliography is a useful feature of this work.

Littlewood, S. R. *Elizabeth Inchbald and Her Circle: The Life Story of a Charming Woman, 1753-1821.* London: Daniel O'Connor, 1921. 126 p.

Elizabeth's life of literary creativity began when as a girl she ran away from her farm home to take part in London's intellectual life and subsequently to become hostess to that city's most elegant and accomplished society. As a personal note, pages 127-130 contain her own balance sheet of happiness *vs.* unhappiness counted by Septembers, beginning with her marriage in 1772. Her literary works are listed in pages 133-135.

Livet, Charles-Louis. *Précieux et précieuses; caractères et moeurs littéraires du XVIIe siècle.* Quatrième édition. Paris: H. Welter, 1895 [1859]. 442 p.

Les précieuses whom Livet eulogizes here are Mme de Rambouillet, Mme Cornuel, and Mlle de Gournay. To Mme de Rambouillet he gives credit for encouraging the refining of

---

[17] Publius Ovidius Nas (43 B.C.-17 A. D.) wrote the *Metamorphoses*, considered the model of elegiac poetry, but his writings on love, *Amores* and *Ars Amoris*, were also influential in delineating the concept of courtly love in the Middle Ages.

language and manners as her influence led to the development of the art of conversation in her *salon,* which became a magnet for notables who willingly joined her select circle. Her accomplishments also led to the founding of the *Académie Française,* formally established in 1635 by Cardinal Richelieu who was one of Mme de Rambouillet's regular guests.

This refinement was echoed in the high quality of the literature of the time, but enthusiasm slowly died out because of the satire of such clever misogynists as Molière who in such plays as *Les femmes savantes* ridiculed women's efforts to be taken seriously in the intellectual sphere.

Loomis, Emerson Robert. *"The Anti-Gothic English Novel."* Unpublished dissertation, Florida State University. Tallahassee, 1957. 431 p.

The anti-Gothic novel rose in support of realism and many of its exponents, as well as characters, were women. Loomis' description of "the female Quixote" (pages 118-160) is of interest as a basis for a comparison with Cervantes' idealistic and bumbling Don Quijote.. Some of the women writers considered here are Jane Austen, Maria Edgeworth, and Ann Radcliffe

Lorichs, Sonja. **The Unwomanly Woman in Bernard Shaw's Drama and Her Social and Political Background.** (Studia Anglistica Uppsalensia, v. 15.) Uppsala: Rotobeckman, 1973. 196 p. Bibliography. Illustrations.

Ibsen's Nora in *A Doll's House* (1879) is seen here as the prototype of many astute heroines who people Shaw's plays, mirroring contemporary views regarding new freedom for women in Western society.

Lorichs selects Barbara in *Major Barbara* as foremost among the "unwomanly" women, along with Edith and Lesbia in *Getting Married,* Fanny and Margaret in *Fanny's First Play,* Eliza and Clara in *Pygmalion,* and Joan of Arc.

A useful appendix contains a chronology of events leading to woman suffrage in Britain from 1792 onward, and a bibliography of works consulted is included.

Lot, Myrrha Borodine. *La Femme et l'amour au XIIe siècle d'après les poèmes de Chrétien de Troyes.* Paris: A. Picard, et Fils, 1909. (Genève: Slatkine Reprints, 1967.) 285 p.

Lot calls her work "un essai de psychologie sentimentale appliqué au roman courtois," and analyzes Chrétien's concepts of womanhood upon which he based the theories that pervade his work. She treats Chrétien's female characters at length after an informative introduction which surveys the works and their background. Some bibliographical notes accompany the text.

Loyd, Dennis. *"Tennessee's Mystery Woman Novelist,"* Tennessee Historical Quarterly, 29, no. 3 (Fall, 1970), pp. 272-277.

Loyd recounts the humorous story of how Mary N. Murfree, writer of regional short stories and novels, passed as a male author under the pen name of Charles Egbert Craddock from 1878 to 1895. During this time she corresponded with such notables as William Dean Howells and Thomas Bailey Aldrich without their being aware that their correspondent was female until she revealed her identity to Aldrich in 1895. In spite of this "exposure," Murfree continued writing until 1906.

MacCarthy, Bridget G. *The Female Pen.* 2 vols. Cork: Cork University Press, 1946-1947.

MacCarthy's ambitious undertaking encompasses writers from 1621 to 1818 and is especially rich in references to generally unknown women.

Agreeing with Virginia Woolf's bitter complaints about the handicaps which have hampered intellectual women throughout the centuries, MacCarthy shows how compelling social forces have impeded development of the gift of writing, how intellectual power can be rendered ineffectual through discouragement. Margaret, Duchess of Newcastle, and Anne, Countess of Winchelsea, are two examples noted here.

A seven-page bibliography will be found at the end of Volume II, and the work is indexed, which makes research abundantly rewarding.

MacCarthy, Bridget G. *Women Writers: Their Contribution to the English Novel, 1621-1744.* Cork: Cork University Press; Oxford: B. H. Blackwell, 1946. 288 p.

An introductory chapter, "Cogent Influences," describes the handicaps facing women writers in this period. Thereafter MacCarthy delves into literary themes and the biographies of such persistent wielders of the pen as the Countess of Pembroke, the Duchess of Newcastle, Aphra Behn, and many others who produced domestic, sentimental, didactic, and picaresque novels. Plentiful quotations from the works are provided, and there is an index.

MacCarthy's sympathetic appraisals belie one of her epigraphs, composed in 1707 by Susannah Centlivre: "Even my own sex, which should assist our prerogative against . . . detractors, are often backward to encourage the female pen." MacCarthy's work, rewarding for researchers, gives well-deserved praise to her own sex.

Machann, Virginia Sue Brown. *"American Perspectives on Women's Initiations: The Mythic and Realistic Coming to Consciousness."* Unpublished Ph.D. dissertation, University of Texas at Austin, 1977. 553 p.

Machann finds great interest in the "coming to consciousness" of six American women as revealed in their autobiographies: Anne Bradstreet, Elizabeth Ashbridge, Margaret Fuller, Margaret Mead, Anne Morrow Lindbergh, and Mary McCarthy. In addition, she makes a detailed assessment of heroines in the novels of Hawthorne and Henry James in relation to this theme.

McKendrick, Melveena. *Women and Society in the Spanish Drama of the "Mujer Varonil."* London and New York: Cambridge University Press, 1974. 346 p. Index and bibliography.

McKendrick's work is a feminist look at Spanish drama, with the term, "mujer varonil" representing a fusion, in time and place, of nearly all the manifestations of the extraordinary woman which history, mythology, and literature could identify, from one of Lope de Vega's heroines taken from a ballad to women like Queen Christina of Sweden. Chapter 7, pages 218-241, deals with the scholar and the unusual "career woman" of the time. Spanish dramatists were not concerned, however, decides McKendrick, with the potential of women's educational or social emancipation, in spite of the brief vogue of liberating ideas set forth by Erasmus and other humanists. The "mujer varonil" remained strictly an echo of the narrow ideas of the times based on the Spanish *ethos* as presented in dramas by pre-Lopistas onward.

Mackenzie, Agnes Muro. *The Women in Shakespeare's Plays.* London: William Heinemann, 1924. 474 p. Index.

Mackenzie sets out to study Shakespeare's changes in his portrayal of female characters. Only Lady Macbeth and Cleopatra have strength that exceeds usual "feminine" qualities, judges Mackenzie (leaving out Portia). But even in their more stereotyped roles as daughters, sisters, mothers, wives, lovers, and friends, Shakespeare's women are delineated with his keen understanding of the dynamics of human relationships, and thus we are presented with "real" human beings, not wooden versions of what a writer might think a woman is, or should be.

Magnin, Charles, éd. *Le Théâtre de Hrotswitha, religieuse allemande du Xe siècle.* Paris: Benjamin Duprat, 1845. 481 p.

Magnin's introduction, "Hrotswitha, son temps, sa vie et ses ouvrages," contains an appreciative overview of the drama of this generally neglected nun. (Her name is spelled in a variety of ways.) As he analyzes her plays one by one in this first French translation of Hroswitha's work, Magnin remarks that the least known of her plays are those which honor women the most and which relieve the tenth century from the accusation of barbarism which has so often been heaped upon it. Noted, too, is Hroswitha's reported skill in music which matched her dramatic ability.

Markow, Alice Bradley. *"The Pathology of Feminine Failure in the Fiction of Doris Lessing,"* Critique, VI, no. 1 (1974), pp. 88-100.

According to Markow, Lessing seems to believe that women fail to *be* (in the existential sense), because they *will* not to be, mesmerized as they are by their belief in romantic love which will relieve them of the necessity of creating their own *essence.* If all the women in Lessing's fiction seem neurotic, the reason is their belief that society, in transition to new values, is neurotic. Markow points out that Lessing has no pat solutions but thinks that the answer may lie in creating a new society.

Mas, Armédée. *La caricature de la femme du mariage et de l'amour dans l'oeuvre de Quevedo.* Paris: Ediciones hispano-americanos, 1947. 415 p.

The mindset of the Spanish writer Quevedo (1580-1645) in regard to women is explored in detail here, as Mas analyzes the conflicts shown in his poetry, which reveals "une âme déchirée." This has led to a bitter misogyny, a disappointment that women are not perfect, because he cannot merge his desires and his beliefs. His satire becomes a weapon again his female victims, for at times he sees them as demons, devilish temptresses peopling Hell. "L'amour venal est senti comme un combat redoutable, meurtrier pour la bourse, pour le corps. . . . L'arme de ce combat, c'est la femme."

Mas includes plentiful quotations from the poetry and from Quevedo's most famous work, *El Buscón.* Mas disagrees with historian Otis Green that "amour courtois" is a unifying theme in Quevedo's work.

Matulka, Barbara. *The Feminist Theme in the Drama of the Siglo de Oro.* (Comparative Literature Series, Institute of French Studies.) New York: Columbia University, 1933(?). 39 p.

Hispanist Maltulka find in the centuries-old European literary tradition surrounding the feminist:anti-feminist debate a "well plenished storehouse" from which Golden Age dramatists (notably Lope de Vega, Tirso de Molina, and Calderón) fashioned *comedias* to bring freshness and subtlety to the "unsolvable" controversy. By eschewing direct man-woman confrontation, they place the conflict within the feminist characters themselves, where the women "are the ones to offer justification for their change of attitude, womanly reasons that emerge . . . from their very nature."

Thus Matulka shows, using many quotations from the original dramas, that the erstwhile disdainful beauty "ends by resigning herself, without regret to her 'subjection' to Man and Love." By so doing, through the artful mediation of the dramatists, the heroine confers "a welcome victory" upon patient suitors (and the male audience) who have been bewildered by her resistance. Thereby the Renaissance concept of the irresistible lover is strengthened.[18]

In sum, according to Matulka's excellent exegesis (which has bibliographical notes for further research), the *comedia,* although presenting in entertaining form every pro-feminist argument, has finally an anti-feminist message: "Está la discreción de una casada/En amar y servir a su marido." ("That is the prudent decision of a wife/To love and serve her husband").

Matz, Gladys Kern. *"Women and Samuel Johnson."* Unpublished master's thesis, Florida State University, 1952. 99p. Bibliography.

Johnson's conception of women in general, finds Matz, is tied to eighteenth century attitudes, with a decided limit to his

---

[18]Compare Shakespeare's *The Taming of the Shrew,* not one of the bard's best plays, in which the suitor uses strong measures to "woo" his ladylove. In this way, as in the *comedia,* the requirement of the "happy" ending is met. Some similarities to the Griselda legend can be found as well.

sympathy for their desires for greater freedom. His ideal for women may have been perfection, but they must always be aware of men's superiority. Johnson thought he had found some such paragons within his circle in the persons of Hester Thrale, Fanny Burney, and Hannah More, as his biographer James Boswell indicates. Although Boswell was not a misogynist, he uncritically recorded the biting anti-feminist epigrams for which Johnson became famous—before their injustice was acknowledged.

Matz describes the "bluestocking clubs" which looked to more freedom than Johnson would have considered deserved by inferior beings. Attention is given here to his wife and mother, who have in the past received little of it.

Maurois, André. *Cinq Visages de l'amour.* New York: Les Éditions Didier, 1942. 253 p.

Maurois' purpose is to show how writers in differnt epochs depict sexual attraction. Five good psychological studies provide the fare offered by Maurois through his perceptive analyses of such fictional women as the Princesse de Clèves (from Mme de LaFayette), Julie (from Rousseau), Mme de Rênal, Clélia, and Mme de Chasteller (all from Stendahl), Mme Bovary (from Flaubert), and certain heroines from Proust, Balzac, and Choderlos de Laclos. The principle themes covered are chivalry, romance, warfare, passion, ideals, and sensuality. An appendix provides pertinent excerpts from works in which the heroines figure.

This work has been translated as *Seven Faces of Love* by Haakon M. Chevalier (New York: Didier).

Mayne, Ethel Colburn, ed. *The Life and Letters of Anne Isabella, Lady Noel Byron.* New York: Charles Scribner's Sons, 1929. 501 p.

"Her life was spring and winter," is the epigraph for Mayne's book which gives a sympathetic portrayal of the generally misunderstood Lady Byron as it draws upon a great mass of comments preserved by the Byron family. These include Anne's own reminiscences of her life with Byron after she was "freed from the necessity of defending her resolve to escape from his hostility."

Meader, William G. *Courtship in Shakespeare.* New York: Columbia University, King's Crown Press, 1971 [1954]. Index, bibliography.

Meader considers the theme of courtship in relation to courtly love, which he sees as a less permanent attachment than romantic love: courtly love, a favorite theme of earlier writers, focuses on seduction, romantic love on marriage. Taking examples from Celtic legend, Chaucer, Shakespeare, and other Elizabethans, he explains that the sickness which was seen as part of courtship ("hereos") has several stages delineated in the literature, three of which are inception, ordeal, and union.

Melián, Lafinur Luis. *Las Mujeres de Shakespeare.* (Colección de Clásicos Uruguayos, Volume 91.) Prólogo de José G. Antuña. Montevideo: Instituto Nacional del Libro, 1965. 170 p. (First published in 1894.)

Melián calls Shakespeare the greatest dramatic genius in literature because of his understanding of human nature. In these pages we see the hearts of a great number of Shakespeare's women characters revealed. Allusions to French literature abound as Melián compares the bard's ideas with those of such writers as Blaise Pascal and Théophile Gautier.

An appendix goes over the Shakespeare *vs.* Bacon controversy over who truly wrote the dramas historically ascribed to William Shakespeare.

Mews, Hazel. *Frail Vessels: Women's Role in Women's Novels from Fanny Burney to George Eliot.* London: University of London Athlone Press, 1969. 209 p. Notes, index, no bibliography.

The flowering of talent among a group of women over a period of eighty years is a phenomenon that reflects the rapidly changing status of women in Britain, observes Mews, even though the climate of opinion seemed to remain constant.

Here this climate is described, along with the women who made the novel the channel of the "working out of their own changed position in society" as they found an eager reading public composed of women all over England—and no doubt the Empire.

Moeller, Aleidine Johanna. *"The Woman as Survivor: The Development of the Female Figure in Heinrich Böll's Fiction."* Unpublished Ph.D. dissertation, University of Nebraska, 1979.

Combing through Böll's *Gruppen bild mit Dame* (1971) and *Die Verlorene Ehre der Katharina Blum* (1974) Moeller analyzes the development of his heroine. Interestingly enough, she finds that Böll's "standard 'good' woman has been transformed into a mature being ready to meet the threats of war, materialism, and the *Wirtschaftswunder*—which refers to the "economic miracle" of Germany's resurgence from the wreckage of World War II, a miracle initiated by the Marshall Plan. It appears that Böll would see a new Germany deserving of a "new" woman.

Moers, Ellen. *"Bleak House: The Agitating Women,"* Dickensian, 69, no. 1 (January, 1973), pp. 13-24.

Dickens has peopled *Bleak House* with twenty women who display a variety of activities which are not limited by sexual stereotypes. Moers interprets their independent actions carried on out-of-doors as symbols of heroism and compares this symbol to its use in Wordsworth and Charlotte Brontë.

Moers, Ellen. **Literary Women: The Great Writers.** Garden City, New York: Doubleday & Company, 1976. 336 p. Illustrated. Index.

There seems to be something for everyone in this richly detailed study of the "great" writers among women, but Moers does not confine herself to literature by women, a decision which increased her book's interest and usefulness, since women sent their books into a man's world to make their mark or be ignored. Moreover, Moers' little comparisons with male writers adds spice to this closely written text.

"Literature," says Moers, "is the only intellectual field to which women, over a long stretch of time, have made an indispensable contribution," and the principal contributors, she adds, have been English, French, and American women from the eighteenth to the twentieth centuries.

Moers, Ellen. *"Money, the Job, and Little Women,"* Commentary, 55: no 1 (January, 1973), pp. 57-65.

"Monday morning realism" characterizes the writings of women in a way unknown to male writers, observes Moers as she ties together such disparate authors as Jane Austen, Charlotte Brontë, Harriet Martineau, Louisa May Alcott, Harriet Beecher Stowe, and Simone Weil with the thematic thread of work.

While illustrating the modernity of Brontë and Alcott in regard to women's need to have employment beyond "household servitude," Moers contrasts Austen's attitude where "marriage makes money a serious business," the one path whereby genteel women could arrive at security, if not always emotional fulfillment.

Moffatt, Mary Jane and Charlotte Painter, eds. *Revelations: Diaries of Women.* New York: Random House, 1974. 411 p. Lists of sources.

The editors have organized this anthology according to three themes: love, work, and power, using fairly short excerpts from thirty-two writers. Under "Love" are two as discrete as Anne Frank and Louisa May Alcott, while in "Work" are found such contrasts as Ruth Benedict and Dorothy Osborne, and "Power" finds Selma Lagerlöf juxtaposed with Carolina María de Jésus. Moffatt in her foreword considers reasons for keeping a diary and interprets the women's personalities within the context of the three themes.

Moorman, Mary. *The Journals of Dorothy Wordsworth.* London: Oxford University Press, 1971. 231 p. Index.

In this edition Moorman has included the *Alfoxden Journal* of 1798 and the *Grasmere Journal* of 1800-1803. In her introduction Helen Darbishise gives the backgrounds of the life of Dorothy Wordsworth, who first achieved fame as the sister of William Wordsworth, but who now is getting her share of attention as "a rare being who has revealed herself in a living world," a creator in her own right.

Two appendices contain the shorter poems of William Wordsworth mentioned in the text of the journals and two poems by Dorothy herself. Explanatory notes clarify the text.

Moraes, Santos. *Heroínas do romance brasileiro.* Rio de Janeiro: Editora Expressão a Cultura, 1971. 199 p.

On pages 197-199 Moraes gives a list and short biographies of the authors he is studying, male writers who have attempted to create believable female characters. The text consists of Moraes' interpretive analyses of twenty four characters taken from the novels he has chosen.

Moulin, Jeanine. *Christine de Pisan.* Paris: Seighers, 1962. 125 p. Illustrations.

The major part of this little book consists of a collection of Christine de Pisan's poems with beautiful illustrations. Moulin has written an introduction in which she calls Christine the first French feminist, "la première en tout," and also takes into account the theories of Christine's detractors.

Muraro, Rose Marie. *A Mulher na construçao do mundo futuro.* Petrópolis, R. J.: Editora Vozes, 1967. 3rd ed. 207 p. Bibliography.

The life of Brazilian women, past and future, is considered in this little treatise, which also contains a group of poems to women, and an appendix, "A nova estrutura da familia," which imagines beneficial changes.

Nahas, Hélène. *La Femme dans la littérature existentielle.* Paris: Presses Universitaires de France, 1957. 151 p.

The changes in thematic orientation developing from the depiction of women as central to novels gives a new approach to the relations between the sexes, asserts Nahas. With this existential approach comes a frankness which allows the downplaying of romantic love, along with the disintegration of other myths. Revealed frankly now are the themes of obscenity, eroticism, prostitution, and deviants as subjects—all in the "chemins de la liberté." The ideas of Jean-Paul Sartre figure heavily in Nahas' analysis, but she does not prove that Sartre presents strong female characters.

Nef, Elinor Castle. ***Letters & Notes, Volume I.*** Edited by John U. Nef. n.p.: W. Ritchie Press, 1953. 499 p. Illustrations.

Elinor Nef, whose passion was literature, bemoaned the fact that being a good wife and hostess for an eminent professor and historian made it impossible for her to pursue her dream of being an author: "I decided women ought not to write books if they are married, unless they are smart women like Mrs. Trollope, who got up early in the morning and wrote a few chapters before she prepared breakfast for her husband and sons." Although Elinor amassed a great deal of material consisting of insightful essays on modern life and literature, personal letters, and jottings, her writings remained unpublished until her husband organized them into the present work shortly after her death.

This is a good book for browsing, for it is not tightly organized; an index would have been helpful both for finding her insightful comments on a multitude of subjects dealing with modern life and the people she knew. Elinor was a keen observer of people, moving easily in the high circles which composed their *milieu* in the United States, England, and

France. This fact made it possible for her to meet many of the luminaries of the day, about whom she writes candidly, including Virginia Woolf (comments on her are on pages 272-331). Elinor admired and understood Woolf's novels, which male critics generally did not, she believed.

Nelken, Margarita. *Las Escritoras españoles.* (Colección Labor, Biblioteca de Iniciación Cultural.) Barcelona and Buenos Aires: Editorial Labor, S.A., 1930. 235 p.

Nelken's work is a scholarly one, carefully documented and replete with quotations from primary sources. This filled a great need, since historically little attention had been paid to women writers in Hispanic culture. Some of the "sabias" (learned women) who figure prominently in this volume are Santa Teresa, Beatriz Galindo, Oliva Sabuco, Luisa Segia, Feliciana Enrique de Guzmán, Caro, Ana, Maria de Zayas y Sotomayor, Luisa de Padilla, Carolina Coronado, Fernán Caballero, and Emilia Pardo Bazán.

Social backgrounds are considered, too, for Nelken states as one of her objectives, "dar idea del ambiente en que se ha desarrollado esta parte nada despreciable de nuestras letras."

Nin, Anaïs. *The Diary of Anaïs Nin.* 6 vols. Edited by Gunther Stuhlmann. New York: Swallow Press,

Author of a 5-volume *roman fleuve, Cities of the Interior,* and the essay *On Women's Liberation* ((1971), Nin has also gathered fame as a diarist. Importance is added to her intimate reportings of her psychological states by the fact that she "moved freely, and sometimes mysteriously, in the cosmopolitan world of international art and society," as Stuhlmann tells us.

These four volumes span a period from 1931 to 1947. An index forms a good guide to subjects that may be especially interesting, but only by reading the diary in its totality can one experience the effect of its undulating prose and soul-searching candor.

O'Connor, Patricia. *Women in the Theater of Gregorio Martínez Sierra.* New York: American Press, 1966. 150 p.

Martínez Sierra, a nineteenth century champion of woman's political liberation, produced plays whose themes dealt almost exclusively (most often romantically) with some facet of women's lives. However, O'Connor points out, as a Spaniard he had few female models except those related to their roles as sexual beings. In spite of this, O'Connor praises him for his insight which allowed him to create heroines who could embody the modern woman.[19] In *Sueño de una noche de agosto* he describes a girl who resents her three brothers' freedom, and in *Seamos felices* he shows a woman who has an opportunity to be a concert pianist.

In an appendix O'Connor gives the plots of the plays she discusses, and a bibliography of books and articles contains materials on Martínez Sierra and other authors referred to in the text.

Olsen, Tillie. *Silences.* New York: Dell Publishing Company, 1978 [1965]. 330 p. (Also published by The Feminist Press.)

---

[19]Martínez Sierra's wife, too, was an ardent feminist and a "modern woman" who could inspire him to write feminist dramas. His plays, however, were usually characterized by happy endings.

This is an excellent book for browsing; its purpose is inspirational. As Olsen describes it, "This book is not an orthodoxly written work of academic scholarship. . . . The substance herein was long in accumulation, garnered over fifty years. . . ." Olsen's incisive comments alternate with illustrative quotations from many well-known writers who have endured the "silences" when for many reasons their creativity was diminished—or absent altogether.

Orléans, Charlotte-Elizabeth, Duchesse d'. *A Woman's Life in the Court of the Sun King: Letters of Liselotte von der Pfalz, Elisabeth Charlotte, Duchesse d'Orléans, 1652-1722.* Translated and introduced by Elborg Forster. Baltimore: Johns Hopkins University Press, 1984. 287 p. Index. Illustrations.

Forsberg notes that these letters "have long enjoyed the status of a literary classic in Germany and a valuable historical source in France." His purpose in translating selections from the great quantity of letters Liselotte wrote to her family after her marriage to the decadent Duc d'Orléans, the only brother of Louis XIV, is to make a portion of this intelligent woman's fifty-year-long commentary available to English speakers, not only because it is instructive but because it is fascinating reading, especially for women.

Although Liselotte was to live all the rest of her unhappy life in France, she thought of herself as German, and that was the principal language she used in her letters (to the irritation of the censors). The letters are very human, and very candid, sometimes humorous (she could even laugh at Mme de Maintenon, the pious wife of the king, when the girls at her St. Cyr academy shamelessly misbehaved). The underlying themes, however, are homesickness (but appreciation for those who are kind to her, including the king himself), disgust at the debauchery she sees everywhere, and fatalism about her own life and death.

Orñate, María del Pilar. *El feminismo en la literatura española.* Madrid: Espasa-Calpe, S. A., 1938. 256 p.

In *Cantar de Mio Cid* (c. 1150), says Orñate, we can see the figure of Jimena as the first tentative ("esbozo") of the ideal which inspired the pages of *La perfecta casada* (by Luis de León, 1528-1591), four centuries later. This perfect Spanish wife was declared to be (by males in authority) one who venerates her husband as master and lord, giving him "la cortesía servil de los tiempos feudales."[20]

Orñate painstakingly follows the centuries, illustrating from literature as she goes, and concludes after her study that although Spanish women of her day had advanced somewhat toward the goal of social justice, the "battle of the sexes" would never achieve satisfying results—"la lucha entre hombres y mujeres está condenada a la esterilidad." (See Ornstein, below, for an example.)

Ornstein, Jacob, ed. *Luis de Lucena: "Repetitión de amores."* (University of North Carolina Studies in Romance Languages and Literatures, No. 23.) Chapel Hill: University of North Carolina Press, 1954. 130 p. Bibliography.

---

[20]These works bear the imprint of the Moorish (Arab, Moslem, Musselman) culture which controlled the Spanish peninsula from 711 to 1492. Strangely enough, although Spanish men battled the Moors for eight centuries, finally chasing them from their lands, they did not appear eager to extirpate the Moorish Koranic teachings which controlled Christian women's lives so rigidly.

Anti-feminist Lucena's work was pivotal in the feminist debate which had flourished among literary men in the Middle Ages and echoed even until the sixteenth century, with Cervantes being anti- and Cristóbal pro-feminist. Ornstein's 32-page introduction to Lucena's text gives a good survey of the debate in Spain, with some references to Latin, Italian, Hebrew, and French ideas. A chart lines up the combatants, and happily the "pros" outnumber the "cons."

"*Repetición de amores,*" remarks Ornstein, is "the most extensive anti-feminist document of early Spanish literature," but it has been neglected by scholars (fortunately). He adds that Lucena "takes his place at the side of the brutal detractors of women in world literature," along with Juvenal, Jean de Meung, and Boccaccio.

Paradis, Suzanne. *Femme fictive, femme réelle: le personnage féminin dans le roman canadien français, 1884-1966.* Québec: Garneau, 1966. 330 p.

Not addressing herself to the literary merit of given works but concentrating on the portrayals of women in general, Paradis isolates about eighty characters from women novelists in Québec and considers each one separately.

Park, Clara Claiborne. *"As We like It: How a Girl Can Be Smart and Still Popular,"* American Scholar, 42, no 2 (Spring, 1973), pp. 262-278.

Park looks at two of Shakespeare's heroines, Rosalind in *As You Like It,* and Beatrice in *Much Ado about Nothing* to illustrate the general principle that audiences like their women characters smart but not too much so. In support of this she cites an analogy from twentieth century popular literature, where

Eric Segal's *Love Story* won readers for allowing a very intelligent girl to sacrifice her own gifts for her husband.

Park notes, however, that Shakespeare departed from this principle when he created Portia: in her person female intelligence carries the day without the restraint of possible audience disapproval.

Parker, David. *"Can We Trust the Wife of Bath?"* Chaucer Review, IV, no. 1 (1970), pp. 90-98.

That is, says Parker, can we trust the words of Chaucer's delightful character enough to give us a reliable idea of what a fourteenth century woman might be like? He objects to critics who say that the Wife of Bath is only a part of the "iconography of the work." He finds the inconsistencies in her attitude toward marriage believable, for these ideas are still vividly recognizable today. He is inclined to trust Chaucer as a superb portrait painter of women as well as men.

Parker, William R. *"Ellen Glasgow: A Gentle Rebel,"* English Journal (College Edition), XX, no. 3 (March, 1931), pp. 187-194.

Glasgow was "the gentlest rebel to whom Virginia has yet given birth," says Parker, but her rebellion against aspects of Southern life she considered mediocre or ugly was uncompromising, and her insistence that the South break away from the outworn habits of the past proves her to be as modern as any writer of the day.

Parton, James. **Daughters of Genius.** Philadelphia, Pennsylvania: Hubbard Bros., 1888. 563 p. Illustrations.

With nineteenth century optimism Parton noted that the most important result of the advances in the culture had been the increased power allowed to women to exercise their talents—"to which we can set no limits." He pays homage to "authors, artists, reformers, heroines, queens, princesses, and women of society, women eccentric and peculiar," praising them for persevering in using their talents "in the teeth of every conceivable disadvantage."

Paz Pasamar, Pilar. *La Mujer y la poesía de lo cotidiano.* Madrid: Ateneo, 1964. 30 p.

The problems of the creative woman ("la mujer creadora"), the woman poet of Hispanic culture, are sympathetically considered, with attention given to the temptation of such a woman to use her pen to escape from the tyranny of the tasks of daily living. Vallejo and Mistral are mentioned.

Pinet, Marie-Josèphe. *Christine de Pisan, 1364-1430: étude biographique et littéraire.* (Bibliothèque du XVve siècle.) Paris: Librairie Ancienne Honoré Champion, 1927. 463 p.

Pinet notes that up to the sixteenth century Christine de Pisan was remembered and praised by such men as Clément Maret, Jean Maret, Jean Bouchet, and William Worster, but in the sixteenth century her name fell into oblivion and was rescued only in the middle of the eighteenth century. Since then respect for her life and work has steadily grown in France and elsewhere. *La Cité des Dames* is the work which has earned for her the title of France's first feminist (although not everyone is convinced that she was truly a "feminist").

In this thorough and well-documented study, Pinet has endeavored to assist the reader in understanding Christine and her work, observing sympathetically that her life was marked by wrenching changes.... "Tu es venue en mauvais temps," she said of herself. ("You have come at a bad time.") After her widowhood at the age of twenty-nine, Christine wrote to earn money, thus becoming the first Frenchwoman to live by her pen. Her complete works are listed on page xix of Pinet's, introduction, and this work is indexed.

Pizan, Christine de. *Le Livre de la Cité des Dames.* Texte traduit et presenté par Éric Hicks et Thérèse Moreau. Stock: Moyen Age, 1986. 291 p. (Originally published c. 1405.)

Comparing Christine to Virginia Woolf, Hicks and Moreau quote passages which echo the theme so familiar in the writings of Mmes de Sévigné, de Lafayette, de Staël and Mlle de Gournay, along with George Sand and countless others: the difficulty of being an intellectual woman in a male-oriented world.

Some writers are not convinced of Christine's feminist convictions, but there is no doubt that she would have espoused the cause of women's liberation if she had lived in the modern world. In her world her quality of pragmatism helped her survive as a widow living upon the income of her books: she counseled women to remain in "their place," for the weight of religion was equal to that of a "caste guerrière," with the power of the ayatollahs of modern Iran, as Hicks and Moreau point out.

This work is plentifully annotated and has a useful chronology of Christine's works from 1364 to 1430. ("Pizan" is a variant of the more usual "Pisan.")

Plomer, H. R. *"Robert Copland,"* Transactions of the Bibliographical Society of London, III (1895-96), pp. 211-25.

Satirist Copland, a sixteenth century translator, lost no time in capitalizing on the widespread interest in the contemporary debate on the subject of women (the English version of the *querelle des femmes*). He kept up with the latest books written in France from 1536 on and through his translations made it possible for English writers to add to the arguments.

Louis B. Wright in *Middle Class Culture in Elizabethan England* (below) mentions Copland's influence on popular thought.

Poe, Edgar Allan. *"Sarah Margaret Fuller,"* in *The Shock of Recognition: The Nineteenth Century,* edited by Edmund Wilson. 2d ed. (Grosset's Universal Library) New York: Grosset and Dunlap, 1955.

Appearing in 1846, this critical essay considers briefly Fuller's *Woman in the Nineteenth Century* (1845), her feminist tract which had been condemned by Poe's fellow critics. Poe, calling himself neutral, evidently felt that much of the condemnation stemmed from a sense of outrage that Fuller would criticize the *status quo*. Nevertheless, he does question Fuller's assumption that all women shared her feelings. Fuller was definitely before her time. Her sincere hope was to be able to awaken women to be aware of their potential, but it is natural that few would wish to be so rudely awakened. (Fuller's ideas were a far cry from Catharine Beecher's advice to create a "pink and white tyranny" in the home in order to assert oneself.)

A description of Fuller's personal appearance closes this essay, which belies the usual epithet "ugly": those who found her ideas abhorrent probably could see less beauty in her appearance than Poe, who, more open-minded than most of his fellow critics, could see that not all of them were handsome—so what had that to do with scholarly accomplishment?

Power, Eileen. *Medieval People.* New York: Barnes and Noble, 1968. (Originally published in 1924.)

Chapter IV, pages 83-95, delves into Chaucer's *Canterbury Tales* to consider the situation of "Madame Eglentyne." Power sees her as a prototype of the contemporary nun, drawing from primary historical sources for her descriptions. Chaucer is thereby shown to have been "one of the most wonderful observers in the whole of English literature." How many know, she asks, that Madame Eglentyne never should have been in the *Prologue* at all, for the Church was adamant in its disapproval of pilgrimages for nuns.

Going in another direction, Power looks at the courtesy book, *Le Ménagier de Paris*, to relate its advice to the contemporary ideal of a wife's deportment, which preached submission. *Le Ménagier,* decides Power, is superior to all other medieval books of behavior for women, since it declares that women should not be slaves to their husbands but should be "helpmeets."

Rackowski, Cheryl Stokes. *"Women by Women: Five Contemporary English and French-Canadian Novelists."* Unpublished Ph.D. dissertation, University of Connecticut, 1978. 315 p. Bibliography.

Margaret Atwood, Marie-Clair Blais, Anne Hébert, Margaret Lawrence, and Claire Martin are the authors whose works Rackowski studies to isolate their techniques in creating heroines who must find some degree of self-fulfillment while leading "cramped lives conforming to (or rebelling against) society's stereotypes of female behavior and roles." Summing up, she presents her assessment of the contrasts between the French and the English writers in the way they handle materials for their fiction.

Raper, Julius Rowan. *Without Shelter: The Early Career of Ellen Glasgow.* (Southern Literary Studies.) Baton Rouge: Louisiana State University Press, 1971. 273 p. (Reprinted in 1982 by Greenwood Press.)

Glasgow lived from 1874 to 1945. Raper here considers a period in Glasgow's life up to 1906 when the influence of Darwinism was evident in her thought and her novels, one of which, *The Voice of the People,* Raper concentrates upon. Social and intellectual aspects relating to Glasgow's work are featured in this work as much as the literary.

Reagor, Margaret. *"Human Aspects of Four Ill-fated Women of Racine."* Unpublished M.A. thesis, Vanderbilt University, 1938. 106 p.

Hermione the vain, Roxane the sensuous, Eriphile the envious, and Phèdre the conscience-stricken are Racine's *femmes damnées,* each of whom has a chapter of her own in Reagor's work.

Quoting from the dramas to illustrate the characteristics of the four women, Reagor sees them comparable in that each allows her heart to conquer both will and reason. Although she finds evidence that Racine was influenced by Jansenist doctrine in his delineation of character, Reagor avers that his genius is not encompassed by it to the extent that his female characters are not credible in the twentieth century.

Richards, Samuel Alfred. *Feminist Writers of the Seventeenth Century.* London: D. Nutt, 1914. 146 p.

It is to France of the seventeenth century that we must look, asserts Richards, if we wish to trace the development of the woman's movement. To this end he cites the pioneer work of *les précieuses* who paved the way for the serious advocacy of equality of the sexes by their literary and social supremacy among their contemporaries. Pointing to the relationship of French ideas with those of Mary Wollstonecraft later, he finds that the French raised first the questions to which she addressed herself so earnestly.

In this work Richards furnishes good research leads for the study of feminists (male as well as female) as he considers their contributions. Some of these, many of them comparatively unknown, are François Poulain de la Barre, Jacques du Bose, Louis Machon, Anne-Marie de Schurman, Jacquette Guillaume, G. de Vertron, C. M. D. Noel, and G. S. Aristophile.[21] In addition, he analyzes works of contemporary fiction for evidence of feminist ideas.

A six-page bibliography enhances the value of this study.

Rivers, Elias L. *"Indecencias de una monjita mejicana,"* in *Homenaje a William L. Fichter,* ed. por A. David Kossoff y José Amor y Vazquez, pages 633-637. Madrid: Editorial Castalia, 1971.

---

[21] Poulain de la Barre wrote *De L'Éducation des dames* in 1674, one of his pro-feminist works. This is available on microfilm (1975).

The "monjita mejicana" is seventeenth-century Sor Juana Inés de la Cruz (1651-1695), and the subject under discussion, the "indecencias," is the pro-feminism (or anti-masculinism) that it is possible to see in her *comedia, Los empeños de una casa,* published in 1692, four years after it was written. Rivers comments upon Sor Juana's great intelligence, as well as upon her daring.

Robert, Roberto, *et al. Las Españolas pintadas por los Españoles.* 2 vols. Madrid: J. E. Morete, 1871. 306 p.

These essays portray more than thirty depersonalized types of women, ranging from "la nerviosa" to "la que lleva perro," with the professed purpose of making Spanish women more understandable. The general effect, however, is one of patronizing, gentle (more or less) humor. Two by Perez Galdós are included, "La mujer del filósofo" and "Cuatros mujeres."

Rocha, Adelaide M. *O diálogo continua.* São Paulo: Herder Editora, 1967. 104 p.

Rocha encourages an existential stance as she advises Brazilian women to assert themselves and says that in literature they will find clues to mark the way. Quoting Malraux, Simone de Beauvoir, and Nietzsche, she exhorts women to take up the inward struggle: "Sempre a considerei como uma heroína atravessando todos os combates" in order to prove their humanity through existential courage in every situation of their lives.

Rodax, Yvonne. *The Real and the Ideal in the Novella of Italy, France and England: Four Centuries of Change in the Boccaccian Tales.* (University of North Carolina Studies in Comparative Literature, No. 44.) Chapel Hill: The University of North Carolina Press, 1968. 136 p.

Chapter V, pages 62-80, "A World in Splints: Marguerite d'Angoulême," characterizes Marguerite as "more mystic than poetic, more *grande dame* than philosopher, and, it appears more feminine than anything else.

Rodax asserts that Marguerite discovered in her maturity the unifying key to her whole cosmos, love. This principle of love, used in a "merry" fashion, is at the base of the *Heptaméron*, through which Marguerite describes the carnal *amour* tempered into "that love of God which can turn a poor muleteer's wife into a martyr in the cause of chastity."[22]

Rosenbaum, Sidonia. ***Modern Women Poets of Spanish America.*** New York: The Hispanic Institute in the United States, 1945. 273 p. Index.

A thought-provoking introductory essay discusses the poets who were precursors of the four whom Rosenbaum considers most important: Delmira Agustini, Gabriela Mistral, Alfonsina Storni, and Juana de Ibarbourou. He sees the "flowering of feminist literature in Latin America coincidental with the triumph of feminism everywhere," although not all these poets are strictly feminist. Passages from the works are included, as well as biographical text. A good bibliography, pages 257-268, will be useful for researchers in Hispanic poetry.

Ross, Ernest C. ***The Ordeal of Bridget Elia: A Chronicle of the Lambs.*** Norman: University of Oklahoma Press, 1940. 232 p.

---

[22] A *Heptaméron* (meaning "seven") was a collection of often spicy stories supposed to be told in seven days for the entertainment of a group. Marguerite's work was published in 1558, seven years after her death. She is variously called Margaret of Navarre, Marguerite de Navarre, and Marguerite d'Angoulême.

Mary Lamb is best known as English essayist Charles Lamb's sister, but Ross reveals that their chief collaborative work, *Tales from Shakespeare*, was preponderantly her creation. Basing his account in great part upon autobiographies and letters as well as numerous biographies of the Lambs, Ross hopes to dispel the myth of Mary's permanent insanity as he shows that in spite of recurrent manic-depressive attacks throughout her long life, she was known among her many friends as a woman of unusual brilliance, a scholar and conversationalist whom William Hazlitt called the only reasonable woman he had ever known.[23]

Ross is perceptive as he highlights many details of the grueling, boring household routine as it adversely affected many women of great intelligence, even genius, who could have accomplished much if time and energy had permitted.

Rubenius, Aina. *The Woman Question in Mrs. Gaskell's Life and Work.* (Essays and Studies on English Language and Literature, No. 5.) Uppsala: Lundequist; Cambridge: Harvard University Press, 1950. 396 p.

Beginning with a survey of woman's position in England from 1800 to 1850, Rubenius turns to Mrs. Gaskell's personal life and her feminist contacts to demonstrate her sympathy for the plight of middle and lower class women in the early days of the Industrial Revolution.

---

[23] During one of her attacks, Mary tragically killed her mother. Charles, however, continued to care for his sister, since much of the time she was able to pursue a fairly normal life. Hazlitt, a writer and critic, was an expert in Elizabethan drama, one of Mary's chief interests.

This work is well-documented, with many relevant passages from Gaskell's novels which underscore her sensitivity to the social and political developments of her times. In creating her novels she believed, as did Charles Dickens, that she could more easily arouse the public through literature than through pressing for legislation to ameliorate the lot of workers.

Gaskell's literary influences are documented in an appendix, and a bibliography will be found on pages 373-386.

Ruddick, Sara, and Pamela Daniels, eds. *Working It Out: 23 Women Writers, Artists, Scientists, and Scholars Talk about Their Lives and Work.* Foreword by Adrianne Rich. New York: Pantheon Books, 1977. Illustrations. 349 p.

This anthology contains a wealth of opinion, and a wealth of references to women who have chosen their work and found success, and those who are still struggling to do so. The essayists put twentieth century touches on the problems faced by women in the past, in spite of the changes which have addressed some of the most pressing ones. There are even new problems, as, for example, the necessity for dovetailing one's own work with one's husband's (in the past women had to follow their husbands), and endeavoring to break into fields which have been inviolably reserved for males (when educational opportunities were not available), and the difficulties of rearing children in urban society without household help (women do not have "wives" to help them as men do).

Rich defines feminism: "Feminism means finally that we renounce our obedience to the fathers and recognize that the world they have described is not the whole world." The task of creating another world—independent or peripheral—is a matter for intense discussion. Tillie Olsen's "One Out of Twelve:

Women Who Are Writers in Our Century" (which is notable for its listing of women writers) is reminiscent of Virginia Woolf's "A Room of One's Own."

Saenz-Alonso, Mercedes. ***Don Juan y el donjuanismo.*** (Colección Universitaria de Bolsillo, Punto Omega.) Madrid: Ediciones Guadarrama, 1969. 330 p.

Scores of interpretations of Don Juan Tenorio's escapades and personality in Tirso de Molina's *El Burlador de Sevilla* have appeared, with only brief notice given to the women who became his victims. Since a "burlador" is one who mocks or plays a rough joke on someone, the title of this play speaks for itself in the context of the traditional attitudes toward women. Saenz-Alonso has addressed this oversight in a study signalling womanly perspectives, with a chapter devoted to *las seducidas* ("the seduced women").

Hispanist Gerald E. Wade remarked that "an added and quite significant value lies in the fact of the book's composition by a woman. Few of her sex in Spain have chosen to express themselves on the Don Juan theme." He notes, however, that Saenz-Alonso is condoning, not challenging, the *donjuanismo* concept. Wide-ranging in scope, this work also looks at how Tirso's *burlador* has influenced music, the arts, philosophy, and several literatures over the centuries. An appendix by Javier Bello Portú details Don Juan's influence on music.

Salomon, Louis Bernard. ***The Devil Take Her: A Study of the Rebellious Lover in English Poetry.*** New York: A. S. Barnes, 1961. 359 p. (First published by the University of Pennsylvania Press, 1931.)

This survey could be called, as Salomon remarks, "a study in masculine unoriginality," for the expressions of rebellion which merge into misogyny are so similar. The rebellion is against the idealization of woman in courtly tradition: "The masculine ego struggles against its ignominious bonds."

Most of the poets viewed are minor, but John Donne, Richard Crashaw, and Robert Herrick also figure here. Two chapters, "Equal Rights" and "Against Women," are of especial interest, and an exhaustive index, pages 298-351, is handily categorized by themes.

Sandelion, Jeanne. *Montherlant et les femmes; avec 45 lettres inédites de Henry de Montherlant.* Paris: Librairie Plon, 1959. 260 p.

The accent of this work is mainly psychological as it views Montherlant in the light of the feminine characters he has created. Sandelion describes the event which inspired her to undertake this project—a dinner with Montherlant, during which they had a conversation which she minutely recorded.

Montherlant's genius is characterized as a synthesis of the "masculine" qualities of *sobriété, sévérité,* and *énergie,* and the "feminine" qualities of *instinct, poésie, nostalgie du bonheur, bovaryisme,* and *humeurs.*[24]

---

[24]"Bovaryisme" is derived from Flaubert's *Madame Bovary*, and "bovaryisme" (relative to Emma Bovary's unconventional actions, refers to a woman's romantic, unrealistic conception of herself, probably stemming from her inability to tolerate the boredom of her life, as Emma Bovary could not. Most male critics have not been sympathetic to this and the term is often used disdainfully. "Nostalgie du bonheur" is akin to "bovaryisme" (English "bovaryism"), but is not so reprehensible, since it may be a passive reaction to unhappiness. Emma stepped outside the bounds of conventional morality, as did Anna in Tolstoy's novel *Anna Karenina,* and both women chose the same

Schiff, Mario. *La Fille d'alliance de Montaigne: Marie de Gournay.* (Bibliothèque de la Renaissance, no. x.) Genève: Slatkine Reprints, 1978. 145 p. (First published at Paris by Librairie Honoré Champion, 1910.)

In spite of the prestige of being Montaigne's adoptive daughter and sharing the intellectual life of her parents, Marie's poignant testimony to her resentment at the inferior status of women is revealed in her two essays, found on pages 61-77: "Égalité des hommes et des femmes" (1622), and "Grief des dames" (1626).

Schiff adds material on variants of the manuscripts and useful bibliographical information, including the Italian reception of Marie's work. Also of great interest is the account of the friendship of Marie and Anne-Marie de Schurman (b. 1607), who had an amazing linguistic ability: she knew Hebrew, Chaldean, Syrian, Arabic, Greek, Latin, French, Italian, Flemish, and Dutch, besides being versed in the arts and sciences of her day.

Schinnerer, Otto Paul. *Women in the Life and Work of Gutzkow.* (Columbia University Germanic Studies, no. 28.) New York: Ams Press, 1966 [1924]. 177 p. Bibliography in German.

Karl Gutzkow, a novelist and poet who was part of the Young Germany movement in the early nineteenth century, held the strange belief that "what men truly love in women is due to the recollections of our mother or of a sister who stood the test

way out of their dilemma.

of unselfishness," while what men hate in women often comes from their wives and *fiancées*.

Chapter III is headed "Women's Emancipation and Free Love." Although Gutzhow was not happy in adult life, he was nevertheless an ardent champion of marriage in his search for woman who would demonstrate the "unselfishness" he had experienced as a child, with, it appears, little thought to be given to the happiness of the "unselfish" wife. Schinnerer notes that more work should be done in analyzing this German writer's attitudes and their influence. His work was first presented as a thesis to Columbia University in 1924.

Schlauch, Margaret. *Chaucer's Constance and Accused Queens.* New York: New York University Press, 1927. 142 p. (Ann Arbor, Michigan: University Microfilms, 1983.)

The focus of this study is Chaucer's *Man of Law's Tale,* for which Schlauch treats the *motif* of an innocent, accused, exiled, and restored queen in relation to other families of stories dealing with this same theme.

Notes are provided, as is an appendix which summarizes the romances under discussion.

Schreiber, S. Etta. *The German Woman in the Age of Enlightenment: A Study in the Drama from Gottsched to Lessing.* New York: King's Crown Press, 1948. 257 p.

The German woman's changing spirit from dependence to self-assertiveness is reflected in the drama of this period as bourgeois ideals gain ascendancy and pave the way for the women in Goethe and Schiller, comments Schreiber. She carefully analyzes the dramatic works of their precursors according to the social philosophies concerning women which appear in a short chapter on "The Moral Weeklies."

Annotations give clues for further research, and there is an excellent bibliography in English and German.

Schwartz, Kessel. *"Eva Canel: Forgotten Psychological Novelist and Conservative Spokeswoman for Hispanism,"* pages 199-212, in *Studies in Honor of Gerald E. Wade,* edited by Sylvia Bowman *et al.* Madrid: Ediciones José Turanzas, S.A., 1979.

Canel, says Schwartz, concentrates on women in society and their idea of love (a vitiating or a redeeming force), as she uses her intuitive knowledge of the "feminine heart" to create characters who suffer from neuroticism, disillusionment, and conflict in relationships. It is Canel's contention that the orthodox Spanish morality, with its view of woman as a subordinate creature, has encouraged the development of neuroticism.

Nevertheless, Schwartz points out as he analyzes her literary output (short stories, dramas, and novels) that she "ambivalently defends" the traditional *ethos,* because—even though her female characters are often immoral—she believes in strict moral codes, especially for the education of the young. To confuse the issue more than ever, Canel herself refused to adhere to the codes completely: if she had, Schwartz opines, she would not have written novels, a disapproved occupation for women. One of these, *Oremus* (Havana, 1893), she wrote in 25 days, "locked up in a stuffy little hotel room," composing it for a friend who wanted a novel to translate. Because of Canel's interest in Cuba and her social work there, she has been looked upon as a Cuban author, also.

Sedwick, Frank. ***A History of the Useless Precaution Plot in Spanish and French Literature.*** (University of North Carolina

Studies, No. 4.) Chapel Hill: University of North Carolina Press, 1964. 84 p.

Sedwick traces the development of the sixteenth century theme of the "useless precaution," referring to the frustrations, often comic, of male protectors of female virtue who have little success in their attempts at managing their unruly charges, and their deceived protectors become laughable figures, with their "honor" compromised.

Here Sedwick considers plays from such solicitous writers as Cervantes, Lope de Vega, and Molière. The paternalism reflects the contemporary *ethos,* but the humor hides a deep anxiety about the ability of society to delay the liberation of women forever. The popularity of this theme finally faded, perhaps owing to the improvement in the status of women.

Sejourné, Philippe. *Aspects généraux du roman féminin en Angleterre de 1740 à 1800.* (Publications des Annales de la Faculté des Lettres, no 52.) Aix en Provence: Gap, Éditions Ophrys, 1966. 568 p.

In a perfect world, where women had found their true place of dignity, the sentimental novel would not have had such overwhelming success, limited as it was and based on formulas of feelings and action, declares Sejourné. In the sentimental novel is reflected a society which smothers its female victims: through an accessible means (the literature of the unbelievable) some showed that they thirsted for deliverance. In spite of their shortcomings, Sejourné praises the novels of this period as precursors of the works of great writers who came later—Jane Austen, George Eliot, the Brontës, and even Sir Walter Scott.

This is an excellent study with a valuable bibliography, pages 515-555, along with an index of names, a list of works of women whose works are analyzed here. Some of these are Charlotte Lennox, Ann Radcliffe, Frances Sheridan, Charlotte Smith, Fanny Burney, and Mary Wollstonecraft

Seymour-Smith, Martin. *Fallen Women: A Sceptical Inquiry into the Treatment of Prostitutes, Their Clients, and Their Pimps in Literature.* (Natural History of Society.) London: Thomas Nelson, 1969. 206 p. Index.

This work contains no close analysis of a few writers but ranges the field of world literature to identify passages substantiating the results of the inquiry. Zola's *Nana,* however, being selected as "the most celebrated" work of fiction to portray the life of a prostitute, is singled out, with Seymour-Smith concluding that Zola has failed to make of Nana a believable human being.

An appendix contains the "Letter from a London Prostitute," reprinted from the *London Times* of February 24, 1858.

Shinn, Thelma J. *"Women in the Novels of Ann Petry,"* Critique, VI, no. 1 (1974), pp. 11-120.

Although Petry is a black writer, comments Shinn, she does not limit herself to ethnic problems, concerning herself instead with the "acceptance and realization of individual possibilities" for all. Nevertheless, the many problems encountered in her novels are usually those of black women, for they are problems characteristic of a society that constricts the individual and makes her or him less "human."

Showalter, Elaine, ed. *Women's Liberation and Literature.* New York: Harcourt Brace Jovanovich, 1971. 338 p.

An anthology designed to be used as a text in women's studies, this collection purports to be objective by presenting samples of a variety of viewpoints. Authors represented include Mary Wollstonecraft, Kate Millett (*Sexual Politics*), Henrik Ibsen (*A Doll's House* is featured), Simone de Beauvoir, and Sigmund Freud (with an *exposé* of the failings of his school of psychology).

Siclier, Jacques. *La femme dans le cinéma français.* (Les Éditions du Cerf.) Paris: Cerf, 1957. 196 p.

Differing attitudes toward women are noted by Siclier in French and American societies, and these differences are reflected in their films, which play out social myths. One difference, Siclier notes, is that the French cinema paints women more realistically, being accepting of their sensuality, while Americans put women on a pedestal and portray their falling from it as reprehensible: this accounts for an element of misogyny because of resentment (on the part of males) that the ideal of woman has been shattered.

This thoughtful analysis traces the French cinema's origins and presents examples of varying images of women on the screen, with photographs of especially memorable scenes.

Smith, D. J. *"The Mem-Sahib in Her Books,"* Literary Criterion, 9, no. 4 (Summer, 1971), pp. 42-50.

Smith takes an overview of authors who have portrayed the Englishwoman in India during the heyday of the British Empire as she graced the landscape with or without male company. Rudyard Kipling and E. M. Forster figure prominently in this article, as well as John Masters, John Kincaid, Maud Diver, and Emily Eden.

Smith, Hugh Allison. *Les femmes dans les chansons de geste.* (Reprinted from Colorado College Studies, X.) Colorado Springs: Colorado College, 1903. 40 p.

Smith assesses the part played by women of the early Middle Ages as wife, mother, and nun, and gives illustrations of the opinions concerning women found in the *chansons de geste.* He concludes that the oft-mentioned equality of women with men at that time did not in fact exist, since the basis of law was physical force, and women were not involved in the use of arms. Consequently life was "monotone et triste." Though short, this work is valuable for the unusual light it sheds upon these epics of male exploits.

Sonstroem, David. ***Rossetti and the Fair Lady.*** Middletown, Connecticut: Wesleyan University Press, 1970. 252 p. Index and bibliography.

The "beautiful lady" *motif* rules Rossetti's work, declares Sonstroem, and he has devoted these pages to delineating the poet's use of this theme under the rubrics of "heavenly," "sinful," "victimized," and "fatale," as well as fantastic and dream-like. Sonstroem's basic premise is that in back of each type there existed an actual woman in Rossetti's life. Many of them appear here.

Sopeña Ibánez, Federico. ***Arte y sociedad en Galdós.*** Madrid: Editorial Gredos, S. A., 1970.

"Sensibilidad artística de la mujer," is found on pages 85-95, a section which considers several of Galdós' female characters according to certain themes not central to this book but of importance in delineating novelist Galdós' interpretation of the Spanish woman's life in the nineteenth century. Sopeña

Ibáñez points out the emphasis on the sewing machine as a symbol of the class changes which caused the formation of a kind of female proletariat, a moving away from home as women's only *milieu,* for good or ill.

Spacks, Patricia. *"Free Women,"* Hudson Review, XXIV (Winter, 1971-72), pp.559-573.

How nineteenth and twentieth century female writers view the problem of freedom for women is analyzed by Spacks as she assesses writers Lillian Hellman, Anaïs Nin, Doris Lessing, Colette, and—to a lesser extent—Mrs. Gaskell, Simone de Beauvoir, Virginia Woolf, Joan Didion, and Ann Richardson Roiphe.

For the talented woman, Spacks opines, Colette's way of reconciliation within the sheltering limits of imaginative creation seems to be the most satisfying freedom for women (as well as many men). For the "untalented" woman the vision is less clear.

Spacks, Patricia. *"Taking Care: Some Women Novelists,"* Novel (6: no. 1 (Fall, 1972), pp. 36-71.

Elizabeth Gaskell, Louisa May Alcott, Virginia Woolf, and Ellen Glasgow are considered in relation to their portrayals of women who take care of others. Spacks shows how the women who are seen spending their lives in devotion to others are thereby affected in their own ability to be integral human beings.

Sparrow, Walter Shaw, comp. **Women Painters of the World, from the Time of Caterina Vigri, 1413-1463, to Rosa Bonheur and the Present Day.** (The Arts and Life Library, vol. 3.) New York:

Hacker Art Books, 1976. (This is a reprint of the original which was published at London in 1905.) 322 p.

In this unusual book Sparrow takes a broad view of women painters in Italy, Britain, the United States, France, Belgium, Holland, Germany, Austria, Russia, Switzerland, Spain, and Finland are represented in this volume, which is copiously illustrated with interesting plates.

Stearns, Bertha-Monica. *"Before Godey's,"* American Literature, II (1930-31), pp. 248-255.

Stearns surveys the field of minor periodicals which catered to American women before the advent of the famous *Godey's Lady's Book*, initiated by Louis Antoine Godey in 1830. Sarah Josepha Hale, who was the first editor, worked for the magazine from 1828 to 1837 in Boston, during which time she wrote astute literary criticism which included approval of the earliest works of Nathaniel Hawthorne and Edgar Allan Poe.

Stegeman, Beatrice. *"The Divorce Dilemma: The New Women in Contemporary African Novels,"* Critique, XV, no. 3 (1974), pp. 81-93.

Stegeman uses R. S. Easman's *The Burnt Out Marriage* and T. M. Aluko's *One Man, One Marriage*, to show how the two novelists use the literary devices of the new woman and the old divorce trial to symbolize the breaking up of traditional family patterns of thought and behavior in Africa, with the concomitant turmoil resulting from the search for new ways.

The African woman's rebellion against the tribal *mores* that made of her a piece of property is made vivid through these two novels.

Stone, Wilbur Macey. *Women Designers of Book-Plates.* New York: Randolph R. Beam, 1902.

This unusual little volume reproduces thirty-six book-plates designed by as many women from Austria, Great Britain, Canada, France, Germany, the United States, and Sweden, with a brief introduction. Stone reasons that since book-plates are essentially a "bit of embroidery or decoration embodying the personality of the owner," by tradition women should be recognized as gifted in this art. Nevertheless, he says ruefully, "writers on this subject have paid scant courtesy to women as a designer of book-plates."[25]

Stowe, Harriet Beecher. *Lady Byron Vindicated; or, A History of the Byron Controversy from Its Beginning to the Present Time.* Boston: Fields, Osgood, and Co., 1870. 480 p.

Contending that Lord Byron's attack on his wife was kept alive by his friends after his death, Stowe uses documents to bolster her championship of Lady Byron. This volume is a sequel to an earlier article, "The True Story of Lady Byron's Life," which raised a storm of discussion and alienated Stowe's British reading public because of her charge that the poet had had an incestuous love for his sister.[26]

---

[25] This is available in microfilm from New Haven, Connecticut: Research Publications, 1977. History of Women, Reel 689, no. 5514.)

[26] Stowe is best known for her 1851 novel, *Uncle Tom's Cabin, or Life Among the Lowly,* which was influential in arousing anti-slavery sentiment before the Civil War.

Sullerot, Évelyne. *Histoire de la Presse féminine en France des origines à 1848.* Preface by Jacques Godechot. Paris: Librairie Armand Colin, 1966. 227 p. Bibliography and index.

After surveying the course of women's periodicals Sullerot decides that they appear "comme le témoin d'une immense frustration de puissance qui fit peu de bruit. La place réservée à la morale dans ces écrits et dans les écrits annexes de ses collaboratrices c'est que l'expression détournée de cette volunté de puissance." Through such insights she expresses the inarticulate desire, and need, of women for more control over their lives, but she understands also their inaarticulated feelings of frustration at their powerlessness to carry out this endeavor, constrained as they were by social taboos.[27]

Swennes, Robert H. *"Man and Wife: The Dialogue of Contraries in Robert Frost's Poetry,"* American Literature, 42 (1970), pp. 363-372.

Swennes provides the reader with analyses of dramatic dialogues in which Frost shows the ubiquitous paradoxes of love and resentment, with the ensuing "contraries" of understanding and lack of communication. Yet Frost believed that the most significant relationship in the world is that of "man to woman."

Extended consideration is given to poems found in *North of Boston* and *Mountain Journal*—"Home Burial," "A Servant to

---

[27] The year 1848, when Sullerot's survey ends, was marked by social ferment and governmental repression. In France Louis Philippe imposed press censorship. He was forced to abdicate, and not long afterward universal suffrage was instituted by the National Assembly—for men only.

Servants," "The Housekeeper," and "The Hill Wife," all of which show Frost's sensitivity to the problems of women.

Sypherd, Wilbur Owen. *Jephthah and His Daughter: A Study in Comparative Literature.* Newark: University of Delaware, 1948. 277 p.

The scholar who likes to trace the changes in the treatment of women in history or fiction (here Biblical lore) can find occupation enough in this detailed volume.[28] The *ethos* of women's destiny is adumbrated as Sypherd looks at the story from Judges 11:30-40, from every possible angle.

Appendix G gives a bird's-eye view of the countries covered, from Africa to Switzerland. This legend is also memorialized by treatments in music (opera, pages 205-225), and the arts.

Tavares de Sà, Irene. *A Condiçao da Mulher: bloqueios e vertentes da personalidade feminine.* Rio de Janeiro: Livraria Agir Editora, 1966. 306 p.

In her analysis of feminine psychology, Tavares de Sà draws from depictions of women in literature, the Bible, cinema, and actual life. For literature she chooses Julien Green's *Adrienne*

---

[28] Jephthah was a judge of Israel who sacrificed his only daughter because of this solemn vow to his god Yahweh (Jehovah) if he were victorious in a battle: "Then it shall be that, whatsoever cometh forth from the doors of my house to meet me . . . shall surely be the Lord's, and I will offer it up for a burnt-offering." Unfortunately, the first one was his only child, a daughter who came to meet him rejoicing. Jephthah was devastated, but his daughter agreed that it should be done as he had vowed, and it was carried out (two months later). Every year thereafter her death was mourned for four days by the women of Israel (not the men, it appears). This is reminiscent of the Greek sacrifice of a daughter by her father in Aeschylus' *Agamemnon*. In this case the mother resented her husband forever after.

Mesurat and François Mauriac's *Thérèse Desqueyroux,* while Simone Weil is the historical figure she concentrates upon.

Tavares de Sà's conclusion is that although women are endowed with great potential for creativity and inspiration, their role is characterized by basic contradictions which inhibit them.

Tavares de Sà, Irene. *Eva e seus autores; ensaio sôbre a mulher modern na vida, no cinema, no teatro, no romance.* Rio de Janeiro: Livraria Agir, 1963. 269 p.

The conflict of the ideal with reality in modern life is perhaps even more pronounced in countries whose ideal woman has been romanticized but whose reality has been limited, ignored or generalized into comforting stereotypes, believes Tavares de Sà. In this thought-provoking analysis, she finds portrayals of women in literature and the cinema especially relevant to the ideal-real dichotomy because of their ability to dramatize dilemmas, making it possible for women to see their problems more objectively.

Here we find praise for many women writers who have contributed toward getting the world to re-evaluate its thinking on the subject of woman's nature and role, women such as Sigrid Undset, Gertrude Von Le Fort, George Eliot, Emily Brontë, Katherine Mansfield, Virginia Woolf, and Pearl S. Buck. Psychologists Marina Leibl, Gina Lombroso, and Karen Horney are also mentioned for their accomplishments.

Tetel, Marcel. *Marguerite de Navarre's "Heptaméron": Themes, Language, and Structure.* Durham, North Carolina: Duke University Press, 1973. 217 p.

According to Totel, Marguerite reveals her own thought through the voices of her narrators in the *Heptaméron*—three women and four men—by means of stories and comment in which are found multifarious considerations of the adjustments women make to secure love or a semblance of it. Sham or integrity in love is one of the recurrent themes in this, Marguerite's masterpiece. For the reader who wishes to pursue this intriguing subject Tetel provides a bibliography.

Thomas, Clara. *Love and Work Enough: The Life of Anna Jameson.* (University of Toronto Department of English Studies and Texts, no. 14.) Toronto: University of Toronto Press, 1967. 252 p. Bibliography.

Anna Murphy Jameson came to the United States from Dublin as a child in 1789. After going to Italy for schooling and spending some time as a governess in England, she began to chafe at the handicaps she suffered because she was a woman. Servility was not part of her nature: she believed that more education would bring her rewards in independence. Through her writings, which were encouraged by her husband, she reached the goals she had set for herself, one of which was to be taken seriously as a writer. Her book on Shakespeare received the critical praise of English poet Gerald Manley Hopkins.

Thomas, Edward. *Feminine Influence on the Poets.* London: Martin Secker, 1910. 352 p. Index.

The poets in question include many of those in England during the eighteenth and nineteenth centuries. Thomas has written this work in an informal, conversational style: in it are found many descriptions of daily life which make more vivid the human fallibility of poets who appear rather austere in the usual anthologies.

Chapter III, "Women as Poets," gives very short sketches of little known female poets, with the comment that to their own disadvantage these women have almost always written "as if they were only an inferior kind of man." Thomas makes plentiful use of quotations from poetry to illustrate his insights throughout the book.

Thompson, Jan. *"The Role of Women in the Iconography of Art Nouveau,"* Art Journal, XXXI, no. 2 (Winter, 1971-72), pp. 158-167.

In this well-illustrated article Thompson traces the development of modern portrayals of women in art as they evolved out of the Pre-Raphaelite school of the late nineteenth century in England.

Thompson sees the *art nouveau* period as one in which artists went overboard in "one last hedonistic fling" at the same time that suffragettes were chaining themselves to public buildings and characterizes this "fling" "as a last-ditch anxiety-ridden attempt to keep women in their traditional places," which in its commercial aspects used representations of women as advertising attractions.

Todd, Janet. *The Sign of Angellica: Women, Writing, and Fiction, 1660-1800.* New York: Columbia Unversity Press, 1989. 328 p. Index.

Aphra Behn is Todd's mentor in this study of fiction from the Restoration to late eighteenth century which focuses on women as outstanding writers apart from the male-dominated literary world. Instead of trying to work within this world, some women chose to use special "female signs and masks" as their point of departure which presaged the nineteenth century achievements of Maria Edgeworth and Jane Austen. Other women whose fame has dimmed are brought to the reader's attention.

Trachman, Sadie Edith. *Cervantes' Women of Literary Tradition.* New York: Institute de las Españas, 1932. 177 p.

In general, decides Trachman, Cervantes' literary personages have been slighted as subjects of scholarly analysis, especially his women, and she endeavors to correct this oversight.

To begin with, her method is to imagine Cervantes' concepts of women from his own life experiences, which were generally negative: perhaps the character Isabel in *La Española inglesa,* for example, can be seen as a counterfoil to his own daughter Isabel.

All in all, Cervantes seemed to have adopted the conventional attitudes current in Spanish thought (and these Trachman explicates in relation to their Hispanic, Italian, Moorish, and Biblical influences), evidently choosing virtuous, demure girls as heroines. Trachman also traces Cervantes' impact on such discrete writers as Thomas Hardy, Beaumont and Fletcher, Thomas Middleton, Nathaniel Field, William Rowley, Augustin Scribe, Victor Hugo, and others.

Trinker, Martha K. *Las mujeres en el Don Quijote comparadas con las mujeres en los dramas de Shakespeare.* Mexico, D. F.: Talleres de la Editorial Cultura, 1938. 115 p.

Trinker finds analogies between Shakespeare and Cervantes, saying, "Shakespeare y Cervantes son los dos caballeros andantes, cujo objeto es la razón y la verdad suprema," and decides that the woman most characteristic of Shakespeare is Lady Macbeth, while Cervantes' is Dulcinea.

In Trinker's opinion Shakespeare's female character is a human being aside from her sex; Cervantes' is an abstract ideal. Other thoughtful comparisons are between Beatriz and Dorothea, Luscinda and Hero, Miranda and Clara, and Imogena and Camila (in *La curiosa impertinente*)).

Tytler, Sarah, and J. L. Watson. ***The Songstresses of Scotland.*** 2 vols. London: Straham & Company, 1871. 662 p.

Certain French women reigned in *salons,* observe the authors, but these unique Scotswomen reigned in the cottage as well as the castle. These two unusual volumes describe the accomplishments of ten "poetesses" of the seventeenth, eighteenth, and nineteenth centuries who have captured the spirit of Scotland in their musical use of the vernacular, examples of which are used to denote their styles. A helpful glossary is provided at the beginning of Volume I, and biographies of the women are included.. This work is invaluable for the student studying women's history in the arts. ("Sarah Tytler" was a pseudonym used by Henrietta Keddie.)

Utter, Robert, and Gwendolyn Bridges Needham. ***Pamela's Daughters.*** New York: Russell & Russell, 1972. (Reprinted from the 1936 edition published by Macmillan, New York.) 512 p.

Pamela, of Richardson's novel of that name, is called "the Eve of the race of heroines" as the authors begin a study of the psychology of the race of "prudes" that followed her, "ladies of sensibility" who peopled novels up to the Victorian era. Here English fiction is gleaned for its diverting and informative clues as to changes in feminine attitudes.

Valency, Maurice J. *The Tragedies of Herod and Mariamne.* New York: Columbia University Press, 1940; New York: Ams Press, 1966. 304 p.

The eighteen-centuries-old story of Herod the Great, King of Judea, and Mariamne his wife comes to us from the first century account of Josephus. Valency feels that Josephus' extended account of it is due to the historian's sympathy with Mariamne, from whom it is said he was descended.[29]

Stirred by the story of the "upstart king" and the "unfortunate queen," writers from the Renaissance onward have used this legend as an inspiration for plays, with their portrayals of the pair (under various names) appearing in classical drama, the Spanish *comedia,* Elizabethan revenge drama, and in nineteen-century writings. This is a fascinating study, and it is indexed.

Vigée-Le Brun, Elisabeth. *Memoirs.* Translated by Sia Evans. Bloomington: Indiana University Press, 1989. 368 p. (The original manuscript was published in Paris in 1835-37.)

Evans calls Mme Vigée-Le Brun a "solitary wanderer," for she, an admired portrait painter of eighteenth century France, found happiness in traveling throughout Europe—Italy, Germany, Russia— alone or with her daughter. Evans confides that a chance encounter with a version of the *Mémoires* at a secondhand bookstall in Paris led her to find a complete version and to translate this intriguing autobiography for English readers and

---

[29] Flavius Josephus (37?-100) was a Jewish historian who wrote the *Antiquities of the Jews,* among other works. He was a great admirer of Roman civilization and is often referred to in ancient histories.

art lovers. A list of paintings, 600 in number, is found on pages 358-368.

Added explicatory notes are helpful, but the work is marred by the lack of an index, which is especially to be regretted since the work is replete with references to persons and places which could offer clues for more research.

Violette, Augusta G. **Economic Feminism in American Literature prior to 1848.** (University of Maine Studies, 2d series, no. 2.) Oron: University of Maine Press, 1926. 104 p.

A brief sketch of the European backgrounds of feminism (from the Greeks to Mary Wollstonecraft) precedes Violette's excellent survey of how American women have fared in regard to freedom.

The correspondence of Mercy Otis Warren with John Adams (who did not show himself enthusiastic about giving women freedom in 1776) sets the tone, and the reference to the Seneca Declaration of Rights (1848) underlines the necessity for strong measures for change.

Vollmer, Sylvia N. *"The Position of Woman in Spain as Seen in Spanish Literature,"* Hispania, VIII, no. 4 (October, 1925) pp. 211-236; 303-348; 369-390.

Women as personal property was the prevailing attitude from the beginning of Spanish literature, reports Vollmer and quotes pertinent lines from *El Poema de Mio Cid* for a point of departure and continues with Juan Ruiz's *El Libro de buen amor,* Martínez's *Archpreste de Talavera,* and similar works through the period of Carlos V.

The second part of this exegesis takes up the Golden Age with its emphasis on the concept of *honra,* which is described well, along with the ideal of "la perfecta casada." In charity, however, Vollmer finds an exception in Cervantes with his lofty (but unsubstantial) portrayal of Dulcinea. The *comedias* of Lope de Vega, Tirso de Molina, and Calderón are also combed for pertinent passages.

The richness of the literature of the nineteenth century is not forgotten, but less space is devoted to it. Vollmer finally concludes that in spite of "bursts of sunshine" here and there, the whole of the literature affords little light for Spanish women. Her final notes deal with hope for the incipient feminism, for "Spain is preparing to have her women take their rightful place in the world." A scholarly bibliography, mostly of primary sources, is included.

Wade, Gerald E. *"The Spanish Woman and the Don Juan Figure,"* Reflexion, II (1973), pp. 97-100.

Wade is intrigued by the interpretation of Don Juan by a Spanish writer, Mercedes Saenz-Alonso (above), because he judges it to be a "significant statement of what is probably the Spanish woman's attitude toward the 'Great Lover,' for she sees him in need of redemption rather than punishment.

In her *Don Juan y e donjuanismo* Saenz-Alonso traces the literary development of Don Juan in the novel, music, drama, poetry, and essay in many countries. Wade recommends the book as a good introduction to the Don Juan theme in Western literature also because of its many comparative references.

Wade, Gerald E. *"Tirso de Molina,"* Hispania, XXXII (May, 1949), pp. 131-140.

Tirso's reputation for creating outstanding women characters, Wade finds, has come largely from his most famous comic situation—"that in which a man becomes merely a pawn in a determined woman's hands."

The Don Juan figure, which is the focus of Tirso's *El burlador de Sevilla*, is often seen as an aggressor, but this legend which Wade asserts "has surely appeared in all the civilized languages," can also be seen as a tribute to the more subtle ways in which woman dominates man, and according to this logic, Don Juan is transmuted into a victim.

Wagner, Geoffrey. *Five for Freedom: A Story of Feminism in Fiction.* London: George Allen and Unwin, 1972. 234 p. Index.

"What woman feels herself to be in a given society" is the theme of this book. Wagner carries it along by analyses of Madame de Merteuil in de Laclos' *Les Liaisons dangereuses*, Tony in Thomas Mann's *Buddenbrooks*, Emma in Flaubert's *Madame Bovary*, and the heroines in Charlotte Brontë's *Jane Eyre* and Thomas Hardy's *Tess of the d'Urbervilles*. Wagner relates these characters to modern feminism as well.

Wasserstrom, William. *Heiress of All the Ages: Sex and Sentiment in the Genteel Tradition.* Minneapolis: University of Minnesota Press, 1959. Index.

Wasserstrom declares that he is trying to "connect the public life of society with the private life of the imagination." The society is that of the United States from 1830 to 1914; the imaginative factor consists of the idea of gentility which, rooted in the eighteenth-century idea of natural nobility, adheres to the twin principles of "manliness" and "womanliness."

Wasserstrom's approach is through literature, with much attention being paid to the heroines of William Dean Howells and Henry James, especially Isabel Archer in the *Portrait of a*

Lady and Maggie in *The Golden Bowl* (where he stresses the ill-effects of too strong an attachment to the father). He sees James indicating in *The Bostonians* that the problems of American women would not be solved by "emancipation," which would be merely a legal victory, but only by a freedom that would be a "moral achievement." These authors, seemingly with regret, verify Wasserstrom's appraisal of a society in which the genteel tradition was completely dead by 1920.

Wellington, Amy. ***Women Have Told: Studies in the Feminist Tradition.*** Boston: Little, Brown and Company, 1930. 204 p.

Mary Wollstonecraft leads the short procession of "unfeminine" women whose lives and writings are considered here. Others are Margaret Fuller, the Brontë sisters, Olive Schreiner, Charlotte Gilman, May Sinclair, Ellen Glasgow, and Rebecca West. "The feminist writers *are* the feminist tradition," declares Wellington.

Williams, Charles. ***The Figure of Beatrice: A Study in Dante.*** London: Faber and Faber, 1943. 256 p.

Beatrice in *The Divine Comedy* has been interpreted as the epitome of the ethereal, feminine woman. Williams does not consider Dante's image of woman innovative; what was new was "the intensity of his treatment and the extreme to which he carried it." Beatrice's meaning must be found in the context of the work. Williams outlines how this ideal arose, as he also emphasizes the inspiration which subsequent male writers found in Beatrice's shadowy *persona*, a proof of the persistence of this ideal throughout the ages world-wide.

Williams, Stanley T., and Leonard B. Beach, eds. *The Journal of Emily Foster.* New York: Oxford University Press, 1938. 171 p.

This intimate and cheerful journal of a young aristocratic girl of the eighteenth century in England reflects a pleasant life without care. Yet there is a more serious dimension to it, since journal-keeping for women often denotes intellectual leanings which were generally frowned upon in that era. Emily's journal does not lack philosophic comments, psychological portraits, and gleanings from her own serious and varied reading, for she was versed in foreign languages. Notes accompany the edited text.

Wilson, Mark K. *"Mr. Clemens and Madame Blanc: Mark Twain's First French Critic,"* American Literature, 45, no. 4 (January, 1974), pp. 537-556.

During her travels in the United States in the late 1880's Thérèse Blanc, a prolific writer for the prestigious *Revue de Deux Mondes,* put to paper her impressions of American women which were published in 1896 as *Les Américaines chez elles* and later translated as *American Women: Images and Realities.*

Mme Blanc became acquainted with American writers, one of whom was Mark Twain, and became a mediator for their works between them and the French reading public.

Winiker, Rolf. *Madame de Charrière: essai d'un itinéraire spirituel.* (Litera 3.) Lausanne: Éditions l'Age d'Homme, S. A., 1971.

Commenting on the fact that Belle de Charrière never attained the fame that she deserved in spite of the praise of

Sainte-Beuve, Godet, Sir Walter Scott, and Kerchove, Winiker introduces the reader to a remarkable woman whose biography offers much to researchers in the eighteenth century, especially those interested in comparative literature.

Although Belle passed most of her married life set apart from the richer life she had had as a girl in her native Holland (then the "carrefour des cultures latine, germanique et anglosaxonne"), she offered hospitality in her *salon* to a host of notables in her day, including James Boswell, who came to visit her.

Winiker is interested in Belle's psychological development, and thus his text is replete with quotations from her own writings, for she was much given to an introspection motivated by untiring efforts to understand herself. At the same time she had a lively interest in the affairs of the day, as is evident by the list of subjects she wrote about (pages 239-242). Winiker mentions many women contemporaries who, like Belle de Charrière, have suffered neglect.

Wolff, Cynthia. *"Lily Bart and the Beautiful Death,"* American Literature, 46, no. 1 (March, 1974), pp. 16-40.

The tragedy of Lily Bart, heroine of Wharton's *House of Mirth*, is that she lives and dies a beautiful object, deluded into viewing herself through others' eyes as part of society's decorative art, yet forced to live in an ugly world of reality from which she is totally alienated. Lily is in actuality only a sample of the American *art nouveau*.

In this novel, says Wolff, Wharton elucidates for the first time what it means to the woman herself to be the beautiful creature whose lover experiences her death. Heretofore authors had focused only upon what the male character feels. Wharton pitilessly reveals "the psychological distortions, the self-alienation, that a woman suffers when she accepts the status of idealized object."

Wood, Ann D. *"The 'Scribbling Women' and Fanny Fern: Why Women Wrote," American Quarterly,* XXIII (Spring, 1971), pp. 3-24.

Using Nathaniel Hawthorne's admiration of Fanny Fern as a reference point, Wood shows how Fern departed from the usual pattern set by women writers who, as Hawthorne remarked irritably, wrote "like emasculated men." This departure from the usual is indicated by Wood to be Fern's refusal to feel guilt for her entrance into the male world of letters, and to speak her mind in language which displeased many critics as much as it delighted Hawthorne. Wood characterizes Fern's first novel, *Ruth Hall,* as "a kind of litmus test . . . for the work of her feminine contemporaries."[30] The sedate, restrained style of the article does not blunt the feeling of shock transmitted by the descriptions of the cruel, though often covert, trammels placed upon intellectual women. Wood's footnotes give leads for further research.

Woodberry, George Edward. *Studies of a Littérateur.* (Essay Index Reprint Series.) Freeport, New York: Books for Libraries Press, 1968. (Originally published in 1921.)

Two sections in this volume, "Mary Wollstonecraft" and "The Courting of Dorothy Osborne" prove that although

---

[30]Fanny Fern has been rediscovered (as are others of the past, especially the nineteenth century), and many of her works are now available.

Woodberry is sympathetic to women, he is not a reliable prophet, since he thought that Wollstonecraft would be forgotten, while Osborne would achieve lasting fame. Of Wollstonecraft he writes, "her name . . . will remain obscure," thinking that her only claim to fame would be that her daughter became Shelley's wife. As for Osborne, he predicts that posterity will find her more favored than ever. Both women, however, deserve the praise he accords them.

Woods, Alice. *George Meredith as Champion of Women and of Progressive Education.* Oxford: Basil Blackwood, 1937. 79 p.

Rhoda (in *Rhoda Fleming* (1865), Diana (in *Diana of the Crossways* (1885), Nesta, and Carinthia, along with those in *Beauchamps's Career* (1876), are foremost among the heroines to prove Woods' thesis that "we women cannot be grateful enough to George Meredith for the position he took in his writing. . . . He filled us with hope."

Meredith (1828-1909) used the novel as an effective vehicle for the character analysis of women who faced personal dilemmas of accommodating to an increasingly sophisticated society which allowed little real freedom and dignity to them.

Woolf, Virginia. *A Room of One's Own.* New York: Harcourt, Brace, and Company, 1929. 199 p.

Woolf's long essay, which has now become a classic in feminist thought, is imbued with a sense of outrage against historical injustices, physical, moral, and intellectual, toward women. Her sympathy for such women as Dorothy Osborne and Margaret, Lady Winchilsea, elicits incisive criticism, as does the persecution of women of the past who were branded as witches. Obvious, too, is her disapproval of some of her male contemporaries who passed as learned critics. The reading of this thoughtful book is *de rigueur* for all students of women's history, whether social or literary.

Wright, F. M. *Feminism in Greek Literature from Homer to Aristotle.* London: George Routledge & Sons, 1923. 222 p.

Aristotle is looked upon by Wright as the *bête noire* of anti-feminism who lent his prestige to a profound error, the rightness of the degradation of women. Thus he "helped perpetuate the malady which had already been the chief cause of the destruction of Greece." Aristotle did not understand the moral aspects of feminism, nor did he see its logic.

On the other hand, Euripides and Plato appreciated woman's real qualities, but they were overshadowed by the fame of Aeschylus and Sophocles, says Wright. Turning from Athens, he praises the social environment of Sparta as more conducive to women's happiness. Males took care of male children in their camps and barracks, and soldiers (which included all fit males) had very little to do with the management of the home.

Instead of generalizing about Greek civilization, Wright identifies ideas in relation to women then current. This is good reading for those who are studying Aristotle especially, for Wright points out how the Greek degradation of women was encouraged by later Aristotelians and how their baleful influence was carried on through the centuries that followed.

Wright, Louis B. *"Popular Literary Tastes,"* in *Middle Class Culture in Elizabethan England,* pages 103-118. (Huntington Library Publication.) Chapel Hill: University of North Carolina Press, 1935.

Chapter IV, pages 103-118, "Popular Literary Tastes," delineates the favorite reading of women in the early seventeenth century. Romances were especially popular then as now, but in that more rigid era such books were considered "idle reading" by Puritans, who called them the road to moral depravity. Nevertheless, writers such as John Lyly, Robert Greene, Samuel Rowland, and Thomas Heyward made a successful bid for feminine approval, as did Margaret Tyler, whose translations of chivalric romances were especially welcomed. In one of her prefaces (in 1578) she countered her carping critics by boldly asserting that women, being equal to men, had the same right to read and write as they pleased.

Wright, Louis B. *"The Reading of Renaissance Women,"* Studies in Philology, XXVIII (1931), pp. 671-688.

A factual, well-documented and comprehensive article which gives perspective on the question of women's literacy in this age. When that is established, Wright gives numerous examples of the varied tastes of these Englishwomen, including excerpts from the works and some critical comments.

Index

Index

A

A Arte de ser mulher (Silva), 178
A Emancipaçao da mulher (Morais), 142
A Mulher no construçao do mundo futur (Muraro), 144
abbesses, 34, 52, 238
Abbott, Edith, 3
Abélard, 38
accomplishments of women, 17, 46, 47, 85, 110, 129, 130, 145, 151 242, 331
Account of the Proceedings on the Trial of Susan B. Anthony, 9
actresses, 215, 239
Adam (biblical character), 271
Adams, Abigail, 35, 149
Adams, Henry, 3, 18, 246
Adams, John, 333
Addams, Jane, 4, 5, 123
Adventurous Thirties, The (Courtney), 51
advertising, 160, 329
advertising industry, 76, 99, 173
Aeneid (Virgil), 281
Afetinan, A., 5
Africa, 87, 152, 323
Africa, tribes in, 129
African Marriage and Social Change (Mair), 128
African women, 43, 87, 125, 129, 159, 189
African-American women, 54, 74, 89, 101, 102, 120, 143, 160, 172, 319
African-Americans, 223
Against Nature and God (Morris), 143
Agoult, Marie d', 201
agriculture, 145
Agustini, Delmira, 310
Aïssé, Charlotte-Elisabeth, 26, 98
Akhmatova, Anna (Russian poet), 237
Alacoque, Marie (Saint Marguerite), 220
Albert, Jeanne d', 246
Alcade, Carmen, 39
Alcott, Louisa May, 235, 294, 322
Alcuin: A Dialogue (Brown), 35
Aldington, Richard (tr.), 207
Alembert, Jean d', 62, 98
alienation, 77, 82, 83, 91, 223, 252
Alliluyeva, Svetlana, 6
Aluko, T. M., 323
Alvarez Quintero, S. y J., 7
Alzona, Encarnación, 8
Amadis de Gaule, 219
American colonies, 57, 110, 121, 172, 176
American Midwest, 115, 127
American Perspectives of Women's Initiations (Machann), 286
American Revolution, 23, 25, 46, 64, 65, 176, 182
American South, 92, 94, 175, 179, 182, 223, 303
American Studies, 127, 192

345

American West, 35, 46, 61, 64, 170, 180
American Women: Fifteen Hundred Biographies (Willard), 202
Amitiés américaines de Madame d'Houdetot, Les (Chinard), 42
anarchism, 87
Anatole France et la femme (Lahy-Hollebecque), 280
Anatolia, 5
ancient civilizations, 89, 119, 163
Anderson, James Edward, 207
androgyny, 219
Anglo-Saxons, 104
Angoulême, Marguerite d', 106
Anne, Countess of Winchelsea, 285
Anne, Princess of Denmark, 10
Anthony, Susan B., 3, 9, 168, 183
anthropologists, 152
anthropology, 10, 19, 31, 90, 107, 122, 133, 135, 144, 152, 162, 189
Anti-feminist Treatise of Fifteenth Century Spain, An (Matulka), 133
Anti-Gothic Novel, The (Loomis), 283
anti-intellectualism, 101
antiquity, 103, 177, 332, 333, 341
  Anatolia, 90
  Babylonia, 16
  Crete, 90
  Greece, 60, 90, 108, 116
  India, 138
  Mesopotamia, 16, 90
  Rome, 60, 72, 75, 77, 90, 105
  Spain, 43
antiquity, scribes in, 238

Aphrodite (Greek goddess), 227
Apollo (Greek god), 108
Appadorai, A., 9
Appignanesi, Lisa, 208
Apprentice Saint, The (Collis), 230
Aquitaine, Eleanor d', 280
Aranguren, J. L., 10
Arblay, Alexandre d', 225
archeology, 16, 133, 227, 255
archetypes (Jungian), 93
Argentina, 162
Aristophile, G. S., 308
Aristotle, misogyny of, 341
Army Letters from an Officer's Wife (Roe), 169
Army, U.S., 169
art, 65, 244, 255, 329
  design of book-plates, 324
  painting, 27, 323, 333
  sculpture, 259
art nouveau, 329
art, commercial, 329
art, Greek, 259
art, nineteenth-century, 239
Arthurian literature, 215
Article 122, on women's equality (Russian Constitution), 155
artists, 27, 65, 185, 241, 312, 323, 324
As You Like It (Shakespeare), 302
asceticism, 34, 96, 180, 263
Ashbridge, Elizabeth, 128, 286
Asia, 9, 26, 37, 48, 63, 87, 90, 108, 144, 145
Aspasia, 150
Aspects of Antiquity (Finley), 72

Astell, Mary, 10, 11, 213
Athens, 150
Atwood, Margaret, 307
Augier, Émile, 235
Aulnoy, Mme d', 218
Aunt Bet, the Story of a Long Life (Hammond), 92
Austen, Jane, 30, 216, 232, 252, 271, 279, 283, 294, 318, 329
Australia, 112, 188
autobiographies, 6, 12, 37, 39, 47, 83, 86, 128, 199, 204, 219, 230, 286, 333
aviation, 45
Azorín, Antonio, 233

B

Bachofen, Johann Jakob, 47
Bacon, Francis, 292
Bagley, Sarah G., 185
Bailyn, Lotte, 123
Bainton, Roland H., 11
Balderston, Katharine L., 208
Baldwin, Monica, 12
Bali, Om Prakash, 209
Balzac, Honoré de, 217, 243
Bantu women, 125
Barbiche, Henry, 229
Bardèche, Maurois, 13
Barine, Arvède, 162
Barish, Jonas A., 209
Baritz, Loren, 13
Barre, Poulain de la, 18
Barreno, Maria Isabel, 210
Barnard, H. C., 14

Barros Vidal, Olmio, 15
Barrows, Isabel C., 185
Barry, James, 248
Basch, Françoisçe, 210
battle of the sexes, 16, 89, 134, 165, 204. *See also querelle des femmes,* controversies.
Baudin, Maurice, 210
Baumal, Francis, 211
Bäumer, Gertrud, 114, 136
Bavière, Isabeau de, 201
Bay, J. Christian, 16
Bayerschmidt, Carl E., 211
Bazán, Emilia Pardo, 7, 39, 221, 297
Beach, John G., 17
Beach, Leonaard R., 336
Beard, Mary Ritter, 4, 17
Beaty, Jerome, 212
Beaumont and Fletcher, 330
Beauty's Triumph (Vigman), 198
Beauvoir, Simone de, 18, 19, 82, 157, 310, 320, 322
Beaver, Robert Pierce, 19
Becker, Lydia E., 140
Bedek, Evelyn B., 20
Bedford, Herbert, 213
Beecher, Catharine, 52, 306
Behn, Aphra, 27, 239, 279, 285, 330
Beirne, M. Francis (Sister), 21
Bembo, Cardinal Pietro, 246
Benedictine convents, 105
Bennett, Arnold, 21
Bennett, Henry S., 22
Benson, Mary Sumner, 23
Benson, Stella, 275

Berkin, Carol R., 23
Berlin, 25
Bernhardt, Sarah, 30
Besant, Annie, 109
Bertaut, Jules, 24
Bethune, Louise, 185
Bettelheim, Bruno, 213
Better Half, The (Sinclair), 180
Beyond God the Father (Daly), 54
Bible, 125, 151, 215, 271, 325, 326, 332
Bible and the Role of Women, The (Stendahl), 184
Bielenberg, Christobel, 25
biographies, 12, 15, 26, 28, 30, 35, 39, 41, 43, 46, 47, 54, 55, 58, 61, 65, 66, 68, 82, 88, 91, 92, 95, 97, 100, 103, 104, 106, 107, 112, 127, 133, 137, 140, 147, 152, 153, 161, 165, 185, 187, 202, 216, 221, 222, 234, 236, 245, 249, 252, 254, 268, 269, 274, 277, 278, 281, 285, 315, 336, 338
birth control, 178
Bishop, Isabella Bird, 139
Blackstone, William (1723-1780), 18
Blackham, Robert, J., 25
Blackwell family, 95
Blackwell, Elizabeth, 95
Blais, Marie-Clair, 307
Blake, William, 163, 248
Blanch, Lesley, 26
Blanche de Castile (1187-1251), 4
Blanche de Navarre, 29
Blandina (martyr), 34

Blashfield, Evangeline Wilbour, 26
Blaze de Bury, Ange Henri, 27
Bloch, R. Howard, 215
Block, Toni, 215
Bloomer, Amelia, 168
bluestockings, 20, 52, 105, 159, 198, 248, 289
Bluestone, George, 216
Boccaccio, 194, 216, 255, 301, 309
Boccage, Anne-Marie du, 253
Bofill, Maria, 27
Böhlen, Helen, 268
Bolivia, 168
Böll, Heinrich, 292
Bolster, Richard, 217
Bolton, Sarah, 28
Bomli, P. W., 218
Bonaparte, Napoleon, 74, 80, 169, 194, 252
Bonheur, Rosa, 28, 323
Bonne, Rena Barbara, 218
Bonny, Anne, 170
Book of the Courtier, The (Castiglione, 1478-1529), 227
book-plates, 324
books, 166, 177, 223, 281, 342
books and prison, 229
books, banned, 234
Booth, Catherine, 28
Bordeau, Henry, 29
Borgia, Lucrèce, 27
Boswell, James, 338
Bouchet, Jean, 303
Bourciez, Edouard, 219

Bourdillon, Anne Francis, 29
Bourignon, Antoinette, 220
Bowman, Frank Paul, 219
Bradford, Gamaliel, 30, 220
Bradstreet, Anne, 128, 286
Brater, Enoch, 220
Braun, Sidney D., 221
Bravo-Villasante, Carmen, 221, 222
Braybrooke, Patrick, 222
Brazil, 15, 144, 162
Brée, Germaine, 222
Breisach, Ernst, 30
Bremer, Frederika, 119
Brenier de Montmorand, Antoine, 222
Brent, Margaret, 35
Brewer, Pat Bryan, 223
Bridenthal, Renate, 31
Briffault, Robert, 31, 32
Brigid of Kildare, 143
Britain, monarchy, 187
British Empire (India), 320
Brittain, Vera Mary, 33
Brittain, Alfred, 33
Broe, Mary Lynn, 223
Bronson, Alcott, 78
Brontë sisters, 145, 270, 279, 319, 336
Brontë, Anne, 250
Brontë, Charlotte, 249, 251, 252, 293, 294, 335
Brontë, Emily, 216, 327
Brook Farm (utopian community), 78, 80
Brooks, Geraldine, 34
Brown, Charles Brockden, 35
Brown, Dee, 35
Browning, Elizabeth Barrett, 111, 270
Browning, Robert, 47
Bryan, Margare B., 224
Buck, Pearl S., 36, 328
Bui Tuong Chieu, 37
Bulliet, Clarence J., 224
Burlador de Sevilla, El (Tirso de Molina), 313
Burma, 9
Burney, Fanny, 30, 154, 208, 224, 270, 292, 319
Burton, Jean, 37
Burton, Isabel, 37
Butler, Pierce, 37
Burundi, 153
By a Woman Writ (Goulianos), 256
Byron, Anne Isabella, 291
Byron, George Noel Gordon, 291, 324
Byzantine empresses, 34
Byzantine Empresses (Diehl), 58

C

Caballero, Fernán, 297
Caburrus, Thérésia, 24
Calderón, 333
Cambridge University, 55
Camden, Carroll, 38
Cameron, Edith, 226
Campo de Alange, Maria, 38
Camproux, Charles, 226
Canada, French, 301, 306
Canel, Eva, 317
Canonesses and Education in the Early Middle Ages, The (Heinrich), 96

Cantar de Mio Cid, 300
Canterbury Tales, 249, 306, 316
capitalism, 84
capitalists, women as, 45
Capmany, Maria Aurelia, 39
Captive Wife, The (Gavron), 82
Carácter femenino: historia de una ideología, El (Klein), 114
careers, 15, 26, 45, 60, 62, 65, 69, 75, 101, 108, 115, 123, 175, 184, 185, 188, 312
Carnegie Fund for International Peace, 78
Caro, Ana, 297
Caroline Chisholm (Kiddle), 112
Carriera, Rosalba, 26
Carroll, Mitchell, 33, 226
Cartas a las mujeres de España (Martínez Sierra), 130
Castiglione, 194, 227, 246
Castresana, Luis de, 39
Castro, Rosalia de, 256
Catalina de Erauso (Castresana), 39
Caterina Sforza, a Renaissance Virago (Breisach), 30
cathedrals, 3, 18
Cather, Willa, 275
Catholicism, 29, 39, 44, 53, 59, 88, 93, 151, 212, 237
Catlin, George, 40
Catt, Carrie Chapman, 146
Cavendish, Margaret, 256
Cazamian, Louis, 228
Cazaux, Yves, 228
Celtes, Conrad, 264

censorship (England), 332
censorship (Portugal), 210
censorship (Spain), 234
Central African Republic, 153
Cervantes, Miguel de, 226, 242, 264, 301, 309, 318, 330, 331, 334
Cespedes, Alba de, 232
Ceylon, 9
Chabrol, Claude, 229
Champagne, Marie de, 280
Chandavarker, Ganesh, L., 41
Changing Social Position of Women in Japan, The (Koyama), 116
Changing Status of Woman in Posence India (Haté), 94
Changing Women in a Changing Society (Huber), 101
chansons de geste, 13, 321
Chantal, Jeanne, 47
Characteristics of Women, Moral, Poetical, and Historical (Jameson), 273
characters in literature, 1, 80, 210, 213, 235, 242, 250, 252, 253, 255, 257, 263, 272, 273, 275, 276, 278, 284, 287, 291, 292, 293, 295, 301, 302, 307, 330, 331, 335, 336, 337
Charlemagne, 96
Charles, Edwin, 229
Charrier, Charlotte, 230
Charrière, Belle de, 278, 338
chastity testing, 255
Chaucer, Geoffrey, 102, 207, 249, 255, 270, 278, 281, 291, 302, 306, 316
Cherel, Albert, 70

Chesterton, Ada, 41
Child, Lydia Maria, 47
children, 5, 8, 60, 79, 89, 111, 121, 122, 176
Chile, 151
China, 36, 87, 127, 128
China, Communism in, 191
Chinard, G., 42
Chinese Revolution (1911), 90
Chinese women, 48
chivalric romances, 278, 280, 284, 342
chivalry, 4, 219
Chombart de Lauwe, M. J., 42
Chombart de Lauwe, Paul Henry, 43
Chrétien de Troyes (1150-1182), 280, 284
Christianity, 17, 18, 44, 52, 54, 60, 61, 119, 121, 132, 133, 143, 164 184
Christianity, early, 33, 96
Christianity, Eastern, 34
Christine de Pisan, 1364-1430 (Pinet), 303
Churchill, Caryl, 220
Cialente, Fausta, 232
Cid, El, 300, 334
Cinderella, 214, 276
cinema, 216, 276, 327
  Brazil, 327
  France, 320
  social thought in, 94
  United States, 265, 320
Cinq Visages de l'amour (Maurois), 290

Cintron, Felipe E., 43
Cité des Dames, La (Christine de Pisan), 304
cities, 4, 25, 26, 39, 41, 42, 74, 90, 125, 127, 147, 154, 181, 183, 237
Civil War (US), 65, 74, 94, 124, 175, 179, 196
Claridge, Mary, 44
Clark, Alice, 45
classical civilizations, 60, 72, 75, 77, 90, 108, 113, 116, 119, 122, 132, 163, 182, 199, 209, 260
Clayton, Aileen, 45
Clement, J., 46
Cleopatra, 220, 287
clubs, women's, 36
Coates, Mary Weld, 46
Code Civile (France), 243
Cognet, Louis, 47
Cohart, Mary, 47
Cohen, Rose, 47
Coke, Edward, 18
Cole, Eunice (Goody Cole), 57
Colette, 218, 322
collections, 111, 161, 207
College, the Market, and the Court (Dall), 53
Collett, Camille, 119
Collins, Marie, 48
Collis, Louise, 230
Colonna, Vittoria, 27, 104, 246
Columbia, 162
comedias, 290
Communism, 61, 86, 141, 144, 237
  China, 23

351

Cuba, 23
USSR, 23
Communism, women and, 6, 23, 59, 73, 92, 155, 191, 196, 251
Comnana, Anna, 102
composers (women), 242
Comte, Auguste, 97
Concerning Famous Women (Boccaccio), 216
Condorcet, 47
Confederacy, American, 94, 179
conferences, 60, 70
conferences on women, 70, 104, 146, 182
consumerism, 160, 167, 172
controversies, 13, 16, 38, 72, 86, 89, 92, 120, 134, 137, 165, 171, 204, 222, 232, 272, 289, 292, 301, 305
convent schools, 97
convents, 12, 26, 39, 52, 88, 105, 126, 138, 262
Conway, Jill, 123
Cooke, Cardinal Terence, 58
Cooper, Elizabeth, 48
Copland, Robert, 305
Corcos, Fernand, 49
Corday, Charlotte, 202
Coriolanus (Shakespeare), 224
Cormack, Margaret Lawson, 50
Corneille, Pierre, 211
Cornillon, Susan Kopelman, 231
Coronado, Carolina, 297
correspondence, 7, 31, 42, 55, 60, 61, 62, 72, 103, 148, 166, 169, 185, 196, 197, 201, 238, 240, 249, 251, 252, 284, 333
costume, 65, 67, 141, 252, 254
Cott, Nancy F., 50
Cotti, Colette, 51
Couch, John Philip 231
courtesy books, 86, 110, 130, 194, 227, 269, 306
Courtisane in the French Theatre, The (Braun), 221
courtly love, 13, 226, 278, 279, 280
Courtney, Janet Elizabeth, 51, 250
Courtney, W. I., 52
courts of love, 4
Courtship in Shakespeare (Meader), 291
Crandall, Coryl, 232
Crane, Thomas Frederick, 232
Crashaw, Richard, 314
Crépuscule des mystiques (Cognet), 47
criminals, 26, 154
Cristóbal (male feminist), 301
critics as censors, 222
Crocenti, Lelia, 232
Cross, Barbara M., 52
Crothers, Rachel, 209
Cruppi, Louise, 233
Crusades (Middle Ages), 153
Cruz Rueda, Angel, 233
Cuba, 162, 256, 318
Culture of the Twenties (Baritz), 13
Cunneen, Sally, 53
Cunnington, C. Willett, 53
Custer, Elizabeth, 36
customs, British (in Australia), 189

D

D'Arc, Jeanne, 38
Dakar, 153
Dall, Caroline H., 53
Daly, Mary, 54
Dames and Daughters of Colonial Days (Brooks), 35
Dames de la Renaissance (De Bury), 27
dance macabre, 270
Dane, Clemence, 275
Daniels, Pamela, 312
Dannett, Sylvia G. L., 54
Dante, 194, 240, 246, 257, 337
Darwin, Charles, 4, 84, 307
Daughters of Eve (Bradford), 30
Daughters of Genius (Parton), 303
Dauntless Women (Mathews), 133
Davies, Emily, 55
Davy, Marie-Magdelen, 55
De la Cruz, Sor Juana Inéz, 269, 309
De passionibus mulierum (Trotula), 102
De Sale, Antoine de, 215
Dean, Rebecca Pennell, 185
Dear-Bought Heritage (Leonard), 121
death camps (World War II), 25, 99
Debower, Lore Loftfield, 233
Decameron (Boccaccio), 255
Declaration of Independence (US), 34
Dédéyan, Charles, 234
Defence of Good Women, The (Elyot), 67
Deffand, Mme du, 30
Defoe, Daniel, 23, 154
Degler, Carl N., 84, 123
Deiss, Joseph J., 55

Dejob, Charles, 235
Delafield, E. M., 275
Delafield, Edmee M. 235
DeLeeuw, Hendrik, 56
Democracy and Social Ethics (Addams), 4
demographics, 178, 188, 193
Demos, John, 57
dependence, women and, 209
Derechos civiles de la mujer (Alvarez Vignoli), 7
Des Roches, Catherine, 246
Descartes, René, 52
Deschamps, Nicole, 236
Deutsch, Helene, 57, 76
Deuxième Sexe, Le (De Beauvoir), 18
Devil Take Her, The (Salomon), 314
Dialectic of Sex, The (Firestone), 73
Diálogo en laude de las mujeres (Espinosa), 68
Diamond, Elin, 220
Diana of the Crossways (Meredith), 247, 265
diaries, 22, 55, 61, 62, 74, 94, 99, 115, 153, 177, 179, 209, 224, 270, 294, 295, 298
Diary and Letters of Madame d'Arblay, 224
Diary of Anaïs Nin, The, 298
Dickens, Charles, 145, 229, 293, 312
Diderot, 62
Didion, Joan, 322
Dido (legendary character in Virgil), 281

Dido en la literature española (Lida de Malkiel), 281
Diehl, Charles, 58
Dirvin, Joseph I., 58
discouragement, effects of, 9, 18, 22, 30, 36, 39, 51, 56, 60, 65, 66, 69, 71, 72, 73, 91, 101, 102, 110, 112, 114, 119, 126, 129, 134, 136, 137, 141, 156, 165, 166, 168, 169, 178, 180, 184, 209, 222, 241, 246, 250, 251, 261, 268, 269, 285, 287, 296, 301, 303, 311, 327, 329, 337, 339
disguises, 46, 253
Dispossessed, The (Longmore), 125
dissertations, 207, 209, 218, 248, 253, 264, 271, 283, 286, 293, 307
Diver, Maud, 321
Divine Comedy, The (Dante), 337
divorce, 67, 106, 108, 156, 158, 182, 188, 194, 221, 229, 234, 258, 260, 323
Doctrine for the Lady of the Renaissance (Kelso), 110
documents, 48, 106
   American, 149, 192
   British, 185
   Hispanic, 151
   Spanish, 142
Dodge, Norton T., 59
Doll's House, A (Ibsen), 284
domesticity, 22, 23, 52, 91, 198, 294, 303, 311
Dominant Sex, The (Vaerting), 196
Don Juan, 313, 334, 335
Don Juan Tenorio, 46

Don Juan y el donjuanismo, 313
Don Quijote, 226
Donaldson, James, 60
Donghi, Beatrice Solinas, 232
Donne della Riforma in Italia, Le (Inguanti), 104
Donne, John, 314
Doubleday, Neal Frank, 237
drama, American, 209, 220, 257
drama, British, 166, 209, 220, 232, 253, 287, 291, 302, 330
drama, French, 69, 210, 221, 235, 282, 307, 318
drama, German, 26, 235, 262, 287, 316
drama, Greek, 116, 341
drama, Irish, 215, 284
drama, Latin, 288
drama, Norwegian, 112, 198, 283
drama, Spanish, 221, 263, 286, 298, 318
dreams, 93
Dreier, Mary E., 60
Dreiser, Theodore, 251
Drexler, Rosalyn, 257
Drinker, Elizabeth, 176
Drinnon, Richard, 61
Driver, Sam N., 237
Dronke, Peter, 238
Drury, Clifford Merrill, 61
Du Bose, Jacques, 308
Duckett, Eleanor Shipley, 238
Dunbar, Janet, 62, 239
Dunbar, Olivia Howard, 239
Dupont-Chatelain, Marguerite, 62

Durning, Russel E., 240
Dutt, G. S., 63

E

Earle, Alice Morse, 35
Early Victorian Woman, The (Dunbar), 62
Easman, R.S., 323
economics, 3, 45, 83, 89, 100, 160, 167, 168, 175, 294, 333
Eden, Emily, 321
Edgeworth, Maria, 240, 283, 329
Educated Woman in America (Cross), 52
education, 245, 258, 271, 317, 328
  Africa, 129
  Australia, 188
  Britain, 11, 33, 53, 55, 67, 148, 154, 165, 166, 185, 200
  France, 14, 21, 70, 71, 89, 117, 119, 138, 165, 171
  India, 95
  Jewish, 108
  Middle Ages, 96
  Morocco, 147
  New Zealand, 189
  Renaissance, 200
  Rome, 78
  Russia, 59
  Spain, 131
  United States, 36, 52, 53, 69, 77, 78, 79, 84, 95, 104, 110, 115, 124, 152, 182
Éducation des femmes du dix-septième siècle (Beirne), 21
Éducation des femmes par les femmes, L' (Gréard), 88
education of nuns, 105
Edwards, Lee R., 241
Effinger, John R., 63
Egoist, The (Meredith), 265
Egypt, ancient, 93, 163
Egypt, papyri found in, 227
eighteenth century, 202, 250, 272, 289, 338
  American colonies, 57, 176, 181
  Britain, 10, 23, 41, 62, 100, 106, 148, 154, 166, 183, 191, 207, 208, 239, 248, 259, 260, 283, 293, 318, 329, 330, 332, 337
  France, 24, 42, 47, 71, 80, 97, 126, 190, 195, 202, 234, 239, 243, 253, 259, 293, 333
  Ireland, 239
  United States, 23, 34, 66, 110, 182, 197
eighth century
  Britain, 208
El Salvador, 162
Eleanor de Guienne (1122-1204), 4
eleventh century, 230, 254
  France, 254
Eliot, George, 28, 145, 212, 231, 241, 250, 270, 279, 292, 319, 327
Eliot, T. S., 163
Elizabeth Inchbald and Her Circle (Littlewood), 283
Elizabeth, Empress of Austria, assassination of, 29

Elizabethan era, 38, 203, 220, 291, 302, 342
Elizabethan Woman, The (Camden), 38
Elizabethan Women (Bradford), 220
Ellen Key, Her Life and Her Work (Nystrom-Hamilton), 147
Ellet, Elizabeth F., 64, 65, 66, 241
Ellis, Havelock, 66, 112, 114, 147
Elson, Arthur, 242
Elyot, Sir Thomas, 67
emancipation, 3, 100, 178, 180, 182, 184, 198
Emancipation of the Turkish Woman (Afetinan), 5
Emancipazione femminile in Italia, L' (Societàs Umanitaria), 182
emigration (Australia), 112
Eminent Victorians (Strachey), 186
Eminent Women of the Age (Parton), 152
Encyclopédistes et les femmes, Les (Dupont-Chatelain), 62
English Domestic Relations, 1487-1653 (Powell), 157
English Woman in History, The (Stenton), 184
English Women Enter the Professions (Franz), 75
English Women in Life and Letters (Phillips), 154
Enter Woman (Moody), 239
environmental issues, 104
epics, Greek, 227
epics, Hindu, 50, 138, 156, 273
epics, Roman, 281

Epstein, Louis M., 67
Epton, Nina Consuelo, 242
Equal Rights Amendment (ERA), 89
ERA (Equal Rights Amendment), 89
Erasmus, Desiderius, 165, 286
Erauso, Catalina de, 39
Erikson, Joan A., 123
Escritoras españolas, Las (Nelken), 297
Eshleman, Lloyd W., 68
Espina de Serna, Concha, 242
Espinosa, Juan de, 68
espionage, 45, 103, 204
Essais (Montaigne), 245
Essay in Defence of the Female Sex (Astell), 10
Essays on Sex Equality (Rossi), 171
Este, Isabelle d', 169
Estudios literarios sobre mística española (Hatzfeld), 265
Eterno femenino, Lo (García Ortiz), 80
ethnic groups, 121, 139
eugenics, 126
Euphrates Valley, 16
Euripides, 341
Europe, 178
Eva e seus autores (Tavares de Sà), 327
Evans, Oliver, 243
Eve (biblical character), 124, 125, 167, 215, 227, 271, 272, 326
Evelina (Burney), 224
Everyone Was Brave (O'Neill), 149
Évolution du droit de la femme (Rigaud), 169
Exeter Book, 207
existentialism, 19, 54, 82, 236, 287,

295, 309
existentialism and feminism, 19

F

fabliaux, 207, 215, 279
factory work, 78, 89, 145, 147, 154, 180
Faerie Queene, The (Spenser), 278
Fagniez, Gustave Charles, 68
Faillie, Maria, 243
Fairchild, Johnson E., 69
fairy tales, 213
Faith of Our Feminists (Jessup), 274
Fallen Women (Seymour-Smith), 319
Family in Classical Greece, The (Lackey), 116
Family in Various Cultures, The (Queen), 159
family patterns, 153, 159, 170
　Australia, 171
　Dutch East Indies, 171
　India, 171
　Indians, North American, 171
　Indonesia, 171
　Malaysia, 171
　Micronesia, 171
Fanshaw, Lady Ann, 236
Farnham, Marynia, 69
Farber, Seymour, 70
farce and women, 278
fashion, 65, 141, 252, 263
fashion in novels, 252

Fauchery, Pierre, 243
Fear of Being a Woman (Rheingold), 166
fear of women (men's), 270
Febvre, Lucien, 244
Female Pen, The (MacCarthy), 285
Feminine Attitudes in the Nineteenth Century (Cunnington), 53
Feminine Character, The (Klein), 114
Feminine Mystique, The (Friedan), 76
femininity (see "themes")
Femininity and the Creative Imagination (Appignanesi), 208
feminism, 5, 17, 210, 213, 247, 259, 261, 264, 274, 300, 305, 333, 334, 335
　American colonies, 181
　Brazil, 15, 142
　Britain, 40, 51, 55, 62, 100, 125, 171, 172, 185, 191, 201, 232, 312, 336, 340, 341
　Denmark, 86
　Ecuador, 80
　Europe, 5, 134, 163
　France, 19, 20, 42, 63, 89, 97, 117, 164, 167, 173, 201, 308
　Germany, 5, 113, 268
　India, 108, 145
　Latin America, 311
　Norway, 258
　Scandinavia, 119
　Spain, 39, 43, 73, 86, 130, 131, 132, 142, 199, 221, 300
　Sweden, 111, 112, 147, 233

Turkey, 5
United States, 3, 50, 60, 73, 76, 80, 83, 84, 91, 99, 108, 115, 120, 123, 135, 137, 147, 149 152, 168, 180, 201, 274, 298, 325
Féminisme au temps de Molière, Le (Baumal), 211
Feminism in Greek Literature (Wright), 341
feminism, Aristotle and, 341
Feminismo en la literatura española, El (Orñate), 300
Feminismo, feminidad, y españolismo (Martínez Sierra), 131
Feminist Writers of the Seventeenth Century (Richards), 167
feminists, male, 8, 10, 13, 23, 31, 33, 40, 41, 47, 49, 60, 62, 63, 66, 67, 71, 72, 78, 80, 83, 118, 130, 131, 132, 133, 137, 142, 147, 152, 165, 166, 171, 172, 180, 199, 201, 213, 217, 233, 243, 248, 265, 269, 283, 287, 288, 298, 301, 303 308, 311, 326
Femme au XVII siècle, La (Reynier), 164
Femme chez les hommes, Une (Casgrain), 39
Femme dans l'Espagne du siècle d'or, La (Bomli), 218
Femme dans la littérature existentielle, La (Nahas), 296
Femme de lettres au XVIIIe siècle, Une: Anne-Marie du Boccage (Gill-Mark), 253
Femme et l'amour au XIIe siècle, La (Lot), 284
Femme et la société française, La (Fagniez), 8
Femme et le destin de l'Afrique, La (Maistriaux), 129
Femme italienne avant, pendant et après la Renaissance, La (Rodocanachi), 169
Femme poète du XVIIe siècle, Une (Brenier de Montmorand), 222
Femmes en Union Soviétique, Les (Pierre), 154
Fénelon (1651-1715), 15, 23, 70, 172
Fénelon on Education (Barnard), 14
Fern, Fanny, 152, 339
Ferrante, Joan M., 245
feudal society, 31, 300
Feugère, Léon
Feytaud, Jacques de, 71
Field, Crystal, 257
Field, Nathaniel, 331
Fifteen Joys of Marriage, The (Aldington, tr.), 207
fifteenth century, 222, 226
Britain, 157
Europe, 110
France, 106, 117, 207, 255, 303, 304
Italy, 169, 194, 323
Spain, 130, 133, 180
Filipino women, 8
Fille d'alliance de Montaigne, La (Schiff), 173
Finland, 284

Finley, M. I., 72
Firestone, Shulamith, 73
First White Women over the Rockies (Drury), 61
Fisher, Marvin, 246
Five Faces of Love (Maurois), 290
Five for Freedom (Wagner), 334
Flaubert, Gustave, 216, 291, 335
Fletcher, Jefferson Butler, 246
Flores, Juan de, 134
Floresta, Nisia, 15
folklore, 132, 133, 213, 214
Forsberg, Elborg, 299
Forsberg, Robert J., 74
Forster, E. M., 321
Forten, Charlotte, 74
Foulché-Delbosc, R., 247
fourteenth century
   Britain, 231
   France, 155, 255
   Italy, 27, 217
Fowler, Lois Josepha, 247
Fowler, W. Warde, 75
Frail Vessels (Mews), 292
France, Anatole, 280
France, Marie de, 254
Frances Wright, Free Enquirer (Perkins), 153
Frank, Anne, 294
Frankfurt (Germany), 90
Franklin, Benjamin, 42, 197, 253
Franz,, Nellie Alden, 75
Frappier, Jean, 276
Frazer, James George, 248
free love concept (USSR), 92

freedom (see "themes")
freedom, ideals of, 202
French Revolution, 23, 51, 169, 172, 202, 250, 259
Freud, Sigmund, 57, 73, 76, 93, 114, 115, 136, 141, 197, 249, 320
Freudian psychology, 57, 73
Friedan, Betty, 76, 115, 161, 162
Friedländer, Ludwig, 77
Frois, Marcel, 78
frontier in America, 192
Frost, Robert, 325
Fryer, Judith, 78
Fryer, Peter, 79
Fulbright, James Stephen, 248
Fuller, Margaret, 28, 52, 55, 79, 80, 128, 201, 286, 305, 336
Fulton, Mary, 275
Fuseli, Henry, 248

G

Gage, Matilda Joslin, 183
Galdós, Benito (Pérez Galdós), 321
Galindo, Beatriz, 297
Gallant Ladies (Rogers), 170
Gandersheim (Benedictine abbey), 263
García Ortiz, Maria, 80
Gardiner, Judith Kegan, 249
Gaskell, Elizabeth, 99, 145, 154, 228, 250, 311, 322
Gautier, Paul, 80, 81
Gautier, Théophile, 292
Gavron, Hannah, 82
Genesis (Bible), 151, 184, 215, 272n.

Genet, Jean, 141
Génie des femmes, Le (Martin), 129
Genlis, Mme de, 126, 250, 266
gentility, 159, 335
Gentle Tamers, The (Brown), 35
George, Margaret, 82
George, Walter L., 82
George Meredith as Champion of Women (Woods), 340
Gerber, Philip, 251
Gerin, Winifred, 251
German Woman in the Age of Enlightenment, The (Schreiber), 316
Germany, 300
Germany vs. France, 195
Ghandi is My Star (Nehru), 145
Ghandi, Mahatma, 145
GI Bill (proposed for women's education), 77
Gibbs-Smith, Charles H., 252
Gilbert, Miriam Anne, 253
Gilbert and Sullivan, 197
Gilette, Julie-Sophie, 143
Gill-Mark, Grace, 249
Gilman, Charlotte Perkins, 68, 83, 83, 201, 336
Gill-Mark, Grace, 253
Ginzburg, Eli, 84
Ginzburg, Natalia, 232
Glasgow (city), 322
Glasgow, Ellen, 223, 254, 275, 302, 307, 336
Glasgow, Maude, 85
Glaspell, Susan, 220
Gloerfelt-Tarp, Kirsten, 85

Godbold, E. Stanly, 254
Goddard, Eunice Rathbone, 254
Goddess of Love, The (Grigson), 259
Godechot, Jacques, 325
Godwin, William, 201
Goebbels, Magda, 136
Goethe, 158, 235, 240, 317
Goldberg, Harriet, 86
Goldman, Emma, 61, 86
Golenistcheff-Koutouzoff, Elie, 255
González, Manuel Pedro, 256
Goode, William J., 87
Gordon, Caroline, 223
Gornick, Vivian, 88
Goulianos, Joan, 256
Goulianos, Ruth, 257
Gournay, Marie de, 72, 120, 167, 173, 245, 278, 282, 315
Graham, Gabriela, 88
Grandgent, Charles H., 257
Grau, Shirley Ann, 223
Graves, Robert, 257
Gravier, Maurice, 258
Graville, Anne de, 222
Gréard, Octavio, 88
Great Depression, 50, 183
Greece, 122, 132
Greek women, 130, 226
Greeley, Horace, 80
Greenwood, Grace, 152
Gregory, Allene, 259
Gregory, Chester W., 89
Griffith, Dudley David, 259
Grigson, Geoffrey, 259
Grimal, Pierre, 89

Grisay, August, 260
Grisel y Mirabella (Juan de Flores), 134
Griselda (legendary character), 255, 259
Grummond, Frances, 36
Grundy, Isabel, 260
Guatamela, 162
Guhl, Ernst, 65
Guiguet, Jean, 261
Guillaume, Jacquette, 308
Guinea, 153
Gutwirth, Madelyn, 261
Guyon, Jeanne-Marie de, 47, 220
Guzmán, Feliciana Enrique de, 297

H

Hadrian, 105
Hahn, Emily, 90
Hahn, Lili, 90
Haig, Stirling, 262
Haight, Anne Lyon, 262
Haiti, 153
Hale, Sarah Josepha, 323
Halkett, Lady Ann, 236
Hall, Edwad B., 91
Halle, Fannina W., 92
Hamlet (Shakespeare), 249
Hamilton, Arthur, 263
Hammond, Harriet Milton, 92
Hampton, New Hampshire, 57
Hanrahan, Thomas S. J., 263
Haraszti, Zoltan, 264

Harding, Esther M., 92
Hardy, Thomas, 330, 335
Harper, Ida Husted, 183
Harris, Sara, 93
Hartley, Susan Rebecca, 264
Harwell, Richard Barksdale, 94
Haskell, Molly, 94
Haté, Chandralkala, A., 94
Hatzfeld, Helmut, 265
Hawkins, Richmond Laurin, 266
Hawthorne, Nathaniel, 128, 237, 286, 323, 339
Hayden, Sophie G., 185
Hays, Elinor, 95
Hays, Mary, 201
healing arts, 102
Healy, Emma Thérèse (Sister), 95
Hébert, Anne, 307
Hecker, Eugene A., 96
Hedda Gabler (Ibsen), 198
hedonism, 198, 199
Heilbrun, Carolyn, 267
Heinrich, Mary Pia (Sister), 96
Heller, Otto, 267
Hellman, Lillian, 322
Héloïse, 38, 102, 111, 201, 268, 269
Héloïse dans l'histoire (Charrier), 230
Henderson, Nancy L., 268
Henri II (France), 219
Henriot, Émile, 268
Henriquez-Ureña, Pedro, 269
Henry VIII (England), 105, 157
Hentsch, Alice Adèle, 269
Heptaméron (Marguerite de Navarre), 244, 309

herbal remedies, 102
Héricourt, Jenny d', 97, 158
Heroínas do romance brasileiro
  (Moraes), 295
Heroines in French Drama of the
  Romantic Period (Ihrig), 272
Heroines of George Meredith
  (Bedford), 213
Herold, J. Christopher, 97
Herrick, Robert, 314
Hertha (feminist novel), 112
Hewitt, Margaret, 98
Heyward, Thomas, 342
High-Caste Hindu Woman, The
  (Ramabai Sarasvati), 161
Hilda of Whitby (abbess), 143, 149
Hildegard (abbess), 238
Hillesum, Etty, 99
Hinduism, 50, 156
Hinkley, Laura L., 270
Hispanic women, 7, 8, 39, 40, 43, 80, 101, 122, 130, 131, 142, 151, 161, 168, 199, 256, 269, 297, 303, 310
Histoire de l'éducation des femmes en
  France (Rousselot), 171
Histoire des femmes (Bardèche), 13
Histoire mondiale de la femme
  (Grimal), 89
History of the Useless Precaution Plot,
  A (Sedwick), 318
History of Woman Suffrage (Stanton), 183
Hitler, Adolf, and women, 18, 114, 136, 141
Hittites, 90

Hobbs, Lisa, 99
Hohman, Daisy Lucie, 100
Holbrook, David, 270
Holcombe, Lee, 100
Holland, Lady, 30
Hollingsworth, Leta S., 145
Holloway, Laura C., 100
homeless women, 41
homemaking, 52, 56, 60, 62, 63, 69, 70, 76, 82, 83, 85, 108, 112, 122, 127, 136, 155
Homer, 227
Honduras, 162
Hong Kong, 103
Hopkins, Gerald Manley, 328
Horner, Matina B., 101
Horney, Karen, 328
Horwitz, Barbara Joan, 271
Hottel, Althea E., 101
Houdetot, Mme d', 42
housework, 22, 60, 63, 91, 136, 172, 311
Howe, Ethel Puffer, 149
Howells, William Dean, 336
Hroswitha, 27, 262, 264, 287
Huas, Jeanine, 271
Huber, Joan, 101
Huch, Ricarda, 268
Hughes, Muriel Joy, 102
Hugo, Victor, 331
Huguès, Micheline, 271
Hull House (Chicago), 4
Hume, David, 14
humor, 318

Hunt, Morton M., 102
Huntington, Annie Oakes, 103
Hutchinson, Anne, 35
Hutchinson, Lucy, 236
Hutton, J. Bernard, 103
hygiene, 190, 199

I

I Leap over the Wall (Baldwin), 12
Ibarbourou, Juana de, 310
Ibibios (African tribe), 189
Ibsen, Henrik, 112, 198, 258, 283, 320
ideal of woman, 96, 108, 139, 155, 159, 258, 274, 277, 278, 309, 327, 334, 336, 337
Ihrig, Grace Pauline, 272
Iliad, The, 227
Images de la femme dans la société (Chombart de Lauwe), 43
imagination, 208, 212, 219, 278, 303, 322, 327, 330, 336
immigration, 47, 50, 61, 87, 115, 120, 172, 328
impersonators, 221, 224
imprisonment, 24, 44, 61, 86, 106, 175, 229
In Darkest London (Chesterton), 41
In Defense of Women (Mencken), 137
Inchbald, Elizabeth Simpson, 184, 259, 283
India, 9, 41, 50, 51, 63, 87, 133, 138, 156, 161, 250
  sacred writings, 156
  women's Freedom Movement (1857-1947), 108
Indians, Brazilian, 15
Indonesia, 9
Industrial Revolution, 5, 45, 50, 173, 228, 246, 312
industry, 3, 145, 180
Influencia de la mujer, La (Lillo Catalán), 123
Inguanti, Maria, 104
insanity, 219, 311
intellect (see "themes")
Intelligence of Women, The (George), 82
International Congress of Women (1933), 104
International Congress of Working Women, 60
international studies, 31, 43, 56, 60, 65, 87, 89, 96, 101, 104, 107, 131, 152, 159, 174, 188, 194
Iowa, 147
Ireland, 240, 328
Irish women, 215
Irwin, Harriet, 185
Isabella, Queen of Spain, 86, 130
Islam, 203. *See also* Moors.
isolation, 77, 82, 83, 136, 175, 180
Israel, 73
Italy, 104, 173, 194, 315

J

Jailed for Freedom (Stevens), 185
James, Bartlett Burleigh, 104
James, Henry, 128, 286, 336

Jameson, Anna M., 273
Jane Mecom, the Favorite Sister of Benjamin Franklin (Van Doren), 197
Janitschek, Maria, 268
Japan, 87
Japanese Woman Looking Forward (Straelen), 186
Japanese women, 116
Jardín de nobles doncellas (Martín), 130
Jardín de nobles donzellas (Goldberg), 86
Jayal, Shaakambara, 273
Jeffers, A. Norman, 274
Jefferson, Thomas, 42, 74
Jephthah (biblical character), 325
Jephthah and His Daughter (Sypherd), 325
Jessup, Josephine Luril, 274
Jeunes filles à la fin du XVIIIe siècle (De Luppé), 126
Jewish Library, The (Jung), 107
Jewish women, 48, 61, 67, 90, 99, 108, 164, 199
Johannesburg, 125
Johnson, R. Brimley, 275
Johnson, Samuel, 101, 224, 289
Jones, Howard Mumford, 275
Jones, Margaret, 276
Jonin, Pierre, 276
Jonson, Ben, 209
Jordan, Ruth, 105
Josephus, Flavius (historian), 332
Jourda, Pierre, 106
Journal of Charlotte Forten, The: A Free Negro in the Slave Era, 74
Journal of Emily Foster (Williams), 337
journalism, 29, 90
Journals of Dorothy Wordsworth, The, 295
Joyce, T. Athol, 107
Judaism, 47, 54, 67, 108, 164
Jung, Carl, 93, 214
Jung, Leo, 107
Jungian archetypes, 214
Justin, Dena, 108
Justin, Linda Levitt, 196
Juvenal (Roman satirist), 209, 301

K

Kane, Leslie, 220
Kaplan, Sydney Janet, 277
Kapp, Julius, 277
Kardiner, Abram, 108
Kaur, Manmohan, 108
Kavanaugh, Julie, 277
Kaye-Smith, Sheila, 275
Keddie, Nikke R., 109
Kelson, Ruth, 110
Kempe, Margery, 22, 231, 256
Kendall, Elaine, 110
Kennedy, Jacqueline, 162
Kentucky, 66
Key, Ellen, 110, 111, 112, 119, 147, 233
Keyssar, Helene, 220
kibbutz concept (Israel) 73
Kiddle, Margaret, 112

Kiefer, Otto, 113
Kingsley, Mary, 139, 140
Kipling, Rudyard, 321
Kirkpaatrick, Clifford, 113
Klein, Viola, 114
Knight, Alan E., 278
Komarovsky, Mirra, 76, 115
Kooiman-Van Middendorp, Gerarda, 278
Koonz, Claudia, 31
Koran, 203, 300
Korea, 133
Koren, 115
Koyama, Takashi, 116

L

La Femme libérée? (Sartin), 173
La Paix? (Corcos), 49
La Sale, Antoine de, 207
La Tour, Mary Jacqueline, 35
Labé, Louise, 246, 267
Lackey, Walter K., 116
Ladies of Dante's Lyrics (Grandgent), 257
Ladies of the White House, The (Holloway), 100
Lady, The (Putnam), 159
Lady Byron Vindicated (Stowe), 324
Lady Chatterley's Lover (Lawrence), 270
LaFayette, Mme de, 162, 234, 262, 290, 291

Lafitte-Houssat, Jacques, 279
Laforet, Carmen, 276
Lagerlöf, Selma, 119, 233
Lahy-Hollebecque, Marie, 279
Laigle, Mathilde, 116
Laiglesia, Edward de, 280
Laird, Donald, 117
Lamb, Mary, 311
Lambert, Juliette, 158, 201
Lan-Ta-Ka, 123
Lancaster, Masika, 85
Langston-Davies, John, 118
language, 79, 266
language, formation of, 248
Larsen, Anna Astrup, 119
Las Antillas, 151
Las Españolas pintadas por los Españoles (Robert), 309
Latin America, 7, 40, 80, 122, 142, 151, 161, 311
Laumonier, Paul, 119
law, 7, 26, 61, 86, 131, 148, 169, 312
law (US) and women, 9
law and women, 8, 9, 18, 37, 41, 53, 243, 321
law in Indian epics, 138
law, Germanic tribes, 208
law, history of, 169, 243
law, medieval, 321
law, tribal, 324
Lawrence, D. H., 141, 243, 270
Lawrence, Margaret, 307
laws (US states, 1914), 96
laws of Manu (India), 156
Le Fort, Gertrude von, 327

Learned Lady in England, 1650-1760
  (Reynolds), 166
Lebedun, Jean, 120
lecturers, 120, 124, 132, 147, 148
lectures, 69, 83, 120, 239
Lee, Helene R., 120
Lee, Mary Ann, 185
legal code, 13th century Spain, 184
legal code, 19th century France, 243
legal status of women, 9, 10, 18, 24,
  26, 27, 28, 41, 53, 145, 153, 161,
  169, 184, 188, 334
legends, 255, 259, 276, 281, 332, 335
legends, biblical, 272, 326
legends, Celtic, 280, 291
Lehman, Rosamund, 277
Leibl, Marian, 328
Lenclos, Ninon de, 30
Lenin, Nikolai, 92
Leningrad, siege of, 181
Lennox, Charlotte, 319
Leonard, Eugenia Andruss, 121
Lespinasse, Mlle de, 30, 98, 130
Lessing, Doris, 288, 322
letters of women, 31, 42, 55, 61, 72,
  91, 103, 105, 126, 165, 169, 176,
  179, 196, 201, 210, 224, 230, 238,
  240, 250, 251, 252, 254, 266, 270,
  319, 333
Lewis, C. S., 280
Lewis, Oscar, 122
liberation, 19, 39, 54, 56, 88, 99, 100,
  129, 146, 236, 298, 304, 318, 320
libraries, 8, 26, 28, 35, 55, 67, 116,
  207, 209, 223, 233, 281
libraries, personal, 223, 225
Licht, Hans, 122
Lida de Malkiel, Maria Rosa, 281
Life and Letters of Anne Isabella, Lady
  Noel Byron, The (Mayne), 291
Lifton Catalán, Victorian, 123
Lilja, Saara, 281
Lincoln, Abraham, 196
Lincoln, Mary Todd, 196
Lindbergh, Anne Morrow, 128, 286
Lindsay, John V., 147
linguistics, 133, 208, 248, 254, 260
literary criticism, American, 275
literary criticism, French, 231
literary criticism, Freudian, 249
literary criticism, Italian, 232
Literary Currents in Hispanic-America
  (Henríquez-Ureña), 269
literature, African, 323
literature, American, 19, 34, 209, 223,
  235, 237, 246, 252, 254, 256, 267,
  274, 284, 288, 294, 298, 302, 307,
  319, 322, 323, 325, 333, 336, 337
  339
literature, Anglo-Saxon, 208
literature, Argentinian, 317
literature, Arthurian, 245, 281
literature, Brazilian, 295
literature, British, 53, 154, 204, 209,
  210, 212, 213, 220, 222, 224, 228,
  229, 230, 235, 241, 247, 248, 252,
  259, 261, 264, 270, 271, 279, 283,
  285, 287, 291, 292, 293, 294, 302,
  305, 306, 316, 318, 320, 321, 322,

330, 332, 340
literature, Canadian, 307
literature, Celtic, 276, 280, 281
literature, chivalric, 219
literature, classical, 209, 238, 281, 282
literature, comparative, 13, 19, 60, 74, 80, 97, 194, 207, 211, 214, 218, 219, 230, 232, 238, 243, 246, 255, 259, 267, 268, 269, 271, 275, 283, 289, 292, 293, 294, 300, 309, 313, 315, 316, 326, 327, 330, 331, 332, 335, 338
literature, French, 167, 172, 211, 217, 221, 222, 226, 231, 234, 244, 245, 255, 262, 265, 267, 271, 272, 275, 276, 278, 279, 280, 282, 284, 290, 292, 294, 295, 296, 304, 307, 308, 309, 314, 315, 318, 321, 328, 330, 333, 335
literature, French-Canadian, 307
literature, German, 174, 255, 259, 264, 267, 268, 288, 293, 315, 316
literature, Greek, 116, 227, 341
literature, Hispanic, 276, 317
literature, Indian (Asia), 138
literature, Irish, 215, 276
literature, Italian, 216, 227, 232, 337
literature, Latin, 282, 287
literature, Latin American, 269, 297
literature, medieval, 13, 238, 244, 245, 262, 269, 271, 276, 278, 279, 281, 284, 316
literature, misogynist, 207, 215, 281, 334
literature, Norwegian, 211, 236, 258
literature, popular, 342
literature, Russian, 237, 249
literature, Sanskrit, 273
literature, Spanish, 86, 134, 218, 221, 226, 233, 242, 247, 263, 266, 280, 281, 283, 286, 288, 289, 297, 298, 300, 303, 313, 318, 330, 331, 334, 335
literature, Swedish, 233
literature, world, 267, 319, 320
Little Sermons on Sin (Simpson), 180
Littlewood, S. R., 282
Livermore, Maria A., 123, 202
Lives of Girls Who Became Famous (Bolton), 28
Lives of the Queens of England (Strickland), 187
Livet, Charles-Louis, 282
Living My Life (Goldman), 86
Living of Charlotte Perkins Gilman, The (Gilman), 83
Livre de la Cité des Dames (de Pisan), 304
Livre de trois vertus de Christine de Pisan, Le (Laigle), 116
Locke, John, 14
Lockwood, Belva Ann, 185
Log-Cabin Lady, The (Anonymous), 124
Lombroso-Ferrer, Gina, 328
London, 8, 26, 41, 154, 192, 283
London Ladies: True Tales of the Eighteenth Century (Stebbins), 183
Long Road of Woman's Memory (Addams), 5

Longmore, Laura, 125
Loomis, Emerson Robert, 283
Lorichs, Sonja, 283
Lot, Myrrha Borodine, 284
Louis XIV (France), 300
Louise de Marillac (Dirvin), 58
love (see "themes")
Love and the English, 242
Love Letters of Mary Hays, The (Wedd), 201
Love, Morals, and the Feminists (Rover), 172
Lovett, Clara M., 23
Ludovici, Anthony M., 125, 145
Luis de Lucena: Repetitión de amores (Ornstein), 300
Lukens, Rebecca W., 185
Luppé, Albert, 126
Lutheranism, 52
Luxembourg, Rosa, 195
Lyly, John, 342
Lynd, Robert, 126, 127
Lynd, Helen Merell, 126, 127

M

MacCarthy, Bridget G., 284, 285
Macaulay, Rose, 222, 275
Machann, Virginia Sue Brown, 128, 286
machine age, 155, 246, 322
machismo, 7, 8, 27, 40, 68, 122
Machon, Louis, 308

Mackenzie, Agnes Muro, 287
Madame Bovary (Flaubert), 216
Madame de LaFayette en ménage (Magne), 128
Madame de Maintenon (Mermaz), 137
Madame de Montaigne, d'après les Essais (Laumonier), 119
Madame de Staël and Freedom Today (Forsberg), 74
Madame de Staël et Napoléon (Gautier), 81
Madame de Staël: dix années d'exil (Gautier), 80
Madame Tallien (Bertaut), 24
Magne, Émile, 128
Magnin, Charles, 287
Mahabharata, 138
Maharshi, Karve (Chandavarker), 41
Mailer, Norman, 141
Maine, Duchesse du, 98
Maintenon, Mme de, 30, 71, 172, 300
Mair, Lucy, 129
Maistriaux, Robert, 129
Malaya, 9
Male and Female (Mead), 135
Man and Woman (Ellis), 66
Mann, Thomas, 335
Mannheim, Karl, 114
Mansfield, Katherine, 130, 268, 327
Manu, laws of (India), 161
manuscripts, illuminated by nuns, 105
Marcel, Gabriel, 55
Maret, Clément, 303
Maret, Jean, 303
Margaret Clitherow, 1556-1586

(Claridge), 44
Margaret Dreier Robins, Her Life, Letters, and Work, 60
Margaret Roper (Reynolds), 165
Margaret, Duchess of Newcastle, 285
Margaret, Lady Winchilsea, 341
Marguerite d'Angoulême (Jourda), 106
Marguerite de Navarre, 226, 244, 245, 246
Mari (Mesopotamia), 16
Marie de Champagne (1145-1198), 4
Marie de l'Incarnation, 266
marketing, 76
Markow, Alice Bradley, 287
Martin, Claire, 307
Martin, Marie-Madeleine, 129
Martin de Córdoba, Fray, 130
Martineau, Harriet, 235, 294
Martínez Sierra, Gregorio, 8, 130, 131, 298
Martínez Sierra, Maria, 132
martyrs, 44, 52, 55, 163, 238
Marxism, 162
Mary Todd Lincoln: Her Life and Letters (Turner), 196
Mas, Armedee, 288
Mason, Otis Tufton, 47, 132
Mata Hari, 103, 170
Mathews, Winifred, 133
Matriarchal Theory of Social Origins (Briffault), 32
matriarchy, 10, 31, 33, 87, 162, 170, 196
Matulka, Barbara, 133, 288
Matz, Gladys Kern, 289

Maulde la Clavière, R. de, 134
Maurois, André, 290
Mayne, Ethel Colburn, 291
McCarthy, Mary, 128, 286
McClelland, David C., 123
McCuller, Carson, 223
McKendrick, Melveena, 286
Mead, Margaret, 69, 76, 114, 128, 135, 286
Meader, William G., 291
Mecom, Jane, 176, 197
medicine, 55, 85, 94, 95, 102, 107, 151, 152, 180, 190, 197, 198
medicine in convents, 105
medicine, male monopoly of, 102
medicine, medieval, 102
Medicis, Catherine de, 68, 130, 219
Medieval People (Power), 306
medievalism, 254, 278, 321
Meissner, Hans-Otto, 136
Melian, Lafinur Luis, 291
Melville, Herman, 246
Memoir of Mary L. Ware, 91
Mémoires et autres écrits de Marguerite Valois, 228
Memoirs of Catherine Booth (Booth-Tucker), 28
Memoirs of the Loves of the Poets (Jameson), 273
Men and Women of the French Revolution (Whitham), 202
Ménagier de Paris, Le (Pinchon), 155
Mencken, H. L., 137
Merchant of Venice, The (Shakespeare), 302

Meredith, George, 47, 213, 247, 264, 340
Mermaz, Louis, 137
Meung, Jean de, 301
Meyer, Johann Jakob, 138
Mews, Hazel, 292
Mexico, 39, 102, 162, 309
Michelangelo, 27
Michelet, M. J., 97, 139
Michigan, 64
Middle Ages, 3, 13, 18, 22, 26, 37, 86, 96, 97, 102, 119, 130, 153, 211, 215, 230, 231, 238, 277, 301, 321
Middle Class Culture in Elizabethan England (Wright), 203, 342
middle class women, 4, 13, 42, 82, 95, 100, 116, 125, 203
Middle East, 5, 87
Middle East (ancient), 90
Middlemarch (Eliot), 212, 241
Middleton, Dorothy, 139
Middleton, Thomas, 331
Middletown (Lynd), 127
Middletown in Transition (Lynd), 127
Middletown: A Study in American Culture, 127
Miles, C. C, 114
Mill, John Stuart, 40, 140, 171, 185, 197
Miller, Henry, 141, 244
Millett, Kate, 140, 197, 320
Milton, John, 157, 257, 272
Milton, Marie, 158, 257
Minnesingers (Germany), 174

Miriamne (legendary character), 331
Mirrlees, Hope, 275
Mirror of Womanhood (Indian periodical), 145
misogyny, 16, 17, 32, 38, 56, 68, 96, 110, 121, 123, 133, 134, 141, 143, 158, 166, 180, 195, 201, 207, 215, 222, 232, 245, 267, 268, 270, 280, 286, 288, 289, 295, 301, 305, 314, 320
missionaries, 19, 61, 133, 176
Mistral, Gabriela, 269, 303, 310
Mme d'Aulnoy et l'Espagne (Foulché-Delbosc), 247
Mnouchkine, Ariane, 220
Modern Women Poets of Spanish America (Rosenbaum), 310
Moers, Ellen, 293
Moeurs et la littérature de cour sous Henry II, Les (Bourciez), 219
Moffatt, Mary Jane, 294
Mohawk women, 46
Molière, 21, 165, 172, 211, 235, 282, 318
Molina, Tirso de (Gabriel Téllez), 313, 334, 335
Moll Flanders (Defoe), 154
monasteries, 29
monasteries, dissolution of (England), 105
Mont-Saint-Michel and Chartres (Adams),
Montagu, Lady Mary Wortley, 30, 260
Montaigne, Françoise de, 119
Montaigne, Michel Eyquem de, 14, 71, 119, 172, 245, 315

Montana, 170
Montez, Lola, 170
Montherlant et les femmes (Sandelion), 314
Moody, Harriet Converse Tilden, 239
Moore, Doris Langley, 141
Moorman, Mary, 294
Moors in Spain, 300, 330
Moraes, Santos, 295
Morais, Vamberto, 142
Morality of Women, The (Key), 111
Morante, Elsa, 232
Mordaunt, Eleanor, 275
More, Sir Thomas, 165, 166, 200
Morena, Amparo, 142
Morgan, David, 142
Morgan, Lady Sydney, 47
Morley, Griswold, 256
Mormons, 78, 170
Morris, Gouverneur, 74
Morris, Jean, 143
Moslem women, 5, 56, 87, 109, 203
mother right cultures, 170
motherhood, 24, 57, 70, 110, 111, 121, 129
Mothers, The (Briffault), 31
motion pictures, 94, 216, 265, 320
Mott, Lucretia, 28, 53, 168, 182
Moulin, Jeanine, 295
Mountain Journal (Frost), 326
Mozart, Wolfgang, 242
Muccini, Leda, 232
Mujer en España, La (Bofill), 27
Mujer en España, La (Campo de Alange), 38
Mujer en los libros de caballerías, La (Laiglesia), 280
Mujer española ante la república, La (Martínez Sierra, M.), 132
Mujer española, La (Alvarez), 7
Mujer moderna, La (Martínez Sierra), 131
Mujer vestida de hombre en el teatro español, La (Bravo-Villasante), 221
Mujer, La (Catalina), 40
Mujeres de Azorín (Cruz Rueda), 233
Mujeres de los Conquistadores, Las, (O'Sullivan-Beare), 151
Mujeres de Shakespeare, Las (Melián), 292
Mujeres en el Don Quijote, Las (Trinker), 331
Mulheres da América (Ramos), 161
Muraro, Rose Marie, 144, 295
Murfree, Mary N., 284
music, 197, 242, 277, 288, 313, 326, 331
Musset, Alfred de, 272
mysteries, women's, 72, 92, 189
mysticism, 47, 88, 219, 231, 245, 265
mythology, 92, 93, 108
myths about women, 38, 39, 40, 77, 118, 139, 140

N

Nahas, Helene, 295
Nalina, Saroj, 63
Nana (Zola), 319
Napoleonic *Code Civile,* 53, 169
Nath, Raja Narendra, 145
Native American women, 159
Native Americans, 20, 61

Natural History of Love, The (Hunt), 103
natural law, 255, 267, 268
Navarre, Marguerite de, 328
Nazi Germany: Its Women and Family Life (Kirkpatrick), 113
Nazism, 18, 25, 31, 36, 99, 108, 113, 180, 204
Nazism, suppression of feminism, 136
Needham, Gwendolyn Bridges, 331
Nef, Elinor Castle, 296
Neff, Wanda Fraiken, 145
Nehru, Rameshwari, 143
Nelken, Margarita, 39, 297
Neveu, Madeleine, 246
New Harmony (utopian community), 78
New York City Commission on Human Rights, 146
New Zealand, 188
Niger, 153
Nigeria, 189
Nightingale, Florence, 28, 94, 186
Nin, Anaïs, 243, 297, 322
Nineteenth Amendment (US), 185
nineteenth century, 158, 163, 185, 213, 229, 231, 241, 243, 270, 271, 272, 291, 292, 336
    Asia, 133
    Britain, 26, 30, 41, 51, 55, 79, 98, 100, 139, 140, 141, 145, 171, 186, 197, 201, 210, 228, 247, 252, 253, 283, 293, 311, 312, 320, 321, 324, 329, 340
    Canada, 302
    Europe, 29, 335
    France, 24, 30, 74, 97, 129, 139, 158, 290, 294
    Germany, 316
    India, 161
    Italy, 182
    Spain, 298, 309, 322, 334
    The Philippines, 8
    United States, 4, 9, 14, 28, 35, 46, 52, 53, 54, 56, 65, 78, 80, 83, 84, 94, 95, 110, 120, 123, 143, 147, 148, 149, 152, 153, 156, 168, 169, 175, 179, 180, 183, 185, 196, 201, 202, 237, 246, 252, 293, 323, 328, 336, 338
Nobel Prize, women and
    Pearl Buck, 36
    Sigrid Undset, 212, 237
    Hiltgunt Zassenhaus, 204
Noble Deeds of American Women (Clement), 46
Noel, C. M. D., 308
nomadic society, 153
North Africa, 147
North of Boston (Frost), 326
North, Marianne, 139
Norton, Eleanor Holmes, 147
Notable Women of Spirit (Beach), 17
Notables mujeres españoles (Cintron), 43
Nouacer, Khadidja, 147
Noun, Louise R., 147
novels, 213, 217, 243, 253, 264, 271, 275, 285, 286, 288, 302, 340
    African, 323
    American, 120, 128, 251, 267,

294, 319, 325, 336
Brazilian, 295
British, 23, 27, 99, 145, 154, 185, 210, 212, 218, 222, 228, 229, 235, 241, 249, 259, 277, 279, 292, 294, 311, 318, 340
European, 335
Filipino, 8
French, 218, 243, 276, 290, 327
French-Canadian, 302, 307
German, 292, 316
Norwegian, 236
Russian, 250
Spanish, 276, 322
Swedish, 233
Novels into Film (Bluestone), *216*
nuns, 29, 30, 34, 39, 53, 93, 105, 132, 143, 149, 262, 266, 287, 306, 309
nuns and medicine, 102
nuns, knowledge of Latin, 105
nursing, 94, 186
Middle Ages, 102
Nyssstrom-Hamilton, Louise, 147

O

O diálogo continua (Rocha), 310
O'Conner, Flannery, 223
O'Connor, Patricia, 298
occupations, 3, 75, 100, 103, 145, 147
Odyssey, The, 227
Of Men and Women (Buck), 36
Ohio Valley, 64, 66
Old English, 208

Olsen, Tillie, 298, 313
On Understanding Women (Beard), 17
One Woman's Situation (George), 82
Opie, Amelia Alderson, 259
oral history, 5, 64, 66, 120, 144, 312
Orbigny, Alcide d', 248
Order of the Minoresses in England, The (Bourdillon), 29
orders, religious, 29, 30, 88, 105, 143, 262
Orléans, Charlotte-Elizabeth, 299
Orñate, Maria del Pilar, 300
Ornstein, Jacob, 300
Osborne, Dorothy, 154, 294, 340, 341
Osborne, Duffield, 140
O'Sullivan-Beare, Nancy, 151
Ouellette, Lucien, 151
Our Common Cause: Civilization (National Council of Women), 104
Our Women: Chapters on the Sex Discord (Bennett), 21
Out of the Shadow (Cohen), 47
Ovid, 209, 260, 282
Owen, Robert, 78
Owens, Rochelle, 257
Oxford University, 33, 55, 76

P

Pacem in Terris (Vatican), 28
pacifism, 5, 49, 104
Padilla, Luisa de, 297
Páginas intimas de la mujer boliviano (Rico), 168
Paine, Thomas, 181

Painter, Charlotte, 294
painters, 28
Pakistan, 9
Palacio Valdès, Armando, 199
Pamela's Daughters (Utter), 332
Pankhurst family, 172
papyri, discovery of, 227
Paradies, Theresa von, 242
Paradis, Suzanne, 301
Paraguay, 162
Park, Clara Claiborne, 301
Parker, David, 302
Parton, James, 132, 302
Pascal, Blaise, 292
Paston women, 102, 185
Paston, Margaret, 22, 154
Patai, Raphael, 152
paternalism, 118, 160
patriarchy, 10, 31, 33, 87, 141, 162, 188
Paulme, Denise, 152
Paz Pasamar, Pilar, 303
Peg Woffington and Her World (Dunbar), 239
Penington, Mary, 236
Pepys, Elizabeth, 30, 154
periodicals, American, 149, 183, 323
periodicals, British, 62
periodicals, French, 229, 325
periodicals, German, 317
periodicals, Indian, 109
Perkins, A. J. G., 153
Perkins, Charlotte, 145
Pernoud, Régine, 153
Perpetua (martyr), 34, 238

Peru, 151, 162
Peterson, Esther, 123
Petry, Ann, 319
Philippines, The, 9
Phillips, Margaret, 154
philosophy, 52, 78
picaresque novel, 263
Pierre, André, 154
Pinchon, Jerome, 155
Pinckney, Eliza, 176
Pineda, Marina, 132
Pinet, Marie-Josephe, 303
Pinkham, Mildreth Worth, 156
pioneer women, 35, 50, 61, 64, 66, 113, 115, 121, 151, 169, 173, 180, 192
Pioneer Women of the West, The (Ellet), 64
Pioneer Women Orators (O'Connor), 148
Pisan, Christine de, 38, 102, 110, 117, 130, 255, 295, 303, 304
Pivar, David J., 156
Plato, 47, 341
Pleck, Elizabeth H., 50
Plomer, H. R., 304
Poe, Edgar Allan, 305, 323
poetry, 254, 256, 257, 267, 273
  American, 35, 239, 256, 325
  Brazilian, 144, 296
  British, 295, 314, 321, 329
  Cuban, 256
  French, 106, 245, 254, 295
  German, 268
  Greek, 60

374

Hispanic, 162
Irish, 274
Latin American, 310
Old English, 208
Roman, 282
Russian, 237
Spanish, 303
Poitiers, Diane de, 219
Polygamie dans le droit Annamite (Bui Tuong Chieu), 37
polygamy, 37, 79
Pope, Alexander, 260
popular culture, 94, 216
population theory, 178
Port-Royal (France), 192
Porter, Katherine Anne, 223
Portraits de femmes d'Héloïse à Mansfield (Henriot), 268
Portraits of Women (Bradford), 30
Portú, Javier Bello, 313
Potter, David M., 157
Poulain de la Barre, François, 167, 308
poverty, 41, 76, 80, 154, 170
Powell, Chilton Latham, 157
Powell, Marie, 257
Power, Eileen, 306
power, political, 31, 41, 73, 98, 141, 143, 210
power, women and, 4, 24, 58, 77, 83, 88, 173, 190, 211, 253, 294, 335
Précieux et précieuses (Livet), 282
Precursoras brasileiras (Barros Vidal), 15
predictions, 24, 35, 43, 51, 73, 87, 93, 111, 112, 119, 125, 132, 137, 139, 144, 199, 296, 334
prehistory, 89, 90, 107, 162
Prelude to the Past (Waldeck), 199
Pride and Prejudice (Austen), 216
primitive cultures, 93, 107, 108, 119, 132, 133, 135, 170, 182, 189
primitive tribes, 248
Problems of Sex (Glasgow), 85
Problems of Women's Liberation (Reed), 162
Profiles of Negro Womanhood (Dannett), 54
Prohibition era (United States), 14
prostitution, 156, 197, 318
Protestantism, 19, 26, 52
Proudhon, P.-J., 158
Proust, Marcel, 271, 290
prudery, 79, 260, 268, 332
pseudonyms, 51, 233, 250, 262, 284, 331
psychiatry, 243
psychoanalysis, 57, 249, 270
Psychology of Supervising the Working Woman, The (Laird), 117
psychology of women, 16, 25, 31, 36, 38, 50, 57, 66, 71, 73, 76, 92, 114, 115, 118, 123, 124, 127, 128, 129, 131, 138, 139, 141, 160, 166, 192, 196, 198, 207, 214, 229, 233, 247, 249, 253, 270, 273, 280, 284, 286, 290, 307, 326, 327, 332, 335, 336, 338, 340
Psychology of Women, The (Deutsch), 57
publishing, 229, 323, 325

purdah, 203
Puritanism, 56, 342
purity crusade, 156
Purity Crusade (Pivar), 156
Putnam, Emily James, 159

Q

Québec, 301
Queen, Stuart A., 159
Queen Anne of England (1665-1714), 187
Queens of American Society (Ellet), 64
querelle des femmes, 16, 134, 222, 232, 289, 301, 305. *See also* controversies, battle of the sexes.
quests, 252. 270
Quevedo, Francisco de, 264, 288
quietism, 47

R

Rabelais, 226
Rachel (Élisa Félix), 266
Racine, Jean, 211, 307
Rackowski, Cheryl Stokes, 306
Radcliffe, Ann, 283, 319
RAF (British Royal Air Force), women in, 45
Rainwater, Lee, 160
Raamabai Sarasvati, Pundita, 161
Ramayana, 138

Rambouillet, Catherine de Vivonne de, 21, 130, 282
Raper, Julius Rowan, 307
Raphael, 27
Ravenal, Florence Leftwick, 162
Read, Mary, 170
Reading of Renaissance Women, The (Wright), 342
reading of women, 70, 110, 177, 204, 214, 222, 249, 270, 292, 315, 342
Reagor, Margaret, 307
Rebel Generation, The (novel), 114
Rebel in Paradise: A Biography of Emma Goldman (Drinnon), 61
rebellion (see "themes")
Récamier, Mme de, 194
Reed, Evelyn, 162
Rees, Richard, 163
Reeves, Amber, 275
Reformation, Protestant, 11, 26, 31, 52, 143, 174, 223
Reich, Emil, 163
Renard, Marie-Thérèse, 164
Reine Blanche, La (Pernoud), 153
Reisman, David, 123
Relative Creatures (Basch), 210
religion, 4, 11, 12, 16, 17, 18, 19, 21, 28, 29, 34, 39, 41, 44, 47, 52, 53, 54, 58, 61, 67, 70, 78, 88, 92, 108, 109, 121, 134, 138, 141, 143, 151, 156, 164, 184, 187, 188, 189, 203, 212, 215, 220, 223, 228, 234, 265
Religion and Sexism (Reuther), 164
Religion of Beauty in Women, The (Fletcher), 246

Renaissance, 13, 27, 30, 67, 100, 110, 134, 143, 169, 194, 200, 232, 245 342
Renaissance of Motherhood, The (Key), 111
Report from a Chinese Village (Myrdal), 144
repression, political, 9, 74, 81, 141, 199
Resistance (Germany), 204
Reuter, Gabriele, 268
Reuther, Rosemary Radford, 164
Reynier, Gustave, 164
Reynolds, E. E., 165
Reynolds, Myra, 166
revolutions, 5, 23, 24, 30, 31, 34, 38, 45, 46, 50, 51, 64, 65, 73, 79, 81, 86, 87, 90, 98, 141, 155, 162, 169, 173, 176, 182, 202, 217, 228, 246, 250, 259, 312
revolutions, historical, 162
Rheingold, Joseph C., 166
Richards, Ellen H., 167, 185
Richards, Samuel Alfred, 167, 307
Richardson, Bertha Jane, 167
Richardson, Dorothy, 275
Richardson, Samuel, 23, 154, 332
Rico, Heidi K. de, 168
Ride Out the Dark (Bielenberg), 25
Riegel, Robert, 168
Rigaud, Louis, 169
Rights of Man (France), 202
rights of women, 3, 34, 80, 89, 95, 100, 121, 141, 162, 164, 174, 183, 259, 316, 333
Rios, Blanca de Los, 47
Rivers, Elias L., 308
Rizal y Alonso, José, 8
Rizal's Legacy to the Filipino Woman (Alzona), 8
Robert, Roberto, 309
Roberts, Elizabeth Madox, 223
Rocha, Adelaide M., 309
Rodax, Yvonne, 309
Rodocanachi, Emmanuel Pierre, 169
Roe, Frances M., 169
Rogers, Anny Mary Anne Henley, 33
Rogers, Cameron, 170
Rohan, Marie de, 170
Roiphe, Ann Richardson, 322
Role of Women in the Freedom Movement (Kaur), 108
Roman Elegists' Attitude toward Women, The (Lilja), 282
Roman Empire, 34, 72, 238
Roman Life and Manners (Friedländer), 77
Roman women, 72, 75, 77, 113
Roman Years of Margaret Fuller (Deiss), 55
Romance of the Rose, (Meung), 78
Romanticism, 217, 272
Rome, 72, 132, 169
Romieu, Marie de, 246
Ronhaar, J. H., 170
Room of One's Own, A (Woolf), 341
Roosevelt, Eleanor, 123
Roosevelt, Theodore, 61
Roper, Margaret, 67, 165

Rosenbaum, Sidonia, 310
Rossetti, Dante Gabriel, 274, 321
Ross, Ernest C., 310
Rossi, Alice S., 123, 171
Rostow, Edna G., 123
Rousseau, Jean-Jacques, 23, 261, 291
Rousselot, Paul, 171
Rovers, Constance, 172
Rowley, William, 331
Rubenius, Aina, 311
Ruddick, Sara, 312
Ruskin, John, 76, 197
Russian Revolution, 73, 155, 249
Ryan, Mary P., 172

S

Sabuco, Oliva, 297
Saint Simonianism, 172
Sales, François de, 47
Salisburg, Harrison E., 181
Salon, Its Rise and Fall, The (Tornius), 194
salons, 20, 42, 159, 184, 190, 192, 194, 202, 208, 239, 250, 282, 283
Salvation Army, 28
Sand, George, 30, 130, 162, 240, 267, 275
Sandelion, Jeanne, 314
Santa Teresa, 130, 143, 266, 297
Santa Teresa: Her Life and Times (Graham), 88
Santé et le travail des femmes pendant la guerre, La (Frois), 78
Sappho, 60, 227, 260

Sartin, Pierrette, 173
Sartre, Jean-Paul, 296
satires on women, 21, 134, 165, 166, 207, 282, 301
satirists, 207, 209, 305
Sayre, Sylvie Weil, 48
Scandinavian writers, 119
Schiff, Mario, 173, 314
Schiller, 235, 317
Schinnerer, Otto Paul, 315
Schirmacher, Kaethe, 174
Schlauch, Margaret, 316
Schoenfeld, Hermann, 174
Scholars, Saints, and Sufis (Keddie), 109
scholarship, 20, 21, 52, 60, 69, 72, 76, 167, 184, 200
schools, convent, 105
Schreiner, Olive, 175, 336
Schumann, Clara, 242
Schurman, Anne-Marie de, 167, 173, 308, 315
Schwartz, Kessel, 316
scientists, 17, 185
Scotland, 153
Scott, Anne Firor, 4, 5, 175, 176, 182
Scott, Sir Walter, 319, 338
Scribe, Augustin, 331
Scudder, Vida Dutton, 75
Scudéry, Mlle de, 278
sculpture, 244, 254, 259
Second Sex, The (De Beauvoir), 19
Sedwick, Frank, 317
Segia, Luisa, 297
Sejourné, Philippe, 318

Seltman, Charles, 177
Seneca Declaration of Rights (1848), 333
Serious Proposal to the Ladies (Astell), 11
seventeenth century, 210, 229, 269, 271, 288, 300, 308, 342
   American colonies, 35
   Britain, 10, 11, 44, 106, 154, 166, 192, 232, 257, 330
   France, 21, 47, 59, 69, 70, 119, 128, 137, 165, 167, 171, 173, 190, 191, 219, 262, 282, 307, 315
   Germany, 52
   Mexico, 39
   United States, 192
Seventh Day Adventists, 17
Sévigné, Mme de, 30, 130
Sewell, Elizabeth M., 235
Sex and Morality (Kardiner), 108
sex differentiation, 196
Sex Laws and Customs in Judaism (Epstein), 67
Sexual Life in Ancient Greece (Licht), 122
Sexual Life in Ancient India (Meyer), 138
Sexual Life in Ancient Rome (Kiefer), 113
Sexual Politics (Millett), 140
sexual revolution, 24, 73, 100, 172
sexuality, 58
Seymour-Smith, Martin, 318
Sforza, Caterina, 30, 169
Shakers (religion), 78

Shakespeare, William, 224, 239, 253, 273, 287, 291, 292, 302, 311, 328, 331
Shaw, George Bernard, 39, 215, 284
Sheldon, May French, 139
Sheridan, Frances, 319
Shinn, Thelma J., 319
shopping, 160
Short History of Women's Rights (Hecker), 96
Short History of Women, A (Langston-Davies), 118
Shorter, Edward, 178
Showalter, Elaine, 319
Siclier, Jacques, 319
Sidgwick, Ethel, 275
Sidney, Sir Philip, 246
Siege and Survival (Skrjabina), 180
Sigrid Undset, ou le morale (Deschamps), 236
Silences (Olsen), 299
Silva, Carmen da, 178
Simkins, Francis Butler, 179
Simon, Angela Gonzales, 68
Simone Weil (Davy), 55
Simone Weil: A Sketch for a Portrait (Rees), 163
Simpson, Leslie Byrd, 180
Sinclair, Andrew, 180
Sinclair, May, 275, 277, 336
singers, Scottish, 331
Sir Richard Burton's Wife (Burton), 37
Sisters, The (Harris), 93
Six Medieval Men and Women (Bennett), 22

sixteenth century, 219, 222, 229, 271,
    301, 305
  Britain, 44, 158, 165, 200, 203, 204,
    287, 305, 342
  Europe, 16, 110
  France, 20, 71, 245, 267, 315
  Germany, 12
  Italy, 12, 104, 228, 232
  Latin America, 151
  Mexico, 39
  Spain, 86, 88, 266, 334
sixth century
  Spain, 44
slavery, 95, 120, 153, 169, 175, 325
Smith, Charlotte, 259, 319
Smith, D. J., 320
Smith, Frank, 181
Smith, Hugh Allison, 320
Smith, Margaret Chase, 121
Smith, Sheila Kaye-Smith, 222
social change, 14, 26, 30, 43, 73, 75,
    89, 93, 94, 101, 117, 124, 129
    137, 147, 152, 188, 193, 198, 221
  Britain, 44
  Japan, 116
  Spain, 28, 38
  United States, 147
social conditioning, 196
social Darwinism, 4, 84
social justice, 76, 80, 153
Social Life at Rome (Fowler), 75
social sciences, 178
social theory, 141
social thought, 23, 70, 74, 75, 82, 84,
    86, 156

social work, 4, 28, 41, 58
socialism, 73, 75, 193
society, evolution of, 32
Socrates, 150
Sojourner Truth, 120
Some Dickens Women (Charles), 229
Some Goddesses of the Pen
    (Braybrook), 222
Some Reflections upon Marriage
    (Astell), 11
Some Women of France (Watson), 200
Sonstroem, David, 321
Soong Sisters, The (Hahn), 90
Sopeña Ibáñez, Federico, 321
Sophie Dorothea (Jordan), 106
Sophie Dorothea, 106, 175
Sor Juana Inés de la Cruz, 269, 309
Soul of Woman, The (Lombroso), 124
South Africa, 125, 133
South America, 248
South Pacific cultures, 135
Soviet Union. *See* USSR, Russia.
Spacks, Patricia, 321, 322
Spain, 132, 218
  Moorish influences, 330
Spain, legal code, 184
Spanish Golden Age, 218, 221, 242,
    286, 288, 289, 334
Spanish Inquisition, 234
Spanish Royal Academy, 47
Sparrow, Walter Shaw, 322
Sparta, women in, 177
Spencer, Anna Garlin, 182
Spencer, Elizabeth, 223
Spencer, Herbert, 47
Spenser, Edmund, 47
Spinoza, 196

Spruill, Julia Cherry, 182
St. Bonaventure, 96
St. Bridget, 230
St. Cyr (girls' school in France), 71, 172, 300
St. Emmeram (Benedictine abbey), 264
St. Francis of Assisi, 29
St. Helena, 34
St. Paul (Bible), 121
St. Teresa (Santa Teresa), 7
Staël, Germaine de, 28, 74, 80, 98, 162, 194, 201, 261, 278
Stalin, Josef, 6
Stanton, Elizabeth Cady, 2, 168, 183
Starr, Belle, 170
status of women, 9, 25, 31, 130, 168, 174. 273
Stearns, Bertha-Monica, 322
Stebbins, Lucy Poate, 183
Steffen, Christine Cecelia, 184
Stegeman, Beatrice, 323
Stendahl (Henri Beyle), 217, 291
Stendahl, Balzac, et le féminisme (Bolster), 217
Stendahl, Kristen, 184
Stenton, Doris Mary, 184
Stephens, Ann S., 185
Stern, Madeleine B., 185
Stevens, Doris, 185
Stevenson, Brenda, 74
Stone, Lucy, 95, 168
Stone, Wilbur Macey, 323
Storni, Alfonsina, 310
Stowe, Harriet Beecher, 28, 120, 294, 324
Strachey, Lytton, 186
Straelen, H. J. J. M., 187
Strange, Sad Voices (Anderson), 207

Strickland, Agnes, 187
Strong-Minded Women (Noun), 147
Stuart, Marie, 246
Studies on Women at Mari (Batto), 15
Subjection of Women (Mill), 40, 140
Sullerot, Évelyne, 188, 324
Summerskill, Edith Clara, 188
surveys, 85, 101, 116, 127, 160
Sutch, W. B., 189
suttee (India), 109, 156, 161
Sweden, 149, 184, 189
Swennes, Robert H., 325
symbolism, 243, 246
symbolism, religious, 243, 245
Sypherd, Wilbur Owen, 325

T

Tacitus (Roman historian) 185
Tagore, Ragindranath, 63
Taine, Hippolyte, 123
Talbot, D. Amaury, 189
Tallentyre, S. J., 190
Tavares de Sà, 326, 327
Tavris, Carol, 191
Taylor, Annie, 139
Taylor, G. R. Stirling, 191
Taylor, Harold, 69
Taylor, Lucy Hobbs, 185
Taylor (Mill), Harriet, 171
technology and homemaking, 175
temperance crusade, 46, 95, 124, 148
Tencin, Mme de, 98
Tennessee, 64
Tennyson, Alfred, 47
tenth century

Germany, 262, 264, 288
Tepoztlan (Mexico), 122
Terman, L. M., 114
Testament of Happiness (Huntington), 103
Tetel, Marcel, 327
Teutonic peoples, 105
Thackeray, William Makepeace, 145
Thailand, 9
That Chinese Woman (McAleavy), 127
theater, 69, 183, 215, 239, 257
Théâtre de Hrotswitha (Magnin), 287
themes:
   femininity, 36, 53, 70, 111, 114, 159, 183, 195, 197, 198, 228
   freedom, 6, 34, 36, 51, 74, 80, 81, 92, 104, 111, 112, 118, 123, 131, 156, 199, 201, 211, 226, 247, 249, 253, 289, 322, 325, 333, 335
   intellect, 10, 15, 20, 22, 36, 69, 83, 85, 101, 110, 120, 125, 129, 132, 137, 212, 268, 302, 303, 311, 315, 322, 337, 339
   love, 13, 92, 97, 103, 111, 122, 134, 138, 155, 200, 228, 236, 237, 246, 258, 260, 262, 270, 273, 274, 277, 279, 280, 282, 284, 291, 294, 310, 313, 325, 328
   marriage, 11, 41, 67, 71, 75, 91, 97, 111, 112, 117, 119, 122, 124, 126, 128, 137, 138, 139, 156, 157, 159, 161, 171, 182, 190, 193, 199, 200, 207, 209, 236, 255, 257, 259, 260, 263, 264, 265, 270, 279, 300, 302, 323, 325
   rebellion, 3, 5, 8, 12, 26, 29, 87, 108, 153, 161, 210, 225, 237, 241, 277, 283, 303, 307, 309, 324
   self-sacrifice, 125, 229, 243, 302, 315, 316, 301, 322
   work, 3, 4, 50, 123, 127, 144, 145, 148, 175, 176, 182, 228, 294, 312
Theodora, Empress, 34
Theodorus, 105
theologians, Protestant, 16
theosophy, 109
Thieme, Hugh P., 192
Third Reich (Germany), 90, 136, 204
thirteenth century
   France, 153
   Italy, 29
   Spain, 184
Thomas, Antoine Léonard, 181
Thomas, Clara, 327
Thomas, Edward, 327
Thomas, M. Carey, 52
Thomas, W. I., 114
Thompson, Helen B., 114
Thompson, Jan, 328
Thompson, Roger, 192
Those Extraordinary Blackwells (Hays), 95
Thoughts on Some Questions Relating to Women (Davies), 55
Thrale, Hester, 159, 208, 225
Thraliana, or The Diary of Mrs. H. L. Thrale (Balderston), 208
Three Marias, The (Barreno), 210

Titmuss, R., 193
Tocqueville, Alexis de, 192
Todd, Janet, 329
Tolstoy, Nikolai, 76, 252
Tornius, Valerian, 194
Toth, Karl, 195
Trachman, Sadie Edith, 329
traditions, 67, 109, 324
Tragedies of Herod and Mariamne, The (Valency), 331
Traité de L'Éducation des filles (Fénelon), 70
translations:
    Chinese into English (McAleavy), 128
    Danish into English (Gloerfelt-Tarp), 85
    Dutch into English (Hillesum), 99
    English into French (Mead), 135
    English into French (Mencken), 137
    English into German (Sarasvati), 161
    English into Italian (Bettelheim), 214
    English into Italian (Dronke), 238
    English into Italian (Lewis), 278
    English into Italian (Mead), 135
    English into Portuguese (Bolton), 28
    English into Spanish (Briffault), 32
    English into Spanish (Firestone), 73
    English into Spanish (Graham), 88
    English into Spanish (Huber), 102
    English into Spanish (Klein), 114
    English into Spanish (Lewis), 278
    English into Spanish (Reed), 163
    English into Spanish (Watson), 200
    French into English, 181, 261
    French into English (Bell), 58
    French into English (Blanc), 338
    French into English (De Beauvoir), 19
    French into English (Fénelon), 14
    French into English (Guiguet), 261
    French into English (Héricourt), 97
    French into English (Maulde la Clavière), 134
    French into English (Maurois), 291
    French into English (Michelet), 139
    French into English (Paulme), 152
    French into English (Sullerot), 188
    French into English (Tornius), 194
    French into English (Vigée-Le Brun), 333
    German into English (Feininger), 244
    German into English (Friedländer), 77
    German into English (Hahn), 90
    German into English (Halle), 92
    German into English (Kapp), 277
    German into English (Kiefer)), 113
    German into English (Licht), 122
    German into English (Meissner), 136
    German into English (Orléans), 300
    German into English (Schirmacher), 174
    German into English (Toth), 195
    German into English (Vaerting), 196
    German into English (Heller), 268
    Italian into English (Boccaccio), 216
    Italian into English (Dante), 257
    Italian into English (Lombroso-Ferrer), 124
    Latin into French (Hroswitha), 287
    Norwegian into English (Undset), 212
    Portuguese into English (Barreno), 210
    Russian into English, 180

Russian into English (Akhmatova), 237
Russian into English (Alliluyeva), 6
Russian into English (novels), 251
Russian into English (Trotsky), 195
Spanish into English (De Castro), 256
Spanish into English (Martínez de Toledo), 180
Swedish into English (Key), 110, 111, 112
Swedish into English (Myrdal), 144
Swedish into English (Nystrom), 147
Swedish into English (Stendahl), 184
Swedish into French (novels), 233
travel, 26, 37, 39, 51, 139, 140, 218, 247, 250, 338
Treatise on the Education of Girls (Fénelon), 70
Treatment of Marriage in the Plays of Rachel Crothers (Bali), 209
tribal customs (Africa), 128, 129, 152
Trinker, Martha K., 330
Tristan and Isolde (legend), 276
Trotsky, Leon, 195
Trotula of Salerno, 102
troubadors, 226
Turner, Frederick Jackson, 192
Turner, Justin G., 196
Twain, Mark, 337
twelfth century, 230
  Europe, 245, 277
  France, 254, 280, 284
twentieth century, 144, 147, 193, 275
  Africa, 129, 153
  Australia, 189
  Bolivia, 168

Brazil, 142, 144, 178
Britain, 12, 45, 82, 100, 120, 125, 175, 188, 218, 268, 277, 294, 336, 341
Canada, 302
China, 90, 144, 190
Ecuador, 80
France, 5, 51, 55, 130, 164, 169, 173, 218, 293, 296, 314
Germany, 25, 90, 113, 136, 268, 293
Holland, 99
India, 145
Israel, 73
Italy, 182
Japan, 116, 187
Latin America, 161, 310
Middle East, 203
Morocco, 147
Norway, 236
Portugal, 210
Russia, 6, 73, 92, 154
South Pacific, 135
Spain, 27, 131, 132, 199
Sweden, 111, 147
United States, 3, 5, 13, 47, 54, 56, 69, 73, 76, 83, 87, 88, 89, 101 104, 120, 127, 136 137 140, 146, 157, 160, 167, 168, 185, 201, 223, 254, 256, 257, 265, 294, 312, 319, 325, 336
Uruguay, 8
USSR, 60, 250
Tyler, Margaret (translator), 342
Tytler, Sarah, 320

U

Uncle Tom's Cabin (Stowe), 120
Undset, Sigrid, 211, 236, 258, 327
UNESCO, 5, 43, 116
unions (trade), 60
United Nations, 5
United States Constitution, 143, 177
United States, pre-Revolutionary, 183
universities, 33, 50, 55
　United States, 54, 110
Unsung Champions of Women (Cohart), 47
Unwomanly Woman in Bernard Shaw's Drama (Lorichs), 283
Uruguay, 7, 162, 292
USSR, 6, 73, 141. *See also* Russia.
Utah, 170
utopian communities, 78
Utter, Robert, 331

V

Vaerting, Mathias, 114, 196
Vaerting, Mathilde, 114, 196
Valency, Maurice J., 331
Valois, Marguerite de, 228
Van Doren, Carl, 197
Vatican, 28, 53, 151
Vedas, 50
Vega Carpio, Lope de, 264, 318, 334
Venus, 259
Vertron, G. de, 308
Vicinus, Martha, 197
Victorian Ladies at Work (Holcombe), 100
Victorian Lady Travellers (Middleton), 139

Victorian Working Women (Neff), 145
Victorianism, 26, 62, 79, 186, 197, 210, 235
Vida y obra de Émilia Pardo Bazán, La (Bravo-Villasante), 221
Vietnam, 9, 37
Vigée-Le Brun, Elisabeth, 332
Vigman, Fred K., 198
Vigri, Caterina, 323
Vindication of the Rights of Women, A (Wollstonecraft), 40, 168, 177, 191
Violette, Augusta G., 332
Virey, Julien-Joseph, 198
Virgil, 281
Virgin Mary, 4, 245
Virginia (state), 66, 92
Vives and the Renascence Education of Women (Watson), 200
Vives, Juan Luis, 165, 200
Voice of the People, The (Glasgow), 307
Vollmer, Sylvia N., 333
Voltaire, 253, 272

W

Wade, Gerald E., 276, 313, 334
Wagenheim, Leah, 199
Wagner, Richard, 277
Waldeck, Rosie Goldschmidt, 199
Wales, 100
Walls: Resisting the Third Reich (Zassenhaus), 204
war and women's health, 78
war work, women and, 45, 49, 89, 117
war, women and, 5, 23, 25, 45, 49, 50, 59, 61, 65, 78, 79, 89, 90, 94, 99,

120, 131, 136, 137, 162, 179, 180, 186, 199, 204
Ward, Lester Frank, 47, 84
Ward, Mary Augusta, 279
Warren, Mercy Otis, 333
Warwick, Ann, Countess of, 236
Wasserstrom, William, 335
Watson, Foster, 200
Watson, J. L., 330
Watson, Paul Barron, 201
We, the Women (Stern), 185
Wedd, A. E., 201
Weil, Simone, 163, 294, 327
Weininger, Otto, 114
welfare state, 193
Wellesley College, 75
Wellington, Amy, 201, 335
Wells, H. G., 131
Welsh, Jane, 184
Welty, Eudora, 223
West, Rebecca, 336
Wetherell, Elizabeth, 235
Wharton, Edith, 275, 339
Wheeler, Candace, 185
White House (U.S. Presidents), 101
White, Ellen G., 17
Whitham, J. Mills, 202
Whitman, Walt, 131
Wife to Mr. Milton (Graves), 257
Wilder Shores of Love, The (Blanch), 26
Willard, Frances Elizabeth, 202
Williams, Charles, 336
Williams, Stanley T., 336
Wilson, Mark K., 336
Wilson, Martha, 66

Wilson, Roger H. L., 70
Wilson, Woodrow, 143, 185
Winiker, Rolf, 337
Wisconsin, 124
witchcraft, 57, 279
wives, cruelty to, 156, 255, 259
wives, recruitment of, 182
Wolff, Cynthia, 338
Wollstonecraft, Mary, 23, 40, 82, 148, 168, 177, 191, 201, 248, 259, 308, 319, 320, 333, 336, 340
Woman (Michelet), 139
Woman and Rococo in France (Toth), 195
woman as ideal, 245, 314, 339
Woman as Image (Ferrante), 245
Woman in All Ages and in All Countries (series), 33, 37, 63, 104, 174, 191, 226, 238
Woman in Fashion, The (Moore), 141
Woman in Soviet Russia (Halle), 92
Woman in the Nineteenth Century (Fuller), 80, 240, 305
Woman Movement, The (Key), 112
Woman Movement, The (O'Neill), 149
Woman of India, A (Dutt), 63
Woman Question in Mrs. Gaskell's Life and Work (Rubenius), 311
woman suffrage, 9, 31, 35, 61, 132, 142, 145, 147, 150, 171, 172, 176, 185, 193, 325, 329
Woman Who Spends, The (Richardson), 167
Woman's Doom in Genesis 3:16 (Ouellette), 151

Woman's Philosophy of Woman, A
(Héricourt),, 97
Woman's Record (Hale), 91
Woman's Share in Social Culture
(Spencer), 182
Woman's World, A (Summerskill), 188
Woman, Change, and Society
(Sullerot), 188
Woman, the Dominant Sex (DeLeeuw),
56
Woman: Her Position and Influence
(Donaldson), 60
Woman: In Honour and Dishonour, 25
Womanhood in America (Ryan), 172
women
  in Africa, 43, 101, 129, 152, 323
  in American colonies, 57, 121, 176, 192, 197
  in American West, 169
  in ancient Egypt, 89, 90, 197
  in ancient Greece., 177
  in antiquity, 17, 60, 72, 75, 89, 159
  in Argentina, 317
  in Asia, 101
  in Australia, 112, 188
  in Austria, 43
  in Babylonia, 16
  in Bolivia, 168
  in Brazil, 15, 40, 142, 144, 178, 296, 310, 327
  in Britain, 12, 13, 18, 20, 22, 26, 33, 37, 38, 41, 45, 51, 53, 55, 62, 75, 82, 83, 100, 140, 145, 148, 149, 152, 154, 159, 166, 171,183, 184, 192, 193, 197, 208, 228, 242, 283, 292
  in Canada, 39, 43, 101
  in China, 48, 90, 127, 144, 190
  in Denmark, 85, 119
  in Ecuador, 80
  in Egypt, 130
  in Europe, 13, 31, 101
  in feudal society, 31
  in France, 4, 13, 15, 21, 24, 37, 42, 43, 47, 48, 51, 53, 55, 59, 62, 68, 69, 71, 74, 78, 80, 97, 106, 117, 119, 126, 129, 138, 153, 155, 158, 159, 164, 167, 169, 171, 173, 190, 192, 195, 201, 202, 211, 243, 250, 272, 300, 304, 320
  in French Canada, 301
  in Germany, 5, 12, 13, 31, 52, 106, 108, 113, 174, 190 ,204, 293
  in Greece, 34, 116, 159
  in India, 41, 50, 63, 94, 108, 138, 145, 156, 161, 274
  in Israel, 73
  in Italy, 12, 13, 18, 27, 30, 104, 124, 169, 182, 232
  in Japan, 56, 116, 187
  in Latin America, 151, 162, 269
  in Mexico, 163
  in Morocco, 147
  in Nazi Germany, 18, 25
  in New Zealand, 188
  in Nigeria, 189
  in Norway, 119, 236, 258
  in Poland, 43
  in Portugal, 210
  in primitive cultures, 133

in Rome, 72, 159
in Russia, 13, 56, 73, 154
in Scotland, 331
in South Africa, 125
in South Asia, 9
in Spain, 7, 10, 27, 38, 39, 43, 46, 63, 68, 86, 88, 131, 132, 142 184, 221, 264, 301, 309
in Sparta, 341
in Sweden, 119, 147, 149, 233
in the American South, 159, 175, 179, 183
in the Middle East, 56, 101, 203
in the Philippines, 8
in the United States, 3, 4, 13, 14, 18, 23, 28, 35, 46, 50, 52, 53, 54 55, 56, 60, 61, 64, 65, 69, 74, 76, 80, 83, 84, 88, 89, 92,9 4 1 101, 103, 110, 115, 117, 120, 123, 124, 127, 135, 13 6 147 149, 152, 156, 159, 160, 168, 170, 179, 180, 185, 202, 265, 312, 336
in the USSR, 6, 59, 92, 250
in Turkey, 5
in Uruguay, 7
in Yugoslavia, 43
Women According to Saint Bonaventure (Healy), 95
women and armed forces, 102
women and civilization, 70
Women and Economics (Gilman), 83, 84
Women and Labour (Schreiner), 175
women and religion, 11, 12, 17, 19
Women and Samuel Johnson (Matz), 289
Women and Society in the Spanish Drama (McKendrick), 286
Women and the French Tradition (Ravenal), 162
Women Artists in All Ages (Ellet), 65, 241
women as *art nouveau,* 329
women as consumers, 160, 167
women as demons, 279, 288
women as designers, 324
Women as Force in History (Beard), 17
Woman as Survivor, The (Moeller), 292
Women at Oxford, The (Brittain), 33
Women Designers of Book-Plates (Stone), 324
Women Have Told: Studies in the Feminist Tradition (Wellington), 201
Women Healers in Medieval Life (Hughes), 102
Women in Antiquity (Seltman), 177
Women in Defense Work During World War II (Gregory), 89
Women in Eighteenth-Century America (Benson), 23
Women in Espionage (Hutton), 103
Women in Industry (Abbott), 3
Women in Primitive Motherright Societies (Ronhaar), 170
Women in Shakespeare's Plays (Mackenzie), 287
Women in Soviet Fiction (Gasiorowska), 248
women in Spanish colonies, 151
Women in Stuart England and America

(Thompson), 192
Women in Subjection (O'Malley), 148
Women in the Community (Gloerfelt-Tarp), 85
Women in the Golden Ages (Mason), 132
Women in the Modern World (Komarovsky), 115
Women in the Modern World (Patai), 15
Women in the Sacred Scriptures of Hinduism (Pinkham), 156
Women in the Soviet Economy (Dodge), 59
Women in the Theater of Gregorio Martínez Sierra (O'Connor), 298
Women of All Nations (Joyce), 107
Women of Early Christianity (Brittain), 33
Women of Modern France (Thieme), 191
Women of the American Revolution, The (Ellet), 65
Women of the Confederacy, The (Simkins),
Women of the Reformation (Bainton), 11
Women of the Renaissance (Maulde la Clavière), 134
Women of the Salons, The (Tallentyre), 190
Women of the Teutonic Nations, 174
Women of Tropical Africa (Paulme), 152
Women through the Ages (Reich), 163
Women with a Cause (Sutch), 188
Women Writers (MacCarthy), 285
Women Writers in France (Brée), 222
Women Writers of the Middle Ages (Dronke), 238

Women's Institute Movement (India), 63
Women's Liberation and Literature (Showalter), 320
women's liberation movement (US), 147
Women's Life and Work in the Southern Colonies (Spruill), 182
women's movement (Britain), 62, 100, 148
women's movement (France), 167
women's movement (United States), 148
women's movement (Germany), 5
women's movement and religion, 54
women's movement, wages and, 100
Women's Mysteries of a Primitive People (Talbot), 189
Women's Mysteries (Harding), 92
women's rights movement, 140, 145
Women's Role in Contemporary Society (New York City), 146
Women's Share in Primitive Culture (Mason), 132
women, forgotten, 11, 46, 47, 48, 54, 65, 85, 91, 104, 129, 143, 145, 151, 152, 218, 238, 242, 246, 264, 268, 275, 285, 287, 288, 304, 317, 324, 330, 338
women, Latin names for, 260
women, sacrifice of, 326
women, self-education of, 165, 166, 223, 225, 315
Women, Society, and Sex (Fairchild), 69
Wood, Ann D., 338
Woodberry, George Edward, 339
Woodhull, Victoria C., 185
Woolf, Virginia, 21, 33, 39, 57, 218,

224, 256, 261, 268, 275, 277, 285,
    297, 313, 322, 327, 340
Woods, Alice, 339
Woodsmall, Ruth Frances, 203
Wordsworth, William, 295
work (see "themes")
work, hazardous (USSR), 155
*Working Life of Women in the
    Seventeenth Century* (Clark), 44
working women, 3, 4, 42, 44, 51,
    61, 82, 85, 89, 98, 100, 118, 145,
    147, 148, 154, 164, 172, 175, 182,
    188, 197, 312
Workingman's Wife (Rainwater), 160
Workman, Fanny Bullock, 139
world peace, 131
World Revolution and Family Patterns
    (Goode), 87
World War I, 5, 13, 49, 78, 82, 128,
    131, 137, 155, 168, 175, 199
World War I, effect on women, 336
World War I, postwar, 275
World War II, 25, 45, 85, 89, 90, 99,
    104, 117, 120, 163, 180
World War II veterans (U.S. males), 77
Worster, William, 303
Wright, F. M., 340
Wright, Frances, 153
Wright, Louis B., 204, 341, 342
Wright, Martha, 168
Wright, Thomas, 204, 255
Wuthering Heights (E. Brontë), 216
Wylie, Eleanor, 256
Wyoming, 66

X

Xantippe (Socrates' wife), 150

Y

Y Service (British RAF), women in, 45
Yeats, William Butler (1865-1939), 274
Yonge, Charlotte, 235

Z

Zassenhaus, Hiltgung, 204
Zayas y Sotomayor, Maria de, 297
Zola, Émile, 319

DATE DUE

DEMCO, INC. 38-2931